AFRICAN LANGUAGE REVIEW

Formerly the Sierra Leone Language Review

This Volume is Dedicated to
SAMUEL AJAYI CROWTHER
1806–1891

Bishop of the Niger Territory, Previously Tutor at Fourah Bay
Pioneer of African Language Studies

AFRICAN LANGUAGE REVIEW

Formerly the Sierra Leone Language Review

VOLUME 8   1969

THE AFRICAN LANGUAGE YEARBOOK OF FOURAH BAY COLLEGE, UNIVERSITY OF SIERRA LEONE, IN ASSOCIATION WITH THE AFRICAN STUDIES PROGRAM OF INDIANA UNIVERSITY

Editor: DAVID DALBY

Associate Editors: CARLETON T. HODGE
W. MICHAEL MANN   A. K. TURAY

Routledge
Taylor & Francis Group
New York London

First published by
FRANK CASS AND COMPANY LIMITED

This edition published 2013 by Routledge

711 Third Avenue, New York, NY 10017
2 Park Square, Milton Park, Abingdon, Oxon OX14 4RN

*Routledge is an imprint of the Taylor & Francis Group,
an informa business*

First issued in paperback 2016

ISBN: 978-0-714-62690-1 (hbk)
ISBN: 978-1-138-98835-4 (pbk)

CONTENTS

	page
Editorial	4
Samuel Ajayi Crowther—a Biographical Note: *P. E. H. Hair*	5
A Provisional Comparison of the English-based Atlantic Creoles: *Ian F. Hancock*	7
The Language Situation in Mauritius, with Special Reference to Mauritian Creole: *Philip Baker*	73
Tone-Marking an African Language, with Application to Bemba: *W. Michael Mann*	98
Focus and Entailment—Further Problems of Transitivity in Swahili: *W. H. Whiteley* and *J. D. Mganga*	108
Some Lexical Differences among Verbs in Kenya Coastal Swahili Dialects: *Carol M. Eastman*	126
Sanye and Sandawe—a Common Substratum?: *Eric ten Raa*	148
Hausa *nàà*—'To be' or not 'to be'?: *Carleton T. Hodge*	156
A Hausa Poet in Lighter Vein: *Neil Skinner*	163
Diola-Fogny Funeral Songs and the Native Critic: *J. David Sapir*	176
La Langue Manjaku et l'Alternance Consonantique Initiale: *J. L. Doneux*	193
Language, Script and Vernacular Literature in West Africa: *Petr Zima*	212
An Ethnolinguistic Inventory of the Lower Guinea Coast before 1700—Part II: *P. E. H. Hair*	225
Studies devoted to S. W. Koelle's *Polyglotta Africana*:	
Etsako: *John Laver*	257
Le Gio: *J. L. Doneux*	263
La Langue de Tumbuktu: *A. Prost*	272
Bibliography of the Somali Language and Literature: *John William Johnson*	279
Research Review	298
Publications Received	305
Notes for Contributors	307

EDITORIAL

SINCE its establishment in Sierra Leone, the expansion of the *African Language Review* (formerly the *Sierra Leone Language Review*) has been due entirely to an annual subvention from Fourah Bay College, University of Sierra Leone. Commencing with the current volume, however, a further increase in size and scope has been made possible by a generous grant from the African Studies Program, Indiana University. Especial thanks in this regard are due to Professor J. Gus Liebenow, chairman of that program, who has shown a close interest in the development of the *African Language Review* since the time of its inception, when he was himself associated with Fourah Bay College. Although the geographical scope of the *African Language Review* has been widened during this period, consistent attention has been devoted throughout—in keeping with its Sierra Leonean origin—to the study of creoles as well as of indigenous African languages. This dual focus becomes especially important today, with the increasing interest which is being shown in the scholarly study of European-based creoles in Africa and the New World, and—perhaps even more important—of the structure and African heritage of Black American English. In this situation, the development of a comprehensive yearbook embracing the study of both African and Afro-American languages and literatures will serve to strengthen the lines of communication between Africanists and Afro-Americanists, as well as helping to meet the need for a periodical devoted to creole language studies. The editors will be pleased to consider contributions on any theme involving the languages or literatures of Africas or Afro-America, and intending contributors are invited to consult the note at the end of this volume.

The present volume is dedicated to the memory of Samuel Ajayi Crowther, one of the major nineteenth-century pioneers of African language studies and among the first students and African tutors of Fourah Bay College (then the Fourah Bay Christian Institution). Dr. P. E. H. Hair, himself long associated with Fourah Bay College and with the *African Language Review*, has kindly compiled the following biographical note on Bishop Crowther and his contribution to African linguistics.

Samuel Ajayi Crowther: a Biographical Note
P. E. H. HAIR

THE son of Yorubaland who is commonly known today as Samuel Ajayi Crowther—though his original African name appears on none of his printed works—probably first came into contact with linguistic studies by acting as an informant of the Reverend John Raban and of Mrs. Hannah Kilham in Freetown in the later 1820s. Crowther, a student at Fourah Bay Christian Institution and then a mission school-teacher, is believed to have supplied Yoruba vocabularies for Raban's and Mrs. Kilham's publications, and also to have attempted to acquire and study Temne, the language neighbouring the Freetown colony.[1] During the 1830s, Crowther may have begun a serious study of his mother-tongue: his selection in 1840 as a mission representative on the forthcoming Niger Expedition suggests that his interest in African linguistics was known, and his companionship on the expedition with the Reverend J. F. Schön, an experienced linguist, most probably encouraged him to prepare the grammar and vocabulary of Yoruba which was published in 1843.

After 1844, Crowther lived and worked in what is now Nigeria. At Abeokuta, he translated a large part of the Bible into Yoruba, and later supervized the translation of most of the remainder. His contribution, through the Bible translation and through his enlarged grammar and vocabulary of 1852, to the shaping of subsequent Yoruba printed literature—and Yoruba has today one of the largest printed literatures among African languages—in terms of orthography, dialect stabilization and stylistics has not yet been adequately assessed but was certainly considerable; and the subsequent development of a unified written form of Yoruba, along with the parallel convergence of spoken dialects, certainly owes much to his intervention. In 1857, Crowther transferred his mission activities to the River Niger, and during the next thirty years, in collaboration with Schön, he published material on Nupe and Ibo, and encouraged the preparation and publication of material on Hausa, Ijaw, Igala and Igbira. Much of Crowther's linguistic activity was directed to a practical object, the education and evangelization of Western Africa. Many of his fondest hopes in this direction foundered with the decline and virtual disbandment of the Niger Mission, in the later 1870s and 1880s, when he himself was a very old man; and it is easy to see his last years as tragic.[2] But Crowther's work also contributed to the linguistic exploration of Africa and to the scientific investigation of African languages. His outstanding contribution in this respect was undoubtedly his insistence on the role of tone in many West African languages, though he unfortunately failed to convince his European colleagues on this point. His linguistic achievement is of course highlighted by the well-known dramatic circumstances of his life: his arrival in Freetown as an illiterate youth, after liberation from slavery, his education and years of obscurity in Sierra Leone, his return to his linguistic homeland in middle age, and his pioneering travels on the Niger and Benue, eventually as a bishop. Though not the first West African to publish in his mother-tongue, Crowther was the first son of Black Africa to make a significant contribution to African linguistics; and until the present generation he remained the most distinguished African linguist of African birth.

NOTES

1. Details on all the points in this note can be found in P. E. H. HAIR, *The Early Study of Nigerian Languages*, C.U.P., 1967. See also two forthcoming reprints by Frank Cass & Co. Ltd., SAMUEL CROWTHER, *Journal of an Expedition up the Niger and Tshadda Rivers* (1855) and J. F. SCHÖN and Samuel CROWTHER, *Journals of the Rev. James F. Schön and Mr. Samuel Crowther* (1842).

2. In the sense that the final disaster was partly due to his own failings: a point stressed by a countryman of Crowther in a recent thesis, Godwin TASIE, 'Christianity in the Niger Delta, 1864–1918', Aberdeen, 1969.

A Provisional Comparison of the English-based Atlantic Creoles*

IAN F. HANCOCK

1.0.0. INTRODUCTION

The accompanying word lists comprise up to 570 items in eight related English-derived creoles, arranged under twelve headings. They are not primarily tables of cognates, although inevitably most entries share cognate features in each language. This must be so, since by definition these creoles are English-derived, i.e. the total present-day lexicon in each is for the most part clearly traceable to English.[1] On the basis of this one criterion China Coast Pidgin, Neo-Melanesian, etc., would fall into the same group; lexical items derived from languages other than English, however, and—still more important—the occurrence of common syntactic structures, serve to indicate a clear relationship among the English-derived creoles on both sides of the Atlantic, distinguishing them from English-derived pidgins and creoles outside that geographical area. On the other hand, Atlantic creoles derived from metropolitan languages other than English, e.g. Haitian Creole French, the (moribund) Virgin Islands Dutch Creole, and the Creole Portuguese of Guiné, etc., share many syntactic features and non-European-derived lexical items with those Atlantic creoles deriving from English. The wider genetic classification of pidgin and creoles is a vexed problem, and will not be discussed here.[2]

1.0.1 The hypothesis presented in this paper maintains that the English-derived creoles spoken today on the West African coast, and in South, Central and North America, represent the modern descendants of a single early pidgin spoken probably with local variants along the West African coast from the early sixteenth century. This will be referred to as the 'Proto-Pidgin', English-derived unless otherwise stated. Despite the fact that there is today only a minimum of mutual intelligibility among the eight languages dealt with here, it would seem possible to extract a common pidgin 'core', and Hall would even like to construct a form of 'Basic' Pidgin.[3]

1.0.2 The designation 'Atlantic', although purely geographical, seems more appropriate than Schneider's 'Central Atlantic' since it

---

* A slightly enlarged version of a paper originally presented *in absentia* at the Conference on Pidginization and Creolization of Languages, held at Mona, Jamaica, in April 1968.

allows for subdivision into Western (or American) and Eastern (or African) groups. The term 'Pacific' could similarly be employed to include pidgins and creoles spoken in that area, 'Indian Ocean' for pidgins and creoles spoken there, and so on.

2.0.0. EARLIER COMPARATIVE STUDIES

Apart from a brief comparison of the English-derived pidgins and creoles of the Americas with West African Pidgin English by Herskovits,[4] a short discussion of a possible African/West Indian origin for Gullah by Stoney and Shelby,[5] and the suggestion that a link may exist between the American and African creoles and pidgins in an article by McDavid,[6] the only detailed comparison between the English-derived creoles of the Old World and those of the New is to be found in F. G. Cassidy's 'Toward the Recovery of Early English–African Pidgin'.[7] It is significant that none of these sources mentions Krio, historically perhaps the most important African representative of the entire group.

3.0.0. THE CREOLES

The languages dealt with here in detail are Krio, Sranan, Saramaccan, Djuka, Cameroons Pidgin, Guyana Creole, Jamaican Creole and Gullah. Briefer reference has been made to Liberian English, so far inadequately documented, Hawaiian Pidgin English, and Pitcairnese. Throughout, particular attention has been devoted to Krio, since this is the language with which the writer is most familiar, and since in many instances it provides a link between the south-western group (consisting of Sranan, Saramaccan and Djuka) and the north-western group (consisting of the Caribbean creoles).

3.1.0 *Krio* serves as the mother tongue of the Creole population in Freetown, Sierra Leone, and is also spoken as such by the inhabitants of various Creole villages in the Sierra Leone Peninsula, on Bonthe Island and in the Banana Islands. Krio, 'Pidgin Krio', and Pidgin English are also employed as lingue franche throughout the country, and often between the local and expatriate populations there. The estimated number of native speakers ranges from 20,000[8] to 120,000[9] according to different sources. Allowing for the great number of urbanized and de-tribalized Sierra Leoneans who have settled in and around Freetown, and for whose descendants Krio has become a first language, the number of *native* speakers may now be in the region of 200,000. The number of 'true' Creoles is dwindling as a result of intermarriage with non-Creole Sierra Leoneans, but the overall number of Krio speakers is gradually increasing. The language is also spoken in Bathurst, the Gambia, by an estimated Creole population of 3,500.[10] Gambian Krio, more often called *Aku* or 'Patois' in that country, differs from that of Sierra Leone principally in intonation and lexicon, including a number of words from local African languages which are unknown in Freetown. The reverse situation also applies. According to reports, a more conservative form of Krio is preserved in several small enclaves in Guinea and Senegal, where Creole traders have formed their own Krio-speaking communities in non-English-speaking environments. Another more conservative form of Krio, known as *Poto* or 'Porto Talk', is spoken by Creoles whose ancestors came originally from Freetown, and who are now living on Fernando Po (cf. 4.4.0) and São Tomé (in Krio, *Sɛntɔmi*).

3.1.1 'Creole' is used in Freetown as a generic term to describe the descendants of the Liberated Africans (rescued from illegal slave ships at sea before ever reaching the Americas), the Maroons (from Jamaica direct, and also via Nova Scotia), the Nova Scotians (British and American slaves assembled at Halifax, Nova Scotia, and taken to Freetown), and the Black Poor from Britain, all of whom were settled in Freetown between 1787 and as late as the third quarter of the nineteenth century.

3.1.2 It is generally maintained that Krio represents a modern offshoot of the speech of the Jamaican Maroons who arrived in the Colony in 1800.[11] This is not entirely true, for a pidgin or creole was in use in the area prior to this date (cf. 4.1.1.). However, whatever was spoken in what is now Freetown was affected to some degree by the speech of the incoming Maroons.

3.2.0 *Sranan*, variously known as *Krioro*, *Taki-Taki*, *Nengre Tongo* or 'Neger-Engels', is the predominant language in Paramaribo and surrounding districts in Surinam, in north-eastern South America. Like Krio, it also serves as a lingua franca throughout the country. Stewart lists the number of Sranan speakers as 80,000.[12]

3.2.1 The language occurs in several markedly differing dialects, the extremes being at the eastern and western ends of the country, and is spoken differently by people of different ethnic backgrounds, by Negro, Javanese, Chinese, etc.

3.3.0 *Saramaccan* is spoken in the interior of Surinam, by descendants of runaway Maroons who fled from the Dutch plantations towards the end of the eighteenth century and who are now settled along the banks of the Suriname and Brownsweg Rivers. Like Krio, Saramaccan has lexical tone, a feature not shared by Sranan. *Matwari* and *Kwinti*, creoles spoken in villages along the Saramacca River, may prove to be dialects of Saramaccan. Nearly all Saramaccan speakers are familiar with Sranan, and in some areas of close contact between the two groups (such as in Berg en Dal) the two languages have become inter-intelligible.

3.4.0 *Djuka*, also called *Ndjuka* (by its speakers), *Aucan*, or *Djoe-Tongo*, is spoken along the banks of the Marowijne River, having an island of *Paramaccan* speakers in the middle and another of *Boni* speakers to the south. These latter languages may be dialects of Djuka, as are *Opo*, *Bilo* and Cottica River Djuka. Some varieties are also spoken along the French Guiana bank of the river.

3.4.1 Little documentation is available for Djuka; it appears to be lexically closer to Sranan, but with a phonological system approaching that of Saramaccan.[13] It is unique among the creoles in that it has an indigenous syllabic script[14] invented by one of its speakers in 1910. It is from a Dutch translation of a religious pamphlet in this script that the majority of the present Djuka items in the accompanying lists is drawn.[15] According to Herskovits[16] the total number of all 'Bosnegers' (Saramaccan, Matwari, Djuka, Paramaccan and Boni) was 18,000 in 1936.

3.5.0 *Cameroons Pidgin* ('Cameroons Creole', 'Bush English', 'Broken English', 'West Coast', *Wes Kos*) has been well documented, and boasts of a weekly news-sheet and various biblical translations. According to Schneider[17] this language is spoken by upwards of 1 million people. It is used throughout West Cameroon by three-quarters of the population, in East Cameroun by perhaps one-third, and by many thousands more in Eastern Nigeria.

As well as the Cameroons Pidgin employed widely throughout the country and for broadcasting, there are at least four other distinct dialects of the language: a creolized variety, which may be the same as the Porto-Talk surviving in Fernando Po, spoken by the descendants of the Sierra Leonean Christian followers of Alfred Saker who settled in small numbers in Victoria on the Cameroons Coast (via Fernando Po); a lexically cosmopolitan and now probably extinct variety propagated by the Germans during their period of occupation (1884–1914); a somewhat artificial variety employed by Catholic missionaries for their religious publications; and a fourth archaic dialect existing in East Cameroun (see note for item 476).

Cameroons Pidgin is easily understood by a Krio speaker from Sierra Leone, although a speaker of Cameroons Pidgin has some difficulty in comprehending a Krio speaker.

3.6.0 *Guyana Creole*, called 'Creolese' by its speakers, is understood by the majority of the population of Guyana (*c.* 436,500 in 1956[18]), although it exists in its more conservative form only in rural areas. Because of the heavily forested terrain, settlements within the country are separated from each other and from those in neighbouring countries, resulting in the retention of features reflecting the varied origins of the language. Three sources still more or less

Pidgin), Barbadian and Sranan. There are reports that a creole similar to this latter language is spoken in several small communities in the eastern part of the country; this may be a retention of a very early creole which became established at the same time as the Surinam creoles, or the speech of Surinamers who have settled over the border. Guyana was Dutch-controlled until 1803.

3.7.0 *Jamaican Creole* ('Broken English', *Jagwa-Talk, Bungo-Talk, Quashee-Talk*) is used in one form or another by most of Jamaica's nearly 2 million inhabitants, but as in Guyana, the most conservative forms are to be found in isolated rural communities, and the distinction between the creole and the metropolitan language is blurred. There are innumerable 'shades' of speech along a spectrum having the fully creolized language at one extreme and standard Jamaican English at the other, with speakers often being able to operate on several levels in both directions, according to the social situation.[19]

3.8.0 *Gullah*, known also as *Geechee* or *Geedgee*, is spoken in several local varieties on the U.S. mainland (as far inland as twenty miles) and on the Sea Islands, along 250 miles of the South Carolina and Georgia seaboard and in part of northern Florida, by several thousand American Negroes. It has retained its creole features due to the comparatively late arrival of the last Africans in the area, and to the lack of adequate educational and communication facilities. This region of the United States also has the smallest percentage of non-Negro Americans, its inhabitants consequently being in less direct contact with more standard varieties of American English. With improving public amenities in the Gullah-speaking area the language is losing, although slowly, its creole features, approximating more and more to southern American speech.

4.0.0 HISTORICAL BACKGROUND

It is known that a Portuguese-derived pidgin was in use along the West African coast as early as 1470. As seamen who had probably sailed to Mediterranean ports as well as to the African coast, early Portuguese sailors were probably familiar with *Sabir*, the lingua franca current in the Mediterranean seaports at that time.[20] It is a possibility that the use of Sabir stimulated the establishment of a Portuguese pidgin on the West African coast; but modern descendants of the early pidgin, such as the creoles of Cape Verde, São Tomé, etc., bear only superficial resemblance to Sabir. As pointed out by Taylor,[21] many Africans were acquainted with the Portuguese-derived pidgin (or even by that time, creole) before ever leaving their homeland for the Americas; it is also known from early slave-auctioneering posters that Africans with a knowledge of some European language commanded much higher prices in the slave markets.

4.0.1 The Portuguese carried their trade language to the Orient as well as to the Caribbean, where it gave rise to Indo-Portuguese (in India and Ceylon), Malaccan (in Malaya), Makista (in Macao), etc. Whinnom says: 'Even at the beginning of the eighteenth century English trade at Canton was carried on through Eurasian Portuguese interpreters, who translated the Cantonese into a Portuguese pidgin comprehensible to the English sailors.'[22]

4.0.2 Just as a Portuguese-derived lingua franca developed between the Portuguese seamen and their African contacts along the Guinea coast, so with the coming of the English to West Africa in the sixteenth century an English-derived pidgin became established concurrently with the Portuguese, and was almost certainly much influenced by it. It is likely that in some communities Africans were familiar with both the Portuguese-derived and the English-derived pidgins, as indicated by the traces of Portuguese surviving in the Atlantic creoles today.

4.0.3. A suggestion which has gained wide currency is the so-called 'relexification hypothesis',[23] which maintains that all the European-language-derived creoles—even those outside the Atlantic area—originated as varieties of an earlier Portuguese-derived pidgin, but in the process of creolization drew on English, French, Dutch, Spanish, etc. for their vocabulary, the grammatical structure of each having already been established. This may well have taken place, but if so it is surprising that so few traces of Portuguese remain in the Atlantic creoles today; Gullah and Krio each have less than 1%, Jamaican Creole about 2%, and Sranan 4%. Saramaccan, with 27% of its lexicon traceable to Portuguese is an exception, and may represent the only certain example of large-scale relexification among the languages dealt with here.[24] A pidgin, however scant its word-stock may be, incorporates sufficient essential vocabulary to cope with its environment, and it seems unlikely that such basic items as pronouns, numerals, and words like *man, woman, eat, work, kill*, etc., would need to be replaced wholesale. A better term than *relexification* is perhaps *supralexification*, implying lexicon-building rather than lexicon-replacement; in any case, in the instances where relexification does occur supralexification must occur also, two items being used concurrently, with one gradually falling out of use.[25]

4.1.0 Evidence in print pointing to a reduced form of English in use along the West African coast during these early years is tenuous;[26] one Portuguese source from 1594 tells us '... depois de terem amizade com os Ingleses, foram ja a Inglaterra aprender a lingúa inglesa e ver a terra, por mandado do alcaide do pôrto de ale que serre de reador da fazenda de el rei' (i.e. '... after making friends with the English, they immediately went to England to learn the language and to see the country, at the command of the Mayor of the port of Ale, who acts as the king's teasurer').[27] A later mention occurs in an account published by Francis Moore in 1734, who comments: 'The English have in the River Gambia much corrupted the English language, by Words or Literal Translations from the Portuguese or Mundingoes'.[28]

4.1.1 Documentation of a pre-1800 English-derived pidgin on the West African coast may also be found in several eighteenth-century travel accounts, one of the most notable being a log-book written in one type of pidgin from Eastern Nigeria between 1785 and 1788.[29] The pidgin in which it is written, however,[30] differs considerably from both Krio and modern Cameroons Pidgin, the latter being spoken today in the same area. A more striking example of pre-1800 pidgin is recorded in the journal of Captain Hugh Crow,[31] written c. 1780, in which he tells of a 15-year-old African boy being brought to England on his ship: 'When we got further north, the cold began to pinch him severely, and ... he one morning came shivering to the side of my cot, and said "Massa Crow, something bite me too much, and me no can see 'im, and me want you for give me some was' mouth, and two-mouth tacken." I knew that "wash mouth" meant a dram, and he soon gave me to understand by getting hold of my drawers, what he meant by two-mouth tacken ...'.[32] Taking into account that the youth may firstly have been trying to approximate his speech to a more comprehensible form of English, secondly that Crow's transcription is probably inaccurate, and thirdly that this represents a form of pidgin spoken two centuries ago, the youth's speech bears a marked resemblance to modern Freetown Krio.[33] This also adds weight to the argument that an English-derived pidgin or creole was in use on the coast before the arrival of the Jamaican Maroons in Freetown. A type of pidgin spoken in Sierra Leone before 1800 is illustrated in a journal compiled in 1791,[34] including the phrases 'Oh! he be fine man, rich too much, he got too much woman', and 'God amity sen me dat peginine, true, suppose he no black like me, nutting for dat, my woman drinkee red water, and suppose peginine no for me, he dead'. In Crow's account are also found samples of pidgin recorded in Bonny, Eastern Nigeria, in 1807,[35] differing from that mentioned above and approximating much more to the present-day idiom. He also gives interesting examples of the Jamaican Creole of that period.

4.2.0 The date of the arrival of the first Africans on the Guiana coast is not known, but the Dutch had a settlement at 'Pormurbo'[36] in 1613. At this time there was no cultivation intensive enough to warrant the importation of slave labour, but, as Rens points out, 'this does not mean that there were no Negro slaves to be found in Guiana during the first few decades of the seventeenth century. On the contrary, it would have been surprising if the Caribbean, lying between Portuguese and Spanish America—both slave-importing regions—had not had its share of African Negroes. The more so, as English, Dutch and French pirates often captured slavers bound for the Spanish plantations in the Islands or on the mainland. In a letter from the cabildo (municipal council) of Santo Thomé, dated April 11th, 1637, we read about a settlement of the Dutch on the River Essequibo "with two forts well supplied with artillery and soldiers, and a quantity of Negroes" . . .'.[37]

4.2.1 The English flag was raised over Surinam in 1651, some twenty-five years after an unsuccessful attempt to establish a settlement there by the French.[38] At this time, the English owners of sugar plantations in Barbados were looking for room to expand their growing business, and not unnaturally cast their eyes towards Surinam. Consequently by 1661 this colony already numbered 1,000 inhabitants.[39] That the number was not even greater at the end of this ten-year period is due in part to the fact that the colonial administration in Barbados was opposed to the transportation of slaves from the island, since it viewed Surinam as a potential rival to its own sugar industry. Thus after the first few years slaves were not brought into Surinam from Barbados, but directly from the English-controlled territories in West Africa.

4.2.2 English rule came to an end in 1667, when under the Treaty of Breda England exchanged Surinam for the Dutch colony of Nieuw Amsterdam (New York). As a result, the English planters and their slaves in Surinam were brought to Saint Elizabeth in Jamaica.[40] Their total number was 1,231, almost one thousand of these being Africans. The population of Jamaica at this time was about 7,000.[41] (By 1700, just twenty-three years later, the population had reached nearly 40,000.)

4.2.3 In 1630 the northern coastal regions of Brazil were occupied by the Dutch. As a result of the open door policy of the Netherlands government, many Portuguese Jews expelled from their own country were able to find refuge in Dutch-occupied Brazil. However, the subsequent reconquest of that country by the Portuguese caused large numbers of Dutch and Portuguese Jewish settlers to leave, many of the latter finding a new homeland in Surinam where their knowledge of sugar cultivation acquired in Brazil proved to be an invaluable asset; thus the Jews were welcome immigrants in the new colony.

4.2.4 Not all the English left Surinam when it passed into Dutch hands; some remained, hoping that the colony would once more revert to England. Little by little, however, the English moved out to other English colonies such as Antigua and Jamaica, so that by

1681 only thirty-nine English subjects remained in Surinam. The Portuguese-speaking Jews on the other hand were politically unaffected by the change, and remained in the colony. By the end of the seventeenth century they constituted 75% of the entire European population of Surinam.[42]

4.2.5 Rens maintains that Africans arriving in Surinam during the period of English control had no knowledge of English, the use of Sranan having been initiated in Surinam after their arrival. He states: 'The slaves learned to speak the language of their masters, and so it seems reasonable to suppose that Negro English was the first "Creole" language spoken in Surinam',[43] and 'Though it would be more than rash to conclude that in those fifteen years [i.e. of English rule] Negro English was formed, it seems a safe assumption to state that during that period the African slaves had acquired the habit of expressing themselves in English of a sort when talking to the whites, and of interspersing their own conversation among each other with a growing number of English words'.[44] In these passages, and elsewhere in his book, Rens intimates that the language had its origins in Surinam. The facts which are evident from this brief synopsis of Surinam's early history, however, are that the country was an English possession for only sixteen years, from 1651 to 1667. The English language was used by a rapidly dwindling population for perhaps forty years, i.e. between c. 1650 and 1690. For two brief periods (1799–1802 and 1804–16), Surinam was again under British rule,[45] but for nearly three centuries the major linguistic influence upon Sranan has been Dutch. One might therefore suppose that Sranan had originated during the period of maximum English-language influence, and been "fortified' by the English speakers who remained in Surinam until the end of the century. This is not implausible, and—if it were not for our increasing knowledge of Sierra Leone Krio—Rens' theory might well have remained unchallenged.

4.2.6 An alternative hypothesis would be that the original slaves were already speaking Negro-English when they arrived in Surinam from Barbados. If this were so, then the total number of years of English-language contact would be extended by twenty-five years, Barbados having been settled in 1625. However, in Barbados '... there was no considerable demand, and perhaps insufficient capital, for the purchase of slaves, and the original settlers had been content to work in the fields they owned, or to hire other white men to work for them'.[46] By 1650, the Negro population of Barbados had reached 25,000.[47] Thus, allowing for the first few years of colonization when practically no slaves were imported, the bulk of the Barbadian slave population must have arrived during the previous fifteen or twenty years. If it were true that early Negro-English, i.e.

the ancestor of modern Sranan, had originated in Barbados and was subsequently carried to Surinam from 1651, then it would have had just fifteen years or so in which to develop, the last stages of its formation having taken place in Surinam during the years after 1651. Yet it would seem that the Barbadian Negroes probably had a better command of the English language than did slaves in other English-owned islands; in 1650 there were nearly as many Europeans in Barbados as there were Africans, unlike the situation elsewhere, and this may have hastened the slaves' acquisition of metropolitan, rather than pidgin, English. In 1673, the representative of the Royal Africa Company in Sierra Leone requested '40 or 50 negroes from Barbadoes that have been bred up their [sic] and speake only the English tongue',[48] serving to illustrate that of the whole Caribbean area Barbadian slaves were noted for their command of English. Of all present-day creole dialects of the West Indies, 'the Barbadian dialect is grammatically closer to Standard English . . . due no doubt to the much higher proportion of Whites to Negroes during the formative period up to 1750'.[49]

4.3.0 Saramaccan is the most deviant of the eight creoles, containing far more lexical items from Portuguese and from African languages, notably Kikongo. Because of this an examination of the Dutch slave trade during these years seems worthwhile, as it may help to shed light on the idiosyncratic lexical content of Saramaccan.[50]

4.3.1 The Dutch West India Company (here abbreviated to DWIC) was founded in 1621, and three years later became involved in the slave trade. In 1637 the Dutch took Elmina from the Portuguese, and in subsequent years several more West African forts fell into their hands. According to the Dutch historian K. Ratelband,[51] the Dutch at that time employed Portuguese officials because Portuguese was still the lingua franca on the West African coast.

4.3.2 In 1636 the DWIC sent a slave ship to Angola, and a certain Jan de Sousa, a Portuguese, was stationed there at São Paola de Loando, because he knew not only the principal language of Angola, but Dutch and Portuguese as well. In 1641 the Portuguese forts in Angola were conquered by the Dutch. From that date until 1648 (when the Portuguese regained their former forts) the DWIC managed to sell about 15,000 Angolan slaves to the Americas, mainly to Brazil. After 1667, when Surinam was ceded to Holland, the DWIC began shipping slaves there, both from the Guinea coast and from Angola. A contract drawn up in 1713 between the government of Surinam and the DWIC stated that of all slaves brought into that country, two-thirds were to be from Ardra on the Guinea coast, and the remaining third from Angola (although there is no evidence that this ruling was maintained).

4.3.3 After 1730 slave trading began to decline as far as the DWIC was concerned, being taken over more and more by private companies. Documents of one of these, the 'Middelburg Commercie Compagnie', are preserved in full, and from these it is known that between 1732 and 1808 one hundred and eight slaving voyages were made, during which time 31,095 slaves were shipped from Africa, 27,344 landing alive in the Americas. During this period of seventy-six years the majority of Africans were taken from the Guinea coast: forty-five ships with 10,245 slaves, as opposed to fourteen ships (4,583 slaves) from Angola, two ships from both Guinea and Angola (481 slaves), and twelve ships from unspecified African ports (2,896 slaves).

4.3.4 Thus it seems evident that at least one-third of the slaves imported into Surinam were from Angola. It would appear that this fact is not highly significant when explaining the Portuguese elements in Saramaccan;[52] Africans on the Guinea coast would also have been familiar with the Portuguese trade language at this time, so a slave from any area under Portuguese influence may well have spoken it. It does, however, help to explain why so many Bantu words are evident in Saramaccan; since the Bush Negroes of Surinam are the descendants of runaway Maroons they would have tended to preserve words which have subsequently disappeared elsewhere. Djuka, while also a Bush Negro dialect, shows far less influence from Portuguese. The Djuka were probably at one time Sranan speakers who fled into the bush, there evolving their own distinctive speech.[53]

4.3.5 Rens refers to an early Negro-Portuguese creole developing in the Jewish-owned plantations, which gave way to the Negro-English spoken by slaves from the English-owned plantations as a result of their going to work for the former when their English owners left (these were not allowed to take their slaves out of the country after 1677). In fact, the influence of the Jews in Surinam from a linguistic point of view has generally been overestimated. The first Portuguese-speaking Jews did not arrive in Surinam until after 1660,[54] and despite their superior numbers they were far more localized than the Dutch, who by 1687 had five times as many plantations as the Jews.

4.4.0 Cameroons Pidgin represents one modern form of West Coast Pidgin, with influences (especially lexical influences, i.e. words traceable to indigenous Sierra Leonean and Gambian languages) from Krio. It appears to have begun to take on its present form only during the nineteenth century, when intercourse between Freetown and the Cameroons region became more frequent. Examples of pre-1800 Sierra Leone Pidgin are far closer to modern Krio than are examples of Bight of Biafra Pidgin from that period (cf. 4.1.1) to the modern pidgin spoken in the area today. LeVine has written that 'In 1827 [the British] obtained permission from the Spanish to occupy Fernando Po, which had fallen to the latter in 1777, and to base a squadron there to control the shipping of slaves from the Bights of Biafra and Benin. The British took advantage of their settlement on the island to encourage several Bristol and Liverpool enterprises to set up floating hulks as trading posts in the Cameroons River. It is interesting to note that the use of pidgin English, still spoken as a lingua franca along the West African coast, began its spread during this period. ... When the British, with Spanish permission, settled Fernando Po in 1827, they brought with them a number of manumitted slaves from Freetown, center of their anti-slavery activities in West Africa. The presence of these freed slaves and the supression of the slave trade spurred English missionary societies into establishing missions on the Cameroons coast, long known as the most active slave-trading region in West Africa'.[55]

4.4.1 A discussion of West Coast Pidgin (although not specifically Cameroons Pidgin) may be quoted also from A. W. Lawrence: 'No European before the nineteenth century is known to have spoken an African language [an exaggeration; cf. 4.3.2]; short vocabularies provided for the simpler needs of trade and person, and there was no lack of interpreters. The castle slaves must have acquired the rudiments of their masters' language in childhood, while mulattoes were probably bilingual. Free Africans too, could often make themselves understood in some form of European speech, either pure or pidgin. The earliest medium, Portuguese, outlasted the dominance of Portugal, remaining the *lingua franca* of the coast (where words and turns of expression still persist). But the languages of successor nations gradually replaced it, each in the appropriate neighbourhood. As early as 1679 Barbot found "good English" spoken by canoemen he encountered at sea, within sight of Elmina—probably they lived at Cape Coast. But at Axim, though the Dutch had evicted the Portuguese thirty-seven years earlier [i.e. in 1642] the *lingua franca* was still known, he asserts, "by the greater part of the population" '.[56]

4.4.2 Although the influence of Krio on Nigerian and Cameroons Pidgin was great (Western-educated Creoles from Sierra Leone were for many years employed in administrative positions in British colonies in West Africa, including Nigeria and the Cameroons), the reverse situation is also true. Curtin and Vansina have demonstrated[57] that the vast majority of liberated Africans who were landed at Freetown between 1820 and 1870 were from the Nigeria–Cameroons region; by 1848 fully 39% of the population of Freetown were of Yoruba extraction, and Yoruba, Ibo and Dahomean represented the three major non-local linguistic groups in the colony.

Over 400 Yoruba-derived lexical items can be found in modern Krio. It would also be surprising if none of these settlers had been familiar with the pidgin of that part of the coast, and this no doubt has also increased the number of features which it shares with modern Krio.

4.5.0 As previously mentioned (3.6.0) Guyana Creole exhibits features demonstrating influences from at least three distinct sources. Forms of Sranan, used by Surinam seamen, are current in the seaports of the Guianas. It is not surprising therefore to find words common to both Sranan and Guyana Creole (such as Sranan *périn*, Guyana *pélin*, 'fence', or Sranan and Guyana Creole *máti*, 'friend', etc.). This coastal contact, and (if substantiated) the existence of a creole similar to Sranan in eastern Guyana, can account for the similarity between certain aspects of Guyana Creole and Sranan.

4.5.1 In the 1740s, under the direction of the Dutch commander S. van 's Gravesande, the colonies at Essequibo and Demerara were thrown open to all nationalities. The Barbados planters were again eager to take advantage of the offer (cf. 4.2.1), and many moved to the new colonies, taking with them all their slaves. This, it seems, constituted another factor in the formation of Guyana Creole, for as Cruickshank maintains,[58] 'The Demerara Black did not get his English direct from the Englishman. He got it at second-hand. He got it from the Barbados Black'.

4.5.2 The last influence on Guyana Creole appears to have been from Krio or West African Pidgin, and to have occurred after the Abolition of slavery. Cruickshank writes that '... during the [18]40's ... there were brought to British Guiana—as also to Jamaica, Trinidad, &c.—to supplement the diminishing labour supply, several thousands of Liberated Africans. Upwards of thirteen thousand Africans were brought to British Guiana between 1838 and 1865. According to the Census Commissioner 706 native-born Africans were alive in British Guiana on April 2, 1911'.[59] Although Cruickshank claims that these Liberated Africans acquired their knowledge of English from the earlier Negro population, it seems possible that at least some of these Africans had arrived with a knowledge of Krio or some variety of West Coast Pidgin. Krio and Guyana Creole share such lexical items as *tobó*, 'chilblains', and *okú*, 'a Yoruba', which are not apparently found anywhere else in West Africa or the New World.

4.6.0 The linguistic history of Jamaica has already been well-documented and needs no elaboration here.[60] Apart from the Proto-Pidgin substratum uniting both languages, Jamaican Creole shares lexical and grammatical features with Krio as a result of more recent influences such as the *c*. 800 Jamaican Maroons who arrived in

Freetown in 1800 (although many of these did not remain for long and their influence may have been overestimated), and the disbanded troops of the 2nd and 4th West India Regiments who remained there between 1819 and 1896. The 5,000 Sierra Leoneans who were sent to Jamaica and other parts of the West Indies between 1841 and 1850 as a liberated African labour force may also have contributed several Krio items to various Caribbean Creoles, Jamaican included.

4.6.1 Jamaican semi-secret societies and religious cults are reported to have preserved quasi-African languages—such as *Kromanti*—intact, for use in communicating with the spirits; this is not unusual, cf. the reported existence of *Lángu* in Surinam, *Efí* and *Lukumí* in Cuba, etc. One such cult language, used in Kingston, is worth mentioning. A tape recording of this language[61] was found upon analysis to contain about 50% Kikongo-derived items. It would be interesting to compare this with the work undertaken by Father Jan Daeleman on Kikongo items in Saramaccan; he has found that this language accounts for about 8% of the collected lexicon (139 items out of a total 1,700).[62] It is also noteworthy (4.5.2) that Cruickshank mentions Kikongo as one of the two African languages which had survived in Guyana into this century,[63] the other being Yoruba.

4.7.0 Gullah provides further possible evidence of an English-derived pidgin or creole having been taken to the New World from the West African coast. From *c.* 1700 it is estimated that over 100,000 Africans had been imported directly into the lower Atlantic coastal region of the U.S.A., and were distributed from Charleston and other points up and down the coast to work in the cotton, indigo, sugar and rice plantations. Despite the Slave Trade Act which came into effect in 1808, slaves continued to be landed on the North American coast illegally, and as late as 1858 four hundred African slaves were landed in Georgia.[64]

4.7.1 It was customarily the practice of the slave-owners to break up the parties of slaves, firstly to hasten their acquisition of English, and secondly to minimize the risk of insurrection being plotted in the secrecy of the tribal tongues. However, there is little evidence to show that slaves brought into the Charleston area *were* widely dispersed. It is perhaps possible that this was because many of the Africans were already familiar with some form of English upon arrival, or at least sufficient English to enable them to understand the orders of the plantation owner. The fact that so many Africanisms have been preserved in Gullah would indicate that these early arrivals did stay in sufficiently homogeneous a group to preserve their characteristic speech. As already mentioned (3.8.0), the fact that Gullah has survived here and not elsewhere (although it was undoubtedly spoken over a much wider area at some earlier time) is due in part to the isolation of the Sea Islands, and to the fact that the last Africans arrived only one hundred years ago.[65]

4.7.2 Nearly 47% of the approximately 4,000 African and supposedly African items listed by Turner[66] as being current in modern Gullah appear to have originated in the Sierra Leone area: this has already been commented on by Hair.[67] Parsons, another student of Gullah folklore, has also noted the similarity between the structure and idiom of Gullah and that of Sierra Leone Pidgin English.[68] A few phrases will indicate these similarities (using I.P.A. notation):

1. 'He told him that he should shut his eyes'
    Gullah: *i tɛ́l əm sɛ́ i ɸə ʃɛ́t i jáj*
    Krio: *i tɛ́l ã sé i fɔ sɛ́t ĩ jáj*

2. 'Brer Alligator usually comes out of the river to sun himself'
    Gullah: *bə gédə bláŋ kʌm áwtn di ríβə ɸə sʌ́n isɛɸ*
    Krio: *bra aligéta blánt kɔmɔ́t na di ríva fɔ sán ĩsɛf*

3. 'My sister is taller than you (pl.)'
    Gullah: *mi ʃíʃə tɔ́l pas únə*
    Krio: *mi sisí tɔ́l pas úna*

4. 'She heard the bird but she cannot see it'
    Gullah: *i jɛ́ɽi äi bʌ́jd bʌt i cã̄ ʃʌ́m*
    Krio: *i jɛrí äi bʌ́d bɔt i cã̄ sí ã*

5. 'They are carrying the drum there'
    Gullah: *dɛn də tót di gɔ́ma gó de*
    Krio: *dɛn de tót di gumbé gó de*

6. 'Where is it?'
    Gullah: *βésaj i dé?*
    Krio: *úsaj i dé?*

7. 'I want to see what a xylophone looks like'
    Gullah: *a wã̄ sí aw bála tã̄*
    Krio: *a wã̄ sí aw balándʒi tã̄*

8. 'They'd taken a stick to beat us soundly'
    Gullah: *dɛn dʌ́n tɛk tík ɸə ɸlág βi gúd ɸáʃin*
    Krio: *dɛn dɔ́n tɛk tík fɔ flág wi gúd fáʃin*

9. 'That morning when they should have gone...'
    Gullah: *dá mɔ́ːnin βe dɛm bĩ ɸə gó...*
    Krio: *dá mɔ́nin we dɛm bĩ fɔ gó...*

10. 'You're not going anywhere'
    Gullah: ju ɛ̃ də gwʌ́jn nɔ́βe
    Krio: ju nɔ́ de gó nɔ́we

11. 'Leave me alone, sonny, please!'
    Gullah: lɛ́f mi bʌ́bə, dú
    Krio: lɛ́f mi bɔbɔ́, dú

12. 'Give it to her at once'
    Gullah: ɟi əm tə rʌm βʌ́n tájm
    Krio: gí ã to rã wán tɛ́m

13. 'Are you warm now?'
    Gullah: ju dʌ́n βʌ́m naw?
    Krio: ju dɔ́n wám náw?

14. 'He/it is there'
    Gullah: i líβ de
    Krio: i líb de

15. 'Both his feet'
    Gullah: ɔl tú i ɸút
    Krio: ɔl tú ĩ fút

16. 'They were there to help catch the muskrats'
    Gullah: dɛm βin dé ɸə hɛ́p kɛ́c dɛm mʌ́scat
    Krio: dɛm bin dé fɔ ɛ́p kétʃ dɛm múscat

17. 'You took it and gave it to the young men who are working over there'
    Gullah: ju βin cá rʌ ɟi dɛn ɲʌ́ŋ mán βe də βʌ́k oβə jánd
    Krio: ju bin kɛ́r ã gí dɛn yɔ́ŋ mán we de wók oba jánda

18. 'They're fine' (reply to enquiry after family, etc.)
    Gullah: dɛn dé de
    Krio: dɛn dé

19. 'Hurry up and run and get some kind of rope'
    Gullah: mɛcés rʌ́n ɟít sʌ́m cánəbə róp
    Krio: mɛkés rɔ́n ɟés sɔ́m kánaba róp

20. 'Both of the men were courting the girl'
    Gullah: ɔl tú di mán bin ə kót di ɟál
    Krio: ɔl tú di mán bin de kót di ɟál

4.7.3 Turner lists examples of Gullah songs containing fragments of Mende and Vai, both of which languages are spoken in Sierra Leone. As is apparent from the above, morphological and phonological correspondences are numerous; Gullah shares with Krio traits not evident in any other New World creole, such as the habitual auxiliaries *blaŋ/blant* (No. 2, above),[69] and the similarly-used *cin/kin*. The completive auxiliary *dʌn/dɔn*, while not restricted to these two creoles, occurs in each with much greater frequency than in any other.[70] A further link may be found in the speech of the so-called 'Americo-Liberians'[71] of Monrovia, Liberia. This type of English, spoken some 200 miles along the coast from Freetown, represents in part a retention of Southern U.S. Negro speech-forms arrested during the last century and left to flourish in an environment less affected by Standard American English. Examples of this speech[72] include: (1) *ma gɛ́: tʃa:j wã kōw hɔ hɛ́:*, 'my daughter wants to comb her hair'; (2) *ow hów ẽ fá, jɔ nɔ́ŋ gó dɛ bifó*, 'our house isn't far; you've gone there before'; (3) *wɛ́ jɔ gɔ̃:j, mɛ̃?*, 'where are you going, man?'; (4) *há ól jɔ?*, 'how old are you?'; (5) *aj sʌ gɔ̃:j hɛ́p jɔ kɛ́: da rák*, 'I'm going to help you carry that rock'; (6) *a ẽ nó wɔ́ jɔ nẽ ɔ trá:j*, 'I don't know (what's) your name or tribe'; (7) *di tʃílrən lɛ kɛ́tʃ gahápa*, 'the children are catching grasshoppers'; (8) *tẽ: só!*, 'it isn't so!'; (9) *á kʌ́mi, ɛn í gɔ̃*, 'I'm coming, and he's gone'; (10) *das di lá:s tã:j a gɔ̃:j tɛ́l jɔ tə kã já*, 'that's the last time I'm going to tell you to come here'; (11) *jɔ lɛ dʒájb mi wid jɔ ásre*, 'you're teasing me with your silly talk'.

4.7.4 The first Negroes to arrive in Gullah country were from Barbados, having been carried from that island in 1671 by Sir John Yeamans to work in his Carolina plantation. In the years following, others were brought to the region from the Antilles, the Bahamas, Antigua, Jamaica, Bermuda and the Leeward Islands, but slaves from the West Indies were not popular in the southern States. At one period the head-tax on a West Indian slave was five times greater than that on a slave brought directly from Africa.[73] By 1803 in fact, the importation of slaves from the West Indies had become illegal, and apart from some small-scale slave smuggling from the Caribbean into the United States, all the slaves purchased after that date came directly from Africa. Although it is probable that many of these were already sufficiently familiar with the English-derived pidgin or creole of the West African coast to influence radically the character of what is today Gullah, Turner has suggested that 'presumably the slaves coming to South Carolina and Georgia direct from Africa, unlike those who had spent some time in other parts of America and the West Indies, had, on their arrival, little or no acquaintance with the English language'.[74]

5.0.0 After the initial years of establishment in the seventeenth century, little contact occurred between Surinam and other creole-speaking areas. There is no historical evidence to show that any Sranan-speaking Negroes ever returned to Freetown—or indeed to any part of Africa—and the fact that there are no Dutch-derived words in Krio, although increasingly since 1667 a great many in Sranan, indicates that the similarity between the two languages is the result of a one way shift—from the West Coast of Africa to South

America. The possibility that the Sranan language was propagated by the descendants of the handful of Surinamers who were resettled in Jamaica (4.2.2) and that their Sranan-speaking [?] descendants were among the Jamaican Maroons who were taken to Freetown in 1800, is exceedingly remote.[75] Therefore that Sranan and Jamaican Creole have less features in common than do both these languages with Krio, is understandable. Whereas the link between what are today Krio and Sranan may be dated to 300 years ago, much more recent two-way communication has taken place between Jamaica and Sierra Leone. It is feasible then to assume that an English-derived contact vernacular had established itself on the West African coast *prior* to the period of mass exportation of slaves from there. Cassidy brought this point to light in 1962.[76]

5.0.1 Sranan shares too many lexical similarities with Krio and other members of the Atlantic group to have produced them independently. The fact that these cognates exist may be explained by their having a common origin in an earlier English-derived pidgin spoken in the English-owned factories and slaving stations along the Guinea coast, this same Proto-Pidgin being the progenitor of all present-day English-derived pidgins and creoles in the Atlantic area. That this was a pidgin, and not a creole, would also explain why modern English-derived creoles in this area are not more similar than they are.

5.0.2 The Surinam creoles appear to have been more conservative than Krio in retaining features of the original Proto-Pidgin. They are spoken in a country where Dutch is the official language, and were subject to a continuing influence from English for only a very short time. Krio, on the other hand, as with Gullah and the Caribbean creoles, has been under constant pressure from English for two centuries or more. Sranan has tended to retain the final open syllables characteristic of the majority of West African languages; Krio, while sharing this feature has either lost (or perhaps in some cases never had) the final vowel on words derived from English items with a closed final syllable. Specimens of Krio recorded in the late eighteenth and early nineteenth centuries indicate that pronunciations such as *gɔdu, meki, driŋki* and *disi* ('God', 'make', 'drink' and 'this', cf. Sranan *gádo, méci, drípi, dísi*) were then in use. Today, such pronunciations are considered by Krio speakers to be typical of the Pidgin Krio used by certain up-country speakers. Besides influence from English, this lack (or loss) of an added final vowel may be due to influence from Temne, an African language with many closed final syllables which is spoken alongside Krio in Freetown. In Gambian Krio, however, despite its co-existence with Wolof (which also admits of closed final syllables), such forms as *frédi* ('afraid') continue to be used where Krio now has *fred* (cf. Sranan *fréde*). In Krio the process has been extended to produce such forms as *les* and *kres* for 'lazy' and 'crazy'.

6.0.0 THE NAUTICAL ELEMENT

As mentioned earlier, evidence points to the first English-derived pidgin having been developed between English seamen and the indigenous peoples along the Guinea coast at watering points and on board ship, in the early sixteenth century. The Sierra Leone estuary, situated as it is on one of the finest natural harbours in West Africa, and also being nearer to Europe, would have been one of the first centres of a trade language.

6.0.1 It is known that buccaneering communities, whether on land or at sea, were composed of Africans (perhaps runaway slaves), Mulattoes and Europeans—many of whom were not English-speaking (fourteen different nationalities, for example, were represented in the crew of Nelson's H.M.S. *Victory* at Trafalgar). It is quite likely that these seamen would have developed a 'common denominator' language for use amongst themselves, as described by Traven in his novel *The Death Ship* (New York, 1934) and commented on by Reinecke.[77] By nature of their renegade profession these people kept themselves well-isolated from civilization and the law. In such isolation their composite vernacular would have been doubly reinforced. Thus many items in Krio and the other Atlantic dialects are of nautical origin, many of them in Krio exhibiting phonological features indicative of early adoption into the lexicon. Examples are *cápin* ('captain'), *cábin* ('cabin'), *dʒɛb* (from archaic 'gybe', i.e. 'to smuggle or hide from sight'), *ɟáli* ('kitchen'), *ib* ('throw'), *drif* ('edge towards'), *wɛr* (in one sense, 'to barely touch, scrape through',— EDD has 'wear: to veer, used of a vessel'), *flag* ('beat, flog'), *es* (from archaic 'heis', NED 'raise up'), *dʒam* ('be stalemated', from 'jam', listed in the NED as nautical, origin unknown), *dʒɔg* ('snatch away', from 'jog', NED nautical, etym. unknown), *slam* ('to berth'), *fuŋkás* ('bellows type'), *gaf* ('withhold, keep at arm's length', from 'gaff'), *pájlɔt* ('procuror', i.e. 'one who guides'—this item occurs in Barbados and in Malacca Creole Portuguese with the same meaning), *capsáj* or *kapsáj* ('overturn'), *bambót(-ɟál)* ('prostitute', i.e. a girl who waited on shore for the bumboats to bring sailors from the ship), and possibly *tʃak* ('drunk').

6.0.2 Since pirates left few written records, much of the early rôle played by them in the formation of Proto-Pidgin must remain conjecture. Jules Faine, whose field is primarily French-derived creoles, has denied an African substratum for the creoles,[78] but admits that they originated as an 'espèce de "lingua franca" en usage sur les vaisseaux marchands'. Goodman on the other hand establishes a West African influence in the French-derived creoles, but considers the idea of a nautical origin to be an inadequate explanation for the grammatical similarities among them.[79] He feels too, that Faine's evidence, in the form of a few French Creole terms of nautical origin, is insufficient proof.[80]

6.0.3 Slaves were often kept on board ship for upwards of six months while captains assembled a full cargo in port; together with the few more months spent on the trans-Atlantic voyage this would have given slaves who knew no pidgin sufficient time to acquaint themselves with it from fellow captives and the crew. Thus, on arrival, many slaves would have already become familiarized with the basic vocabulary and syntax of the pidgin in addition to their own languages. In order to continue communication among themselves, having once arrived in the New World, they would have retained this common form of speech. New generations of children, although in the first instance probably having some knowledge of the mother's language, would of necessity have conversed with each other in pidgin, but—since the very nature of a pidgin makes it inadequate as a vehicle for expressing a very wide range of human experience—the children would have soon encountered difficulty in attempting to communicate their thoughts. It is not unlikely that under such circumstances the children would have looked for guidance to the adult slaves (who would have been experiencing the same difficulties). The adults, being still more familiar with their tribal tongues than with the pidgin, would have drawn upon them in order to 'expand' this pidgin, thus producing the extensive calquing and Africanization of the creoles, and the individual characteristics of each in its own area.[81]

7.0.0 SUMMARY CHART

Although linguistic 'family trees' are not altogether in favour nowadays, tending to present data too rigidly, they do serve to indicate the interrelationship of languages in simple diagrammatic form. The following chart is merely tentative, and makes no reference to the time factors involved.

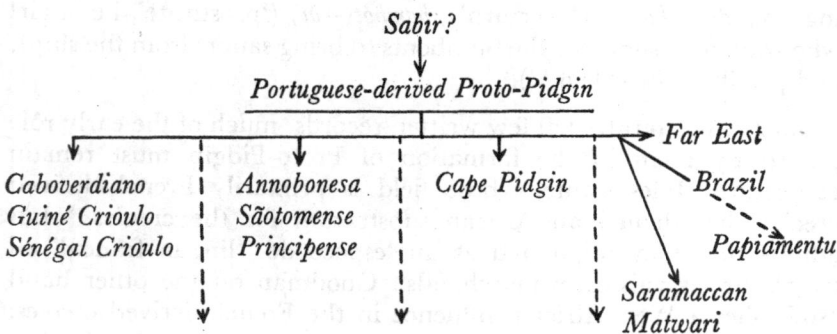

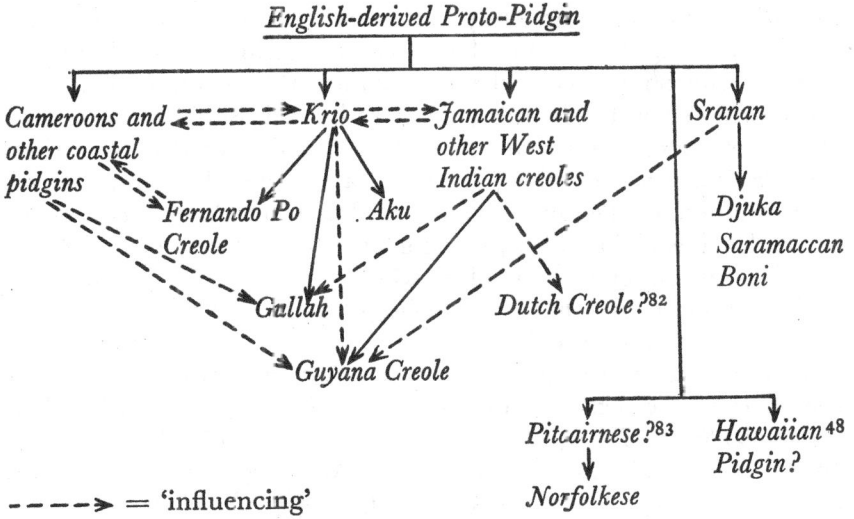

- - - → = 'influencing'

8.0.0 THE WORD-LISTS

Where occurring, cognate forms with identical or near-identical meaning in each creole have been entered. Where items which are etymologically traceable to the same source differ semantically, this has been noted (e.g. item 89, for Sranan). Those entries accompanied by additional notes at the end of the lists are marked with an asterisk.

For the purpose of providing a general Creole English glossary, non-cognate translations have been included where a cognate form does not exist, and often in addition to the cognate form. Blanks in the lists indicate that these items have not been traced in the sources available, or that the items do not occur in the language (e.g. item 384, 'loincloth', where such a garment is not normally worn by Gullah speakers). I.P.A. orthography is employed. It should be noted that for Guyana Creole and Gullah especially, the phonetic spellings are sometimes only approximations, adapted from sources in which these creoles are spelled according to English orthographic convention.

In all languages except Saramaccan and Djuka, syllables are marked for prominence (high tone/'stress'), which is also lexically significant for Krio and possibly Jamaican Creole.[85] Saramaccan is marked for tone, also lexically significant, but for Djuka no data are available.

Not all free variant forms have been included for each language; thus in Jamaican Creole, Guyana Creole and Krio, /b/ may occur as an allophone of /v/ in some words. Similarly initial /s/ before a plosive may or may not be retained. Since it is likely that the older forms of each creole approximate more to the assumed common

Proto-Pidgin and consequently to each other, obsolescent items and old-fashioned pronunciations have been recorded—especially in the case of Guyana Creole—where available. Where more than one Krio form occurs for an item, they are listed in order of currency. Items not widely known are marked with a dagger (†). Note that Krio /r/ is a velar fricative, Gullah /ɽ/ a retroflex flap, and that in Krio, Cameroons Pidgin, Guyana and Jamaican Creole, /c/ and /ɟ/ are realized as [kj] and [gj], being generally more retracted than in Sranan, Saramaccan and Gullah, where they represent [c] and [ɟ]. In most dialects of Jamaican Creole, /o/ is realized phonetically as a half-close central vowel.

Written sources for the word-lists in addition to those mentioned elsewhere in the text, include for Sranan, J. VOORHOEVE, *Woordenlijst van het Sranan Tongo, Glossary of the Surinam Vernacular*, Paramaribo, 1961; H. R. WÜLLSCHLAGEL, *Deutsch-Neger-Englisches Wörterbuch*, Löbau, 1850, reissued Amsterdam, 1965, and G. C. WEYGANDT, *Gemeenzame leerwijze om het Bastert of Neger-Engelsch op een gemakkelijke wijze te leeren verstaan en spreken*, Paramaribo, 1798; for Saramaccan, A. DONICIE and J. VOORHOEVE, *De Saramaccaanse woordenschat*, Amsterdam, 1962; H. SCHUCHARDT, *Die Sprache der Saramakkaneger in Surinam*, Amsterdam, 1914, and M. DELAFOSSE, 'Survivances africaines chez les Nègres "bosch" de la Guyane', *L'Anthropologie*, XXXV, 1925, pp. 475–94; for Djuka, A. G. BARNETT, 'Colonial Survivals in Bush Negro Speech', *American Speech*, VII, 1932, pp. 393–7; M. KAHN, *Djuka, the Bush-Negroes of Dutch Guiana*, New York, 1931, and C. N. DUBELAAR and J. W. GONGGRYP, 'Het Afakaschrift, een nadere beschouwing', *Nieuwe West Indische Gids*, 1968, 3, pp. 232–60; for Cameroons Pidgin, D. DWYER, *An Introduction to West African Pidgin English*, Michigan State U.P., 1966; for Guyana Creole, S. R. R. ALLSOPP, 'The English Language in British Guiana', *English Language Teaching*, XII, 1958, pp. 59–55 and I. VAN SERTIMA, *The Creole Tongue of British Guiana*, New Amsterdam, 1905; for Jamaican Creole, T. RUSSELL, *The etymology of Jamaica grammar*, Kingston, 1868, and for Gullah, A. GONZALES, *The Black Border*, Columbia, 1922; H. P. BLOK, 'Annotations to Mr. Turner's "Africanisms in the Gullah Dialect"', *Lingua*, VIII, 1959, pp. 306–21; *Animal Tales Told in the Gullah Dialect* (with notes, texts and glossary), Library of Congress Recordings (three records), Washington, 1949; L. D. TURNER, 'Notes on the Sounds and Vocabulary of Gullah', *Publication of the American Dialect Society*, III, 1945, and 'Problems Confronting the Investigator of Gullah', *Publication of the American Dialect Society*, IX, 1948; M. CRUM, *Gullah, Negro Life in the Carolina Sea Islands*, Durham, 1940; R. SMITH, *Gullah*, Columbia, 1926 (re-issued Charleston, 1969), and J. BENNETT, 'Gullah, a Negro Patois', *South Atlantic Quarterly*, VII, 1908, pp. 332–47, and VIII, 1909, pp. 39–52.

The bulk of the entries were collected from informants; these included for *Krio*, Miss Rosamunde Davies (16 years), Mrs. Agnes Parker (55 years) and Mr. Bayo Bright (35 years), all of Freetown, Mrs. W. Johnstone of Leicester Village (*c.* 80 years) and Mrs. Modu Bright (30 years) of Sussex Village; for *Sranan*, Mr. L. J. Modell (72 years) of Paramaribo; for *Cameroons Pidgin*, Mr. John Ndembuisi (34 years) of Afikpo; for *Guyana Creole*, Mrs. Yvonne Gayle (24 years) of Georgetown and Mr. Raj Lakraj (37 years) of Demerara; for *Jamaican Creole*, Mr. Michael Gayle (16 years) of Kingston and Mr. Sonny Haughton (28 years) of Clarendon; for valuable contributions on *Trinidad Creole English* thanks are extended to Mr. and Mrs. David Field, both of Port-of-Spain. Thanks also go to Professor F. G. Cassidy at Wisconsin, who personally checked a large part of the Jamaican material, and likewise to Professor Jan Voorhoeve at Leiden, who provided additions and corrections to much of the Sranan and Saramaccan material, and without whose encouragement and suggestions this paper would never have been written. I should also like to thank my friend and tutor, Dr. David Dalby, for his criticism and advice during the preparation of this paper, at the School of Oriental and African Studies.

NOTES ON THE TEXT

1. Slightly *less* than half the available lexicon for Saramaccan is clearly derived from English.
2. For further discussions on the classification of pidgin and creole languages, see M. EMENEAU, 'Bilingualism and Structural Borrowing', *Proc. Amer. Phil. Soc.*, 106, 1962; L. GÖBL-GÁLDI, 'Problemi di sostrato nel creolo francese', *Rev. de Ling. Romane*, IX, 1933; R. A. HALL Jr., 'The Genetic Relationships of Haitian Creole', *Word*, XIV, 1958; D. H. HYMES, 'Genetic Classification, Retrospect and Prospect', *Anthrop. Ling.*, I, ii, 1959; R. MORGAN Jr., 'St. Martin Creole and Genetic Relationships', in A. H. MARCKWARDT (ed.), *Studies in Languages and Linguistics*, Ann Arbor, 1964; D. TAYLOR, 'Language Shift or Changing Relationships?', *Int. Jour. Amer. Ling.*, XVI, 1960, and U. WEINREICH, 'On the Compatibility of Genetic Relationship and Convergent Development', *Word*, XIV, 1958. Many languages not usually considered to be creoles nevertheless exhibit creole features—Santali, Mundari, Romanes, Beja, Mbugu, Yiddish, and even English—and it is likely that this linguistic process is far older and much more widespread than is generally realized.
3. See R. A. HALL Jr., 'Pidgin English and Linguistic Change', *Lingua*, III, ii, 1952, pp. 145–6.
4. M. and F. HERSKOVITS, *Surinam Folklore*, New York, 1936, pp. 117–75.
5. S. G. STONEY and G. M. SHELBY, *Black Genesis*, New York, 1930, p. xi. The authors suggest an original West African (Bantu) pidgin as the source of both the West Indian creoles and Gullah, which began to acquire their English-derived lexicon when the Africans arrived in the Caribbean. Gullah took on its own characteristics when its speakers were taken from the West Indies to North America. They claim that Gullah is the 'strongest linguistic connection between America and the Antilles and Africa'. A similar suggestion, i.e. that an *African* inter-language had developed on the Guinea coast and formed the basis for the Atlantic creoles, was put forward by L. LICHTVELD, in his article 'Enerlei creools?', *Nieuwe West Indische Gids*, XXXV, 1954, pp. 59–71. Both these works forerun the relexification theory. A very brief note on the similarities between Gullah and Sierra Leone Pidgin in particular was

made some years earlier by E. C. PARSONS, in his *Folk-lore of the Sea Islands, South Carolina*, Mem. Amer. Folk Lore Soc., XVI, 1923. See also J. J. Thomas, 'Creole Philology', *Trübner's American and Oriental Record*, December 1870, pp. 57–8.

6. R. and V. McDAVID, 'The Relationship of the Speech of American Negroes to the Speech of Whites', *Amer. Speech*, XXVI, 1951, p. 11.

7. In *Symposium on Multilingualism* (3nd meeting of the Inter-African Committee on Linguistics), Brazzaville, 1962, pp. 267–77.

8. See J. BERRY, 'English Loanwords and Adaptations in Sierra Leone Krio', *Creole Language Studies*, II, 1961, p. 1: 'Krio is spoken as a mother tongue by some 20,000–30,000 inhabitants of Freetown ...'.

9. R. J. HARRISON-CHURCH, *West Africa*, London, 1963, p. 307, where Krio is stated to be the first language of 65,000 urban and 55,000 rural speakers (1955 estimate).

10. According to *The Gambia in Brief*, 1955, p. 11. Between 1821 and 1888 the Gambia was placed under the administration of the Government of Sierra Leone (but had its own colonial administration between 1843 and 1866). There have always been fairly strong ties between the two countries.

11. See A. VON S. BRADSHAW, 'Portuguese in the Languages of Sierra Leone', *African Language Review (Sierra Leone Lang. Rev.)*, IV, 1965, p. 12: '... Krio, which may be said to have begun with the arrival of the Maroons in Freetown in 1800'; R. W. THOMPSON, 'A Caribbean Sister for Krio', *Sierra Leone Studies*, June 1962, p. 227: '... we shall soon be able to ascertain in some detail how far Krio is the development of one or more New World dialects ...'; L. D. TURNER, *Krio Texts, with grammatical notes and translations in English*, Chicago, 1965, p. 8: 'The English of the West Indians and the American ex-slaves of the late eighteenth and early nineteenth centuries serves to form the base [of Krio] to which have been added important features of many differing African languages'; J. BERRY, 'Creole as a Language', *West Africa*, September 19, 1959, p. 745: 'It would appear to have developed from a pidginized type of English spoken in the contact situation in the early nineteenth century', and 'The Origins of Krio Vocabulary', *Sierra Leone Stud.*, December 1959, p. 298: 'Krio is a creolized language, based on a reduced or pidginized type of English spoken in the contact situation in the early nineteenth century', and R. A. HALL Jr., *Pidgin and Creole Languages*, New York, 1966, p. 17: 'An offshoot of Jamaican Creole is found in Africa ... under the name of Krio'.

12. 'Creole Languages in the Caribbean', p. 35, in F. A. RICE (ed.). *Study of the Rôle of Second Languages in Asia, Africa and Latin America*, Washington, 1962. During the early nineteenth century the name 'Talkee Talkee' (cf. *Taki-Taki* for Sranan) was given to the vernacular used in Freetown between Africans and Europeans.

13. According to J. VOORHOEVE, 'A Project for the Study of Creole Language History in Surinam', *Creole Language Studies*, II, p. 102.

14. Compared with scripts originating in West Africa in an article by D. DALBY, 'The Indigenous Scripts of West Africa and Surinam: Their Inspiration and Design', *Afr. Lang. Stud.*, IX, 1968. Note that it was the three great pidgin/creole-speaking areas, viz. Sierra Leone/Liberia, the Cameroons and Surinam, which produced the earliest indigenous scripts.

15. The pamphlet is reproduced in J. GONGGRYP and C. DUBELAAR, 'De geschriften van Afaka in zijn Djoeka schrift', *Nieuwe West Indische Gids*, XLII, 1962. Djuka items in the lists from this source are left in Dutch orthography. Further lexical material on Djuka, not available at the time of going to press, will be found in J. E. Grimes, ed., *Languages of the Guianas*, S.I.L., in press (Djuka–Sranan–Saramaccan wordlist by Dr. G. L. Huttar). Note that a Djuka pidgin is also used between the Djuka Bush Negroes and the Trío Amerindians.

16. Op. cit., p. 759.

17. In his *Cameroons Creole Dictionary, first draft* (privately circulated), Bamenda, 1961, p. 10.

18. According to R. T. SMITH, *The Negro Family in British Guiana*, New York, 1956, p. 3.

19. Although this is an over-simplification.

20. Material dealing with Sabir includes H. SCHUCHARDT 'Die Lingua Franca', *Zeitschr. für Rom. Phil.*, XXXIII, pp. 441–61; C. TAGLIAVINI, 'Franca, Lingua', *Enciclopedia Italiana*, Vol. XI, p. 837, and H. KAHANE *et al.*, *The Lingua Franca in the Levant*, Urbana, 1958. A sample of Sabir, taken from A. COELHO, *Os dialectos românicos ou neolatinos na Africa, Asia e América*, Lisbon, 1881–83, is given here: 'Bon giorno Signor; comme ti star? —Mi star bonu, e ti?—Mi star contento mirar per ti.—Grazia.—Mi pudir servir per ti per qualche cosa?—Muciu grazia.—Ti dar una cadiera al Signer. —Non bisogna. Mi star bene acousi.—Comme star il fratello di ti?—Star muciu bonu.' ('Good-day, sir; how are you?— I am well, and you?—I am happy to see you.—Thank you.—Can I help you in any way?—Thank you very much.—(You) give a chair to the gentleman—I don't care. I am fine as I am.—How is your brother?—(He) is very well.') This highly Italianized Sabir or Lingua Franca is, however, hardly representative of the more cosmopolitan variety used in earlier centuries.

21. D. TAYLOR, 'The Origin of the West Indian Creole Languages', *Amer. Anthrop.*, LXV, 1963, p. 802.

22. K. WHINNOM, *Spanish Contact Vernaculars in the Philippine Islands*, Hong Kong U.P., 1956, p. 7, n. 13. Even later evidence pointing to the widespread use of the Portuguese-derived pidgin is found in the journal of John BARBOT (*c.* 1679; British Museum Add. MS. XXVIII, 788), in which he says that a knowledge of this trade language was necessary to those travelling to both the Caribbean and the Guinea Coast. He does not specify, however, the precise areas in which the language was then current.

23. See STEWART (op. cit., n. 12 above), and TAYLOR (op cit., n. 21).

24. The same applies to Papiamentu, the creole spoken in Aruba, Bonaire and Curaçao. The Portuguese elements in Saramaccan and Papiamentu represent the original pidgin substrate, the English and Dutch (or, in the case of Papiamentu, Spanish and Dutch) elements subsequently being adopted into the languages during the process of developing into a creole and later. Had contact with Portugal been maintained in Surinam and Curaçao, both Saramaccan and Papiamentu would presumably be Portuguese-derived creoles today.

25. It is possible that there were two main periods of supralexification: in the first instance it might have taken place during the earliest years of pidgin acquisition in the settlements along the Guinea coast, when it was used only sporadically between Africans who shared a common tribal language, and Europeans. The Africans would have soon discovered that their Portuguese-derived pidgin proved of little use when attempting to communicate with English sailors, and concurrence of the Portuguese- and English-derived items would have been short-lived, the latter taking prominence as England established her own footholds in West Africa, and as contact with Portuguese speakers subsequently lessened. The second period of supralexification would have been perhaps a century later, i.e. around the middle of the seventeenth century, when the slave trade was well-established and the coast pidgin sufficiently deep-rooted for its retention. During this second period the pidgin would have been employed less between African and European than amongst Africans of different linguistic backgrounds. The process of supralexification may have taken three courses: firstly, the items in the earlier pidgin being quickly forgotten, as happened during the first period (e.g. the word '*kollilu*', the name of a spinach-like vegetable, listed as having been used in Sierra Leone 250 years ago—according to ASTLEY in his *Voyages*—but now surviving only in French-speaking West Africa and the West Indies); secondly, both items being retained in the pidgin with the same meaning and frequency (e.g. Krio *blaj*, from Portuguese, and *baskit*, from English, both meaning 'basket'), or else one gradually superceding the other (e.g. Sranan *ánson*, 'attractive', from English, which is being ousted by Dutch-derived *moj*), and thirdly, the retention of both terms with specialized meanings (e.g. Krio *pikin*, Portuguese-derived and meaning 'baby, child', and *bebi*, English-derived and meaning 'doll').

26. For a detailed study of the history of English in West Africa, see J. SPENCER (ed.), *The English Language in West Africa*, London, in press.

27. A. Alvares D'ALMADA, *Tratado breve dos Rios de Guiné*, 1594 (repr. Lisbon, 1946), in a reference to the island of Gorée (Dakar), on the Senegal coast. For this, and several other historical references cited in this paper I am indebted to Dr. P. E. H. Hair and Dr. David Dalby.

28. F. Moore, *Travels into the Inland Parts of Africa* London, 1734, p. 294.
29. D. Forde (ed.), *Efik Traders of Old Calabar*, London, 1954.
30. An example of which is as follows: '... *about 6 am in aqua Landing with fine morning so I go on bord and com back in 10 clock time so I have drink in my house 6 clock I brow* [i.e. 'blow'] *all wawa Egbo to again cutt firs wood in morning for putt to Town plaver house* ...'. On p. viii, Forde writes: 'In their relations with the European traders, who were for the most part fleeting visitors with neither the interest nor the training to learn an African language, the Efik soon appreciated the importance of acquiring a trade language in which to carry out their transactions. Thus at Old Calabar, and at other trading centres of the Oil Rivers, there developed, through intercourse with English traders and seamen, a jargon which was mainly English in vocabulary, although the constructions were often modelled on those of Ibibio. Europeans adopted it in their dealings with Africans, and it was carried from place to place on the West Coast, where it merged with other jargons, similarly developed, to become in the eighteenth century a fairly standardised pidgin English'.
31. In G. Williams, *History of the Liverpool Privateers*, London, 1897, p. 628.
32. In modern Krio, the youth's words would read *Mása Kró, sɔntin de bɛ́t mi túmɔs; a nɔ́ ébul fɔ si ā. A wā mɛ́k ju gi mi sɔ̄ wasmɔ́t, ɛ̄ wā trɔsis.*
33. Other Krio forms are possible, for example *nɔ́ kī* (or *cánt*) *si* and *a wā ju fɔ gi mi* instead of *nɔ́ ébul fɔ si* and *a wā mek ju gi mi*. One Krio informant has provided independently the expression *tikín pantín* (cf. 'tacken') meaning 'underpants', but no other speaker has so far been able to verify this.
34. A. M. Falconbridge, *Narrative of Two Voyages to the River Sierra Leone During the Years 1791-2-3*, 2nd edn., London, 1802, pp. 77 and 82.
35. Op. cit. (n. 70 above), p. 650: ... *you and me sabby each other long time and me know you tell me true mouth ... for you sabby me have too much wife it be we country fash ... and we no sabby book, and we no havy head for make ship for sen we bad mans for more country.* ... *But we tink trade no stop for all we Ju-Ju-man tell we so for dem say you country no can niber pass God A' Mighty.*
36. S. van Brakel, *Een Amsterdamsche factorij te Paramaribo in 1613*, Utrecht 1914.
37. L. Rens, *The Historical and Social Background of Surinam Negro English*, Amsterdam, 1953, p. 16.
38. Rens, op. cit., p. 13. In 1626 over 500 French subjects settled on the Saramacca River, but left at the end of three years. In 1639 three hundred and seventy-eight more Frenchmen attempted to establish a colony in the same region, but Amerindian attacks made settlement impossible.
39. Rens, op. cit., p. 14.
40. R. Le Page, 'Jamaican Creole', *Creole Lang. Stud.*, I, London 1960, p. 17.
41. See the population tables in R. Le Page 'General Outlines of Creole English Dialects in the British Caribbean', *Orbis*, VII, 1958, pp. 54-64. The tables appear on pp. 58-9.
42. Rens, op. cit., p. 22.
43. Rens, op. cit., p. 15.
44. Rens, op. cit., p. 25. This is also the opinion held by Hall, who writes: '... Saramaccá and town Sranan are so closely related that it is clear that both are developments from a common ancestral form, seventeenth-century Guianan Pidgin English (which in its turn was a replacement for, and took over a great many features from, an even earlier Guianan Pidgin Portuguese)', op. cit. (n. 11 above), p. 36.
45. Cassidy, op. cit., p. 270.
46. A. Burns, *A History of the British West Indies*, London, 1954, p. 69.
47. According to the tables in Le Page (n. 41 above).
48. P. Kup, *A History of Sierra Leone 1400-1787*, Cambridge, 1961, p. 69.
49. R. Le Page, 'General outlines ...', p. 63. Despite this remark, he indicates that the proportion of Europeans to Negroes in 1650 (20,000 Europeans, 25,000 Negroes), had become 17,000 Europeans to 60,000 Negroes by 1750. This represents a drop from 80% to around 28% in one century.

50. For details concerning the history of the Dutch slave trade I am entirely indebted to Mr. H. C. van Renselaar, Research Fellow at the Koninklijk Instituut voor de Tropen in Amsterdam, who provided them in personal communication.

51. In his *Vijf dagregisters van het kasteel São Jorge da Mina aan de Goudkust, 1645–1647*, Series Linschotenvereningen, VAN RENSELAAR suggests that the best studies of the history of the Dutch slave trade are W. S. UNGER, 'Bijdragen tot de geschiedenis van der Nederlandse slavenhandel' [a general survey], *Econ. Hist. Jaarboek*, 's-Gravenhage, dl. 26, 1956, pp. 134–74, and 'Bijdragen tot de geschiedenis van de Nederlandse slavenhandel' (the 'Middelburg Commercie Compagnie 1732–1808'), *Econ. Hist. Jaarboek*, 's-Gravenhage, dl. 28, 1961, pp. 3–148.

52. Suggested by Mr. van Renselaar.

53. For further information on the Surinam Maroons, see H. LARSEN and M. PELLATON, *Behind the Lianas*, London, 1958, pp. 16 and 61–2.

54. See CASSIDY, op. cit. (n. 7 above), and M. HERSKOVITS, 'On the Provenience of Portuguese in Saramacca Tongo', *West Indische Gids*, XII, 1930–31.

55. *The Cameroons, From Mandate to Independence*, Los Angeles, 1964, p. 18. A little-known source for Fernando Po Creole is R. P. MARIANO DE ZARCO, *Dialecto inglés-africano o broken-english de la colonia española del Golfo de Guinea. Epitome de la gramatica seguido del vocabulario español-inglés y inglés-español*, 2nd edn., Turnhout, 1938.

56. A. W. LAWRENCE, *Trade Castles and Forts in West Africa*, London, 1963, p. 69. See also BARBOT's journal (op. cit., n. 22 above).

57. In their 'Sources of the Nineteenth Century Atlantic Slave Trade', *Jour. Afr. Hist.*, V, 2, 1964, pp. 185–208.

58. However near to standard English modern Barbadian speech may be, a pidgin, if not a creole, must have been in use during the early years of colonization in Barbados. And while it is possible that whatever form of English the Barbados Negroes spoke may have contributed to the formation of Sranan, this in itself does not imply that it had a purely Caribbean origin. If, as Cruickshank has remarked, the Barbadians were speaking Negro English when they arrived in Essequibo and Demarara in the 1740s, their speech in Barbados much have developed toward standard English in the years following this date (but cf. 4.2.6.). As a source for common words and expressions in the modern dialect of Barbados, consult F. COLLYMORE, *Notes for a Glossary of Words and Phrases of Barbadian Dialect*, Bridgetown, 1955.

59. J. G. CRUICKSHANK, *Black Talk, being notes on the Negro dialect of British Guiana, with (inevitably) a chapter on the vernacular of Barbados*, Demarara, 1916, p. 4.

60. Especially R. LE PAGE and D. DECAMP, *Jamaican Creole*, London, 1960; F. CASSIDY, *Jamaica Talk*, London, 1961, and F. CASSIDY and R. LE PAGE, *Dictionary of Jamaican English*, London, 1967 (esp. introductory chapters).

61. Mentioned in LE PAGE, *Jamaican Creole* (n. 60 above), p. 94, and again in his 'General outlines...' (n. 41 above), p. 381.

62. Presented at the Conference on Pidginization and Creolization of Languages, held at Mona, Jamaica, April 1968.

63. In addition, over one-third of the African-derived religious items in Haitian Creole French appears to be traceable to Kikongo, according to an examination of the material in S. and J. COMHAIRE-SYLVAIN, 'Survivances africaines dans le vocabulaire religieux d'Haïti', *Études dahoméennes*, XIV, 1955, pp. 3–20. For material dealing with the impact Portuguese has had on Kikongo, see W. BAL, 'O destino de palavras de origem portuguesa num dialecto quicongo', *Revista Port. de Filologia*, XV, 1 and 2, 1969, pp. 49–102.

64. L. D. TURNER, *Africanisms in the Gullah Dialect*, Chicago, 1949, p. 1.

65. Apart from this, conditions of legalized subjection very similar to slavery continued to exist for thousands of Negro Americans, in the form of peonage, until 1907. 'Extra-legal forms of peonage have been tolerated since that time' (quoted from R. I. McDAVID Jr., review of TURNER, *Language*, XVI, 1950, p. 324, n. 7).

66. TURNER, op. cit., pp. 42–208.

67. P. E. H. HAIR, 'Sierra Leone Items in the Gullah Dialect of American English', *Sierra Leone Lang. Review*, IV, 1965, pp. 79–84.

68. See n. 5 above. His source for Sierra Leone Pidgin is M. CRONISE and H. WARD, *Cunnie Rabbit, Mr. Spider and the Other Beef*, New York and London, 1907.

69. In Gambia Krio, this is regularly pronounced *blan*. The *English Dialect Dictionary*, ed. J. WRIGHT, London, 1905, has *belong to, belang, belangt*, 'be accustomed, be in the habit of', as occurring in the dialects of Lincolnshire and Cornwall. It also occurs in some U.S. dialects.

70. *Dɔn* is used in the same way in Trinidad, Creole English; see C. R. OTTLEY, *Trinibagianese, Words and Phrases, Old and New, Peculiar to the Speech of Trinidadians and Tobagonians*, Port-of-Spain, 1966. B. L. BAILEY, in her *Language Guide to Jamaica*, New York, 1962, includes on p. 11 both *mi don iit* and *mi iit don* ('I have finished eating'), but does not discuss the first construction in her later *Jamaican Creole Syntax*, Cambridge, 1966. A similar use of *done* occurs in the English dialect of Tristan da Cunha, as in 'when you done went' (see A. ZETTERSTEN, 'The Linguistic Situation on Tristan da Cunha', *Folia Linguistica*, 1, 1–2, 1968, pp. 119–24), and in the now probably extinct so-called 'Butler English' of Madras: '. . . the preterite indicative being formed by "done", thus . . . I done tell, I have told; done come, actually arrived'. (H. YULE and A. C. BURNELL, *Hobson Jobson*, London, 1886, pp. 133–4). A further similarity between Gullah and Krio lies in their respective syllable-stress patterns; as is apparent from the word lists, many English-derived words in Krio have an un-English final syllable stress (e.g. *dadí, watá, Krió*, etc.), and, according to M. S. WHALEY, in *The Old Types Pass*, 1925, p. 162, '. . . the Gullah, contrary to English usage, places the accent on the last syllable of a number of words which otherwise they speak correctly or with little change'.

71. Not a popular term in Liberia.

72. Known as 'Waterside English', 'Brokes' or 'Merico Talk'. These sentences were collected by the writer from Liberians resident in Sierra Leone. There is very little documentation on Liberian English; William A. STEWART discusses it briefly in his 'Foreign Language Teaching Methods in Quasi-foreign Language Situations', *Nonstandard Speech and the Teaching of English*, Cent. for Applied Linguistics, Washington, 1964, pp. 1–15, and there exists a Liberian English glossary (of limited use) published by the American Peace Corps, *Some Terms from Liberian Speech*, by W. L. D'AZEVEDO, Monrovia, 1967.

73. TURNER, op. cit., pp. 256–7.

74. TURNER, op. cit., p. 4. An earlier viewpoint in contrast to Turner's was held by G. P. KRAPP, who maintained that 'it is not improbable that the English of the original Gullah negroes was a kind of Pan-African English, used all along the slave coast . . .' (*The English Language in America*, New York, 1925, p. 253).

75. Further details on the historical connection between Surinam and Jamaica may be found in G. B. JOHNSON, *Folk Culture on St. Helena Island, South Carolina*, Chapel Hill, 1930, p. 112, n. ii, and in F. CUNDALL, 'The Migration from Surinam to Jamaica', *Timehri*, VI, September 1919.

76. CASSIDY, op. cit., p. 268.

77. J. E. REINECKE, 'Trade Jargons and Creole Dialects as Marginal Languages', *Social Forces*, XVII, 1938, pp. 107–08, and also in D. HYMES (ed.), *Language in Culture*, New York, 1966. In other words, a type of pidgin was already in formation before the European sailors arrived on the West African coast, and it was this that the Africans learned as the European speech. The Africans would naturally have tried to speak in a way most like the visiting Europeans, in order to be better understood. An example of a much more recent nautical pidgin, with no African influence at all, is furnished by Russonorsk (see O. BROCH, 'Russenorsk', *Archiv für Slawische Phil.*, 41, 1927, pp. 209–62, and G. NEUMANN, 'Russenorwegisch und Pidginenglisch', *Nachrichten der Giessener Hochschulgesellschaft*, 34, 1965, pp. 219–23).

78. J. FAINE, *Le créole dans l'univers*, Port-au-Prince, 1939, p. 16.

79. M. GOODMAN, *A Comparative Study of Creole French Dialects*, The Hague, 1964, pp. 127–32.

80. In his *Vocabulaires comparatifs*, Paris, 1904, M. DELAFOSSE says of the French-derived pidgin dialects of West Africa ('Petit-Nègre' or 'Pitinègue'), that there is 'emploi fréquent de mots empruntés ... à la terminologie maritime', and gives some examples (p. 265).

81. STEWART (op. cit., p. 44) says '... none of the Caribbean Creoles are now mutually intelligible with their lexically related standard, and if early accounts are to be trusted, they apparently never were'. WHINNOM, in 'The Origin of the European-based Creoles and Pidgins (1)', *Orbis*, XIV, 1965, p. 509, similarly remarks that 'Standard French and the French Creoles are not mutually intelligible (and almost certainly never were: which fact must cast doubt on the "baby talk" theory)'. These statements possibly exaggerate the situation; a pidgin in its initial stages is usually comprehensible to metropolitan speakers (although not vice versa). Mutual unintelligibility would come about later during the process of creolization, and supralexification away from English, French, etc. At this stage the Europeans must learn the creole from the Africans. While in the New World the establishment of the creoles was due to African language fragmentation, these languages in West Africa probably became creolized by Mulatto speakers, large numbers of whom lived in and around the factories on the coast.

82. This language is fast giving way to a variety of English Creole. An examination of the lexicon of Virgin Islands Dutch Creole indicates considerable earlier influence from English.

83. Pitcairnese and Norfolkese developed as a result of a voluntary settling on Pitcairn Island in 1790 by mutineers from H.M.S. *Bounty*—nine British seamen accompanied by nineteen Polynesian men and women. Their very different cultural and linguistic backgrounds combined to form a unique miniature society, and an English-derived creole developed within the community. The Pitcairn Islanders were moved *en bloc* in 1859 to Norfolk Island for economic reasons. Many were later to return to Pitcairn, leaving two isolated communities separated by over 4,000 miles of ocean. It appears from examining texts (in S. Ross and A. MOVERLEY, *The Pitcairnese Language*, London, 1964), that the type of English which contributed to the lexicon and syntax of Pitcairnese was a nautical pidgin rather than the metropolitan speech. Of the nine non-Polynesians, four were English, two Scottish, one American, one a West Indian from St. Kitts and one from Guernsey whose first language was French. Within the first five years of settlement several of them died, leaving two Englishmen, a Scot and the West Indian. It seems strange that with such a difference in numbers it was not Tahitian or some other Polynesian language which came to be spoken on the island; yet the creoles are English-derived, and share far more features in common with the Atlantic Creoles than with Neo-Melanesian (see note for item 553 below).

84. Like Pitcairnese, the English-derived pidgin/creole of Hawaii appears to share more features with the Atlantic group than with Neo-Melanesian, China Coast Pidgin, etc. (although an attempt to show a link between the latter and the Hawaiian pidgin/creole, and a discussion of an earlier Portuguese influence upon each, may be found in E. C. KNOWLTON, 'Pidgin English and Portuguese', *Proc. of the Symp. on Historical, Archaeological and Linguistic Studies on Southern China, S.E. Asia and the Hong Kong Region*, ed. F. S. DRAKE, Hong Kong U.P., 1967, pp. 228–237). Examples of Hawaiian speech include: *by'm by 'e say 'e going come inside one-time*, ('after a while he said he was going to come in immediately'); *this strong; you no can broke 'm*, ('this is strong; you cannot break it'); *he go fool me*, ('he will fool me'); *us go stay sweat*, ('we will be sweating'); *we been get plenty rice een Tony house*, ('we got plenty of rice in Tony's house'); *one basket I been buy da fair*, ('a basket I bought at the fair'), and *we going da town foa get barb*, ('we're going to town for a haircut'). See J. REINECKE and A. TOKIMASA, 'The English Dialect of Hawaii', *American Speech*, IX, 1934, pp. 48–58 and 122–31; S. M. TSUZAKI, 'Coexistent Systems in Language Variation: The Case of Hawaiian English', in D. HYMES (ed.), *Proceedings of the Conference on Pidginization and Creolization of Languages* (Jamaica, 1968), London, in press, and 'Problems in the Study of Hawaiian English', *Working Papers in Linguistics*, III, 1969, pp. 117–33, and E. NEMETHY, *Da tree leedle peegs*, Honolulu, 1953.

85. See D. L. LAWTON, 'The Implication of Tone for Jamaican Creole', *Anthrop. Ling.*, X, 6, 1968, pp. 22–6.

COMPARATIVE WORD-LISTS

English	Krio	Sranan-(Djuka)	Saramaccan

LIST A. VERBS

#	English	Krio	Sranan-(Djuka)	Saramaccan
1.	abuse	kɔs, bjus	kɔ́si, frúku	kósi
2.	agree	gri	gri	
*3.	annoy	ambɔ́g, trɔb	mɔ́feri, trɔ́bi	toóbi
4.	ask	aks	áksi	hákísi
5.	attend	tambáj	stambáj	
6.	awaken	wek	wéci	wéki
*7.	be (equating)	na	na, da, (na)	na, da
8.	be (locating)	de	de, e, (de)	de
9.	be (resembling)	tã	tã, (ta, tang)	tán
10.	beg	beg	béɟi, (begi)	bégi, pidí
11.	begin	bigín, (s)tat	biɟín, (bigi)	bigí
12.	believe	bilív	bríbi, (bilibi)	bílbi
*13.	bend down	butú	bukún	sijá
*14.	bite	bɛt	béti, (biti)	kukuɲáŋ-kukuɲán
*15.	bleach	britʃ	bréci	
16.	boil	bwɛl	bɔ́ri	bói
17.	bore, drill	bo	bɔ́rɔ	bólu, avíti
*18.	borrow	lɛnt, trɔs	léni	júu
19.	break	brok	brɔ́kɔ, (broko)	boóko
20.	brush	brɔs	bɔ́srɔ	bɔ́sɔ̀
21.	burn	bɔn	bron, (bron)	cumá, boónu
22.	burst	bɔs	bɔs, báster	
23.	buy	baj	baj, (baj)	bái
24.	can, be able	kin, ébul	kan, maŋ	kan
25.	care	bísin, kíja	ke	kɛ́
*26.	carry	tot	cári, ca, (tjari)	cá
27.	carry on the head	†panteté	cá na éde	agbágba
28.	catch	ketʃ	císi, (kisi)	kísi
29.	chew	tʃam	betbéti, kaw	kukuɲáŋ-kukuɲán
30.	choke	tʃok	jóko	ɟukú ['vomit']
31.	chop	tʃap	cápu ['hoe']	
32.	climb	klem	kren	subí
33.	cock, tilt up	kak	káka	
34.	cohabit	ab, †sɔkísɔki	sɔ́ki, bɔ́mbo	kú
35.	come	kam, kã	kɔm, kɔ̃, (kong)	kó
36.	cook	kuk	kúku	kúku, fɛ̀ɛ́bɛ́
37.	cover	kɔ́ba	cíbri	cubí
38.	crush	mas	mási, (masi)	masiká
*39.	curtsey	kɔtʃí	kósi	sijá

(see 8.0.0 above for phonological conventions)

	Cameroons	Guyana	Jamaican	Gullah
1.	kəs	kɔs, bju:z	kos, bju:z	kʌs
2.	gri	gri:	gri:	gri:, lɔ
*3.	ambɔ́k, trɔ́bu	trʌbl	trábl, ambóg	trʌβl
4.	aks	a:ks	(h)a:ks	(h)ʌks
5.	tandá	stambáj	tambáj, tan	tambáj
6.	wekɔ́p	wek	wiɛk(óp)	βek
*7.	na, bi	a	a, dá	dʌ, də, de
8.	də, di	de	de	dʌ, də, de
9.	tan	tan	tam, stíɛ	tã
10.	bɛk	bɛg	bɛg	beg
11.	bigín, sitát	bigín, sta:t	bigín, ta:t	biJin, stat
12.	bilíf	bli:b	bli:b	bli:β
*13.	butú	bɔwdɔ́wŋ	butú	bɛndáwŋ
*14.	bajt	bajt	bajt	bajt
*15.	muf-kɔ́la	bli:tʃ	bli:tʃ	bli:c
16.	bɔ́ja	bajl	bwajl	bʌjl
17.	bɔ	bo, bɔr	buo	bo
*18.	bɔ́rɔ, trəs	lɛn, trɔs	lɛn, tros	lɛn
19.	brok	brek	brok	brʌk
20.	brum	brɔʃ	brɔʃ	brɛʃ
21.	bən	bɔn, bɔrn	bon	bʌn
22.	bəs	bɔs	bos	bʌs
23.	baj	baj	baj	baj
24.	fit, ébu	can, kan	ca:n	ciʀ, ku
25.	kíja	ke, kir	ca, kir, bíznis	ca, ke, bídnis
*26.	tut	car, cɔr	caj, ca	toː, ca
27.	tút fɔ hɛ́t	cár an di hɛ́d	car a hɛd	tóː pan də héd
28.	kas	ketʃ	kɛtʃ	cɛc
29.	tʃɔp	tʃɔ:	tʃa:, tʃu:	tʃɔ:m
30.	tʃok	tʃok	tʃuík	cok
31.	tʃɔp	tʃap	tʃap	cʌp
32.	klajm	klajm	klajm	klajm
33.	kak	kak	kak	kæk
34.	mbumbú, tu	fɔk	fok	ɸut
35.	kɔm	kɔm	kom	kʌm, kʌ̃
36.	kuk	kuk	kuk	kuk
37.	kɔ́ba	kɔ́bə	kíba	kíβə
38.	maʃ	maʃ	maʃ	maʃ
*39.	kiní	kɔ́rtisi	kótʃi	kʌ́ci

	English	Krio	Sranan-(Djuka)	Saramaccan
40.	dare	díjas	dɔ́rfu	póli
*41.	dip	dɔk	dɔ́ki, dukún	dɔ́ki
42.	do	du	du, (doe)	dú
43.	dream	drim	dren	suɲá
44.	drink	driŋk, fuŋk	dríɲi, (dirigi)	diíŋgi
*45.	drive	drɛb	dríbi	diípi
46.	drop	drap	drópu, (saka)	sáka, disá-kaí
*47.	eat	ɲam, jit, wak	ɲã, (njang, nja)	ɲam, kɔmɛ́
48.	edge (towards)	drif	drífi, dríbi	pusá
49.	exchange	tʃendʒ, tʃendʒí(n)	cénci, céɲi, (kengie)	tooká
*50.	fall	fɔdɔ́m	fadɔn, (fadom)	kaí
*51.	fasten	fáʃin, klif	fási	namá, peká
52.	fight	fɛt	féti, (feti)	féti
53.	fill	ful(ɔ́p)	fúru	fúu
54.	find	fɛn	féni, (fene, fende)	féndi
*55.	flatter	kúfa, korí, swit-mɔ́t	kɔ́li, kɔ́ri	gaɲá
56.	flog, whip	flag, laʃ, wip	wípi, fɔm	húpi
57.	fly	flaj	frej	buwá
58.	forget	fɔgɛ́t	friɟíti, (figete)	fɛ̀ɛkɛ́tɛ̀
59.	forgive	fɔgív	párdon, (parato)	paádon
60.	give	gi	ɟi, (gi)	dá
61.	go	go	gɔ, (go)	gó
*62.	gossip	koŋgosá	gɔŋgɔsá	goŋgosá
63.	grow	gro	gro	gɔ́ɔ
64.	hang	ɛŋ, ɛŋg	áɲa	hɛ́ŋgi
65.	have	a, ab, gɛ(t)	a, ábi, (abi)	hábi
66.	hear	jɛrí	jére, jɛ́rɛ, (aliki [?])	jéi
67.	help	ɛp	jépi, (jeepi)	heépi
68.	hold	ol	ɔ́ri, (oli)	hói
69.	hunt	ɔnt	ɔ́nti, (jaki)	hɔ́ndi
70.	hurry	mekés	mecési, (feti)	
71.	hurt	at	áti, (ati)	háti
*72.	jump	dʒomp	dʒɔ́mpɔ, (djompo)	ɟómbo
73.	keep	kip, ol	ɔ́ri, (oli)	hói
74.	kill	kil	círi, (kila)	kíi
75.	kiss	kis	bósi	bósi
76.	knock	nak, †gens	náci, ɟens, (naki)	náki

	Cameroons	Guyana	Jamaican	Gullah
40.	dɛ:	dir	dir	de
*41.	put	dip	dok, dip	dʌk
42.	du	du	du	du
43.	drim	dri:m	dri:m	dri:m
44.	driŋ	driŋk	driŋk	driŋk
*45.	draf	drajb	drajb	drɑjβ
46.	drɔp	drap	drap	drʌp
*47.	tʃɔp, wak	ɲam, ji:t	ɲam	ɲam, ɲɔ:m
48.	drif, nĺja	drif	drif	drif
49.	tʃens	tʃendʒ	tʃiɛndʒi	cenɟ
*50.	fɔl	fa:l dówŋ	fadóŋ	ɸʌdáwn, kan
*51.	tajt	fa:sn	fa:sn	ɸʌʃn
52.	fajt	fajt	fajt	ɸajt
53.	fulɔ́p	ful	ful(óp)	ɸul
54.	fajn	fajn	fajn	ɸajn
*55.	jawó	swi:t-mówt	swi:t-mówt	sβi:t-mawt
56.	flɔk, wip	flag, laʃ, wip	flag, fom, wip	ɸlag, βip
57.	flaj	flaj	flaj	ɸlaj
58.	frubáj	fɔrgét	figát	ɸĺgət
59.	sɔ́ri fɔ	fɔrgiv	fagíb	ɸaɟiβ
60.	gif	gi	gi	ɟi:
61.	go	go	go	go
*62.	kuŋgusá	kɔŋgəsá	koŋgosé, sesé	ʃiʃi
63.	bik	gro	gruo	grɑ, tánda
64.	haŋ	hɛŋ	hɛŋ	haŋ, hɛŋ
65.	gɛt	a, ha, gɛt	ha, hab	ha
66.	híja	héri, híə	hiɛ, jɛ́ri, háriki	jɛ́ri, hárci
67.	hélɛp	hɛp	hɛp	hɛp
68.	hol	hol	huol	hol
69.	hánta	hɔnt	hɔnt, prag	hʌnt
70.	hɔrihɔ́ri	mekés, pulfút	mekíɛs	mɛcés, sazúka
71.	háti	ha:t	ha:t	hʌt
*72.	dʒɔm	dʒʌmp	dʒomp	ɟʌmp
73.	kip	ki:p	ki:p	ci:p
74.	kil	kil	kil	cil
75.	tʃɔp-mɔ́f	kis	bos	cis
76.	nak	nak	nak	nak

	English	Krio	Sranan-(Djuka)	Saramaccan
*77.	know	no, sabí	sábi, (sabi, konni)	sábi, sá
78.	laugh (at)	laf	láfu	jábi-jábi
79.	leave, go out	kɔmɔ́t	kmɔ́tɔ, (koemoeta)	kumútu
80.	leave, let alone	lɛf	líbi	disá
81.	lie down	lidɔ́m	lidɔ́n, didɔ́n	
82.	lift	es, bumbú	ési	ési
*83.	live	lib	líbi, (libi)	líbi
84.	look (at)	luk	lúku, (luku)	lúku
85.	look after	mɛn, ʃad	méni	
86.	make	mɛk, mek	méci, (moke)	mbéi
87.	marry	máred	trow	tɔ́u
*88.	menstruate	si mun	mɛf	faági, dé na tén
89.	move	muf	muf [= 'go away!']	
90.	must	mɔs, gɛ(t) fɔ	mu, músu, (moe)	músu
91.	nag	bre, dʒadʒá	tánteri, spéti	
92.	(be) named	nɛm	nẽ, (ning)	nɛ́
93.	need	nid	(notoe)	
94.	open	ópin	ópo	jábi
95.	pull, take off	pul	púru, (poe)	púu, hái
96.	push	ʃub, ʃɔb, puʃ	ʃɔ́bu	
97.	push into	trɔs	trúsu	tuúsi
98.	put	put	póti, (poti)	butá
99.	remember	mɛ́mba	mémre	mɛ́mbɛ̀
100.	resemble	fíba, tã lɛkɛ	tã léjci	taŋ kúma
101.	rest	blo	(ar)bró, lɔ́stu, (boro)	bɔ́ɔ
102.	ride	rɛd	re	lé
103.	scratch	kratʃ	krási	kaási
104.	see	si	si, (si)	si
105.	shake	ʃek, ʃɛk	séci	séki
106.	shout	ála	kre, bári, (bali)	kɛ̀ɛ́, bái
107.	shut	klos, sɛt	tápu	tapá
*108.	singe	swindʒ	brɔn, (bron)	boónu
109.	sit	sidɔ́m	sidɔ́n, (sidom)	sindɔ́
110.	slap	slap, †kɔf	kɔ́fu	
111.	sleep	slip	srtíbi, (siibi)	duúmi
112.	slip	slípul	skɔ́jfi, gráti	
113.	spill, throw away	trowé	trowé, (towe)	túɛ
114.	split	plit	príti	piíti, lacá

	Cameroons	Guyana	Jamaican	Gullah
*77.	sábi	no	nuo, sábi	no, sábi, ndɔ
78.	laf	la:f	la:f	laɸ
79.	kɔmɔ́t	gó ɔ́wt	komɔ́wt	guajnáwt
80.	lɛf	lɛf	lɛf	lɛɸ
81.	ladɔ́ŋ	ledɔ́ŋ	lidθŋ	lɛdáwŋ
82.	lif	ajs	ajs	hajs, bumbú
*83.	lib, lif	lib	lib	liβ
84.	luk	lúk(u)	lúk(u), ku	luk
85.	majn	majn, wátʃman	majn, ɬa:d	majn
86.	mek	mɛk	mɛk	mɛk
87.	méri	márid	márid	sɔ́mpa, mári
*88.	si mun	há di kɔ́rsiz	mu:n	sumɨ́ci
89.	muf	mu:b	mu:b	mu:β
90.	mɔs, gɛt fɔ	mɔs, gɛ́fu	mós(i), mósa	mʌs, háfə
91.	hála	nag	nag, bonɨ́sz	ɬáɬa, ribré
92.	nem	nem	niɛm	nem
93.	wan	ni:d	ni:d	ni:d
94.	ópan	opm	uopm	ópi
95.	pul	pul	pul, púli	pu, pul
96.	puʃ	ʃɔb, ʃub	ʃob, ʃub	ʃʌb, pʌʃ
97.	puʃ	trɔs	tros	cʌs
98.	put	put	put	pit
99.	mímba	mɛ́mbə	mɛ́mba	mɛ́mbə
100.	fíba	féba	fɨ́eba	táŋkə
101.	rɛs	blo	bluo	rɛs
102.	rajt	rajd	rajd	rajd
103.	kras	kratʃ	kratʃ	krɑc
104.	si	si:	si	si:
105.	ʃek	ʃek	ʃiɛk	ʃɛk
106.	hála	hála	hála	hálə
107.	ʃɛt	ʃɔt	ʃɛt	ʃɛt
*108.	bən	swindʒ	swindʒ	sβiɲɬ
109.	ʃidɔ́ŋ	sidɔ́wŋ	sidóŋ	sɛt, sɛsáwŋ
110.	siláp	kʌf	kof	kʌɸ
111.	silíp	sli:p, dódo	sli:p	sli:p
112.	slajt	slajd	sipl, slip	slip
113.	trowé	trowé	trowɨ́ɛ	cʌráj, cʌré
114.	brok	(s)plit	plit, plik	plit

	English	Krio	Sranan-(Djuka)	Saramaccan
115.	spoil	pwɛl	póri, (pori)	pói, póndi
116.	squat	dʒɔŋkɔ́n [Bathurst]	dʒokotó, dʒoŋkó ['nod head']	ɟɔkɔ̀tɔ́
117.	squeeze	kwis	kwínsi	kpíɲi
118.	stab	tʃuk, stɛb	dʒʌ́ku	tuká
119.	stand	tináp, tanáp	tnápu, (tanopo)	tan
120.	stay	te, tap, lɛf	te, fiká, (te)	te, fiká
121.	steal	tif	fufúru	fufúu
122.	stop	tap	tápu	tapá
123.	stutter	stɔ́ma	gágu	ŋgáku
124.	swallow	swɛ́la	swári, (gobe)	gulí
125.	take	tek	téci, (teki)	téi, ba
126.	take (accompany)	kɛr, kɛ́ri	cári, ca, (tjari)	ca
127.	talk	tɔk	táci, (taki)	táki
128.	thank	tɛl téŋki	táɲi, (tagi)	taŋgí
129.	think	tiŋk, ⁺sájfa	déŋki, prákseri, (pakisiri)	tíŋga
130.	tickle	tiklís	tígri	abokíki
131.	tie up	tajɔ́p, triŋ	triɲi	mindí
132.	tilt	liŋ, cant	kánti, (kanti)	kándi
133.	tremble	trímbul	béjfi	tɛ̀ɛmɛ́ [earlier trèmɛ́]
134.	walk	wáka	wáka, (waka)	wáka
135.	want	want, wã	wáni, wã, (wanni)	kɛ́
136.	wash	was	wási, (wasi)	wási
137.	wear	wɛr	wéri	wéi
138.	wipe	wep	fiɟí	féki
139.	work	wok	wróko, (oroko)	wokó, woóko
140.	write	rajt, rɛt	skrífi	sikífi
141.	yawn	ɟap	gápu	hóha

LIST B. ADJECTIVES

	English	Krio	Sranan-(Djuka)	Saramaccan
142.	abundant	nɔf, bɔkú	nɔ́fɔ	ndófu
143.	afraid	fred, frédi [Bathurst]	fréde, (fele, fede)	fɛ̀ɛ̀ɛ̀
144.	all	ɔl	ála, (a)	hǐi, túu, ála
145.	angry	vɛks	mándi	máti
146.	bad	bad	tákru	táku
147.	better	bɛ́tɛ	bétre	bɛ̀tɛ̀
148.	big	big	bíɟi, gran, (bigi, garan)	bígi, gaán
149.	black	blak	bláka	baáka

THE ENGLISH-BASED ATLANTIC CREOLES 43

	Cameroons	Guyana	Jamaican	Gullah
115.	sipɔ́l	spajl	pwajl	spʌjl
116.	sidɔ́ŋ fɔ fút	ni:l dɔ́wŋ	saŋkúku	ní:l dáwŋ
117.	mas	kwi:z	kwi:z	kβi:ʃ
118.	tʃuk	dzuk	dʒuk, tʃuk	ɟuk
119.	tanɔ́p	stanɔ́p	tanáp	tanʌ́p
120.	tif	ti:f, prápra	ti:f, prápra	ti:f, húma
121.	te	ste	te	te, laŋ
122.	sitɔ́p	stap	tap	tap
123.	sitáma	stáma	táma	táma
124.	swɔ́lo	swálo	swála	sβʌ́lə
125.	tek	tɛk	tek	tɛk, tʌk
126.	kɛ́ri	ca:	ca:, caj	ca
127.	tɔk	ta:k	ta:k, tá:ki	tʌk
128.	taŋ	táŋki	táŋki, tɛ́ŋki	táɲci, tɛ́ɲci
129.	tiŋ	tiŋk	tiŋk	tiŋk, sájfə
130.	tíku	tikl	tikl	tikl
131.	taj	tajɔ́p	triŋóp, tajɔ́p	triŋʌ́p
132.	ban	tip(-ɔ́p)	li:ŋ, tip	cant, tip
133.	ʃek	trimbl	trimbl	trí:mbl
134.	wɔ́ka	wa:k	wa:k	βɔk
135.	wan	wan(t)	wa:n(t)	βɔ̃, βã
136.	wɔs, wɔʃ	waʃ	waʃ	βʌʃ
137.	wíja	wir	wiɛr	βe
138.	wajp	wajp	wajp	βajp
139.	wɔk	wɔrk	wok	βʌk
140.	rajt	rajt	rajt	rajt
141.	ópan-mɔ́f	ja:n	ja:n	ɟap
142.	bɔkú	nʌʃ	nof	nʌ́фə
143.	fíja	frajkn	friɛd	фed, fjed
144.	ɔl	a:l	a:l	ɔl
145.	bɛks	bɛks	bɛks	βɛks
146.	bat	bad	bad	βad
147.	bɛ́ta	bɛ́ta	bɛ́ta	βɛ́ɽə
148.	bik	big	big, grán(di)	βig, gən
149.	blak	blak	blak	blak, báka

	English	Krio	Sranan-(Djuka)	Saramaccan
150.	blind	blɛn(-jáj)	bréni	
151.	blue	blu	braw	
152.	bogus, fake	bógro	bóŋgrɔ	
153.	bold	drajáj	drejáj	póli
154.	broken	bróko	brɔ́kɔ	boóko
155.	casual	dɔ́ŋca, ízi, wajwɔ́	doŋcé	
*156.	chock-full	tʃak, ful-pí, tʃɔkɔ́p	tʃok	
157.	clean	klin	krin, (kiri)	limbá, límbo
158.	cold	kol	kówru	kɔ́tɔ̀
159.	crooked	bɛmbɛ́n	krúktu	kuúkútu
160.	cunning	kɔní	kɔ́ni, (konni)	kɔ́ni
161.	dark	dak	dúŋru	dúŋgu
162.	dead	déde, daj	dede	dɛ́dɛ̀
163.	deaf	dɛf(-jés)	dɔ́fu, dúfu	
164.	deep	dip	dípi	fúndu
165.	drunk	drɔ́ŋgɔ, tʃak	drúŋu	dɔɔ́ŋgɔ̀
166.	dry	draj	drej	dɛ́ɛ̀, caka
*167.	dumb	mumú	stɔn	
168.	every	ébri	íbri	íbi
169.	far	fáwe, poŋ	farawé, (farawej)	lóŋgi
170.	fine	fajn, fɛn	fíni	fínu
171.	first	fɔs	fɔ́si, (fosi)	fósu
172.	foolish	tʃúpit, lawláw	lawláw	láu
173.	glad	gládi	bréti	wái
174.	good	gud	bun, (boeng)	búnu
175.	greedy	biɟáj, grídi	biɟáj, grídi	gíti
176.	green	grin	grun	guúnu
177.	heavy	ébi	ébi, (hebi)	hébi
178.	high	aj(-ɔ́p)	ej	héi
179.	hoarse	os	grɔ́fu [also 'stern']	
180.	hot	ɔt	áti	
181.	impudent	sas, fítjáj	asránti, frépostu	saánti, póli
182.	insolvent	brok	browk	
183.	jealous	dʒálas	ɟárusu	ɟalúsu, haún
184.	lazy	les	lési	malɛ́ŋgɛ̀
185.	long	láŋga	láŋa, lápa, (langa)	láŋga
186.	many	plɛ́nti, bɔkú	fúru	híla
187.	mean	krabít, grídi, kɔvɛ́tfɔs	grídi	gíti

THE ENGLISH-BASED ATLANTIC CREOLES 45

	Cameroons	Guyana	Jamaican	Gullah
150.	blajn	blajn	blajn	blajn
151.	bilú	blu:	blu:	blu:
152.	fɔls		bogubóu	
153.	drajáj	traŋáj	drajáj, traŋáj	βol
154.	brok	brok	brokóp	brʌk
155.	ísi	í:zi	duoŋcá	í:zi, diŋcá
*156.	tʃək	tʃak	tʃak	cʌk
157.	klin	kli:n	kli:n	kli:n, túnija
158.	kol	kol	kuol	kol
159.	bɛmbɛ́n	krúkid	krúkid	krúkiti
160.	kɔ́ni	kɔ́niŋ	kóni	skí:mi
161.	dak	dark	da:k	da:k, dáki
162.	daj	dɛd	dɛd	ded, bu
163.	mumú	dɛf	dɛf	di:f
164.	dip	di:p	di:p	di:p
165.	drəŋ	drɔŋk, bú:zi	drɔŋk, tʃa:dʒ	drɔŋk
166.	draj	draj	draj	draj
*167.	mumú	mumú	mumú	dʌm
168.	ɔl	ɛ́bri	ɛ́bri	ɛ́βə
169.	fawé	farawé	farawíɛ	ɸa, pon
170.	fajn	fajn	fajn	ɸajn
171.	fəs	fɔs	fos	ɸʌs
172.	fúliʃ	fú:liʃ	tʃúpit	ɸú:liʃ, tʃúpit
173.	glat	glad	glad	glad
174.	gut	gud	gud, bun	gud
175.	bigáj	bigáj	bigáj	biɟáj, gʌtlin
176.	girín	gri:n	gri:n	gri:n
177.	hɛf	ɛ́bi	hɛ́bi	hɛ́βi
178.	háj-fɔ-ɔ́p	ḣaj	haj	haj, hɔj
179.	rɔf	ḣos	ha:s	hósi
180.	hɔt	ḣat	hat	hʌt
181.	trɔŋ-hɛ́t	ru:d	ru:d, fíɛsti	sási, impí:din
182.	no gɛt mɔ́ni	brok	brok	brok
183.	laŋgatrút	dʒɛ́lɔs	dʒálas	ɟɛ́ləs
184.	lési	lézi	líɛzi	lézi
185.	lɔŋ	laŋ	laŋ	lʌŋ
186.	plɛ́nti, bɔkú	nʌfnʌ́f, plenti-plɛ́nti	plɛnti-plɛ́nti	nʌ́ɸə, tɔ́kɔ
187.	laŋgatrút	kɔbitʃɔs, bɔrí:di	krábit, kóbitʃ	tába, kʌ́βic

	English	Krio	Sranan-(Djuka)	Saramaccan
188.	mediocre	afáf, †basabása	afáfu	
189.	middle	mídul	míndri	míndi
190.	naked	nékɛd	soso-scín	pɛ́nɛ́pɛ́nɛ́
191.	new	ɲu	ɲun	ɲúɲú
192.	occasional	wãwán	wãwán, (wawang)	wãwán ['sole']
*193.	old	ol, wol	ówru, (olo)	awoo, gasá
194.	old-fashioned	óltɛm	owrutén	awooté
195.	only	sóso, nɔ́mɔ	sóso, sɔ́sɔ, (soso)	sɔ́sɔ̀
196.	other	(n)ɔ́da, nɛ́da	tra, (taa)	óto
197.	own	jon	éjɟi	éigi
198.	painful	so, sáwa	sɔ́rɔ	gáŋgi
199.	poor	po	póbri, póti	pená
200.	pretty	fajn	mɔj, ánson, (moi)	hánso, cénce
201.	red	rɛd	rédi	bɛ́
202.	rich	dʒɛ́ntri, ritʃ	dʒéndri, gúdu	ɟɛndɛ̀
203.	ripe	rɛp	lépi	lépi
204.	rotten	rɔ́tin	rátin, frɔ́tu	fɔ́ɔtu
205.	second	sɛ́kɛn	di-fu-tú	
206.	shaky	dɛgɛdɛ́gɛ	dégedége	dɛ̀ŋgɛdɛ̀ŋgɛ
207.	short	ʃɔt	ʃátu	sáti
208.	small	smɔl, líli	smára, pcin	pikí
209.	soft	saf	sáfu, (safoe)	mɔ́i
210.	softly	sáful, sáfli	sáfri, (safri)	sáápi
211.	sour	sáwa	swa	sóa
212.	square	skwája	kwéri	
213.	strong	tráŋga	tráŋa, (taraga)	taáŋga
214.	tasty	swit	swíti, (soeiti)	súti
*215.	thin	draj	máŋri	máŋgu, cólólóó
216.	third	tɔd	di-fu-drí	
217.	tired	tája, wíri	wéri	wéi
218.	tough	tɔf, galút	tɔf, típsi, kaŋkán	vuŋgá
*219.	ugly	wɔwɔ́, wogrí	ógri, (ogiri, ogi)	wógi
220.	untidy	dʒagadʒága	jagajága	
221.	warm	wam	wárã	
222.	wet	sok, wɛt	náti	muɲá
223.	white	wet	wéti	wéti
224.	yellow	jála	géri	donú, fòkò

THE ENGLISH-BASED ATLANTIC CREOLES

	Cameroons	Guyana	Jamaican	Gullah
188.	hafháf	bugú:di	só:so	bíti
189.	míndru	midl	migl	midl, mil
190.	nékit, soso-sikín	nékid	niɛkid	néciti, be, ɸut
191.	nu	ɲu:	ɲu:	ɲu:
192.	wanwán	wanwán	wanwán	βã̃βán
*193.	ol	ol	uol	ol
194.	oltájm	óltajm	úoltajm	óltajm
195.	sóso	sóse	sóso, oŋgl	sóɾo, nʌmə
196.	áda	ɔ́da	tára, (n)áda	tʌ́ɾə
197.	ɔn	jon, on	uon, úona	joɴ, jont
198.	sɔ	sɔr	so, suor	so
199.	pɔ	po	puo	po
200.	fajn	príti, fajni-fájni	príti, príki	píti
201.	rɛt	rɛd	rɛd	rɛd
202.	ris	ritʃ	dʒɛ́ntri, ritʃ	ric
203.	rɛt	rajp	rajp	rajp
204.	sipɔ́l	ratn	rátn	rʌtn
205.	nəmba tú	sɛkn̩	sɛ́kan	sɛkŋ
206.		dʒɔgadʒɔ́ga	rúkurúku	
207.	ʃɔt	ʃa:t	ʃa:t	ʃɔt
208.	simɔ́l	sma:l, kʌ́ntʃi, líli	sma:l, likl, líli	smɔ:l, lí:li, li
209.	sɔf	saf	sa:f	saɸ
210.	sɔ́fri	sáfli	sá:fli	sɛ́ɸli
211.	sáwa	sówər	sóuwa	sáβə
212.	sikwía	skwir	skwiɛr	skwe
213.	trɔŋ	traŋ	traŋ	trʌŋ
214.	ʃwit	swi:t	swi:t	sβi:t
*215.	no fat	má:ga, pí:ni, slɛ́ŋgəri	ma:ga, pí:ni, krá:ni	drəjbón, pí:ni
216.	nəmba trí	tɔrd	tri: tajm, tod	tʌd
217.	taja	tajə	tája	tájəd, βɛ:ri
218.	trɔŋ	tɔf, basabása	tof	tʌɸ, ɬalú:t
*219.	wowó, wawá	wɔ́rɔ, ɔ́gli	hogli, úogli	ɔ́kli, ógli
220.	dʒagadʒága	dʒúgadʒúga	jágajága	ɬug
221.	wɔm	wɔrm	wa:m	βʌm
222.	sok, kol	wɛt	wɛt	βɛt
223.	wajt	wɛt, wajt	wajt	βajt
224.	rɛt	jála	jéla	jálə

	English	Krio	Sranan-(Djuka)	Saramaccan

LIST C. ANIMALS

	English	Krio	Sranan-(Djuka)	Saramaccan
225.	alligator	alig(r)éta	kájmã, aligéta	akalí, káima
226.	animal	bif	méti	mbéti
*227.	ant	antʃ	míra	ánsi
228.	ape	babú	babún	babúnu
229.	bee	ɔní, bɔŋgrɔbí	ɔ́ni	hɔ́ni
230.	bird	bɔd	fówru	fóu
231.	boa constrictor	bomán	abóma	bòmà
232.	cat	pus, cat	puspúsi	pusipúsi
233.	centipede	santapí	lusúmbe	ahalala
234.	cow	kaw	kaw	káu
235.	dog	dɔg	dágu, (dago)	dágu
*236.	duck	dɔks	dɔ́ksi	patupátu
*237.	elephant	ɛ́lifant, dzɔmbó	asáw	zaun
238.	fowl	fɔl	fówru	fóu
239.	goat	(raŋ)gót	krabíta	kaábíta
240.	hawk	ak, akák	áka	gabián
241.	hen	umanfɔ́l	m:áfowru	mamáfóu
242.	iguana	gwaná	legwána	wajamáka
243.	louse	lɔs	lósu	lósu
244.	monkey	mɔŋkí	mɔŋkimɔ́ŋki	ɬakài, keskési
245.	mosquito	maskíta	mascíta	máku
246.	mouse	aráta	mɔjsmɔ́jsi	alátu
247.	parrot	pɔlí	popokáj	faágima
248.	pig	ɔg, bɛsí	águ, (hago)	hágu
249.	rabbit	rábit	kɔŋkɔ́ni, (koni)	kɔ̀kɔ́ni
250.	rat	aráta	aláta, (alata)	alátu
251.	rooster	kak	káka, (kakafulu)	ómiganía
252.	sandflea	dʒigá	síka	síka
253.	scorpion	kaktél	krúktutere	kúkútulábu
254.	snake	snɛk	snéci, (sineki)	sindéki
255.	spider	spájda, (nansí)	anâ:nsi	aɬaánsi
256.	tortoise	trɔkí	sɛkrepátu	tɔ́ti
257.	vulture	júba, dzɔŋkró	jaŋkɔrɔ́, opéte	ɬaŋkóo, opéte
258.	wasp	waswás	waswási	wasiwási
259.	worm	wɔrɔ́m	wɔrɔ́n, (worom)	gbícu, wánu

LIST D. PLANTS AND FOODSTUFFS, ETC.

	English	Krio	Sranan-(Djuka)	Saramaccan
260.	bean	bintʃ	bɔ́ŋci, pési	pési
*261.	beancake	(bintʃ-)akára	akará	akala
262.	bread	bred	bréde, (bede)	bɛ̀ɛ̀

	Cameroons	Guyana	Jamaican	Gullah
225.	áligetɔ	aligéta	haligéta	kɔ́jma, gétə
226.	bif	ánimal, mi:t	hánimal	krí:tə
*227.	ans	antʃ	antʃ, ans	ans
228.	babún	babú:n	babú:n	
229.	hɔ́ni	bi:,	bi: boŋgabí	βi:, bʌməlabí
230.	bɛt	bɔrd	bod	bʌjd
231.	mbóma			bʌ́mə
232.	púsi	pus, cat	pus, cat	pus, cat
233.	sɛntipít	santapí	santapí	sɛ́nəpi:
234.	kaw	kɔw	kow	kaw, caw
235.	dɔk	dag	dag, da:g	dɔg, hawn
*236.	dɔ́kfawu	dɔk	dok	dʌk
*237.	ɛ́lifan	ɛ́lifant, asúnu	asúnu	oliɸóm, ɬámba
238.	fáwu	fɔwl	fowl	ɸawl
239.	got	(raŋ)gót	(raŋ)gúo:	got, búdi
240.	hɔk	ha:k	ha:k	hʌk, címbi
241.	wúmanfawu	hɛn	húmanfowl	úməcikin
242.	ŋgɔ́mbɛ	gwɔ́:na	gwá:na	
243.	karáŋgwa	lɔws	lajs	laws, úla
244.	mɔ́ŋki	mɔŋkí	mɔ́ŋki	mɔ́ŋci
245.	mɔskítu	maskí:ta	maskíta	scí:də
246.	aláta	mɔws	musmús, músu	maws, púku
247.	bɛ́t-we-i-tɔ́k	pá:rɔt	pá:rat	kúcu
248.	ʃwajn	hag, bára	ha:g	hag
249.	buʃbíf	rábit	rá:bit	rátit, kándi
250.	aláta	ráta	táta	rat, ʃiɬi
251.	mánfawu	fɔwíkák	kak	máncikin
252.	tʃíga	dzíga	dzíga	ɬígə
253.	sikɔpiɔn	skɔ́rpiən	ká:pjan	
254.	sinɛ́k	snek	sniɛk	sni:k
255.	sipáda	anánsi	aná:ŋsi	nánsɛ
256.	trɔ́ki	tɔrtl	kúta, tɔrkl	kútə
257.		búnəbɔrd, karjaŋkró	opete, ca:ŋkrúo	ɬʌŋkró, bʌ́zəd
258.	manawá	wɔs	waswás	βʌs
259.	wɔm	wɔrm	wɔrom	βʌ́rʌm
260.	bin	bi:n	bi:nz, pi:z	bi:nz
*261.	akára		ákra	
262.	brɛt	brɛd	brɛd	brɛd

	English	Krio	Sranan-(Djuka)	Saramaccan
263.	burnt food	*bɔmbɔ́n, krawó*	*brɔ́mbrɔ́n*	*aɟáɟa*
264.	bushland	*bus*	*búsi, (boesi)*	*mátu*
265.	calabash	*kalbás, ɔ́bɔrɔ*	*krabási, páci*	*kúja*
266.	cashew	*kuʃú*		
267.	cassava	*kasáda*	*kasába*	*kasába*
268.	coconut	*koknát*	*kɔkrɔnɔ́tɔ*	*kɔkɔnɔ́tɔ̀*
269.	dried fish	*drajfís, stɔkfís*	*tɔkɔfísi, (bat jau [?])*	
270.	egg	*eg*	*éksi, (eksi)*	*wóbo*
271.	flower	*fláwa*	*brɔ́ŋki*	*foló*
272.	food	*jajám, ɲaɲám*	*naɲán*	*ɲaɲá*
273.	fruit	*frut*	*frɔ́ktu*	*fuúta*
274.	fufu	*fufú*	*afufú*	*fufú*
275.	fungus	*dʒondʒó, ɔkpɔlɔ́-ós*	*popolípo, tɔ́dɔ-prásɔrɔ, (búnɟi)*	*fúŋgu*
276.	garlic	*ɟálik*	*kúnofróku*	
277.	ginger	*dʒíndʒa*	*ɟinɟa*	*aɟinɟa*
278.	gourd	*ɔ́bɔrɔ*	*gɔ́dɔ*	*kúja*
*279.	lagniappe	*būjá*	*bakafíɲa, baksís*	
280.	mango	*máŋgro*	*máɲa*	*máŋgo*
281.	mangrove	*sɔlwatá máŋgro*	*máŋgro*	*máŋgo*
282.	meat	*bif*	*méti*	*mbéti*
283.	nut	*nat*	*nɔ́tɔ*	
*284.	ochra	*ɔ́krɔ*	*ɔ́krɔ, (okoro)*	*lalú*
285.	onion	*jabás*	*ajún*	*ajón*
*286.	peanut	*granát, gra(w)mpí*	*pindá, gobogóbo*	*pindá, gobogóbo*
287.	pepper	*pɛ́pɛ*	*pɛ́prɛ*	*pɛ́pɛ*
*288.	pineapple	*pajnápul, (nanás)*	*nanási*	*naná*
289.	potato	*pɛtɛ́tɛ*	*patáta*	*batáta*
290.	pumpkin	*pɔŋkín*	*pampún*	*pampú*
291.	rice	*rɛs*	*aléjsi*	*alísi*
292.	rind	*kandá*	*búba, (boeba)*	*kákísa*
293.	root	*rut*	*rútu*	*lútu*
294.	salt	*sɔl*	*sówtu*	*sátu*
*295.	thorn	*tʃuktʃúk*	*máka*	*maká*
296.	tobacco	*tabáka*	*tabáka*	*tabáku*
297.	tomato	*tamatís*	*tomáti*	*tomáti*
298.	tree	*tik*	*bõ*	*páu*

THE ENGLISH-BASED ATLANTIC CREOLES   51

	Cameroons	Guyana	Jamaican	Gullah
263.	bɔmbɔ́n	bɔrnbɔ́rn	bɔrnfú:d	bʌnɸú:d
264.	buʃ	buʃ	buʃ, búʃiz	búʃiʃ, ɸínda
265.	krabás	calǝbáʃ, gúbi	calabáʃ, báki	cílǝbaʃ, túmbu
266.	káʃu	cáʃu	kúʃu, cáʃu	cáʃu
267.	kisáda	casá:ba	casáda, casába	casá:βǝ
268.	kokonɛ́t	kókǝnʌt	kuoknát	mɲ́ncinʌt
269.	sitɔkfís	sá:ltfiʃ	sa:lfíʃ	
270.	ɛk	ɛg	hɛgz	eg
271.	fláwa	flɔ́wa	flóuwa	ɸláβǝ
272.	náma, tʃɔp, wakís	ɲam	niɲám	ɲám(-ɲam)
273.	frut	fru:t	fru:t, bɪɛrin	fru:t
274.	fufú	fufú	fufú	ɸuɸú
275.	dʒundʒú	dʒondʒǘ, dʒʌmbí-ɔmbrɛ́la	dʒondʒó, dʒundʒú, dopi-cáp	mʌʃrú:n
276.	gálik	ɬá:lik	ɬá:lik	ɬá:lik
277.	dʒíndʒa	dʒíndʒǝ	dʒíndʒa	ɬɪɬa
278.	krabás	gɔrd	gúodi	god
*279.	daʃ-dáʃ, dʒára	bra:ta [?]	brá:ta, ɲápa	brɔ́:tǝs
280.	máŋgo	máŋgu	máŋguo	máŋgo
281.	máŋgro, matánda	máŋgro	máŋgruo	mánŋgro(β)
282.	bif	mi:t	mi:t	mi:t
283.	nǝt	nat	nat	nɔt
*284.	ɔ́kra	okró, gúma	ókro, górnba	βʌ́krǝ, gʌ́mbo
285.	áɲɔs	ɔ́ɲǝn	óɲan	ʌ́ɲʌn
*286.	gránɛt	gúba	pínda, gʉbgúb	pínda, gú:ba, grʌ́nʌt
287.	pɛ́pɛ	pɛ́pǝ	pɛ́pǝ	pɛ́pǝ
*288.	ranás, pánapu	pajn	pajn	pájnapl
289.	pɔtéto	pɔtéto	pitlɛda, táta	tʌ́tǝ, tɛ́tǝ
290.	pɔ́ŋki	pɔ́ŋkin	póŋkin	pʌ́ɲcin
291.	rajs	rajs	rajs	rajs, káɸa
292.	ŋkandá	(s)kin	kin	s(c)in
293.	rut	ru:t	ru:t	ru:t
294.	sɔl	sɔlt	sa:l	sɔl
*295.	tʃukatʃúka	pímplʌ	máka	
296.	tǝbáko	tǝbáko	tabáka	tǝbá:kǝ, makápa
297.	tǝmáto	tǝmá:ta	tumátis	tǝmédǝ
298.	sitík	tri:	tri:, tik	tri:, ci:, kri:

	English	Krio	Sranan-(Djuka)	Saramaccan
*299.	vine species	brokobák	brɔkɔbáka	boókobáka
300.	water	watá	wátra, (wata)	wáta
301.	wood	tik, wud	udu, (oedoe)	údu
302.	yam	jams, ɲams	jámsi	ɲámísi

LIST E. NATURAL PHENOMENA

	English	Krio	Sranan-(Djuka)	Saramaccan
303.	ash	ásis	asísi, ás:i	sínɟa
304.	coast	watásaj	wátrasèj	wátasɛ́
305.	copper	kɔ́pa	kɔ́prɔ	kópu
306.	country	kɔ́ntri	kɔ́ndre, (konde)	kɔ́ndɛ̀
307.	dawn	do-klín	dé-brɔ́kɔ	
308.	day	de	dej, (dej)	dáka
309.	day after tomorrow	nɛkstumára	trátamára	óto-amaɲá
310.	ditch	gɔ́ta, gwáta	gɔ́trɔ	gɔ́tɔ̀
311.	earth	dɔtí	dɔtí, (doti)	dɔtí
312.	fire	fája	fája, (faja)	fája, vɛ̀vɛ́, zo
313.	gold	gol	gówtu, (goro)	góutu
314.	ground	grɔn	grɔ̃, (gorong)	goón
*315.	iron	ájɛn	ísri, (aje)	félu
316.	midday	sántɛm	dinatén, bákadína, (dinatem)	sapaté
317.	midnight	midul-nɛ́t	míndri-néti	míndi-ndéti
318.	moon	mun	mun, (moeng)	líba
319.	morning	mɔ́nin	mamantén, (mamating)	mámaté
320.	mud	pɔtɔpɔ́tɔ	pɔtɔpɔ́tɔ, mɔtɔmɔ́tɔ	pɔ́tɔ́pɔ́tɔ́
321.	night	nɛt	néti, (neti)	ndéti
*322.	powder	póda	pwíri, frúa	fanía
323.	rain	ren	alén, (areng)	vulá, cubá
324.	rainbow	rémbo	alémbo	mucáma
325.	river	ríba	líba	líjo
326.	rock	akpáta	s(i)tɔ̃, (sitong)	sitónu
327.	sand	sansán	sánti	sándu
328.	smoke	smok	smóko	sumúku
329.	star	sta	stári, (sitari)	teéa
330.	sun	san	son, (son)	sónu
331.	swamp	swamp	swámpu	
332.	thunder	ténda	dɔ́ndru	giíta
333.	time	tɛm	tẽ, (ting)	ten
334.	today	tidé	tidé, (tide)	tidé
*335.	tomorrow	tumára, tamára	tamára	amaɲá

THE ENGLISH-BASED ATLANTIC CREOLES 53

	Cameroons	Guyana	Jamaican	Gullah
*299.				
300.	wɔ́ta	wá:ta	wá:ta	βɔ́:tə
301.	sitík	wud	wud, hud	ud
302.	ɲámas	jam	ɲa:mz	ɲam
303.	áʃis	áʃiz	háʃiz, áʃiʃ	(h)áʃiʃ
304.	kos	wɔ́:təsajd	wá:tasɑjd	βɔ́:təsaj
305.	kɔ́pa	kápa	kápa	kɔ́pa
306.	kóntri	kɔ́ntri	kóntri	kʌ́ntri
307.	dé-klía	de-klí:n	diɛ-klí:n	dé-klí:n, dé-brʌ́k
308.	de	de	diɛ	de
309.	nɛkstumálo	dé á:fta tumáro	díɛ a:tɑ tumáro	dé ʌ́tə təmárə
310.	wɔtarót	ditʃ, gɔ́ta	góta	dic
311.	dətí	dɔ́rti	dóti	dʌ́ti
312.	fája	fájə	fája	ɸájə
313.	gol	gol	guol	gu:l
314.	grɔŋ	grɔwŋ	groŋ	grawŋ
*315.	ájan	ájan	hájan	ajn, ájən
316.	sɔ́n-di-mídu	midé	migl-díɛ	sʌnʌ́p
317.	míndru-nájt	mídnajt	migl-nájt	mídl-najt
318.	mun	mu:n	mu:n	mu:n
319.	mónin	ma:nin	má:nin	mɔ́:nin
320.	pətəpɔ́tə	pʌ́tapʌ́ta	potopóto, mokɔmóko	mʌd, pɔ́ti, mʌʃ
321.	najt	nɛt, nájt	najt	najt
*322.	páwda	pɔ́wda	powda	páwɽə
323.	ren	ren	riɛn	ri:n
324.	rémbo	rémbo	riɛmbuɔ	rí:mbo
325.	bik-wɔ́ta	ríbə	ríba	ríβə
326.	sitón	rʌkstón	rakatúon	rʌk(-stón)
327.	sansán	san	san	san
328.	simók	smok	smuok	smok, sísı
329.	sitá	star	sta:	sta
330.	sən	san	san	sʌn
331.	swɔm	swamp	swamp	mʌʃ
332.	tɔ́nda	tɔ́nda	tónda	tʌ́nə
333.	tajm	tɛm, tajm	tajm	tajm
334.	tudé	tudé	tidé	tidé
*335.	tumálo	tumáro	tumárɔ	təmárə

	English	Krio	Sranan-(Djuka)	Saramaccan
336.	wind	*bris*	*wínti, (winti)*	*véntu*
337.	world	*wɔl, dúnia*	*grɔntápu, (gorontapoe)*	*múndu*
*338.	yesterday	*jɛ́stade, éside*	*és(re)de, (esrede)*	*éside*

LIST F. HOUSEHOLD, ETC.

	English	Krio	Sranan-(Djuka)	Saramaccan
339.	backyard	*(bijɛn-)jád*	*bákaɬári*	*ɬái*
340.	bed	*bed*	*bédi*	*bédi*
341.	boat	*bot, kunú*	*bóto*	*bóto*
342.	book	*buk*	*búku, (boekoe)*	*búku*
343.	bucket	*bókit, kítul*	*bóciti*	
344.	buoy	*búwi*	*búwi*	
345.	candle	*cándul*	*kándra, (kandra)*	*kandéja*
346.	church	*tʃɔtʃ*	*cérci, snóga*	*kéíki*
347.	court	*kot*	*krútu*	*kuútu*
348.	cowshed	*kawpɛ́n*	*kawpɛ́n*	*kaupéni*
349.	doorway	*domɔ́t*	*dɔ́rɔmɔ́fɔ*	*dɔ́ɔmɔ́fɔ*
350.	fence	*fɛntʃ*	*périn, skótu*	*cáŋga*
351.	fork	*fɔk, stíka*	*fɔ́rku, (forku)*	*cɔkɔ́*
352.	funeral	*bɛ́rin*	*béri*	*béi*
*353.	game played with counters	*warí*	*awarí-báni*	
354.	hammock	*amáka*	*amáka*	*amáka*
*355.	house	*os*	*ɔ́sɔ, (oso)*	*wósu*
356.	job	*dʒab*	*dʒóbu*	*woóko, wokó*
357.	kettle	*tikítul*	*kétre, (ketre)*	*kɛ́tɛ*
358.	knife	*nɛf*	*nɛf, néfi, (nefi)*	*ndéfi*
359.	mat	*máta*	*matamáta*	
360.	mortar	*mata-odó*	*máta*	*máta*
361.	mortuary	*dede-ós*	*déde-ɔ́sɔ*	*dɛ́dɛwósu*
362.	oven	*óvin*	*ófu, ōfu*	
363.	pestle	*mata-tík,-pɛ́nsul*	*mátatíci*	*tatí*
364.	pigsty	*ɔgpɛ́n*	*águpén*	*hágupéni*
365.	place	*ples, saj*	*pe, prési*	*pɛ́, kamía*
366.	pot	*pɔt*	*pátu, (patu)*	*pɔ́tɔ, gansɛ́*
367.	proverb	*parébul*	*ɔ́dɔ, (odo)*	*ɔ́dɔ, nɔ̀ŋgɔ́*
368.	portion	*dʒoŋk, pis*	*móŋki, písi*	*písi*
369.	school	*skul*	*skɔ́rɔ, (sikolo)*	*sikɔ́ɔ*
370.	scissors	*sízas*	*siséj*	*seséi*
371.	song	*siŋ*	*síni*	*kandá*

	Cameroons	Guyana	Jamaican	Gullah
336.	bris	briːz	briːz	briːz
337.	wɔl	wɔrl	wol, wuːrl	βʌl, at, βɔ́rəl
*338.	jɛ́səde	jɛ́stəde	jɛ́sidiɛ	íːstidi
339.	ját-fɔ-bák	jard	jaːd	jad
340.	bɛt	bɛd	bɛd	βed
341.	bot	bot, bató	buot, kʌ́nu	boː, kʌ́nu
342.	buk	buk	buk	buk
343.	bɔ́kɛt, mulúŋga	bɔ́kit	bókit	bʌ́cit
344.	bɔj	baj, bɔj	bwaːj	búwi
345.	kándu	candl	caŋgl	cándl
346.	tʃɔs	tʃɔrtʃ	tʃotʃ, tʃaːtʃ	cʌc
347.	kɔt	kɔrt	kuort	kot
348.	háws-fɔ-káw	kɔ́wʃɛd	kowpɛ́n	cǽwpɛn
349.	dɔmɔ́t	dɔrmɔ́wt	duomówt	dɔ́mawt
350.	fɛns	fɛns, pɛ́lin	fɛns, paláŋka	φɛŋc
351.	fɔk	fɔrk	fok	φɔk
352.	bɛ́ri-tajm, kráj-daj	fínərəl	bɛ́rin	fjúːndrəl, bɛ́rin
*353.	warí		wári	
354.	hámak, tajtáj	hámɔk	ámak	hámək
*355.	haws	hos, hows	hows	haws
356.	dʒɔp	dʒab	dʒab	ɟʌb
357.	kɛ́tu	kɛtl	kɛtl, kitl	citl
358.	najf	nɛf	najf	najφ
359.	mat	mat	mat	mat
360.	mɔ́ta	mɔ́ːta	máːta, dɛ́ŋki	mɔ́ːtə
361.	háws-fɔ-dáj-pípu	mɔ́ːtʃəri	dɛdóws	dɛ́d-haws
362.	plɛ́s-fɔ-kúk	ɔːbm	huobm	óφən, obm
363.	mɔ́tasitík	mɔ́ːtastík	máːtatík	pɛsl
364.	háws-fɔ-ʃwájn	ɔgpɛ́n	háːgpɛn	hǽgpɛn
365.	ples, saj	ples	pliɛs	plɛs
366.	pɔt	pat	pat	pʌt, píŋgi
367.	pánabu	praːbl	próbaːb	pɔ́βəb
368.	pat, pis	tʃɔŋk	dʒɔŋk, pɛg	cʌŋk
369.	sikúl	skuːl	(s)kuːl	skuːl
370.	sísas	sízərz	sízaz	sízəz
371.	siŋ	sáŋ	siŋ, saŋ	siŋ

	English	Krio	Sranan-(Djuka)	Saramaccan
372.	spoon	pun	spun, (spoen)	kujɛ́
373.	story	torí	tóri	kóntu
374.	street	trit	stráti, pási	kamína, pási
375.	town	tɔŋ	fɔ́tɔ, (foto)	fóto
376.	verandah	viránda, pijéza	barkón, gadrí	baákon, gadií
377.	word	wɔd	ɔ́dɔ	ɔ́dɔ

LIST G. CLOTHING, ETC.

	English	Krio	Sranan-(Djuka)	Saramaccan
378.	clothes	klos, áfɔ	krósi, (kojo [?], krosi)	koósu
379.	earring	jerín	jésliŋa	jésilíŋga
380.	handkerchief	pɔkɛtán	sakaɲísa	
381.	hat	at, cap	áti	
382.	head-pad	katá	cacári	àkàtà
383.	headscarf	ɛŋkíntʃa, edtáj	aɲísa, tajéde	haŋgísa
*384.	loincloth	kɔmíʃɔn, vɔmí	kámsa, páɲi, (kamisa, bolo)	kamísa
*385.	maraccas	ʃaká, ʃɛgurɛ́, ʃɛkʃɛ́k	saká	caká
386.	pipe	pɛp	pípa	pípa
*387.	sandal	sampatá	páta	saapátu
388.	shoe	sus	súsu, s:u	súsu
389.	trousers	trɔsís, paŋks	brúku	buúku
390.	umbrella	ɔmbwéla, brɔlá	prásɔrɔ	paazóo
391.	walking-stick	wakatík	wákatíci	kokotí

LIST H. PERSONS

	English	Krio	Sranan-(Djuka)	Saramaccan
*392.	bastard	awsaj-pikín, basta-pikín	básra, dɔrɔséj-pcín	bása
393.	boy	bɔbɔ́, bɔj	bɔj	womimtí
394.	brother	bróda, bra	bráda, (bada)	baáa
*395.	child	pikín	pcin, (piki)	miíi
*396.	co-wife	met	méti, kabósa	mbéti, kambósa
397.	creole	krió	krióro	kióo
398.	devil	débul	didíbri, (didibi)	didíbi
399.	Englishman	iŋgliʃmán	íŋlisimán	iŋgitsimá
400.	family	fámbul	fámiri, (famiri)	bɔ̀ŋgɔ̀, mbe
401.	father	dadí, papá	tatá, papá, (tata)	tatá
402.	girl	ɟal, tití	wénce, búli, (wendje)	wɛnɟɛ̀

THE ENGLISH-BASED ATLANTIC CREOLES 57

	Cameroons	Guyana	Jamaican	Gullah
372.	sipún	spu:n	pu:n	(s)pun
373.	tóri	tóri	túori	(s)tóri
374.	lɔŋtrí	tri:t	tri:t	(s)tri:t
375.	tɔŋ	tɔwŋ	toŋ, towŋ	tawŋ
376.	varánda	piéza	pίεza	pajázə
377.	wɔt	wɔrd	wuord	βʌd, ŋgo
378.	kilós	kloz	kluoz	kloz
379.	íariŋ	íriŋ	ίεzriŋ	jέrin
380.	háŋgis	kə́rtʃif	héŋkitʃif	héŋkʃə
381.	hat, kap	hat, cap	at, cap	hat, cap
382.	káta		kóta	
383.	tajhέt	hédtaj	tajhέd, hədtáj, bandú:	héŋkʃə
*384.	kilós		raprówŋ	
*385.	ʃekʃék	ʃakʃák	ʃaká	ʃéka
386.	pajp	pajp	pajp	pɔjp, sáka
*387.	sándu	sandl	sámpata	
388.	ʃus	ʃu:z	ʃu:z	ʃu:ʃ
389.	trósas	trɔ́wzərz	trózaz	pʌns, bríciz
390.	ɔmbréla	ɔmbréla	ombrájla, párasəl	hʌmbrájlə
391.	wɔkasitík	wɔ́kinstik	wá:kintik	wɔkiɲcén
*392.	dʒabú-pikín	ɔwsájd-tʃajl	outadúo-píkini	búʃ-cajl, βúdz-cajl
393.	bɔj	bɔj, bwɔj	bwa:j	bʌ́βə, bɔj
394.	bráda	bróda	bréda, bɾa	bʌ́βə, brέɾə
*395.	pikín	píkni, tʃajl	píkini	cajl, do
*396.	mbáɲa			kə́ɲciβajn
397.	sa:ró ['Sierra Leone Creole']	krió	kriúol	
398.	wíʃman	dεbl	dεbl	dεβl
399.	iŋgrismán	iŋgliʃmán	hiŋgliʃmán	
400.	fámli	fá:mli	fá:mbl(i)	ɸá:mbli
401.	bába	táta, púpa	bába, táta, púpa	dǽdi, tátə
402.	gεl, ŋgɔ́ndεli	gɔrl	ɟal, ɟol	ɟal, títə

	English	Krio	Sranan-(Djuka)	Saramaccan
403.	girlfriend	swɛtɛ́, fɛdʒɛ́	swíti	súti [?]
404.	God	gɔd	gádɔ, (gadoe)	gádu
405.	hunter	ɔntimán	ɔ́ntiman	hɔ́ndima
406.	liar	lajmán	léman	lɛ̀gɛ̀dɛ̀má
407.	man	man	man, (man)	(w)ómi
408.	master	mása, másta	másra, (masa)	mása
409.	mermaid	mamiwatá	wátramamá	
410.	mother	mamá, mamí	mamá, m:a, (mama)	mamá
*411.	mulatto	maláta, ⁺paná	maláta	maáta
412.	negro	blakmán	néŋre, (ninge)	nɛ́ŋgɛ̀
413.	overseer	obasía	báʃa	basiá
414.	peer, comrade	kɔ́mpin	kómpe, máti, (mati)	kómpe, máti
415.	people	pípul	pípɛl, líbisma	sɔ̀mbɛ̀
416.	person	pósin	sma, súma	sɔ̀mbɛ̀
*417.	portuguese	podogí	potogísi	potigé
418.	sister	sísta, sisí	sísa, (sisa)	sísa
*419.	spirit	dʒombí, spírit	dʒumbí, jéje	dʒombí, jéje
*420.	term of address	bo, bɔ, ba	ba	ba
421.	white man	wɛ́tman, ojmbó	bakrá, jóbo	bakáa
422.	wife	wɛf	wéfi	mujɛ̀ɛ́
423.	woman	úman	úma	mujɛ̀ɛ́
*424.	workman	wokmán, worók	wrókoman, (orokomang)	woókomá
*425.	Yoruba	okú, nagó		

LIST I. ANATOMICAL, ETC.

	English	Krio	Sranan-(Djuka)	Saramaccan
426.	arm/hand	an	ánu, (ana)	máu
427.	armpit	ɔnda-án, amól	ɔndránu	básumáu
428.	back	bak	báka, (baka)	báka
429.	beard	bjabjá	bárba, balúba	bía
430.	birthmark	gɔ́dmak	gadumárci, (gadoemariki)	gádumaáka
431.	blood	blɔd	brúdu, (brodu)	buúu, saŋgá
432.	body	bɔdí, skin	scin, (siking)	siŋkíní
433.	bone	bon	bóɲo	bónu
434.	brain	bren, mudumúdu	tɔntɔ́n	tɔnzɔ́
435.	breast	bɔbí	bɔ́bi, bɔ́rsu	bobí
*436.	buttocks	batí, ras, baksáj	gogó, lási, bakaséj, (gogo)	gogó, kú
437.	bump, callous	kókó	kúndu	agó

THE ENGLISH-BASED ATLANTIC CREOLES 59

	Cameroons	Guyana	Jamaican	Gullah
403.	ſwitát	swi:tá:t, bʌ́stə	switá:t, ɛpar	díndin
404.	gad, gɔt	gad	gad	φaɾə
405.	hɔ́ntaman	hɔ́nta	hontamár.	hʌ́ntə(-man)
406.	lajmán	lájad	lájad	lájə
407.	man	man	man	mæn, ma:n
408.	mása	má:sta	má:sa	mɔ́:sə
409.	mamiwáta	mɔ́rmed	mɔ́rmiɛd	
410.	mamá	mámi, múma	má:mi, múma	mámi, mɔ́:mə, mʌ́ɾə
*411.	múkala, dío	məlátʌ	maláta	məlá:də
412.	blakmán	nígə	nɪɛga	nígə
413.	obasía	obəsí:r	búſa	óβſe
414.	kɔ́mbi	máti, mí:tʌ	kómpini	βʌ́di, φrin
415.	pípu	pi:pl	pi:pl	pí:pl
416.	pəsin	pɔrsn	pɔrsn	pʌsn
*417.	pɔtſugi	potigi	puotagí:	pʌcéɬi
418.	sísta	sísta	sísta	títi, ſiſə
*419.	sipírit	dʒʌ́mbi, bakú	dópi, dʒémbi, dʒídʒi(-wajna)	(s)périt, plátaj
*420.	bo	bo	bo, ba	bo
421.	bákara, bákala	bákra	bakra, bókra	bʌ́krə
422.	mɛ́ri	wɛf	wajf	βajφ
423.	wúman	úman	húman	úmə
*424.	wɔ́kman	wɔ́rkman	wokmán	βʌ́kmən
*425.	jɔ́rəbamán	ɔkú, járiba	nagó	
426.	han	han	han	jæm, han
427.	əndahán	ɔndahán	a:mhuól	
428.	bak	bak	bak	bak
429.	bjabjá-fɔ-fés	bird	bi:d, bɪɛd	βed
430.	gádimak	bɔ́rtmark	gadmá:k	
431.	blət	blʌd	blod	blʌd, méŋga
432.	sikín	bɔ́di	bádi	bɔ́:ɾi
433.	bon	bon	buon	bən, bo:n
434.	hɛt	bren	brɪɛn	bren
435.	bábi	bʌ́bi	bóbi	ɲini, bʌ́bi, brɛs
*436.	las	báti, ra:s, baksáj	báti, ra:s, báksaj	bʌ́ti, baksáj
437.	bɔm	lɔmp	kóko	bʌmp

	English	Krio	Sranan-(Djuka)	Saramaccan
438.	ear	jes	jési, (jesi)	jési
*439.	excreta	kaká, pupú	kaká, pupú, kuŋkún	kaká
440.	eye	jaj	aj, (aj)	wójo
441.	finger	fíŋga	fíŋa, (finga)	fíŋga
442.	groin	grajn	lis	baŋgáti
443.	gullet	gɔŋgɔ́ŋgɔŋ	gorogóro	gaŋgáa
444.	hair	íja	wi(ri)wíri	wiwíi, uwíi
445.	head	ed	éde, (ede)	hédi
446.	heart	at	áti	háti
447.	hunger	áŋgri, gapé	áŋri, (agiri)	áŋgi
448.	knee	ni	cindí, (kini)	kiní
449.	leg/foot	fut	fútu, (futu)	fútu
450.	leprosy	lɛ́prɔsi	kokobé	ɟɛmbɛsí, kína
451.	liver	líba	léfre	
452.	lung	fukfúk	fokofóko	fugufúgu
453.	mouth	mɔt	mɔ́fɔ, (mofo)	mɔ́fu, búka
454.	nipple	bɔbímɔt	bɔ́bimɔ́fɔ	bobíbúka
455.	nose	nos	nóso, (noso)	núsu
456.	nostril	nosól	nosóro	núsufúla
*457.	penis	ton, bɔtú	ston, p:i	pipí
458.	pleasure	plɛ́fɔ	prísiri	peésa
*459.	pubic hair	wiriwírí	stón-wiwíri	wiwíi, uwíi
460.	pus	mɔ́ta, tɔf	mántɛri	
*461.	skin	kandá	búba, scin, (boeba, siking)	búba
462.	stomach	bɛlɛ́	bére, bɛ́lɔ, (bele)	bɛ̀ɛ, báika
463.	thigh	fut, lɛg	bɔ́wtu	asákpáa
464.	thirst	tɔ́sti	drejwátra	
465.	tongue	tɔŋ	tɔ́ŋɔ	tɔ́ŋgɔ
466.	tooth	tit	tífi, (tifi)	tánda
*467.	vulva	bombó, píma, totó	bɔmbó, píma, fesɛ́j	kú
468.	yaws	jɔs	jási	jási

LIST J. PRONOUNS AND VERBAL MARKERS

469.	I	a, mi	mi, (mi)	mi
470.	you (sing.)	ju	ju, i, (ioe)	ju, i
471.	he, it	i	a, ē, (a, eng, ing)	a, hɛn
472.	she	i	a, ē, (a, eng, ing)	a, hɛ́n
473.	we	wi	wi, ũ, (wi)	wi

THE ENGLISH-BASED ATLANTIC CREOLES

	Cameroons	Guyana	Jamaican	Gullah
438.	hía, hɔ́a	e:z	iɛz	jez
*439.	ʃit	kuŋs, pups	pupú, kaká	tútu, túβi
440.	aj	aj	haj, jaj	je, jaj
441.	fíŋga	fíŋga	fíŋga	ɸɨŋgə
442.	grɔjn	grɔjn	gra:jn	
443.	trut	trot	truot	gu:zl, trot
444.	bjabjá-fɔ-hɛ́t	hir	hir	he
445.	hɛt	hɛd	hɛd	hed
446.	hat, bɛ́li	hart	a:t	hʌt
447.	hɔ́ŋgri	hɔ́ŋgri	hoŋgri	hɔ́ŋgri, stɛ́pni
448.	kiní	ni:	ni:	niβo
449.	fut	fut	fut	ɸut
450.	lɛ́pa	kʌkʌbɛ́	kokobiɛ	
451.	líba	libə	líba	líβə
452.	lɔŋ	lʌŋ	lownz	ɸukɸúk, ɸugɸúg
453.	mɔf	mɔwt	mowt	mawt
454.	mɔf-fɔ-bábi	nipl	títi, nipl	tít(i), ɲíni
455.	nos	noz	nuúz	noz
456.	mɔf-fɔ-nós	nozól	nuozúol	nʌ́ʃrəl
*457.	mbrakɔ́t	ston	tútu, hud, wud	
458.	lajf	plɛ́dʒa	plɛ́dʒa	plɛ́ɟə
*459.	bjabjá-fɔ-mbrakɔ́t	hir	tutuhír	
460.	wájtwɔ́ta	máta, pɔs	kwíta, matamáta	
*461.	ŋkandá, sikɨn	skin	kin, kánda, búba	(s)cin
462.	bɛ́li	bɛ́li	bɛ́li	βɛ́li
463.	fut	taj, fut	taj, fut	ʃɛŋk
464.	tɔ́sti	tərs	tɔrs	tʌs
465.	tɔŋ	tɔŋ	tɔŋ	tʌŋ, tɔŋ
466.	tik	ti:t	ti:t	tut, ti:t
*467.	mbumbú, píma, tutú	púsi, tiŋ	bómbo, nú:na	púsi
468.	jɔs	ja:z	já:zi	
469.	aj, mi, mí-a	a, mi	a, mi	a, mi
470.	ju	ju	ju	ju, unə, i
471.	i	hi, i	im, i	i
472.	i	ʃi, hi	ʃi, im, i	ʃi, i
473.	wi	wi, á:wi	wi, á:wi	βi

	English	Krio	Sranan-(Djuka)	Saramaccan
474.	you (plur.)	úna, únu	ũ, únu	u, ũ, únu
475.	they	dɛm	dɛ̃, (de)	de
*476.	durative marker	de, di	de, e, (de)	tá
477.	future marker	go	sa, go, (sa)	sa, ó
478.	past marker	bin	ben, (be)	bi
479.	completive marker	dɔ́n+, +dɔn	+kba, (+kaba)	+kaba
480.	negator	nɔ́, ná	nɔ, (na)	ná

LIST K. NUMERALS

	English	Krio	Sranan-(Djuka)	Saramaccan
481.	one	wã	wã, (wan)	wã
482.	two	tu	tu, (toe)	tú
483.	three	tri	dri, (dri)	díi
484.	four	fo	fɔ, (fo)	fɔ́
485.	five	fajv	féjfi, (fejfi)	féifi
486.	six	siks	síksi, (siksi)	síkísi
487.	seven	sɛ́vin	séjbi, (sebi)	sébɛ̀n
488.	eight	et	ájti, (ejti)	ájti
489.	nine	najn	néjɬi, (negi)	néni, nétɬi
490.	ten	tɛn	tin, (tin)	téni
491.	eleven	lɛ́vin	ɛ́rfu, (elfi)	téni-a-wã
492.	twelve	twɛlv	twárfu, (twálfu)	téni-a-tú
493.	twenty	twɛ́nti	twɛ́nti, (twenti)	tú-téni
494.	thirty	táti	dri-ténti	díi-téni
495.	hundred	ɔ́ndrɛd	ɔ́ndrɔ, (hondro)	hɔ́ndɔ
496.	thousand	táwzɛn	dúsun, (dusen)	dúsu
497.	dozen	dɔ́zin	dúsen	téni-a-tú
498.	all	ɔl	ála, (a)	túu, ála

LIST L. GRAMMATICAL AND MISCELLANEOUS ITEMS

	English	Krio	Sranan-(Djuka)	Saramaccan
499.	again	bak, egén	báka, agén, (baka)	(baka)
500.	against	gɛ̃s	gɛ̃s	banɬa
501.	all right	ɔ́rajt	ɔ́rejt	awá
502.	always	ɔ́ltɛm	alatén	
503.	and	ɛn	ɛn, (en)	ɛn
504.	any	éni	íni	
505.	as, like	lɛ́kɛ, lɛ́ka	léci, (eke)	kúma
506.	because	bikɔ́s	biká(si), (bika)	biká

	Cameroons	Guyana	Jamaican	Gullah
474.	wúnə	á:ju, juwá:l	únu	únə
475.	dɛm, de	dɛm, de	dɛm, de	dɛm, de
*476.	di, də, li	de, di, a	de, da, a	də, ə
477.	go	sa, go, gwajn	wi, gwajn, go	gwʌjn
478.	bin	bin	ɛn, bɛn	βin
479.	dɔ́n+	+dʌn, dʌn+	+don, +fíniʃ	dʌn+
480.	no	nɔ, na, ɛn	no, na:	jɛnt, ɛ̃, dõ, nɔ, nínə
481.	wã	wan	wan	βʌn
482.	tu	tu	tu	tu
483.	tri	tri:	tri:	tri:
484.	fɔ	fɔr	fuor, fo	φa
485.	fajp	fajv	fajv	φaj(β)
486.	síkis	siks	siks	siks, sis
487.	sɛ́bin	sɛbm	sɛbm	sɛbm
488.	et	et	iɛt	et
489.	najn	najn	najn	najn
490.	tɛn	tɛn	tɛn	tɛn
491.	lɛ́bɛn	lɛbm	lɛbm	lɛbm
492.	twɛf	twɛlv	twɛlb	tβɛl
493.	tú-tali	twɛ́nti	twɛ́nti	tβɛ́ni
494.	trí-tali	tɔ́rti	tɔ́rti	tʌ́ti
495.	hɔ́ndrɛt, hɔn	hɔ́ndrɛd	hɔ́ndrɛd	hʌ́nə
496.	táwsan	tɔ́wzn	towzn	táwzn
497.	dɔ́sin	dɔzn	dozn	dʌzn
498.	ɔl	a:l	a:l	ɔl
499.	agén	bak, əgɛ́n	agíɛn	ɟiu, əɟín
500.	agɛ́nsə	gens	gens	gens
501.	ɔ́lrajt	arájt	á:rajt	ɔ́rajt
502.	ɔ́ltajm	álwez	á:lwiɛz, á:zwiɛz	ɔ́:βez
503.	na, an	an	an	ɛn, na
504.	ɛ́ni	ɛ́ni	ɛ́ni	ɛ́ni
505.	lájka	lájka	láka, síɛŋka	lʌ́kə, sʌkə, sɛ́ŋkə
506.	séka	(bi)kázn	(bi)ká:zn, (bi)cá:ŋ	ke, kez

	English	Krio	Sranan-(Djuka)	Saramaccan
507.	before	bifó	bifɔ́, (fesisej)	bifɔ́, ufɔ́
508.	behind	bijén, na bák	báka, (baka)	báka
509.	but	bɔt	ma, (ma)	ma
*510.	contention	plába, kasí, kuskás	koskósi	kósikósi
511.	even	sɛf, íbin	sréfi	seépi
512.	everywhere	ɔlsaj, ébriwe	álaprési	alapɛ́
513.	for	fɔ	fu, (foe, fi)	fu, u
514.	formerly	(fɔs)fɔstɛm	(fos)fostén	fosufósu
515.	hello	adú	ɔ́di, (odi)	odi, ũɟi
516.	here	najá, ja, jasó	ɟa, ɟasó	akí
517.	how	aw, a	fa, o, (fa)	ũfá
518.	how many	ɔ́mɔs	ɔméni	homéni
519.	if	if, ɛf	éfi, éfu, (ifi, efoe)	é
520.	in, at	na	na, (na)	na, a
521.	inside	ĩsáj	inisé (insej)	déndu
522.	(verbal) intensifier	soté, teté	soté	tɛ́ɛ́, poi
523.	interjection of disgust	tʃɔ!	tʃɔ!, ʃa!	sia!
524.	interjection of incredulity	swɛ-to-gɔd!	ʃwɛ!	
525.	interjection of pain	waj!	wɔj!	wooló!
526.	interjection of surprise	ʔɛ ʔɛ!	ʔɛ ʔɛ!	ʔɛ ʔɛ!
527.	just	dʒis, dʒɛs	dʒɔ́nsnɔ	
528.	magic	dʒudʒú	óbia	óbia
529.	manner, way	fáʃin	fási	fási, fa
530.	mercy	mási	sári	sáa
*531.	more than	pas	mɔ́ro, psa, (moro, pasa)	mɔ́ɔ́
532.	never	nɔ́ba, nába	néba, némre, nɔ́jti	
533.	news	jus	ɲūs	ɲūsu
534.	nothing	nátin, dondó	nɔ́ti, (noti)	ná-sɔ́ndi
535.	now	naw, nɔ, wántɛm	nɔw, wãtrɔ̃	nɔ́ɔ́
536.	on top (of)	pantáp	tapsé, (na-tapoe)	tápu
537.	only	nɔmɔ́	nɔmɔ́, (namo)	nɔ́ɔ́
538.	outside	nadó	nadɔ́rɔ	
539.	over	óba	abrá	

THE ENGLISH-BASED ATLANTIC CREOLES

	Cameroons	*Guyana*	*Jamaican*	*Gullah*
507.	bifɔ́	bifó	bifúor	ɸo, biɸó
508.	fɔ bák	biájn	bihájn	bəhájm
509.	bət, an	bɔt	bot	bʌt
*510.	kɔskɔ́s, palába	kaskás, rándan	kaskás, plába	kʌskʌs, kwajl
511.	sɛf	sɛf	sɛf, sɛlf	sɛɸ
512.	ɔ́lsaj	ɔ́briwe	ɔ́briwe	ɛβəβe
513.	fɔ	fu	fi	ɸə, ɸɔ
514.	(fəs)fəstájm	fʌstájm	fóstajm	biɸótajm
515.	ha-ju-dú	hɔ́wdi	hówdi	hʌ́di
516.	hía	ja, ɲe	ja, jasó	jʌ, jʌsó
517.	ha	hɔw	how	haw
518.	háməʃ	hɔ́wmɔtʃ	hómotʃ	hʌ́mʌtʃ
519.	ífi	ɛf	if, ɛf	ɛɸ
520.	na, fɔ	a, iɲ	a, í:na	í:n, í:nə
521.	ĩsáj	insájd	insáj(d)	insájd
522.	soté:	soté:	soté:	so-iβɔ́l
523.	ʃa!	tʃa!	tʃo!	cɛ!
524.	ʃwɛ!	swɛːr!	swiɛr!	sβé-ti-gɔd!
525.	waj!	waj!	(w)aj!	aj!, kaj!
526.	ʔɛ́ ʔɛ̀!	ʔɛ́ ʔɛ̀!	ʔɛ́ ʔɛ̀!	ʔɛ́ ʔɛ̀!
527.	dʒəs	dʒʌs	dʒós, dɛs	ɟis, ɟɛs, dɛs
528.	dʒudʒú	óbia	óbia	ɟúɟu, βúdu
529.	fáʃan	faʃn	faʃn, wiɛ	βe, ɸáʃin
530.	sɔ́ri	mɔ́rsi	máːsi, mɔ́rsi	mʌsi
*531.	pas	móuən	múoran, paːs	mórə, pas
532.	nɛ́ba	nɛ́va	nɛ́ba	nɛ́βə, nʌβə
533.	nus	ɲuːz	ɲuːz	ɲuːz
534.	nɔ́tiŋ	nɔtn	notn	nʌtn
535.	na, wantájm	nɔw, wantájm	now, wantájm	naw, wantájm
536.	ntɔp	pantáp	pantáp, tápsaj(d)	pantáp
537.	nomɔ́	nɔmɔ́	nomó	nʌ́mə
538.	awsáj	ɔwsájd	owtaduó	awsájd
539.	óba	ɔ́ba	úoba	óβə

	English	Krio	Sranan-(Djuka)	Saramaccan
540.	own	jon	éjɟi	éigi
541.	pardon	pádin	párdɔn	paádon
*542.	perhaps	sɔntέm, paravέntʃɔ	sɔntén, (somtem)	sɔnté
543.	recently	tradé	tradéj	óto-dáka
544.	someone	pɔ́sin, sɔmbɔdí	súma, sma, (sama)	sɔ́mbɛ́
*545.	soon	dzísnɔ, bambáj	dzɔns(nɔ́), bambaj, (bambej, djusnu)	dzúnsu
546.	speed	es	ési	hési
547.	that	dá, ná, dát	dá, dáti, ná, (da, dati)	dáti, dí
548.	then, that time	dεn	ne	de
549.	then, so then	najĩ, dɔ̃	dan, (da)	hεn
550.	there	de	de, dapé	naadέ, alá
551.	these	dɛ̃(....ja)	dísi	déé
552.	this	dis(....ja)	dísi	dísi
*553.	to (preverbal)	fɔ	fu, (foe, fi)	fu, u
554.	to (locative)	na, to	na, (na)	na, a
555.	too	tu	tu, (toe)	tu
556.	too much	pasmák	psamárci	pasámáu
557.	under	ɔ́nda	ɔ́ndrɔ, ɔ̃ru	básu
558.	until	soté, teté, té	soté, té, (te)	téé
559.	very much	túmɔs	túmsi, (toemisi)	túmúsi
560.	what	wétin	san, (sanni)	andí
561.	when	ústεm	ɔtén	té, hέn
562.	where	úsaj, úspat	ɔpέ, úsaj	ũsέ, ká
563.	which, that	we	di, (di)	dí
564.	who	udá, udát	ɔsúma	ambέ
565.	why	wetin-dú?	san-éde?, sájde?	andí?
566.	with	wit	náŋa, (aga)	ku
*567.	without	bitáwt	zɔ́ndrɔ	sɔ́ndɔ
568.	yes	jεs, jε	aj, (aj)	awá
569.	yet	et, jet	éte	jéti
570.	yonder	jánda	jána, (janda)	alá, aá

THE ENGLISH-BASED ATLANTIC CREOLES 67

	Cameroons	Guyana	Jamaican	Gullah
540.	ɔn	jon	uon, úonc	jon, jont
541.	sóri	pa:dn	pa:gŋ	pa:dn
542.	səmtájm	sɔmtájm, mébi	míɛbi, parabɛ́ntʃa	mɛ́βi, pəháps
543.	no-fawé	di óda dé	wedíɛ	tʌrədé
544.	sómbədi	sɔmbádi	smá:di	səmbɔ́:ri
*545.	dʒəsná, bambáj	dʒɔsnów, bambáj	dʒosnów, bambáj	ɟɛ́snaw, bambáj
546.	hɔrihɔ́ri	hes	hiɛs	hes
547.	da, dat	a, da, dat	da(t), dára(-dɛ́)	da, na, dat
548.	dɛn	dɛn	dɛn	dɛn
549.	dɛn	(so) dɛn	(so) dɛn	(so) dɛn
550.	de	de	de	de
551.	dɛm	dɛm	dɛm(-já)	dɛm . . . . jʌ
552.	dis	dis	dis(-ajá)	dis, díʃɛ
*553.	fɔ	fu	fi	φə, φɔ
556.	fɔ	a	a, da	də, tə, ə
555.	tu	tu:	tu:	tu:
556.	pasmák	tú:mɔtʃ	pa:smá:k	tʌmʌ́tʃ
557.	ónda	ónda	anda(ní:t)	ɔ:ní:t
558.	soté	soté, sotíl	súté	tβə!
559.	túməʃ	tú:mɔtʃ	túmotʃ	tʌmʌ́tʃ
560.	wáti	wa, wat	awá, wat	βʌ, βʌt
561.	hústajm	wítɛm, a-wén	wɛ́ntajm	βʌ́tajm
562.	húsaj	wísaj, a-wé	wépa:t	βísaj
563.	we	witʃn	we	βe, βis, βʌt
564.	hu	hu(dát)	hu:(dát)	húdat
565.	hu?	wɔ-mɛ́k?	wa-mɛ́k?	mɛ́k-so?
566.	wíti	wid	wi, wid	lʌŋ(ə), βid
567.	nó-gɛt	biówt	widówtn	βidáwt
568.	jɛs	jɛs	jɛs	jɛ:, jas
569.	jɛt	jɛt	jɛt	jɛt
570.	jánda	jánda	jánda	jan, jánd(a)

NOTES ON THE WORD-LISTS

3. Hawaiian Pidgin English has *hámbʌg*, and Neo-Melanesian *hámbak*, with the same meaning.

7. *Na* has so far defied a satisfactory etymological explanation; cf. similarly-used *na* in Virgin Islands Dutch Creole, British Honduras *da*, Guyana and Tobago *a* and Jamaican *a/da*. In each case the verbal form is identical with the locative prepositional form (cf. items 520 and 554). In Crioulo, the Portuguese-derived creole of Guiné, *na* is both a progressive action marker (the other being *ta*, cf. Saramaccan *tá*), and the locative preposition. Verbal *a* occurs in Cayenne French creole as well: *a pa mo fot* ('ce n'est pas ma faute'), *a aswé*, ('c'est le soir'). For discussions of *na*, see n. 1 in H. SCHUCHARDT, 'Zum Negerholländischen von St. Thomas', *Tijdschr. v. Nederl. Taal en Letterk.*, XXXIII, 1914, pp. 131–2, and L. LICHTVELD, 'Afrikaansche resten in de creolentaal van Suriname', *West Indische Gids*, X, 1928–29, pp. 515–16 and 81–3.

13. Cf. Akan *butu*, 'lie, lie on the belly' (CHRISTALLER).

14. English /aj/ becomes Krio /ɛ/ (sometimes /e/) and Sranan/Saramaccan /e/, a fairly regular shift not shared by other creoles, although occurring in a few Guyana Creole items. Variant forms are found in Cameroons Pidgin according to SCHNEIDER (see n. 17), but not in his later works on the language. Cf. also items 45, 52, 54, 85, 102, 140, 150, 194, 203, 291, 321, 333, 358, 386 and 422. These may be English dialect-form retentions rather than sound-shifts within the creoles; Standard English /aj/ is often /e/ or /ɛ/ in the dialects of Northumberland and several other counties in the north of England above Liverpool. See the wordlists in J. WRIGHT, *English Dialect Grammar*, republished London, 1968. In the case of items 16, *bwɛl* ('boil') and 115, *pwɛl* ('spoil'), the shift to /ɛ/ may have occurred at a time when English had /ai/ for orthographic 'oi' (up to c. 1750—cf. Krio *pɔk-pɛ́nt*, 'porcupine', from sixteenth century 'porkpoint'), or may represent a less common sound shift, with /ɔi/ becoming /ɛ/. /ai/ for /ɔi/ is a regular phonological feature in Jamaican and other Caribbean creoles. Such sound shifts may occasionally present problems of etymology; Krio *gwɛbá* ('guava') for instance may derive from English 'guava', with /a/ becoming /ɛ/—another frequent sound shift in Krio—or from Portuguese 'goyava' (cf. Mende *goyaba*, Temne *a-koyaba*, etc.), with /ɔi/ becoming /ɛ/.

15. For confusion of /l/ and /r/ in Krio, cf. also *dɔŋglín* ('dungarees'), *rapɛ́l* ('lapel', also 'jacket-type'), *lapá* ('wrapper', 'garment-type'), and item 219.

18. *Trɔs* is usually restricted to the borrowing of money in Krio.

26. Cf. Kikongo *tota* ('pick up') and similar forms in related dialects. Anglo-Saxon, however, also had *totian*, 'lift, elevate', as in *totodun ut tha heafdu*, 'lift up your head'. 'Tote' for 'carry' occurs also in Trinidad.

39. *Curchie* is a widespread dialect form (EDD). The Guyana entry is also used in Barbados.

41. English 'duck', cf. item 236. While a product of natural linguistic development, this morphological distinction between words identical or near-identical in the source-language is significant. Cf. also 136 and 258, 327 and 330, and 47 and 302.

45. 'Drive off', 'shoo away'. In Krio, to drive a vehicle is *drajv*. Both Krio and Sranan feature couplets derived from the same source word but differing semantically and phonologically, and which probably entered the languages at different periods. Examples from Krio include *ol* ('old') ∼ *wol* ('senile'); *pot* ('complain about') ∼ ∼ *ripɔ́t* ('report'); *trɛk* ('affect') ∼ *strajk* ('strike'); *triŋ* ('tie up') ∼ *striŋ* ('string'), and more recently *lɛk* ('love') ∼ *lajk* ('like'). Compare also items 19, 154 and 182, and the Sranan and Krio *kápa/kɔpɔ́* ('money') ∼ *kɔ́prɔ/kɔ́pa* ('copper').

47. *Njam* is a very widespread African root. Also Scots and Dutch dialect, and even Chinese: *ŋjàm-ŋjàm* (Hakka dialect, 'to pick at food'). *Wak* is probably Yorkshire, Scots, etc. dialect *whack*, 'large quantity of food or drink' (EDD).

50. Eng. 'fall down'. Saramaccan entry is from Portuguese *cair*, cf. *kaj* in all the Creole Portuguese dialects of West Africa and Asia. This may also survive in Krio, in the children's refrain ... *a dúmba dúmba káj káj, a fufú plɛ́t i bɔ́s* (where *a* may also represent an earlier variant of *na*, cf. n. 7, supra). The refrain would then mean '(it is)

dumba dumba fall fall, it is a fufu plate he broke', *dumba dumba* being onomatopoeic. (Although Cheshire dialect has *'dumber (-dash)'*, 'a smash, breakdown' (EDD).)

51. Cf. item 528.

55. Krio *korí* in its primary sense means an (untrue) tale, usually in the phrase *gi korí*. 'Flatter' is only one of its possible meanings. Cf. English 'cully' or 'curry'.

62. *Kɔŋkɔnsá* in Trinidad. The Jamaican Creole entry, with variant forms *koŋkoŋsá, koŋkoŋsé*, etc., means 'connive, flatter, curry favour' (DJE). Cf. Twi *ŋkɔŋkɔnsá*, 'falsehood, hypocrisy'. In Gullah, *ʃiʃi tʌk* is 'female gabble' (cf. Barbados *ʃiʃi*, 'effeminate').

72. The vowel /o/ rather than the expected /ɔ/ is unusual in the Krio entry. Cf. the Saramaccan form, and items 343 and 362. Krio *dʒómbo* is retained only in the name of a species of fish, *dʒombofis*, 'mudfish'.

77. Portuguese *sabé* or *sabeir*. See R. A. HALL, Jr., 'Romance Sapère in Pidgins and Creoles', *Rom. Phil.*, X, 1957, pp. 156–7. According to J. G. WILLIAMS, in his 'A Study in Gullah English', *The Sunday News*, February 10, 1895, Charleston, South Carolina, 'sabbe is never heard from any other than a regular rice field Gullah negro'.

83. Krio, Cameroons Pidgin and Gullah use this verb to infer a state of being even for inanimate items.

88. A calque from African languages. Dominica French Creole has *ué lalin* (lit. 'see moon'), with the same meaning. Cf. also items 153, 192, 253, 275, 309, 316, 349, 361, 392, 409, 427, 430, 454, 456, 512, 514, 556, 560, 561 and 562. Other possible calques are Krio *a ték Gɔd bég ju!* and Sranan *mi téci Gádo béji ju!* as an expression of incredulity (cf. Yoruba *mo f'Ɔlɔrun bɛ ɔ!* with the same meaning), and Krio *ju dʒis de tráj fɔ ptk mi mɔ́t* and Gullah *ju jɛs dɔ tráj fɔ ptk mi mɔ́wt*, 'you're only trying to make me say something I don't want to'.

108. *Swindʒ* also in Barbados.

156. In Krio the meaning of *tʃak* is restricted to 'intoxicated', i.e. *chock* full of liquor. Compare Louisiana Creole French *tʃak*, 'être à demi ivre', (MORGAN), and Yorkshire dialect 'chark' [tʃák], 'to drink to intoxication' (EDD). In Jamaican Creole it may be used in the sense of 'entirely', e.g. *im wa:k tʃák op a Kiŋstan*, 'he walked all the way to Kingston' (cf. *ʒuk a*, 'as far as', alongside *ʒiska*, 'jusqu'à', in the Creole French dialects of Cayenne, Martinique and Haiti). In Jamaican Creole the expression *tʃák an bilte*, of nautical origin, occurs with the meaning of 'cram-full'.

167. Malacca Creole Portuguese has *múmu*, 'dumb person'.

193. The Krio form *wol* ('senile, aged') may have been brought in by the Maroons, cf. Jamaican Creole *uol*. Similarly Krio *jet*, ('gate') may be from the same source, cf. Jamaican Creole *gtet*. Compare also item 442.

215. The Saramaccan entry *cólóló* means 'thin' only of liquids, and may derive from Fon *tʃrololo*, 'much diluted'. Compare Martinique Creole French *còlòlò* with the same meaning.

219. Cf. Fanti *wɔwɔw*, 'ugly', (CHRISTALLER). Krio *wogri* in its primary sense means '(affected by) an unhealthy, unattractive skin condition', usually on the face. Guyana Creole *wɔ́wɔ* means 'sickly'.

227. Derived from the English plural form. Cf. also items 236, 260, 264 (for Jamaican Creole and Gullah), 270, 297, 303, 307, 388, 438, 452 (for Jamaican Creole) and 466.

236. The Saramaccan entry is from Portuguese *pato*. Virgin Islands Dutch Creole has *patpát* also from this source (or possibly Spanish *pato*), and *páto* for 'duck' even occurs in Neo-Melanesian.

237. Martinique Creole French has *zámba* for 'elephant'. While some creole form may have produced English 'jumbo', Krio *dʒɔmbó* probably entered the language via English; in Krio the word is used as the name of an elephant character found in storybooks of British origin, and never for the animal in general. Note that African words for this beast have survived in areas where the elephant does not exist, but English-derived forms are used in the West African pidgins/creoles, spoken in areas

where elephants may still be found. Restricted vocabulary items are often of non-English origin in all the creoles.

261. Cf. Yoruba, Ibo and Brazilian Negro Portuguese *akara*, 'fritter made from ground blackeyed peas fried in palmoil'. Martinique Creole French has *akrá* with the same meaning; in Trinidad English Creole *akrá* is a flour-and-saltfish fritter.

279. That is, a little extra thrown in with a purchase. The Krio entry occurs in Mandinka, Bambara, Soso, Bullom, Temne, etc., with the general meaning of 'gift'. The Sranan entry is probably of East Indian origin (cf. *baksheesh*). The Guyana Creole, Jamaican Creole and Gullah entries are from English *brotus*, widespread in the Caribbean. The word *lagniappe* is itself originally from Louisiana French Creole, and derives from Quechua *yapa*. It occurs widely in Central and South America in various forms: *yapa*, *ñapa* (American Spanish), *nhapa* (Brazilian Portuguese), etc.

284. Virgin Islands Creole Dutch has *jámbo*, and Puerto Rican Spanish *kiŋgɔmbɔ́*. Cf. Chiluba *tʃiŋgɔmbɔ*, or Angola *kiŋgombo*, 'ochra'.

286. Cf. Virgin Islands Dutch Creole *góbgɔb*, and the dialect forms 'pinder' and 'goober (-peas)' in the U.S. Compare also Kimbundu *ŋgúba* and Kikongo *mpínda*, both meaning 'peanut'.

288. *Nanás*, ultimately from Tupí, via Portuguese, while not considered a Krio word, occurs in this form in Mende, Temne and Fula (all spoken in Sierra Leone), and is understood and used by many Krio speakers.

295. Guyana Creole *pímplʌ*, also occurring in Barbados and Trinidad, originally meant a species of cactus known as the prickly pear, and derives from *pín pílʌ*, a pin-cushion or 'pillow'. This is retained in Jamaican Creole *plímpla*, 'pin-cushion'. Krio has *píla*, 'pillow'. *Máka* has also become generalized, originally meaning the macaw-palm, noted for its prickles (which meaning is also retained in Jamaica). The word is probably of Carib origin (DJE). St. Andrew (Colombia) English Creole has *júka*, 'thorn'.

299. Probably 'broken bark' rather than 'broken back'. In Krio it is the vine species *dichapetalum toxicarium* ('ratsbane'), and in Sranan *mikania atriplicifolia*. The word may have been influenced by Fanti *ɔ-tokotáká*, 'a species of creeper, *bauhinia reticulata*', (CHRISTALLER).

315. Interestingly, the Sranan entry is Dutch-derived (<*ijzer*), the Djuka entry English-derived, and the Saramaccan entry Portuguese-derived (<*ferro*).

322. Krio *póda* is losing ground to the more anglicized *páwda*. It is heard more frequently in *gɔmpóda*, 'gunpowder'.

335. The Krio pronunciation *tamára* is now seldom heard.

338. Krio *éside* has almost entirely given way to *jéstade*, but like *póda* and *tamára* may still occasionally be heard, especially from elderly rural Creoles.

353. *Warri* in Barbados.

355. The English Creole of St. Andrew and Providence, off the Nicaragua coast, has 'hose'. The speech of these islands, which have been under Colombian government for c. 160 years, has been briefly described by N. S. FRIEDMANN, 'Miss Nansi, Old Nansi and other folk material from the islands of San Andres (Colombia)', *Revista Colombiana de Folclor*, IV, 9, pp. 215–233, Bogotá, 1967.

384. In Krio, in the verb phrase *táj kɔmíʃɔn*, 'to don a loincloth'. Cf. Portuguese *camisa*, 'shirt', and English cant *commission* with the same meaning.

385. In both the English and French creoles of Trinidad *ʃakʃák*, and in Martinique French Creole *ʃaʃá*. In Barbados the name 'shakshak' is given to a species of plant with rattling seed-pods. Cf. English *shake*, French *secouer*, Portuguese *sacudir*, Yoruba *ʃɛkɛre*, Hausa *tʃaki*, Kra *saklɛɛ*, Arabic *ʃagʃág*, etc.

387. Cf. Portuguese *sapato*, Cuban Spanish *zapata*, Trinidad *sampát*, Martinique *capát* and Temne (via Krio or Portuguese) *aŋ-sampatha*. One Jamaican Creole (English) spelling possibly deriving from folk etymology is 'sand patter'.

392. Haitian Creole has *āfā-dɔhɔ́* ('enfant-dehors'), and Liberian *awsáj-tʃaj*.

395. The plural 'children' exists in Guyana Creole (*tʃtrʌn*) and Gullah (*ctlən*).

396. The Sranan and Saramaccan entries derive from Portuguese *combaça*, 'rival in love', also occurring in Haitian Creole as *kɔmbɔ́s*.

411. Krio *paṇá* or *paṇamán* probably derives from Portuguese *apanhar*, 'seize', rather than from 'Spaniard'. *Panyaring* was used in West Africa as well as the East Indies as a term meaning slave-seizing, and it may sometimes have been Mulattoes rather than Europeans who carried out the bargaining for slaves with the African chiefs, since they were invariably familiar with both an African and a European language. In Jamaican and British Honduras Creole, *páṇa* means 'Spaniard'.

417. The Jamaican Creole entry is retained only as the name of a species of fish.

419. Cf. also Barbados *dʒímbi*, Virgin Islands Dutch Creole *zúmbi*, Haitian French Creole *zómbi*, and English (via Haitian) *zombie*. Mbundu has *nzúmbe* and *zúmbi*.

420. E. PARTRIDGE, in *Slang Today and Yesterday*, London, 1933, lists this item as American slang, and writes 'Bo, short for *hobo*, and not French *beau* Americanized. Often a term of address (–1895)'. The word is more likely to be dialectal *bor* or *bo*', 'a term of familiar address applied to persons of either sex, and of all ages', in use in Norfolk, Cumberland, Essex and Suffolk (WRIGHT, EDD). Vai has *bɔ*, 'friend, fellow, companion' (KOELLE).

424. Cf. Krio *worók ó!*, shouted out by porters in the markets of Freetown in order to make known their availability.

425. Cf. Haitian, Trinidadian and Brazilian *nagó*, and Cuban Spanish *ınagó*. The Nago are a coastal subtribe of the Yoruba, from the Dahomey border region.

436. *Gogo* in the Caribbean French Creoles.

439. *Kaka* or variants of it, occurs in English, Dutch, Portuguese, French, Spanish, Polish, etc. Forms of *pupu* are likewise widely evident in European languages. The Sranan *kúŋkun* and Guyana Creole *kuŋs* (properly, the faeces of an infant), may be connected with Krio and Trinidad English Creole *kuŋkú*, 'vulva'.

457. Cf. Krio *bɔtú*, Sranan *bówtu* (item 463). In East Indies Dutch, and in Indonesian, *butu* means 'penis'. Vai has *bɔ́tu* with the same meaning.

459. Reduplication of English 'weed', cf. Sranan *stri*, 'seed' (but Krio *sid*). This item occurs in Papiamentu with the Krio meaning, and in Guyana Creole *wíriwíri pɛ́pɛ*, the name of a species of pepper.

461. Jamaican Creole *kánda* is restricted to mean only the skin or fibrous sheath around the base of a palm branch; *búba* is similarly restricted in this creole, applying to the cabbage palm. Krio has *bubá* (from Yoruba), meaning a type of upper garment worn by women.

467. Cf. Temne *a-bómbo* ('labia'), Zulu *-búmbu* ('pubic region'), Xhosa *-bhómbho* ('vagina'), South American Spanish *bombó* ('buttocks'), Trinidad and Tobago English Creole *bombóm* ('buttocks'), and English *bum*. Cf. Saramaccan *kú* with Malacca Creole Portuguese *ku* ('buttocks'). *Toto* is also a widespread word: cf. Trinidad English Creole *tóti* or *tóto* ('penis'), and *tutú* ('excreta'), Gullah *tútu* ('excreta'), Cameroons Pidgin *tutú* ('vulva') and Jamaican Creole *tútu* ('penis'). *Pima* is probably Fanti *ɛ-pím* ('clitoris'). That there is such a high frequency of sex-term correspondences among the creoles is hardly surprising; women were a much sought-after commodity when pirates and slavers came ashore after months at sea.

476. Use of the Cameroons Pidgin form *li* is restricted to an isolated area of East (French) Cameroun. It may be connected with the more widespread *də* or *dɛ*, or be a form of *lib/lif* (item 83), with which it may alternate, cf. Jespersen's 'he live for hup', 'Massa no live'. Charles Gilman, currently doing research on Cameroons Pidgin at the Université Libre du Congo, regards this as an archaic retention (personal communication). The Liberian English durative marker is *lɛ* or *də* (see 4.7.3).

510. *Plaba* (<Portuguese *palavra*, 'word') occurs in Gullah in the form *pəlá:brin*, but means '(to make) suggestive or flirtatious talk to a girl'. In Krio this is *bɛl, jan*, or *ib tak*.

531. Sranan *mɔ́rɔ* may also be used verbally in the sense of 'get the better of': *korsu de moro mi*, 'fever is getting me down' (FOCKE). Krio has the verb *mɔ́na* used in much the same way: *fiva de mɔ́na mi* 'fever is making me fed-up'. Probably from English

dialect 'more nor', (cf. Gullah *mónə*), although Yoruba has *mɔnamɔna*, 'trouble, worry', Temne has *mɔnɛ*, 'poverty', and Yorkshire dialect has *mauner*, 'confused, helpless' (WRIGHT, EDD). Trinidad Creole English has *dat 'ooman moe-dan me*, 'I cannot tolerate that woman' (OTTLEY).

542. Krio *paravέntʃɔ* is rare.

545. Virgin Islands Dutch Creole and Papiamentu both have *bambáj*. The word was also adopted into Ceylon Creole Portuguese and the now extinct Ceylon Dutch. In the form *mbambai* it occurs in Fanagalò and Zulu, but does not appear to exist in Afrikaans. Cf. Eng. *by and by*, Spanish *vamos vai*.

553. Derivatives of English 'for' with this function are widespread in the creoles, but do not occur in any non-creolized variety of English outside Britain. The EDD gives several examples of dialect sentences with 'for': *bin yo ready for go?*; *I bain't gwain vor let you hab-m*, etc. (Devonshire, Somerset). While not evident in China Coast Pidgin, Australian Pidgin or Neo-Melanesian, 'for' occurs in Hawaiian Pidgin English (*'you gimme dose grasses foa build myself one house'*), Pitcairnese (*aj nó bin nó wɔ́siŋ fə dú*, 'I didn't know what to do') and Norfolkese (*aj gɔ́wɛn fə kɛtʃ sʌm fíʃ fə íːt lɔ́ːŋə də jám*, 'I'm going to catch some fish to eat with the yams').

567. Krio *bitáwt* is rare.

The Language Situation in Mauritius with Special Reference to Mauritian Creole

PHILIP BAKER

INTRODUCTION

Mauritius is a small island in the Indian Ocean situated about 500 miles east of Madagascar, 20° south of the equator. It has an area of 724 square miles and a rapidly expanding population currently approaching 800,000. Though now one of the most densely populated territories in the world the island remained uninhabited until comparatively recent times.

Arab sailors are thought to have visited Mauritius in the Middle Ages but if they did so they left no trace behind them.[1] Early in the sixteenth century the Portuguese discovered the island but they made no attempt to establish a settlement and called there merely to forage their ships. In 1598 the Dutch formally took possession, naming it Mauritius after the Stadtholder, Prince Maurice of Nassau. They made two successive attempts to colonize the island, brought slaves to exploit the then extensive ebony forests and introduced sugar-cane and other crops. Neither settlement was very prosperous nor very large and the Dutch withdrew finally in 1710 leaving a few runaway slaves behind them.[2] In 1715 the French East India Company claimed possession of Mauritius, renaming it Île de France. Six years later a first group of Frenchmen and slaves crossed over to Île de France from neighbouring Bourbon Island (later known as Réunion).[3] The recorded continuous habitation of Mauritius dates from this event.

From 1721 onwards the peopling of Mauritius may be seen as a series of overlapping waves of immigration, each wave bringing with it new customs and languages. The aim of this article is to describe how, in Mauritius, these languages fared in the past, and how those which have survived co-exist at the present time, and to give some indication of how the situation may be expected to develop in the future. The information given here is largely based on a period of more than two years (1965-67) spent in the island. This has been supplemented by bibliographical sources and by conversations and correspondence with Mauritians and others with experience of local conditions.

MAURITIUS: POPULATION BY ETHNIC GROUP AND DISTRICT (1962)

District	Numerical total	Percentage of district by ethnic group:			
		Hindu %	Muslim %	General population %	Chinese %
Plaines Wilhems	208,184	42	13	42	3
Port Louis	119,950	25	28	37	10
Flacq	73,061	67	14	19	1
Grand Port	69,023	59	14	25	2
Pamplemousses	55,899	68	15	16	1
Rivière du Rempart	53,309	70	13	16	1
Savane	46,380	59	18	21	2
Moka	37,245	67	17	15	1
Black River	18,568	56	2	40	2
Island Total	681,619	50·5	16·2	29·9	3·4

THE IMMIGRANTS

The French held Île de France from 1721 to 1810. During this period three kinds of immigrant came to the island: the French, the slaves and Indian traders. The French came initially from Bourbon Island which they had held since 1644, but later settlers came from Normandy, Brittany and other parts of France. The majority of slaves are known to have come from East and South East Africa and Madagascar and, according to one authority, those of Mozambique descent formed two-fifths of the island's population by 1806.[4] Other slaves are believed to have come from India and West Africa.[5] As the settlement grew it was visited by traders from Kutch, Surat and other ports on the western coast of India, and some of these subsequently made their homes in the island.

In the ensuing polyglot situation a lingua franca was clearly needed and this role was fulfilled by a language later termed 'Creole' which may not originally have been the mother tongue of any immigrant. The exact origin of the French-based Creole languages currently spoken in many parts of the Caribbean and the Indian Ocean is not known, but their remarkable similarity suggests that they may all have stemmed from a common source.[6] Since the term 'Creole' is later applied to a section of the population of Mauritius it is proposed to adopt the phonetic spelling 'Kreol' for the Creole language spoken in this island.

The British captured Île de France in 1810 and restored the Dutch name, Mauritius. The treaty of capitulation gave continued sanction to French language, culture and law and to the Roman Catholic church. The business of government was, however, to be conducted in English, a language known to very few islanders at that time, with the result that the early administration included expatriates performing minor tasks. The British government abolished slavery in 1833 and the emancipation of the slaves in Mauritius took place two years later, at which time the population exceeded 100,000 and comprised about 76% slaves, 17% *libres* and 7% white.[7] The term 'libres' was applied both to free coloureds and to Indian traders.

It was intended that the ex-slaves should serve a four-year period of apprenticeship before being permitted to leave the estates, but the plan was not successful since many fled immediately after emancipation and others got away as soon as they could. This led to a grave labour shortage and to the introduction of indentured labourers from India. The latter were to serve five-year contracts after which they could re-engage or return to India. Small numbers of indentured labourers had been arriving in the colony since 1830, but from 1835 their rate of arrival increased on a quite massive scale. Between 1834 and 1866 more than 365,000 labourers arrived in Mauritius, while only 81,000 returned to India in the same period.[8] People of Indian descent now formed more than two-thirds of the population. Conditions for Indians in the island were often thought to be so bad that on a number of occasions the Indian government suspended immigration. Indentured labourers continued to arrive sporadically from 1867 until 1904 although arrivals (55,000) were fewer and largely offset by departures (45,000).[9]

Precisely which parts of India the labourers came from is not known, but of those coming in the period 1834–1900 inclusive, 60% left from Calcutta, 33% from Madras and 7% from Bombay.[10] Labourers did not necessarily originate from areas close to these ports and there is evidence to suggest that many leaving from Calcutta came from areas of what is now the state of Bihar.[11] This is further supported by the development of a dialect of Bihari known as Bhojpuri as a kind of lingua franca in rural areas of Mauritius in the nineteenth century.[12]

Small numbers of Indian traders continued to settle in Mauritius throughout the nineteenth century and in the early part of the present century. From about 1890 onwards Chinese immigrants from Hong Kong and mainland China began to appear in the island in increasing numbers.[13]

THE DEVELOPING SITUATION (TO 1939)

For those coming as slaves or as indentured labourers the first few years spent in the island must have been an extremely unpleasant experience. In an isolated society the disagreeable treatment of one's ancestors is not easily forgotten and continues to influence contemporary attitudes to a considerable degree. Yet as each group of immigrants adjusted to local conditions, so their members sought ways to improve their lot. Until the outbreak of the Second World

War social change took place at a leisurely pace and may be summarized as follows:

The French: After capitulation the Franco-Mauritians (as they became known) remained somewhat apart from all other communities, although they continued to play a dominating role in commerce, especially in the sugar industry. Though forming only about 2% of the population in 1939 they remained a major political force because of the financial and property-owning requirements of the franchise.

The slaves and free coloureds: At the time of emancipation slaves and free coloureds formed distinct social classes. This distinction became increasingly blurred but was not entirely forgotten as the term 'gens de couleur' (coloured person) was often applied to those of partial European descent. Nevertheless the two groups were slowly merging into a 'Creole' community subdivided in a very complex manner according to ancestry, financial position, education, etc. All Creoles were Christians and led lives modelled on a European cultural pattern. Economically they occupied a wide variety of jobs, ranging from well-paid civil servants to impoverished fishermen. Creoles who could meet the requirements of the 1886 franchise could vote in all subsequent elections and pre-war political contests were largely between Franco-Mauritians and Creoles.

The British: The number of people from Britain was always too few for them to form a separate ethnic group in the island. Most of them were government employees who returned to Britain on completing their service. Some members of early British administrations appear to have intermarried with Creoles, and a few later British settlers have been assimilated into Franco-Mauritian society.

The Indians: The Indians gradually regrouped themselves into separate Hindu and Muslim communities with those descended from Indian traders forming something of an elite in each. Hindus generally remained in agriculture, and many now owned small plots of land. Small but increasing numbers found other kinds of employment. By 1939 few Muslims remained as agricultural workers, the descendents of Muslim indentured labourers having mostly found other kinds of jobs, such as messengers, chauffeurs, artisans, etc. Hindus and Muslims were always under-represented politically.

The Chinese: The Chinese rapidly established general stores throughout the island and soon dominated the retail trade. Many became Christians and intermarriage with Creoles was commonplace.

Since they depended on the goodwill of their customers they refrained from taking part in island politics.

1939–68

Soon after the outbreak of war able-bodied men of all backgrounds were encouraged to join the British army. Many did so and were later stationed in Italy, Egypt and elsewhere. Locally there was some distress as supplies of certain basic foodstuffs ran out and there was concern over rumours of a possible occupation by the Japanese. British troops were subsequently stationed in the island in considerable numbers and, for the first time since 1810, there was a substantial British 'presence'. The war caused many to recognize that they were all involved in the future of the colony, although not equally represented politically. Hindus and Muslims pressed for a fairer deal and in 1948 a new constitution—the first for sixty-two years—was introduced, which extended the franchise to all who could pass a simple literacy test.[14] The electorate increased six-fold and in elections held the same year Hindus (40% of the electorate[15]) won eleven of the nineteen seats. Creoles and Franco-Mauritians (41%), classed together for the first time by the ambiguous term 'general population', won the remaining eight. Muslim (17%) and Chinese (2%) minorities were unrepresented. Muslims voiced their discontent, while there was disquiet in other quarters at the prospect of 'Hindu rule'.

During the next few years a new concept was to win general approval: that in all matters concerning religion privileges should be related to the number of adherents each religion had. In this way, a government subsidy previously paid only to Christian churches was extended to all the main religions in proportion to their numerical strength. This concept caught the imagination of the Mauritian public, who termed it 'fair-play'. Its principle was applied in many spheres and changes recommended by its logic were usually adopted. As 'fair-play' flourished, 'new' minorities appeared with spokesmen ready to stake their claims. Tamils, Telegus and Marathis were apparently no longer satisfied to be classified with the 'Bihari'[16] majority as simply 'Hindus'. Such claims were given some degree of recognition as the number of languages in which there were regular broadcasts increased from two to eleven, and public holidays multiplied until by 1968 there were twenty-eight.[17]

In the late 1950s universal adult suffrage was introduced. New political parties claiming to represent specific communities were formed with names such as Tamil United Party and Comité d'Action Musulman. Sections of the Press were disturbed by the trend and termed it 'communalisme', yet this was not a new feature of island life since the nominally non-racial Scouting Movement had locally developed into five separate organizations (Hindu, Christian,

Muslim, Tamil and Telegu, and Chinese Scouts) and football teams with names like Young Tamils and Hindu Cadets abounded. However, 'communalisme' in politics caused rather more concern.

In 1966 a new electoral system was introduced which, while refusing to recognize sub-divisions of the Hindus (i.e. Telegus, Marathis, etc.), ensured by means of 'correctives' that the numbers of Hindus, Muslims, Chinese and General Population elected would be substantially in proportion to their percentage of the total electorate. 'Fair-play', as originally conceived, was now part of the constitution. Elections were held the following year and interest centred on the question of independence. Candidates favouring the latter won about 55% of the votes cast and a clear majority of seats. Mauritius became independent in 1968.

THE LANGUAGES OF MAURITIUS TODAY

In order to arrive at the exact number of languages currently in use in Mauritius it would be necessary to define the word 'language' very precisely and to have undertaken a far more exhaustive survey than has been attempted here. The task may be simplified if the following are eliminated, since their influence at the present time in Mauritius is minimal:

1. Languages acquired by Mauritians while resident abroad, but which are not currently the mother tongue of anyone born in the island.

2. Languages spoken by people born outside the island, who have subsequently become Mauritian citizens, but where these are not the mother tongue of any native-born Mauritian (e.g. Réunion Creole).

3. Languages in which instruction is available in certain educational establishments, but which are never, as yet, used in ordinary conversation (e.g. Russian, German).

4. Languages such as Sanskrit, Latin and Arabic which are used in certain religious ceremonies performed by Hindus, Christians and Muslims respectively, but which are never used in ordinary conversation.

From the widely differing opinions of Mauritian informants it has been possible to draw up the following alphabetical list of languages, each of which was described to the author at some time as being the mother tongue of some Mauritians currently living in the island: Bengali, Bhojpuri, Cantonese, English, French, Gujerati, Hakka, Hindi, Hindustani, Kokni, Kreol, Kutchi, Mandarin, Marathi, Punjabi, Tamil, Telegu and Urdu. It is proposed to examine such claims, and the spheres in which each of these languages is currently used, but it will first be useful to consider first the official statistics relating to languages:

The Censuses

In the 1952 census Mauritians were asked (1) which language was their mother tongue; (2) which language they most frequently used at home; (3) which languages they could speak; and (4) which languages they were able to read and/or write. In the 1962 census it appears that, of the questions relating to languages, only the first two were asked. The answers are tabulated below in percentages of the total population of the island,[18] where not otherwise indicated by a lettered footnote. A number of special factors need to be considered in interpreting these figures:

1. Census forms were delivered to all households and were written in both English and French. Not all Mauritians were literate in either of these two languages and such people had to seek help from friends or from persons whose job it was to collect completed forms. Few of those who filled in census forms could have had any linguistic training.

2. Of the two most widely used vernaculars in the island, Kreol, which few Mauritians readily acknowledge as a language proper (i.e. it is seen as a substandard form of French) does appear, while Bhojpuri does not, being presumably hidden under the guise of Hindi and, perhaps, Urdu. It is difficult to know either how people whose mother tongues these were would have described them on the census forms ('broken French', 'Hindi patois', etc.) or how such replies were treated by the statisticians.

3. Several Mauritians consulted during the preparation of this article understood the term 'mother tongue' to mean 'language spoken by one's ancestors at the time of their arrival in Mauritius'. This view was held by a number of educated people and must have influenced the answers given on census forms.[19]

4. In many homes more than one language is regularly used and it would be difficult for people from such a background not to be influenced by considerations of status or ethnic group in selecting one of these as that most frequently employed.

5. Both censuses took place at times when 'fair-play' was a growing influence in island affairs. Since languages provided a way in which to register the numerical strength of sub-divisions of the three permitted ethnic groups (Indo-Mauritian, General Population or Sino-Mauritian), there was some incentive for minorities to list languages associated exclusively with them as their mother tongue and even as the language most frequently used at home. Certainly the apparent fall in those listing Kreol in the first category between 1952 and 1962 and the apparent rise of other languages conflicts strongly

not only with personal experience but also with the opinions of all Mauritians consulted in the preparation of this article.

Language	Mother tongue 1952 %	Mother tongue 1962 %	Currently spoken most often at home 1952 %	Currently spoken most often at home 1962[a] %	Able to speak[b] 1952 %	Able to read and/or write[c] 1952 %
Chinese[d]	2·7	2·8	2·1	2·0	2·9	1·8
English	0·2	0·2	0·2	0·3	2·8	27·7
French	7·1	6·9	7·6	8·1	24·4	39·8
Hindi	40·8	36·4	38·9	32·5	42·0	8·3
Kreol	36·9	29·2	44·6	45·5	94·2	40·8
Tamil	4·3	6·5	2·0	2·9	3·3	0·9
Telegu	1·3	2·4	0·8	1·0	1·0	0·2
Urdu	5·3	13·6	2·7	6·4	4·4	2·1
Other Indian languages[e]	1·4	2·0	1·1	1·3	1·4	0·5
	100·0	100·0	100·0	100·0	176·4	122·1
Bhojpuri/Hindi/Urdu[f]	46·1	50·0	41·6	38·9	46·4	in Arabic script 2·1% in Devanagari script 8·3%

a Based on 93·6% of the total population and compensated pro-rata to facilitate comparison with other figures. The remaining 6·4% were listed as 'not applicable or not stated' (see BENEDICT, *Mauritius*, 1965).
b Based on a population aged 3 years and over.
c Based on a population aged 5 years and over.
d Varieties of Chinese were not distinguished.
e Mainly Marathi. This obscures the remarkable fact that of 796 who listed their ability to speak Gujerati in 1952 762 claimed to be literate in this language (BENEDICT, *Indians in a Plural Society*, 1961, p. 37).
f These are the figures of Hindi and Urdu combined together (see discussion of these languages on subsequent pages).

Bengali

There were undoubtably some Bengali speakers amongst the Indian labourers who came in the nineteenth century. At the present time Bengali does not appear to be in use as either a written or a spoken language and the only person encountered who claimed Bengali as his mother tongue had been unable to converse in this since the death of his father, the only other speaker known to him.

Bhojpuri

Bhojpuri is a dialect of Bihari spoken in parts of the Indian state of Bihar. It was brought to Mauritius by indentured labourers and appears to have flourished initially as a kind of lingua franca used by Indians from diverse parts of the subcontinent. It has been modified by contact with Kreol[20] and has borrowed many words from the latter including: *lakdʒin* 'kitchen' from Kreol *lakuzin* (ultimately from French 'la cuisine') and *dʒalmet* 'matchstick' from Kreol *zalimet*

(French 'les allumettes'; Bhojpuri lacks z and replaces this by $dʒ$ in loan-words).

Bhojpuri is usually described as ɛ̃djɛ̃, 'Indian', by its speakers though the terms 'Hindi patois', 'broken Hindi' and 'Bhojpuri' are also used occasionally. It is currently the mother tongue of a substantial proportion of those of Indian descent including some whose ancestors must originally have spoken Dravidian languages. The rapid spread of Kreol in recent years has deprived Bhojpuri of much of its former importance as a lingua franca but it remains a widely spoken vernacular especially amongst women and is known as a second or additional language by some Creoles and (rarely) Chinese in certain villages. Bhojpuri is not a written language[21] and is permitted very little broadcasting time. Political speeches are sometimes made in Bhojpuri in rural areas. There are also locally-composed folk songs in Bhojpuri which adopt the rhythmic musical form of the *sega*, a traditional Creole dance.

Cantonese

Cantonese is one of at least two mutually unintelligible varieties of Chinese spoken by Sino-Mauritians. All four Chinese newspapers printed in the island in 1967 could be read by literate speakers of any variety since written Chinese ideographs are not related to spoken sounds. Cantonese is permitted one hour of radio broadcasting per week. There are fewer speakers of Cantonese than of Hakka (see below).

English

English has been the only official language of Mauritius since 1810. As such it is the exclusive written language of the civil service and the spoken language of High Court proceedings. It is taught in primary schools and is the medium of instruction in some primary classes and in secondary education for all subjects except French. English is much used in correspondence, especially for business purposes and although there is currently only one newspaper appearing mainly in English there are at least a dozen in other languages which regularly include some articles and advertisements in English. The British Council maintains a library and reading rooms and conducts a cultural programme. In addition a specialist in teaching English as a foreign language is on the British Council staff and, with a language laboratory, organizes intensive courses in English.

English is the mother tongue of very few Mauritians and, until quite recently, was rarely spoken outside the homes of such people. The rapid increase in recent years of the numbers of children attending both primary and secondary schools has made some knowledge of English commonplace and those whose mother tongue is not French often prefer to speak imperfect English rather than imperfect French in circumstances calling for a 'status' language. One reason for this may be that Mauritians generally are far more aware of errors made in French than in English. This is discussed elsewhere but it appears to be partly responsible for the increasing though still limited use of English in the civil service and for the fact that in the Legislative Assembly, where speakers may use either English or French, at least three-quarters of the discussion took place in English in 1967.

In the arts English has won varying degrees of acceptance. There are relatively few English-language films shown in the island's cinemas,[22] but about 10% of radio and about 50% of television programmes are in English. There are a number of amateur novelists and playwrights writing in English and local dramatic groups occasionally perform plays in English. Most libraries include a large proportion of books in English, especially non-fiction works. English and American popular songs are frequently heard on the radio and in local dance halls, etc.

The emergence of English as a widely understood language is too recent a phenomenon for there yet to have arisen a predictable form of 'Mauritian English' though this may appear in due course. In the meantime spoken and written English are substantially influenced by translation from other languages, especially French and Kreol.

French

Mauritian French appears to have developed semi-independently of metropolitan French in the past and to have retained some archaic terms. In recent years mass communications have made islanders familiar with current terminology and the most striking feature of Mauritian French is now no longer vocabulary but pronunciation. Particularly noticeable is the presence of regularly distributed, strongly-stressed syllables and a very wide range of pitch which caused a French government official to comment in private recently: 'Les Mauriciens ne parlent pas le français. Ils le chantent!' 150 years of British rule has naturally led to the borrowing of many terms from English and to the adoption of phrases modelled on English constructions, such as 'Il est en charge de . . .' (modelled on English 'He is in charge of . . .') for normal French 'Il est chargé de . . .'. Cultural bodies such as the Alliance Française, which maintains a centre at Curepipe and has recently established several regional 'centres d'animation française', are currently very active in encouraging islanders to adopt metropolitan French forms.

French is the mother tongue of Franco-Mauritians and the Creole élite. Since such people held most of the better-paid jobs in the past the French language became associated with the well-to-do and Kreol speakers occasionally endeavoured to speak French at home as a means of acquiring a more cultivated image. Outside the home

French is the language most frequently used in the smarter shops and restaurants and in some offices. As a written language it is used a great deal in correspondence, especially private correspondence, and is the medium adopted for most of the contents of nine daily and several weekly journals. Most poster advertising is in French. In broadcasting French is allotted about 60% of radio and over 40% of television broadcasting time. More than half the films seen in the island have French dialogue. There are many authors who write in French including several professionals and French plays are occasionally performed locally. French popular songs are frequently played on the radio and performed by local dance bands.

French is the medium of instruction of most primary education and this language is also taught in secondary schools. There has thus been a vast increase in the numbers of people able to read, write and speak French, although there does not seem to have been any commensurate increase in the volume of French spoken. Indeed in offices there seems to be a growing trend to regard French as a formal register of Kreol, the former being used with one's superiors and the latter with one's equals. This reflects the social, political and financial rise of those whose mother tongue is not French and may be a continuance of the pattern adopted in primary schools where children speak Kreol with their friends and French with their teachers.

Gujerati

Gujerati is the mother tongue of some Muslims and Hindus whose ancestors originated from parts of what is now Gujurat state. It is allotted a small but regular proportion of radio broadcasting and is offered as an optional subject in a few primary schools. Most Gujerati speakers belong to comparatively wealthy trading families and an unusually high proportion are literate in their language. Some are said to write their account books in Gujerati.

Hakka

Hakka is the main variety of Chinese spoken in Sino-Mauritian homes. There is one hour of radio broadcasting in Hakka per week.

Hindi

In Mauritius the term 'Hindi' usually means 'literary Hindi'. It is also used by some people to describe the following:

1. The language used in some homes in certain villages with an unusually high proportion of Hindus (Triolet and Piton were frequently cited). Asked about the affinities between this and Bhojpuri, informants described the former as being 'purer' and as containing fewer Kreol words. It is tentatively suggested that this form of Mauritian 'Hindi' may be a type of Bhojpuri which has remained fairly close to Indian Bhojpuri.

2. The language used in some Hindu religious ceremonies where this is neither Sanskrit nor Bhojpuri. This appears to be Hindi proper, i.e. a spoken form corresponding to written Hindi and retaining some inflections lost in modern Hindustani.

3. The language spoken in most Indian films and used in some radio and television programmes. This is undoubtably Hindustani (see next entry) except in prayers and readings from religious works.

Literary Hindi is taught as an optional subject in many primary schools. There are two bi-weekly newspapers with about 50% of their contents in Hindi, and Indian books and publications in Hindi are widely obtainable. There have also been some literary works by Mauritians in Hindi.

Hindustani

Hindustani was said to be the mother tongue of some Mauritians but this was not confirmed. Outside the home it is the language spoken in nearly half of the films shown publicly in the island and is allotted about 20% of radio and 5% of television broadcasting time. Hindustani songs enjoy a wide measure of popularity and Indian singers have made a number of successful concert-tours locally. Mauritians who have studied in India sometimes make speeches in Hindustani on formal occasions. In spite of a widespread interest in this language there appear to be no local facilities for its instruction except via its literary variants Hindi and Urdu.

Kokni

A very small number of Muslim families speak a language they describe as 'Kokni'. This appears to be an abbreviation of Konkani, a dialect of Marathi spoken in the Konkun area of western India. It is popularly spelled 'Cockney'.

Kreol

Kreol is the mother tongue of an increasing proportion of Mauritians who probably now form a majority of the total population. It is also known as a second or additional language by virtually all other islanders. Outside the home it is the medium of most informal conversation especially in intercommunal situations. Kreol is thus the language of the street, the playground, the workshop, the political meeting, the Chinese general store, the market-place and the bar. Only in some rural areas does Bhojpuri provide a serious challenge to the omnipresence of Kreol and even here the latter is making rapid progress. In the past Kreol was denied broadcasting time except in the form of lyrics to locally composed songs known as 'segas' to which a popular dance is performed. Within the last decade a regular radio request programme including some interviews with hospital patients in Kreol has been introduced and for the 1967 election the majority of party political broadcasts were in Kreol. The first regular television programme in Kreol—encouraging islanders to grow their own food—began in 1968.

As a written language Kreol has made far less progress. In the nineteenth century Baissac collected Kreol folk tales and wrote a Kreol grammar[23] using a French-based orthography which rendered Kreol *sat* 'cat', *feə* 'do', and *zãfã* 'child(ren)' as 'çatte', 'fére' and 'zenfant(s)' respectively. Similar spelling was accepted as proof of literacy for the 1948 franchise and is currently used by newspapers when quoting the livelier passages from Kreol political speeches which cannot be adequately translated into French, such as: *Nous ti donne zotte learner. Zotte ti fail*, i.e. 'We (the government) gave them (the opposition) a provisional driving licence (i.e. the opportunity of taking part in a coalition government). They failed the test (i.e. later withdrew from the coalition)'. For a few years recently there was a newspaper, *L'Epée*, written entirely in Kreol spelled in this way, and this inconsistent orthography is also used in some private correspondence and for police depositions.

Illiterate Mauritians often speak what is termed 'Créole vulgaire' or 'Vulgar Kreol'. A more appropriate name would be 'Old Kreol' since such speakers retain the older pronunciation of words, such as *posɔ̃* 'fish' (Fr. 'poisson') and *kum* 'as, like' (Fr. 'comme'), as recorded by Baissac in 1880. These are regularly 'corrected' to *pwasɔ̃* and *kom* by literate speakers to conform with French pronunciation. When those whose mother tongue is French speak Kreol they respect its grammatical rules but not its phonological rules, with the result that the consonants ʃ and ʒ, the semi-vowel ɥ and the vowels y, ø, œ and ə are to be heard in such speech. In apparent imitation of this some speakers whose mother tongue is not French attempt to introduce these sounds into their Kreol at the etymologically 'correct' moment. ʃ and ʒ are achieved with comparative ease but y usually emerges as jə and ø and œ are approximated to ə. This Kreol is termed 'Créole raffiné' or 'Refined Kreol'. Refined Kreol is extremely difficult to speak since the would-be speaker must constantly refer to the written French form from which the Kreol term is thought to be derived in order to decide on the appropriate 'refined' pronunciation. In slow speech some consistency of pronunciation may, with considerable practice, be achieved, but in rapid conversation or under emotional stress 'mistakes' are frequently made revealing the speakers' Kreol background. Thus if normal Kreol *disel* 'salt' (Fr. 'du sel') and *dipɛ̃* 'bread' (Fr. 'du pain') are to be 'corrected' to *djəsel* and *djəpɛ̃*, Kreol *dimãs* 'Sunday' (Fr. 'Dimanche') may accidentally emerge as *djəmãʃ*. Erroneous etymology may lead the speaker of Refined Kreol to pronounce normal Kreol *lakaz* 'house' as *lakaʒ*, on the assumption that this is derived from French 'la cage' (*lakaz* is actually derived from French 'la case'). Refined Kreol is largely confined to the smarter residential areas of Plaines Wilhems and appears to be a verbal way of 'keeping up with the Joneses', since it carries the implication that one speaks French at home.

Kutchi

Kutchi is spoken in the homes of a few Muslim families whose ancestors originated from the Rann of Kutch. Kutchi is a dialect of Gujerati.

Mandarin

Mandarin Chinese was said to be spoken in the homes of some Sino-Mauritians but this was not confirmed. Mandarin is regarded as the standard form of Chinese by the Peking government and is taught in the Chinese Middle School in Port Louis.

Marathi

Marathi is spoken in the homes of some Mauritians descended from indentured labourers whose ancestors came from what is now Maharashtra state. It is permitted some regular radio broadcasting time and instruction is available in Marathi as an optional subject in some primary schools.

Punjabi

A small number of Punjabi-speaking Indians came to Mauritius in the present century to work as prison guards and policemen. There do not appear to be any Punjabi-speaking homes at the present time.

Tamil

Tamil is spoken in a very small number of homes said to be mostly in the district of Savanne. There is some regular radio broadcasting in Tamil and this language is offered as an optional subject in some primary schools. About half the contents of the fortnightly paper 'Tamil Voice' are in Tamil and an Indian film magazine in Tamil and English is widely circulated. Tamil-speaking films are occasionally shown publicly and in the past *ségas* with Tamil lyrics were composed locally. Tamil songs and sketches are performed on special occasions.

Telegu

Telegu was said to be spoken in a very small number of homes but this was not confirmed. There is a limited amount of radio airtime in Telegu and instruction in this language is available as an optional subject in some primary schools. There appear to be no local publications in Telegu. Telegu songs and sketches are performed annually to mark Ougadi, Telegu New Year.

Urdu

In Mauritius the term Urdu is applied to the following:

1. The language written in Arabic script which is a literary form of Hindustani. There are two weekly papers written entirely in Urdu and instruction in the language is available at most primary schools as an optional subject.

2. The spoken language used in Islamic religious ceremonies and allotted a proportion of radio broadcasting time. Sketches and songs in Urdu are performed on special occasions.

3. The language spoken by a few older Muslims in their own homes. According to one informant this was a mixture of Urdu and Bhojpuri. According to others this was a mixture of Hindustani and Urdu.

THE ACQUISITION OF LANGUAGES

The Mauritian child learns his first language from the members of his household. Where this is neither Kreol nor Bhojpuri he is likely to come into contact with speakers of one of these vernaculars at an early age and will normally have acquired a working knowledge of this by the age of five. At that age he becomes entitled to free primary education and although attendance is not compulsory most parents send their children to school. (Free primary education became generally available in the 1950s.) In October 1967 there were 140,495 children attending primary schools. This figure represents more than 19% of the estimated total population of the island of whom about 57% are under the age of 21.[24] These figures give some indication of the importance of the education system in determining future language patterns.

On entering primary school all children, regardless of their mother tongue, are familiar to some extent with either Kreol or Bhojpuri. Since the teacher must endeavour to teach in French his first task is to encourage his Kreol-speaking pupils to teach this to their Bhojpuri-speaking comrades. This process is apparently achieved with remarkably little difficulty though it was said to have been a major problem a decade ago. This is seen as a testimony to the structural simplicity of Kreol and may give some indication of the speed with which Kreol is replacing Bhojpuri in many homes. Once his pupils understand Kreol the teacher can begin to make some progress in spoken French but he will often have to modify his pronunciation towards Kreol. As French will probably not be the mother tongue of the teacher such modification is normally achieved readily.

Children are taught to write English and French simultaneously. The unphonetic orthography of French and the wide differences in pronunciation, word class, meaning and usage between French forms and terms derived from these in Kreol create special problems for both teacher and pupil. Although French is the medium of oral instruction, text books for all subjects except French are in English as is all the pupil's written work. English is taught in English. In addition to learning French and English pupils have one period per week where they are offered a choice between 'catechism' and learning an Indian language such as Hindi or Urdu. In some schools instruction in Gujerati, Tamil, Telegu and Marathi is similarly available. This seemingly bizarre choice does not strike the Mauritian as such since French, the language in which catechism is taught, Hindi and Urdu are seen as the religious languages of Christians, Hindus and Muslims respectively, religious texts being likewise used in the teaching of these Indian languages. For those who wish there are ample facilities for supplementing knowledge of Indian languages outside school hours in the premises of religious bodies. During the last two years of primary education the official medium of oral instruction is changed from French to English. In practice it is said that the majority of teachers continue to use French, switching to English only when a school inspector is in the vicinity.

The rapid increase in the number of children attending primary schools naturally brought a much greater demand for secondary education than the existing schools run by government or religious bodies could cope with. This led to the establishment of numerous secular private schools which charged fees. These became known as 'mushroom colleges' and their standards have varied enormously.[25] In almost all secondary schools English is the medium of instruction since the system is orientated towards the Cambridge Overseas Certificate of Education and the (British) General Certificate of Education, both of which require a high standard of English.

Free primary education only became generally available during the 1950s, but in a population which has increased from half a million in 1952 to 800,000 in 1969[26] this has already brought major changes. There can be no doubt that the number able to speak, read and write both French and English has increased on a massive scale since 1952 as has the proportion literate in Indian languages. The effect of the system has been to increase the number of languages with which each child may become familiar to a maximum of six (i.e. for a child whose mother tongue is Marathi who picks up Bhojpuri in his village and learns Kreol, French and English and another oriental language such as Hindi at school, for example). In practice some knowledge of five languages is not unusual and a tolerable fluency in four is now commonplace.

GENERAL TRENDS

In the eighteenth century the influx of immigrants speaking mutually unintelligible languages led to the adoption of Kreol as the lingua franca. French, the language of the master, remained the language of the elite. Other languages may have continued to be spoken for many years but the overwhelming trend was for these to give way to Kreol. In the nineteenth century a change of ownership and a new influx of immigrants provided another status language (English) and an additional lingua franca (Bhojpuri). English made limited progress as a spoken language but its usage as the exclusive written medium of government gave it a special stature. Bhojpuri flourished initially as a lingua franca in rural areas and subsequently became known as an additional language by some Creoles and a very few Chinese. In spite of these changes both French and Kreol continued to make slow but steady progress. Towards the middle of the twentieth century Bhojpuri was still making some progress at the expense of other Indian languages while losing ground to Kreol especially in areas close to the main urban settlements. Kreol was flourishing at the cost of oriental languages generally but losing a little to French as those aspiring to join the elite endeavoured to speak the latter wherever possible. The introduction of mass education has had the effect of accelerating these trends and of boosting the position of English as both a written and spoken language.

Of the twelve Indian languages said to be the individual mother tongues of some Mauritians, two—Punjabi and Bengali—appear to have already become extinct in the local context. Two others—Kutchi and Kokni—are currently spoken by so few people that they seem unlikely to survive for many years. Six languages—Gujerati, Hindi, Marathi, Telegu, Tamil and Urdu—are supported by religious practices, the education system and by sound broadcasting. These factors seem to favour their continued use in Mauritius for some considerable time to come, yet there are no signs that anyone without ethnic or religious reasons for learning these has so far made any effort to avail himself of the opportunities to do so at primary schools.

The two remaining Indian languages are Bhojpuri and Hindustani. The fact that Bhojpuri remains the mother tongue of more Mauritians than any other language except Kreol[27] does not appear to guarantee its future. Those most vocal in demanding equal rights for Indian languages are liable to dismiss it as 'broken Hindi' and since an exclusive knowledge of this is considered a hindrance at school it is perhaps not so surprising that Bhojpuri should be particularly vulnerable to the advance of Kreol. Yet the speed at which Kreol is replacing Bhojpuri in many homes is quite extraordinary and may give some indication of how, in an earlier era, this morphologically efficient language was able to replace the original languages of the slaves. During the period spent in the island many families were encountered where it was said that, until the eldest child had begun to attend primary school, Kreol was never spoken at home, but where it was now the language most frequently employed. The change from

Bhojpuri to Kreol may be observed at different stages of development throughout the island at the present time. It is interesting to note that women, perhaps because they spend most of their time in or near their homes, seem far more reluctant to abandon Bhojpuri than other members of their family. Bilingual conversations in which the mother sticks resolutely to Bhojpuri while her offspring addresses her in Kreol may frequently be witnessed.

As the official language of India, Hindustani remains a potential status language to rival English and French in an island where two-thirds of the population is of Indian descent. That it has not so far taken their place is due to religious considerations which have favoured the teaching of literary Hindi and Urdu rather than their common spoken relative Hindustani.

The Chinese languages appear to be giving way fairly rapidly to Kreol. Outside Port Louis where there are substantial numbers of Chinese, the Sino-Mauritian has very limited opportunities for speaking his traditional languages and this situation is further aggravated by the fact that the two main varieties—Hakka and Cantonese—are mutually unintelligible. Children from traditionally Chinese-speaking homes are sometimes unable to converse in Chinese although they apparently understand some Chinese terms. Such children address their parents in Kreol.

Kreol continues to replace traditional languages in many homes. Since Kreol has generally been regarded as an inferior tongue it would seem that its extreme simplicity is an important factor in persuading islanders to adopt this and abandon their more complex ancestral languages. Kreol is rarely now identified with one particular group (i.e. the Creoles) and is increasingly regarded as *nu koze morisjẽ*, 'our Mauritian language', by many people.

The education system has had the effect of greatly increasing the proportion of people familiar with French yet this does not appear to have brought about any comparable increase in the volume of French spoken outside the classroom. The main reason for this is that the very nature of Kreol makes French an unusually difficult language for Kreol-speakers. The Kreol-speaker does not regard French as being a foreign language since most of Kreol's vocabulary is recognizably derived from French. Yet in order to speak French the Kreol-speaker must:

1. learn to produce consistently several sounds not occurring in Kreol;

2. reintroduce these into Kreol in the etymologically 'correct' places;

3. disentangle traces of French articles which have become an inseparable part of many Kreol nouns such as *duri* 'rice' (Fr. riz), *lezel* 'wing(s)' (Fr. aile), *nam* 'soul(s)' (Fr. âme), etc.

4. grasp several entirely new concepts including elision, inflections, number and gender;

5. reorganize his vocabulary according to a very different and much more complicated set of grammatical rules.

The above list is far from exhaustive but is perhaps sufficient to demonstrate that, in order to speak French, the Kreol-speaker must mentally retrace the processes involved in the original creation of Kreol. In view of this it is not altogether surprising that Kreol is generally preferred to French as a medium of informal conversation and those whose mother tongue is not French will normally speak French only in polite or formal circumstances.

A further hazard facing spoken French in the island is that this language is associated with the traditional elite who in the past held a majority of high-salaried employments. This gave rise to the idea that 'good French' was to be equated with 'good breeding' and, because of the difficulties facing the Kreol-speaker who wishes to speak good French, the latter is liable to make errors which will reveal his Kreol—and thus his socially-inferior—background. This is seen as a contributory reason for the increasing use of Kreol between colleagues in the civil service; since it is undesirable to introduce status factors into conversation with people regarded as one's equals.

The expansion of the education service has led to the rapid increase in the numbers familiar with English but, as with French, this has not so far greatly augmented its usage as a medium of conversation outside the schoolroom. However, whereas French is the mother tongue of perhaps 7% of the population, English is that of a mere 0·2%. There is thus very little informal conversation in English. The failure of any English-speaking minority to emerge, readily identifiable on racial or religious grounds, has currently become a great asset. English is a status language free of class associations and imperfect English does not carry the same kind of social stigma as does imperfect French. It has thus made progress as a medium for formal speeches, especially in rural areas.

THE LANGUAGE PROBLEM

The language problem in Mauritius is not one of simple verbal communication, since Kreol already fulfils this role, but one of finding a language policy for education and broadcasting which will meet with the approval of most of the population. The education system has already been described. The Mauritius Broadcasting Corporation provides about 112 hours of sound broadcasting and about thirty-four hours of television per week. Both services are commercial and accept advertisements in French, English, Hindustani and, especially since 1967, Kreol and Bhojpuri. Advertisements need not be—and frequently are not—in the same language as the programme they interrupt. In March 1969 the percentage of airtime allotted the different languages calculated as far as possible on the basis of the language employed most in each individual programme,[28] was:

Language(s)	Radio %	Television %
French	60·2	40·8
Hindi/Hindustani/Bhojpuri/Urdu [a]	23·8	6·0
English	9·8	51·1
Tamil	1·1	b
Hakka	0·9	b
Cantonese	0·9	b
Mixed [c]	0·9	0·7
Marathi	0·7	b
Telegu	0·7	b
Gujerati	0·7	b
Kreol	0·2	0·7
Other [d]	0·1	0·7
	100·0	100·0

a It has proved impracticable to separate these four languages. It would appear that Hindustani is the most frequently used. Hindi and Urdu are mainly reserved for devotional songs and prayers. Bhojpuri is used in some interviews.

b There are no regular programmes on television in these six languages, but they are used infrequently in special programmes marking religious festivals or cultural events.

c For radio this consisted of a regular one-hour programme, 'Bonne journée aux malades/ Khush raho' in which hospital patients are interviewed in any language of their choice. For television this was a regular programme about 'family planning' which might similarly be multilingual. In both cases it would appear that Kreol, Bhojpuri and French were the three languages most frequently employed.

d For radio this represented two five-minute programmes of readings from the Koran in Arabic. For television this represented fifteen minutes of 'Magazine Musical', 'une programme allemande' which apparently comprised light classical music and songs by German and other artistes.

In the past there have been three basic schools of thought as to how the system of education and broadcasting might be changed and these three may be termed 'pro-Indian', 'pro-French' and 'pro-English' for convenience, although it should be noted that these correspond broadly to ideas expressed by private individuals in the local Press and elsewhere and not to organized pressure groups.

The pro-Indians have sought for a fair representation of several Indian languages in broadcasting and education. They have substantially achieved their aims in broadcasting and primary education but have yet to make much progress with regard to secondary education. The pro-French have argued bitterly against the high proportion of television programmes in English and have stressed that in a country where most people speak 'French or French patois' (i.e. Kreol) it would be logical to eliminate English from the education system and orientate the latter towards French government examinations. This view has been countered strongly by the pro-English who have argued that a French system of education would give those who speak French at home 'an unfair advantage', thereby rejecting the classification of 'French or French patois' as a single entity. They have emphasized the fairness of the present system which puts everyone at the same disadvantage, conveniently overlooking the advantages enjoyed by the tiny English-speaking minority. The pro-English are not vocal in demanding more broadcasting-time in English.

In 1967 D. Virahsawmy introduced some quite novel ideas. In a series of newspaper articles[29] he offered a substantially phonemic orthography for Kreol of his own design and proposed that children be taught to read and write this for the first two years of primary school after which there would be a rapid transition to English in order to obtain maximum advantage from the English-based system. Virahsawmy also argued in favour of giving Kreol joint official status (with English) since this was the only language all Mauritians understood. Any proposal which promised both to lower the status of French and to raise that of Kreol was bound to incur the wrath of the pro-French and in the ensuing controversy the potential importance of a suitable orthography for Kreol has been largely overlooked.

Broadcasting and education are very different spheres but it is interesting to note that the arguments for and against changing the present systems rely mainly on the 'fair-play' principle and the differences of opinion stem substantially from whether Kreol is to be classed as French or not. If the purpose of broadcasting is to entertain and to inform then it must be noted that Kreol is generally used only for the transmission of politically important information (party political broadcasts, programmes encouraging home food production and family planning, etc.) and is very rarely used for entertainment. The use of eleven languages in domestic broadcasting where none of these are known to all islanders and the almost total exclusion of the only language understood by everyone cannot fail to strike the non-Mauritian as odd. Yet it must also be noted that there does not appear to have been any vocal public demand for programmes in Kreol as yet.

So far as the general public is concerned, the purpose of education is to acquire either the Cambridge or G.C.E. 'O' level certificate, the means to obtain a better paid job. If this view is taken, then it is clear that the assumption that a single European language could be used as the medium of instruction in both primary and secondary education once sufficient fluency had been achieved, as implicit in the arguments of the pro-French and of Virahsawmy, is valid. The choice of which is more suitable—English or French—is a very difficult matter. It is not easy to say to what extent Kreol is either a help or a handicap in coping with a French-based system of education. As already described, a prior knowledge of Kreol creates major difficulties when it comes to speaking correct French, but it does not necessarily follow that the other three functions of language—listening, reading and writing—are similarly affected. On the basis of discussions with Mauritians of varying backgrounds it is tentatively suggested that most Kreol-speakers find reading and listening to French much easier than speaking or writing and that the reverse appears to be true for English, at least for those who have completed secondary education. The reasons for this appear to be as follows:

1. It is not necessary to interpret most of the inflected endings of French when listening or reading since tense, for instance, may normally be guessed from context. Inflected endings must often be pronounced in speaking, but must always be written whether sounded in speech or not.

2. Even in primary school most text books are in English. This seems to lead to a familiarity with English spelling at an early age and the fact that English is rarely spoken in primary schools helps, apparently, to cloak the illogicalities of English spelling. There are also some surprising similarities between English and Kreol syntax. English has very few inflections and both languages have roughly comparable systems of displaying tense and aspect in verbs.

If the attainment of qualifications is to be the sole aim of school education then there can be no doubt that *either* French *or* English is superfluous in the present system. If, however, a broader interpretation of 'education' is taken, the present system does have an important virtue since it not only familiarises pupils with the most widely spoken language in the world (English) but also with another important world language (French) which is not only the mother tongue of an important minority but also the parent language of the vernacular spoken by all islanders (Kreol). Mauritians sometimes complain that having to learn two languages at school is an unusually heavy imposition upon children, yet it is commonplace in many parts of the world. However, in other countries the mother tongue of the majority has normally been studied and courses in other languages are designed with this in mind. The unusually heavy imposition upon Mauritian children is surely not that they are required to learn two useful languages but that the mother tongue of the majority and the lingua franca known to the remainder (Kreol) has not been properly studied. As to the continued dispute between the qualities of French vis-à-vis those of English, this surely indicates that a system which provides for the teaching of both cannot be entirely out of step with public opinion.

CONCLUSIONS

The current importance of the 'fair-play' principle favours the continued use of English as the exclusive written language and formal spoken medium of government in Mauritius. Even if the education system were not English-based the growing use of this as a world language and the fact that the island trades mainly with Anglophone countries (Australia, East Africa, Hong Kong, India, New Zealand, South Africa and the U.K.) would probably ensure that English remained an important school subject.

The 'fair-play' principle also encourages the continued expansion of Kreol as the medium of informal conversation and in all situations where it is desirable to be understood by the largest possible number of people. The future of Kreol as a written language is, as yet, unpredictable.

Nine languages—French, Hindi, Urdu, Marathi, Tamil, Telegu, Gujerati, Hakka and Cantonese—are in varying degrees literary, cultural and/or religious languages for different groups of islanders. French retains the additional advantage of being the medium of instruction of most primary school education but, on present trends, it is difficult to see how it can regain its former position as the unchallenged spoken status language.

It is difficult to see any of the remaining languages of Mauritius extending their domain in the near future. Whilst Hindustani remains potentially important the fact that Hindus and Muslims in India and Pakistan continue to develop separate literary varieties of this language hinders its progress locally.

NOTES

1. Mauritius is said to appear on an Arabic map drawn by Edrisi in 1153. See M. EMRITH, *The Muslims in Mauritius*, Port Louis, 1967, pp. 4–5. Also BULPIN, *Islands in a Forgotten Sea*, Cape Town, 1958, pp. 19–20.

2. H. DE RAUVILLE, *L'Ile de France Contemporaine*, Paris, 1908. In his 'avant-propos' the author, writing of the year 1723, states: 'les forêts et les montagnes étaient infestés d'ésclaves *marrons* enfuis autrefois de chez leurs maîtres hollandais et que ceux-ci avaient abandonnés lors de leur départ'.

3. DE RAUVILLE, op. cit.

4. M. V. Jackson HAIGHT, *European Powers and S.E. Africa*, London, 1967, p. 88.

5. J. G. MILBERT, *Voyage pittoresque a l'île Maurice*, Paris, 1812. On pp. 162 and 195 the author mentions the presence of slaves from India and various parts of West Africa, in addition to those from Madagascar and S.E. Africa. In spite of this, it is difficult to find any reason why the French should have brought slaves from West Africa since the slave trade on the East and S.E. coast of Africa had flourished in the hands of the Arabs and later the Portuguese for several centuries. It would also be extremely difficult to find any Mauritian at the present time who could be described as 'West African' in appearance. However, whilst it seems most improbable that there was any regular importation of slaves from West Africa the survival of the name 'Camp Yoloff' for a district of Port Louis supports the view that there had been some shipment of West African slaves (i.e. Yolof or Wolof, in this case).

La route des Îles, compiled by the chief archivist of Mauritius, Auguste TOUSSAINT, Paris, 1968, provides detailed figures for the number of slaves arriving from East and S.E. Africa and from Madagascar in the period 1773–1810 (Appendix 1). Since no slaves appear to have been landed from 1795 to 1800 inclusive the period may be divided in two:

	Numerical total	Percentage from East and S.E. Africa %	Percentage from Madagascar %
1773–94	39,683	93	7
1801–10	18,395	59	41

These figures are for the numbers of slaves put on board ship. The mortality rate for those coming from Madagascar was in the region of 12% and for those from East and S.E. Africa, 21%.

6. See M. F. GOODMAN, *A Comparative Study of Creole French Dialects*, The Hague, 1964, esp. pp. 129–33.

7. From B. BENEDICT, *Mauritius*, London, 1965, p. 15.

8/9. From the immigration records of the Mauritius Archives.

10/11. From B. BENEDICT, *Indians in a Plural Society*, London, 1961.

12. S. BHUCKORY, *Hindi in Mauritius*, Port Louis, 1967, pp. 22–3.

13. TOUSSAINT, op. cit., notes the presence of a Chinese immigrant as early as 1783 (p. 144) but the majority of Chinese immigrants appear to have settled far more recently, many in the present century.

14. Literacy was recognized in nine languages: 'English, French, Gujerati, Hindustani, Tamil, Telegu, Urdu, Chinese and the Creole patois commonly in use in the colony' (BHUCKORY, op. cit. The author appears to be quoting from an official document since these words appear between inverted commas).

15. The percentages are all of the electorate, not of the total population, and are derived from figures appearing in M. EMRITH, op. cit. The author divides the electorate into Hindus, Muslims, General Population and Chinese for each of the five constituencies which existed in 1948, although this division of the population into four groups was first used in 1962 and it would appear that Emrith had applied the later criteria to the 1948 electorate. Emrith's total electorate is almost 3,000 less than that given by BENEDICT, op. cit., p. 30, and may perhaps exclude Christian Indians and others not adequately described by these later terms. An Electoral Boundaries Commission in 1957 estimated the population of Mauritius to be: $46\frac{1}{2}$% Hindus, $32\frac{3}{4}$% General Population, $14\frac{3}{4}$% Muslim and 6% Others (comprising Chinese, Franco-Mauritians, Britons and Christian Indians).

16. 'Bihari' is adopted here as a convenient term to describe Hindus who do not regard themselves as being either Tamil, Telegu or Marathi.

17. This figure does not include four non-recurring public holidays granted that year to mark independence celebrations. More recently a commission of enquiry was appointed to find ways of reducing this number and it is understood that their recommendations have been implemented.

18. 'Total population' refers in all cases to the island of Mauritius only and excludes dependencies such as Rodrigues, 350 miles to the east with a population of more than 20,000.

19. Cf. BHUCKORY, op. cit., p. 138: 'Has one ever heard of an Englishman not knowing English or a Frenchman not knowing French? But there exist in Mauritius many people of Indian origin not knowing their mother tongue ...'.

20. So far as is known no study of Mauritian Bhojpuri has yet been undertaken. The author has no specialized knowledge of Indian languages but from examples of Bhojpuri collected it would appear that this is an inflected language which adds such inflections to its numerous loan-words from Kreol. It has not proved possible to establish whether its structure has, in any way, been 'creolized'.

THE LANGUAGE SITUATION IN MAURITIUS 97

21. A London-based Mauritian who wrote to his mother in Bhojpuri, using the Romanized script sometimes adopted for Hindustani, has been encountered, although this appeared to be an isolated phenomenon.
22. Programmes consist of up to three 'European' films or two Indian films, Indian films being generally longer than 'European'. The latter may come from any source (including the United States) but the majority have French dialogue. In analysing the programmes for a week in March 1969 it was found that:
    63% were French-speaking films;
    33% were Hindustani-speaking films;
    4% were English-speaking films.
   There were no programmes in this sample consisting only of English-speaking films but several consisting of one English dialogue film and one or two French dialogue films. Tamil dialogue films are also presented occasionally and there are also private performances of Chinese films.
23. C. BAISSAC, *Une grammaire du patois créole mauricien*, Nantes, 1880.
24. Based on an estimated population of 782,044 at December 31, 1967 (*The Quarterly Guide of Statistics*, Mauritius, 1967).
25. The government subsequently introduced a system of grading according to quality.
26. In recent years the net annual increase in population has always been in excess of 20,000 and, with no reason to suppose there has been any sharp decrease in the rate of expansion, the present figure can scarcely be less than 800,000.
27. This is based on personal observation, since the census does not list Bhojpuri as a separate language.
28. Record request programmes have been allocated according to the language employed by the disc-jockey since such programmes might include songs in several languages. Compared with a similar set of figures which appeared in the Port Louis *Sunday Express* (September 18, 1966) the proportion of French on the radio has decreased by about 7%, while the proportion of French on television has increased by the same amount. Conversely, the percentage of television airtime in English has dropped by about 8%, while its proportion of radio broadcasting has increased by about 2½%. Kreol dialogue was unknown on television in 1966. There is very little variation in other figures, compared with 1966.
29. The first of these appeared in *L'Express* (Port Louis) in August 1967 and subsequent articles have all appeared in the same newspaper.

Tone-marking an African Language, with Application to Bemba

W. MICHAEL MANN

THE object of this paper is to extend the discussion initiated by Professor A. N. Tucker in his article 'Systems of Tone-marking African Languages'[1] by proposing a system, designed in the first place for Bemba (Guthrie's M42a, Zambia), which makes a new use of some older conventions. The article is in two parts, the first introducing and discussing the proposed system, the second attempting to derive from it a conventionalized tonal orthography[2] suitable for textual use, both locally in Zambia and arguably also for academic purposes. It is possible that a similar system may be of value for some other African languages.

I

The great majority of tone-marks used in the systems described by Professor Tucker indicate the tone-level of a single syllable, usually the relative tone-level as established by tonemic analysis. Thus a high-tone syllable is indicated ˉa by Beach, á by Endemann, ā by Jones, and á by Westermann and subsequently many others following the recommendations of the International African Institute. In some cases the interpretation of a given sign may be conditioned by the occurrence of another sign preceding it in the text. For instance á in the Meeussen system is interpreted as a lowered high (or mid) tone following á, and in Christaller's system zero marking is interpreted as high tone following á.[3]

A few tone-marks indicate not (only) the tone of a single syllable, but a feature of an indefinite number of syllables following, to the end sometimes of the word, sometimes of the sentence. The most obvious case is 'down-step' (or tone-slip or tone-lowering), indicated variously ā, 'a, ¹a, à and á by different authors.

Tone-marks have sometimes been placed on a separate line over the text. More frequently they have been placed immediately over the vowel concerned (diacritics), immediately before the vowel or between syllables.

The principle of the system here proposed is that it indicates not tone-level but change of tone-level, or 'contrast' (i.e. syntagmatic contrast). The symbols indicating the various types of tone-contrast are placed naturally between syllables. (Tone-contrast can be seen as a segmental feature, while tone-level is clearly suprasegmental.)[4]

It proves necessary in devising a tone-contrast orthography for

Bemba to recognize three types of contrast: low to high, or 'rise', symbolized ´, high to low, or 'fall', symbolized `, and high to slipped high, or 'slip', symbolized ʼ. Absence of contrast is unsymbolized, except that where a word has no tone-contrast, ˙ indicates that the level is high and . that it is low. Contrast is not indicated between words, and in cases where in speech the tonal distinctiveness of a final or initial vowel is morphotonemically neutralized (masked by the predominant high tone of a succeeding or preceding vowel), the tonal distinctiveness is preserved in writing.[5]

A tone-level orthography for Bemba requires to distinguish high level (symbolized by the diacritic á) and low level (zero-marked); slipped high tone may be indicated by ā (mid level) or by an intersyllabic ʼ in association with á.[6] Falling tone is confined to long syllables, and is indicated áa, ẃa, áṅ, the tone-contrast orthography treating these syllables similarly a`a, w`a, a`n.[7]

The passage below is printed using first a tone-level orthography, then a tone-contrast orthography; the third passage, in a conventional orthography derived from the tone-contrast principle, is relevant to the discussion of part II of this paper, but is printed here for ease of comparison.

(a)

Abántú nga báléefwaya ukúyá kúkwelá inʼtánshi báfwáya úbuubá. Úbuubá nabó bẃabá imísángó ibili; búmó bálímba múmábálá, bátíila koobámúshi, búmbí báyá múkwimbá múmpangá, bátíila cibómbolwa. Kúlikoobámúshi bábúúlakó amábúúlá, báátwá, leeló kúlicibómbolwa kwéná bábúúlakó imishílá éyo báátwá. Ilyo báápwá úkutwá úbuubá báséndela múmiséké nangu múmitóngá ukúyá kúkámana básúngíláʼmó.

(b)

Aʼbantu .nga baleeʼfwaya uʼkuya kuʼkweʼla inʼtanshi bafwaʼya uʼbuuʼba. Uʼbuuʼba naʼbo bwʼaʼba iʼmisango ˙ibili; ˙bumo balimʼba ˙mumabala, batiiʼla kooʼbaʼmushi, ˙bumbi ˙baya ˙mukwimba mumʼpanʼga, batiiʼla ciʼbomʼbolwa. Kuʼlikooʼbaʼmushi babuuʼlaʼko aʼmabuula, ˙baatwa, leeʼlo kuʼliciʼbomʼbolwa ˙kwena babuuʼlaʼko iʼmishila eʼyo ˙baatwa. Iʼlyo ˙baapwa uʼkuʼtwa uʼbuuʼba basenʼdela ˙mumiseke .nangu muʼmiʼtonga uʼkuya kukaʼmana basunʼgiʼlaʼmo.

(c)

Aʼbantu nga baleeʼfwaya uʼkuya kuʼkwela inʼtanshi bafwaʼya ubuuʼba. Ubuuʼba nabo bwaʼba iʼmisango ibili; bumo balimʼba mumabala, batiiʼla kooʼbaʼmushi, bumbi baya mukwimba mumpanʼga, batiiʼla ciʼbomʼbolwa. Kulikooʼbaʼmushi babuuʼlako aʼmabuula, baatwa, leeʼlo kuliciʼbomʼbolwa kwena babuuʼlako iʼmishila eʼyo baatwa. Iʼlyo baapwa uʼkutwa ubuuʼba basenʼdela mumiseke nangu muʼmitonga uʼkuya kukamana basungilʼamo.

It will be seen that the orthography proposed does achieve some limited economy of symbol. There are however several further grounds for preferring a tone-contrast orthography.

Firstly, it appears that newcomers to the language are more conscious of tone-contrast than tone-level. Perhaps oddly, it is not an uncommon experience to detect tone-contrast, but to be unable to decide whether the change is from a higher to a lower level or vice versa. Whether the Bemba themselves are more conscious of tone-contrast it would take psycholinguistic study to establish. But from another Bantu field it is suggestive that two closely related languages, Shambaa and Bondei (G23 and 24), differ chiefly in that the tonal polarity is reversed in the verbal system—one has high tone wherever the other has low tone and vice versa.[8]

Secondly, it is common experience that symbols having a natural or conventional place in the linear sequence of writing receive more attention from readers and are used more faithfully by writers than diacritic symbols. (Certain tone-level systems are also linear, but they are not among the more popular. A linear system is of course more economical typographically.)

Thirdly, perhaps because of the more pictorial quality of tone-contrast orthography, it is much easier to see the overall pattern of a word than in tone-level orthography, especially where the latter uses zero-marking. For instance the basic similarity of *bálwilé, bálondólwélé* can readily be seen if they are spelt *ba'lwi'le, ba'lon'dolwele*, and their further similarity with *béé'lé* appears when, with careful choice of convention, it is spelt *bee'le*.

II

The system of orthography outlined in the previous section is a tonemic system, in which a one–one correspondence is maintained between the symbol and its realization.

Such a system is however less than ideal for practical use, for a number of reasons. Firstly (and this has been the greatest problem for devisers of tonal orthographies for Africa), Africans will not be tolerant of a system which augments so greatly the number of symbols required to transcribe a given text (given that the present norm is the non-representation of tone in any way).[9] Secondly, students of the language have found the current tone-level system so clutters the text with diacritics that they cannot see the wood for the trees, and rapidly despair of learning anything of the tonal system beyond what they hope to assimilate by repeated listening.

It is possible to devise a more economical system if we abandon a tonemic system for a conventionalized one. The possibility arises from the considerable restriction of tone-patterns that may occur on a word of given grammatical and syllabic structure in a given syntactical environment. In fact, if we take into account these restrictions we could maintain that the type of orthography proposed in the first part of this article considerably over-differentiates.

For instance, let us consider the sentence frame *naa'shi'ta... mwi'shi'too'lo* 'I have bought...in the shop'. If we select VCV–CVCV nouns to complete the frame, we may find the following tone-patterns: *i'cisote, u'mu'pe'ni, u'mu'cele, a'ma'cun'gwa*. Selection of nouns with a monosyllabic prefix yields some different tone-patterns: *i'sumbu, i'la'ya, im'bushi, i'buu'ku*, while selection of nouns with a vocalic stem yields the patterns: *u'mwando, u'bwa'lwa, i'com'bo*. In no case are more than four patterns possible, although the number possible if we considered only general phonetic restrictions would be several times as great. Further variations in tone-pattern are possible if we consider other sentence-frames, such as *naa'shi'ta...EDPmutengo usu'ma* 'I bought a cheap...', or *u'mutengo waa...wa'a'likosa* 'the price of...is high', but in no cases are the possibilities more than four if we consider dissyllabic stems of similar syllabic structure, or, if we consider polysyllabic stems, more than a fraction of the patterns theoretically possible.

There will not be any loss of distinctiveness therefore if we simplify the orthography by leaving out some of the contrasts, choosing for retention wherever possible contrasts that are constant in all syntactical environments. The following list shows the words quoted above first in the orthography we have considered so far, and underneath in the simplified orthography we are proposing; forms occurring in different environments follow in parentheses.

i'cisote (i'ci'sote, 'cisote, 'ciisote, 'pacisote, u'bwa'cisote)
i'cisote (i'cisote, cisote, ciisote, pacisote, ubwa'cisote)

u'mu'pe'ni (mupe'ni, muu'pe'ni, ku'mupe'ni, u'bwa'mu'pe'ni)
umupe'ni, (mupe'ni, muupe'ni, kumupe'ni, ubwamupe'ni)

u'mu'cele (u'mucele, mu'cele, muu'cele, ku'mu'cele, ubwa'mu'cele)
u'mucele (u'mucele, 'mucele,[10] muu'cele, ku'mucele, ubwa'mucele)

a'ma'cun'gwa (ma'cun'gwa, maa'cun'gwa, ku'ma'cun'gwa, ubwa'ma'cun'gwa)
amacun'gwa (macun'gwa, maacun'gwa, kumucun'gwa, ubwamacun'gwa)

i'sumbu (i'sum'bu, 'isumbu, 'liisumbu, 'kwisumbu, u'bwe'sumbu)
i'sumbu (i'sumbu, isumbu, liisumbu, kwisumbu, ubwe'sumbu)

i'la'ya (lii'la'ya, pee'la'ya, ubwe'la'ya)
ila'ya (liila'ya, peela'ya, ubwela'ya)

im'bushi (m'bushi, nim'bushi, kum'bushi, ubwam'bushi)
im'bushi (m'bushi, nim'bushi, kum'bushi, ubwam'bushi)

i`buu`ku (lii`buu`ku, mwi`buu`ku, ubwe`buu`ku)
ibuu`ku (liibuu`ku, mwibuu`ku, ubwebuu`ku)

u'mwando (u'mwan`do, `mwando, `kumwando, u`bwa'mwando)
u'mwando (u'mwando, mwando, kumwando, ubwa'mwando)

u`bwa'lwa (bwa'lwa, bwa'lwa, mu`bwa'lwa, ubwa`bwa'lwa)
ubwa'lwa (bwa'lwa, bwa'lwa, mubwa'lwa, ubwabwa'lwa)

i`com`bo (com`bo, mu`com`bo, ubwa`com`bo)
icom`bo (com`bo, mucom`bo, ubwacom`bo)

The rules on which this orthography is based are set out in an Appendix.

If we attempt a similar simplification in verbal forms, we shall encounter more serious difficulties. Let us for the moment consider sets of verb forms which are identical except that they contain different radicals of similar syllabic structure, the syntactical environment being assumed the same. Under these conditions it will be found there are never more than two possible patterns. We will use the same pair of radicals in each example:

1	baa`fi'kile	ba`a'fumine	4	`baleefika	bale`e'fuma
2	baafi`kile	baafumi`ne	5	na`a`ba`fi`ka	na`a`bafuma
3	balee`fika	bale`e'fuma	6	ba`fi`ke	ba`fu'me

A fall and rise before the radical is characteristic of the second column (examples 1, 3, 4), but it is distinguished from the patterns of the first column in different ways—with a fall and rise around the radical syllable in 1, with a fall before the radical in 3 and with no tone-contrast in 4. In 5 the first column shows a fall and rise around the radical syllable while the second column shows no tone-contrast at that point. In 2 the difference is in the position of a high–low contrast, while in 6 the patterns are not differentiated.

It is still possible to devise a simplification of the tone-marking which nevertheless preserves the distinction between the radicals. However, unlike the nominal stems, where we had one (or at most two) orthographic patterns characteristic of each noun in its different variants and environments, here we have to recognize as many as seven orthographic patterns characteristic of each radical in different environments. The following conventional representations of the above patterns are proposed in the Appendix:

1	baafi`kile	baa'fumine	4	baleefika	balee'fuma
2	baafi`kile	baafumi`ne	5	naabafi`ka	naabafuma
3	balee`fika	balee'fuma	6	bafike	bafume

In addition to the radical the verbal concord prefix and infix both have tonal distinctiveness, and there are a number of tenses distinguished only by tone. It proves easy to distinguish the tonality of concord infixes by the simplified conventions, and it is highly desirable to do so, since at least one pair of forms distinguished only by tone— -mù- 'him' and -mú- 'you'—are frequently not distinguished by the semantic context. On the other hand, hesitation between the concord prefixes ù- familiar 2nd person and ú- Class 3, or tù- 1st person plural and tú- Class 13, or mù- 2nd person plural and mú- Class 18 is contextually less likely, and they are not systematically distinguished in the proposed conventional orthography.[11] The orthographic rules proposed in the Appendix provide for the differentiation of tenses distinguished only by tone where ambiguity remains after the devices for distinguishing radical tone.

Further study might suggest principles for the simplification of the tonal orthography of particles; for the present they are spelt as in Part I, except that the symbols · and . are not used.

The third passage on p. 99 above is an example of the conventional orthography here proposed. The tonal distinctiveness of all lexical items is clearly distinguished, except where the distinctiveness is neutralized in speech. Its economy against the first two representations of the passage will be clearly seen.

Some exception may be taken to the complexity of the rules. Within reason, however, complexity is tolerable in a conventional orthography, since once the convention is established, the majority will learn to reproduce the orthography by imitation and habit, in the same way that an Englishman masters the irrational orthography of his own language. It is relevant that psychologists have observed that for fluent reading we learn to recognize the shape of the word as a whole, and not the shape of the constituent letters, a fact that underlies the modern 'Look and say' approach to the teaching of reading.[12] It is for this reason that I have tried to keep to a minimum the orthographic forms of each word.

I believe that students will similarly find such an orthography less forbidding, and are much more likely to learn a word with its correct tonality when they are used to seeing the simplified representation. Provided they are aware of the lexical distinctions of tone they should be much better equipped to acquire by imitation the variations according to syntactical environment. The use of such an orthography need not represent an academic compromise provided that first a full statement of the tonology of the language has been made, and that second the researcher is continually open to the possibility that there may be tone-patterns he has not yet recorded.

No orthographical innovation can look for ready acceptance by everyone. For this reason I have preferred to use symbols on a level with the ascenders, which will not space letters out appreciably more than in non-tonal orthography, and will consequently not be obtrusive to those who prefer not to take notice of them. It would have been more convenient, for instance for typing, to choose a symbol on a level with the body of the type, taking the full width of a letter, so obviating the need for dead keys and half-spacing. In handwriting it may be possible to devise a cursive form of these symbols; those that the present writer has devised for his own use unfortunately do not seem suited to all hands. The ideal solution is a symbol that is written in its proper sequence rather than added after the word is completed, like the dot of an 'i' or the stroke of a 't', when omission becomes all too easy.

Appendix

The following rules govern the tone-marking proposed in the second part of this article:

(*a*) Nominals

Where nominals regularly have tone-contrast within the stem (tone-groups Ib, IIb, etc.), contrast is marked on the stem and not marked on the prefix or between prefix and stem.

Other nominals have tone-contrast marked on the prefix only, or, where the prefix in the full variant is monosyllabic, and in the stable variant of tone-group II, between the prefix and the stem. In tone-group II the tone-mark is retained in the short variant: '*lubuto*. In tone-group I a rise is marked after the first syllable in the full variant only; the subsequent fall occurring in some syntactical contexts is unmarked.

Addition of an extra prefix or proclitic (*na-*, *nga-*, etc.) never increases the symbols used. If the contrast indicated by the tone-marks in the full variant is unaltered by the addition, it is indicated, otherwise not.

The spelling of the nominal is illustrated on pages 101–2.

(*b*) Verbals

Verbal radicals belong to one of two tone-groups, exemplified by applying the conventions for the nominal to the Independent Nomino-verbals formed from them: *u'kulondolola* (I) 'explain', *u'kupilibula* (II) 'rotate, translate'. We consider separately non-relative verb-forms, relative verb-forms, forms with a concord infix and certain tenses for which the rules need slight modification.

In non-relative verb-forms, all tone-contrasts on the base are retained. Before the radical a rise is shown (unless the rise is confined to first and second person forms), and a fall is shown if no other contrast follows. Exceptionally, a rise before the radical is not shown in a few tenses noted below where there is a rise irrespective of radical tonality.

In verb-forms with a relative tone-pattern, the characteristic rise (or in some cases a slip) before the last syllable is retained, together with any rise or fall before the radical syllable. (This is again omitted in a few tenses where radical tonality is neutralized.) If the radical begins with a vowel fused with a preceding element, a rise following the radical vowel is shown.

Where the radical is preceded by a concord infix, distinctiveness is fully shown (to the extent that it is not neutralized in speech) by marking the final contrast together with any rise preceding either the concord infix or the radical (in the case of a concord infix fused with a radical beginning in a vowel, before or after the fused syllable). These conventions apply equally with the relative tone-pattern, but still with exceptions in a few tenses noted below.

In the dependent (or subjunctive) tense 31[13] with the tense-suffix -e, radical tonality is neutralized except where the concord infix is in tonal contrast to the radical. Other than this last contrast, no contrast is marked.

The weak link immediate past simple tense 24 has tone-slip before radicals of tone-group II, contrasted with level tone or rise before radicals of tone-group I, depending on the tonality of the concord prefix. The only contrast to be marked is the slip before radicals of tone-group II.

There are a number of tenses in which there is regularly a rise between the tense infix and either the radical or the concord infix (except before low-toned concord infix followed by high-toned radical, where the conventions above yield a distinctive spelling). They are the dependent (or subjunctive) tense 32 with the tense infix -lee- and suffix -a, the negative present progressive tense N7 (-lee- -a) and the 'not yet' tense N38 (-laa- -a). In these cases the rise before the radical is not shown, but in the relative tone-pattern (tense N7 only) it is necessary to show the position of the following fall in order to show the full distinctiveness. In tense 32, the fall before the infix-'lee- must be shown to distinguish it from the indicative tenses 7 and 27.

Among the past progressive tenses, it is necessary to distinguish the further and remote past (tenses 12 and 11) by marking the contrast in the tense infix of the latter: *baa'lee'bomba ka'le* 'they were working (before yesterday)' and *baalee'bomba maile* 'they were working yesterday'.

If these rules are applied to the verbs *u'kulondolola* and *u'kupilibula*, the tone-marks on the base (radical+suffix) will assume a number of different patterns according to the tense:

-*londolola* (e.g. *balondolole* [31] 'that they might explain')
-*lon'dolola* (e.g. *baacilon'dolola* [9] 'they explained earlier today')
-'*londolola* (e.g. *baka'londolola* [15] 'they will explain')
-*lon'dolola* (e.g. *naabalon'dolola* [25] 'they have already explained')
-'*londolo'la* (e.g. *baka'londolo'la* [15 rel.] 'which they will explain')
-*londolo'la* (e.g. *twaiondolo'la* [4 rel.] 'which we have just explained')

-pilibula (e.g. bapilibule [31] 'that they may translate')
-'pilibula (e.g. naa'pilibula [25] 'he has already translated')
-ʾpilibula (e.g. baaʾpilibula [24] 'they have just translated')
-pili'bula (e.g. baacipili'bula [9] 'they translated earlier today')
-'pili'bula (e.g. balaʾpili'bula [26] 'they generally translate')
-'pilibu'la (e.g. balee'pilibu'la [7 rel.] 'which they are translating')
-pilibu'la (e.g. twapilibu'la [4 rel.] 'which we have just translated').[14]

Most of the patterns are peculiar to one tone-group. For each tone-group however the first and last patterns quoted are common to both. Sometimes for a given tense, one of these patterns is characteristic of a single tone-group, the other tone-group being distinguished by one of the patterns peculiar to it. (For instance *naabapilibula* [25] 'they have already translated', but *naabalon'dolola* [25] 'they have already explained'; compare *baalilondolola* [22] 'they have explained'.)[15] In other cases there is no distinction in speech between the patterns for the two tone-groups, so no distinction is made in writing.

NOTES

1. *Bull. SOAS*, 27, 3, 1964. I have to thank Professor Tucker and Mr. F. D. D. Winston for their interest, encouragement and criticism.

2. I have used the term 'orthography' in reference to each of the writing-systems applied to Bemba in this article, since they are compared in point of their fitness for all the uses to which an orthography is put. This departs from the usage which restricts the term to writing-systems already established by convention. Both the writing-systems described in Part I of this article are also phonological (in part morphophonological) transcriptions.

3. For detailed references here and in the following paragraphs see Professor Tucker's article. Tone-marks have been displayed in relation to an arbitrary vowel.

4. Christaller's system can indeed be interpreted as representing tone-contrast (although he used diacritic tone-marks), and the present writer acknowledges the inspiration of his system. Indications of down-step are similarly applications of the tone-contrast principle, but they have been used by other writers in systems that otherwise indicate tone-level.

    It should be made clear that the system represents no discovery of linguistic features previously unobserved, but simply an alternative transcription. A tone-level system can be transcribed into a tone-contrast system and vice versa without any recourse to fresh observation of the language.

5. Thus *baleʾeʾbomba iʾmiʾlimo ʾyaabo* is pronounced *baleʾeʾbombeemiʾlimo ʾyaabo*, obscuring the low–high contrast in *iʾmiʾlimo*. (Changes in the tone-pattern conditioned by the *syntactical* environment are indicated in the orthography: thus *iʾmiʾlimo ʾyaabo* but *iʾmilimo iʾinʾgi*.)

    This decision parallels a similar decision that has to be made as to the vowels where a final vowel combines with the initial vowel of a following word, sometimes with some loss of distinctiveness, as is also seen in the first example above. In both cases I have preferred an orthography which keeps to a minimum the orthographic forms in which a given root appears; in the latter case the decision is further dictated by arguments of word-division.

    Indication of contrast between words would not remove the need to use the symbols ʾ and ., as sentences are conceivable without contrast either entirely low-toned or entirely high-toned. Again, omission of contrast here is preferred so as not to augment the orthographic forms in which a root appears.

6. It is arguable that mid-tone should be recognized as distinct from slipped high tone, wherever a low-toned element has coalesced with a following high-toned one immediately before the first high tone of a word. If this is sustained, there are two additional contrasts to be recognized: low–mid and mid–high, but I have not here considered mid–high to be distinguishable from low–high.

7. There would be slight loss in distinctiveness for practical purposes if a falling tone were indicated by ˆ at the end of the syllable, as a high tone later in the word does not reach the level of the earlier one when low tone has intervened, and the distinction between falling–high and high–slipped high is difficult to hear. This would be further advantageous in Zambian use, where a long vowel is frequently not distinguished from a short by the orthographic doubled vowel, and would simplify the operation of intonational rules at the end of the sentence where both contrasts are realized as high–low. The extended 'meaning' of ˆ to high–low at the end of a sentence would be readily grasped, whereas the retention of 'a' in the same circumstances would be difficult.

8. I owe this information to Professor Malcolm Guthrie.

9. There is, as Professor Tucker observes, very little sign that Africans are conscious of a need for the orthographic representation of tone. Nevertheless, there are frequent reports of, for instance, Africans having recourse to an English Bible before being able to read aloud a translation in their own language, and in the reading of original literature I have noted a lack of fluency in Africans whose fluency in reading English is good. While the cause must be in part the absence of sufficient reading-matter, I feel a contributing cause is the gross under-differentiation of the orthography, including the non-representation of tone. However, even if this is true, a tonal orthography will not win acceptance for itself without extreme economy and a maximum compatibility with existing if imperfect conventions.

Dr. Dalby has informed me that out of a dozen indigenous West African scripts, two only make regular provision for indication of tone.

10. The inconsistency of allowing at the beginning of the word a mark normally indicative of tone-contrast was admitted in this one case for the sake of the simplicity of the system.

11. If exceptionally distinction is required, this can be shown by reverting to the orthography of Part I, with the use of a horizontal line between syllables if the form in question is distinguished by lack of contrast where the doublet has contrast—*tu¯leeseka* (Class 13) in contradistinction to *tu'leeseka* (1st person plural).

12. See for instance I. H. ANDERSON and D. F. DEARBORN, *The Psychology of Teaching Reading*, New York, 1952.

13. This and other numbers given to tenses here are those devised by Professor Guthrie, and used in the author's forthcoming *Outline of Bemba Grammar*. The corresponding numbers in J. C. SHARMAN's work ('The Tabulation of Tenses in a Bantu Language', *Africa*, 26, 1956; with A. E. MEEUSSEN, 'The Representation of Structural Tones in Bemba', *Africa*, 25, 1955) are: 7: MO3; 11: M13/4; 12: M23/4; 24: M42; 27: MO4; 31: SO1; 32: SO3/4; N7: MO3 neg.; N38: MO7 neg.

14. In Sharman's tabulation, tenses SO1, M31, M71, MO6, M71R, M41R; SO1, MO6, M42, M31, MO2, MO3R, M41R.

15. In Sharman's tabulation, tenses MO6 and M16.

Focus and Entailment:
Further Problems of Transitivity in Swahili

W. H. WHITELEY AND J. D. MGANGA

INTRODUCTION

In an earlier study[1] certain problems of transitivity were discussed with reference to a group of speakers for whom Swahili is a first language. I (W.H.W.) tried to show there that future lexicographers of Swahili might gain important insights into the syntactic properties of verbs by looking at the various transitivity patterns with which they are associated. I started out from the fact that in Swahili there are a number of sentences of a pattern S(ubject) V(erb) O(bject) from which other sentences may be differentially 'entailed' by transposing the lexical items which are in subject and object relationship to the verb. This procedure yielded the following patterns:

P_0 *mzee yule alikufa njaa*, That old chap died of hunger.
　　No entailment (E-).

Pi *mtoto huyu anapenda ndizi*, This child likes bananas.
　Ei *ndizi zinapendwa na mtoto huyu*

Pii *huyu atafaa kazi*, He'll do for the job.
　Eii *kazi itamfaa huyu*

Piii *mto umejaa maji*, The river is full of water.
　Eiii *maji yamejaa mtoni*

Piv *mgeni wetu amefika nyumbani*, Our guest has arrived (at) home.
　Eiv *nyumbani pamefika mgeni wetu*

P/E sentences can in all cases be inferred from one another, but, as will be shown in the following pages, the precise semantic relationship between them is not, in all cases, either constant or straightforward. Particular P/E patterns were found to be characteristic of different verbs and a systematic study of simple radicals in the language suggested a tentative but extremely interesting basis for verbal classification.

The presence in London during 1967–68 of Mr. J. D. Mganga, for whom Swahili is a second language,[2] made possible a reappraisal of these problems in terms of what is acceptable to him. As a result of this reappraisal some modification of the scheme has become necessary, but as this seems also to be acceptable to such first-language speakers as we have been able to consult, it seems likely that the resulting presentation may be more generally acceptable than for the initial sample from whom it was specifically worked out. The most important modifications are that Eiii should be treated as a Piv sentence and that Piii should be regarded as an entailment (Eiii) of a previously unrecognized Piii sentence, thus:

Piii *maji yamejaa mto* [$NP_S+V(op\pm)+NP_O$], The water is full as to the river.

Eiii *mto umejaa maji* [$NP_S+V(op-)+NP_O$]

A great deal of our most recent work concerns this pair P/Eiii, whose incidence appears to be far wider than had previously been thought, occurring as it does not only as a major pattern for a few radicals like -*ja*-, but also as a minor pattern for a large majority of radicals whose major patterns are Pi/Ei or Piv/Eiv. It has not been noted for radicals whose major pattern is P_O (no minor pattern) nor for P_O (minor pattern Pii/Eii).

The revisions to the schema have meant some modification in the P/E affiliations listed for various radicals in the 1968 study, so for ease of reference a summary of the patterns that are acceptable to Mr. Mganga is given in the Appendix. The most noticeable refinement over the earlier presentation occurs in the radicals for which Piv/Eiv is a major pattern. Two sub-groups can now be recognized:

(a) Those radicals like -*kimbi*-, Run; -*tembe*-, Walk; -*fik*-, Arrive; -*end*-, Go, for which Ei occurs as a minor pattern.

(b) Those radicals like -*ng'a*-, Shine; -*vuj*-, Leak; -*tamba*-, Spread over; -*yeyuk*-, Melt, for which Ei does *not* occur.

It is tempting to suggest that those in sub-group (a) connote 'linear movement' while those in sub-group (b) connote 'dispersion over an area'. This is not wholly borne out by the facts, but the correlation seems strong enough to be significant. A further point to notice is that those radicals for which Piii/Eiii occurs as a major pattern are restricted to -*ja*-, Become full; -*ene*-, Spread over; -*kauk*-, Become dry.

At this point we must consider the relation between P and E sentences. In the earlier study emphasis was placed on the formal differences both between P sentences, and between P sentences and their entailments, but it was also stressed that a sentence was recognizable as Pi, ii, iii or iv by virtue of the entailment associated with it, and vice versa. While many verbs participated in particular P/E patterns, e.g. -*pig*-, -*pik*-, -*fung*- in Pi/Ei, it was also discovered that a number participated in several, even all, of these patterns, and recognized that their number might be increased with further research. It is now clear that a further feature should be recognized, that of the location of 'focus' or 'marking'. It will not be possible within the scope of this paper to do more than make a provisional and partial survey of this feature, but its importance for the P/E framework seems unquestionable. Focus may be broadly divided into two types: paradigmatic focus, in which an item is contrasted implicitly with other items which could occur in that position; and syntagmatic focus, in which an item is contrasted explicitly with other items which usually, but not invariably, occur outside the clause, and serve to link it thematically with other clauses. Such focus is commonly retrospective, in the sense that contrast is made to what has been uttered previously, but it may also be prospective and anticipate subsequent contrast.

A form of weak paradigmatic focus is exemplified for both S and O in very many P sentences (except Piii) and in Eii and Eiv, of the pattern cited above, thus:

Pi *mgeni wetu alinunua nyama,*
Our guest bought the meat,

which might serve as a response to:

nani alinunua nyama?
Who bought the meat?

though such bifocal sentences are perhaps less common than the European grammarian might suppose.[3] Stronger paradigmatic focus on S is exemplified by:

ndiye mgeni wetu aliyenunua (nyama),
It is our guest who bought the meat,

which might form part of a response to some such question as:

nyama hii yanoga, ulinunua wewe Ali? A'a, ndiye ...
This is tasty meat, did you buy it, Ali? No ...

A similar degree of focus on O is exemplified by

ndiyo nyama aliyonunua mgeni wetu iliyoibiwa ...
It was the meat that our guest bought that was stolen ...

where O is front-shifted. Front-shifting of O in Pi sentences may exemplify both paradigmatic and syntagmatic focus, thus:

nyama, alinunua mgeni wetu,

where *nyama* may be contrasted with other things that our guest did not buy, or with the fact that it was our guest who did the buying.

It is possible that paradigmatic focus on V may be exemplified by a sequence $V + NP_O$, NP_S but this is a very infrequent pattern and informants differ widely on whether they will accept it or not.[4]

Piii sentences, which occur as a minor pattern for radicals whose major pattern is Piv, exemplify a strong retrospective syntagmatic focus on O, thus:

> *mgeni wetu ameifika nyumba,*
> Our guest has reached the house (the one we told him to go to)—cf. *mgeni wetu amefika nyumbani,*

but such a focus is not a feature of Piii sentences which occur as a major pattern.

Ei sentences may exemplify either paradigmatic or syntagmatic focus, thus:

> *nyama imenunuliwa na mgeni wetu,*
> The meat was bought by our guest,

where *nyama* may contrast with all the other things which our rather mean guest did not buy. Choice of this pattern rather than that in which the O is front-shifted seems to be correlated with the individual's command of devices to differentiate degrees of paradigmatic focus: Ei, like Eii and Eiv, represent points along such a scale of choice. Yet, Ei seems also—in the example cited—to have a possible prospective syntagmatic focus:

> *nyama ilinunuliwa na mgeni . . . huenda ikawa ngumu,*
> The meat was bought by our guest . . . maybe it'll be tough,

where, again, the choice of this, rather than the front-shifted variety preceded by *ndiyo*, is dictated by the individual's range of choices.

Against this background it is now possible to consider Eiii sentences, which differ from all other P/E sentences in that in the great majority of cases their extra-linguistic status is contra-experiential.[5] Consider the following example:

> Pi *mgeni wetu amepika chakula,*
> Our guest has cooked food,

for which an Eiii sentence occurs as follows:

> *chakula kimepika mgeni wetu*[6].

Clearly, in terms of extra-linguistic experience, no one has yet witnessed food cooking people, but recognition of such a contra-experiential status makes possible the use of the pattern to exemplify strong retrospective focus on S (or on O, if one is thinking of the original P sentence), thus, 'the food (which we have been praising or criticizing as being in some way out of the ordinary) has, as a matter of fact, been cooked by our guest'. In the case of many Piv sentences this kind of focus is exemplified not by Eiii but by Piii:

> *mgeni wetu ameifika nyumba,*
> Our guest has arrived at the house (i.e. the aforementioned one);

> *wezi wamekwenda mji,*
> Thieves have gone to the town (some particular town, or even the urban as opposed to the rural areas).

Eiii is then freed for an alternative, prospective focus, in this case fairly definitely on V+O, thus:

> *mji umekwenda wezi,*
> The town is full of thieves.

Sentences such as these raise problems for the lexicographer as for the grammarian. There are many instances—as here—where a simple gloss on a given radical would not cover cases of Eiii, and it does not yet appear to be possible to abstract some common semantic feature for the verb in these sentences. In the meantime it will be necessary to recognize in the lexicon that since the meaning of a given radical may be a function of its co-occurrent S and O, extended citation of particular cases will be necessary.

Acceptability of the contra-experiential status of Eiii sentences is subject to a number of limitations. For example, the NP_s in the P sentence must be animate, and the NP_o inanimate. If both are animate, then the extra-linguistic status of the resulting entailment is experiential, and the sentence not an E, but a P sentence, thus:

> Pi   *yule kijana anawapiga watoto wangu,*
> That teenager is hitting my kids;

> Pi   *watoto wangu wanampiga yule kijana,*
> My kids are hitting that teenager.

Where both S and O are inanimate, no generalization can yet be made, both Eiii and Pi sentences occurring, thus:

> Pi   *maji yameharibu ngozi hizi,*
> Water has damaged these skins;

> Pi   *ngozi hizi zimeharibu maji,*
> These skins have spoiled the water,

where the second has an experiential status comparable to the first. On the other hand with the same radical:

> Pi   *mvua imeharibu mimea,*
> Rain has damaged the plants,

no transposition at all can be effected, so that one is forced to recognize that the patterning appears to be dependent on the co-occurrence of particular lexical items at S and O. Finally, one may note an example from which either a Pi or an Eiii may be postulated:

> Pi   *maji yatazimua pombe,*
> Water will dilute the beer;

Pi *pombe itazimua maji*,
 Beer will dilute the water (in the sense of making it less pure);

or Eiii *pombe, itazimua maji*,
 Only water will dilute the beer.

Here the focus on S is manifested prospectively, the point being that a number of possible alternatives to dilute the beer have been suggested. Whether the sentence will be interpreted as a Pi or as an Eiii depends on the wider context within which it is embedded. Where O is animate and S inanimate no transposition seems possible at all:

Pi *njaa imepiga watu sana mwaka huu*,
 Hunger has hit people hard this year.

It seems likely that further detailed study of individual radicals will suggest that particular radicals display characteristic co-occurrences at both S and O, with the consequent P/E patterning that this entails.

DETAILED EXAMINATION OF Piii/Eiii SENTENCES

I. *Cases where Eiii is a minor pattern and Pi/Ei the major or minor pattern.*

For a great majority of the minimal radicals listed in Appendix A (1968), Eiii occurs in the manner described above. It is already clear, however, that there are some radicals for which this pattern cannot occur, since the P sentences in which they typically occur manifest one of the limitations noted above, e.g. -*u*-, Kill; -*um*-, Bite (together with -*umi*-, Harm, hurt; -*umiz*-, Do harm to); -*pony*-, Cure.

The following examples serve to reinforce the explanations outlined above:

-*lim*-
 shamba limelima watu ishirini,
  Twenty people have cultivated the field. A reply to one who expressed surprise that such a large area could have been cultivated by a single person.

 shamba halilimi watu wengi,
  Not many people are cultivating the field. Disappointment at there not being a larger turn out at co-operative farming.

-*imb*-
 wimbo utaimba watu mia,
  A hundred people will sing the song. Of a song to be specially performed on the occasion of the President's visit. The whole ceremony is being praised.

 wimbo hautaimba watu wengi,
  This is not a song to become popular.

-kagu-

mji ulikagua mawaziri walipofika hapo,
The ministers inspected the town when they arrived here. Emphasis on the important occasion this was for the town.

-pand-

shamba lilipanda watu wote nyumbani,
All members of the household worked in the field. Again an explanation for an apparently immense area under cultivation. Could also be an explanation for the speed with which a particular area had been cultivated.

-pig-

ngoma ilipiga yule sogora?
Did the professional beat the drum? Reference to a particular drum which only responded well to an expert.

-ruk-

mtoto huyu ameliruka jiwe,
This child jumped onto a stone.

jiwe limeruka mtoto huyu,
The stone is small enough for a child to have jumped on it.

-tag-

mayai yanayotaga kuku wa kizungu.
J.D.M. provides the following explanation for this:

Mtu mmoja alikuwa akitaka kununua mayai kwa ajili ya kufanya biashara. Basi mtu mmoja alimletea mayai chungu nzima ili anunue yale ambayo alipenda. Mayai yaliyoletwa yalikuwa ya aina mbali mbali, mengine yalikuwa mekundu na mengine yalikuwa meupe. Huyo mnunuzi akasema kuwa yeye alitaka mayai yanayotaga kuku wa kizungu.

A man was anxious to buy eggs to start trading. So, someone brought him a whole pile for him to buy those he liked. The eggs brought were of different kinds, some brown, some white. The buyer said that the eggs he wanted were those that European hens had laid.

The focus on these eggs suggests that they were of special size or colour.

-l-

chakula kimekula watu wengi.
J.D.M. provides the following explanation:

Watoto wawili waliachiwa chakula na mama yao kula wakati yeye atakapokuwa amekwenda sokoni. Huko nyuma wao watoto wakaalika wenzao wengine kula chakula, kwa hiyo basi hawakushiba. Mama aliporudi aliwauliza, mbona mnaelekea hamkushiba? Mtoto mmoja akajibu, chakula kimekula watu wengi.

Two children had their food left for them by their mother while she went to the market. After she'd gone the children invited their playmates in for food, so they weren't full. When their mother returned she asked, how is it you don't appear to be full? One of them said, the food had to do for lots of people.

-pand-

mlima umepanda watu.
J.D.M. provides the following explanation:

Ilikuwapo imani tangu zamani katika kijiji fulani kuwa mtu ye yote atakayepanda katika mlima fulani uliokuwapo karibu ya kijiji hicho atakufa papo hapo. Watu wote wakaogopa hata kukaribia mlima huo kwa woga kuwa wasije wakafa kama imani ilivyowaongoza. Kumbe siku fulani wakatokea toka nchi ya kigeni wasiojua kuwa mlima haupandwi, na hata kama wangejua wasingeamini kama wenyeji walivyofanya, wakaupanda. Wenyeji walipowaona juu kileleni waliitana wakasemezana kuwa njoni mwone mlima umepanda watu.

It was believed from time immemorial in a particular village that anyone who climbed a nearby hill would die on the spot. People were afraid even to go near it lest they die according to the superstition. However, one day some foreigners, who were unaware that the hill was taboo—and who wouldn't have accepted local superstition even if they had known—climbed it. When the locals saw them on the summit, they called to one another urging each other to come and see that some people have climbed THE HILL.

-sem-

kesi imesema watu wengi.
J.D.M. provides the following explanation:

Katika kijiji alikuwako mwizi mmoja ambaye aliwaibia watu wengi sana mali zao. Siku moja aliiba katika nyumba tatu, na watu wakamwona na hivyo akashtakiwa mbele ya jumbe. Watu waliofika katika kesi hiyo walikuwa wengi na karibu wote walijaribu kutoa ushahidi juu ya wizi wa yule bwana, naam, kesi hii ilisema watu wengi.

There was a village in which a thief had robbed many people of their goods. One day he burgled three houses, people saw him and he was had up before the headman. Many people came for the case and nearly all tried to give evidence of the man's thieving, yes indeed, this case witnessed a lot of talking!

II. *Cases where Piii/Eiii is a minor and Piv/Eiv the major or minor pattern.*

Group A

-*ng'a*-
    Piii *taa zinang'aa nyumba,*
        Lights are shining in the house (some particular house, that has already been referred to).

    Eiii *nyumba inang'aa taa,*
        As far as the house is concerned it is flooded with light (about which further data will be given).

    Ei *nyumba inang'awa na taa,*
        The house is lit by lamps.

-*fik*-
    Piii *wageni wame(i)fika nyumba,*
        Visitors have come to the house (again one that has already been alluded to).

    Eiii *nyumba imefika wageni,*
        The house is occupied by visitors (a fact of some concern since there is now no room for me!)

    Ei *nyumba imefikwa na wageni,*
        The house has had visitors arrive at it.

-*simam*-
    Piii *watu wengi wame(i)simama njia,*
        Many people are standing in the street (the one, as it happens, that we had intended to go down).

    Eiii *njia imesimama watu wengi,*
        The street is blocked by people. Here the focus is clearly on V, which is associated here with a particularly strong connotation.

-*chez*-
    Piii *vijana wanacheza kiwanja,*
        The youngsters are playing on the field (again, one previously alluded to in some terms or other).

    Eiii *kiwanja kinacheza watu,*
        The field is occupied by people playing (so that we cannot play there), *or* The field is usually available for people to play on. Here there is again some expectation of further data to be supplied.

-*tand*-
    Piii *kamba zimetanda njia,*
        Fronds/lianas/rope-like undergrowth have blocked the path—so maybe I should cut them down.

Eiii *njia imetanda kamba,*
This is a liana-overgrown path. There is a sense here in which what is being discussed is a characteristic of the path, and not something which anyone need do anything about.

-tu-

Eiii *kiwanja kinatua ndege.*
J.D.M. gives the following explanation:

Baada ya kukaa kwa muda mrefu sana bila ya kiwanja chao cha ndege kuanza kutumika kwa ajili ya mvua nyingi ambazo zilinyesha, watu walikata tamaa juu ya mgeni wao ambaye walimtegemea kwa siku nyingi kufika kwa ndege. Hata kulipoanuka sawasawa siku moja katika mastaajabu yao waliona ndege imetua katika kiwanja. Mmoja katika hao watu akasema, jamani tazameni kiwanja kimetua ndege.

During a long period during which their airfield could not be brought into use because of heavy rain, people lost heart regarding a visitor whom they had been expecting to come by air for a long time. Until one day when things had dried out completely, to their astonishment they saw that an aircraft had landed. One of them said to his fellows, look chaps, the airfield is in use!

-lal-

Eiii *jiko limelala paka.*
J.D.M. gives the following explanation:

Bwana mmoja alifanya kazi ya kulima kwa muda wa saa tano tangu asubuhi. Ilipofika wakati wa kuondoka alijiona amechoka sana kwa ajili ya njaa. Alifululiza moja kwa moja mpaka nyumbani kwake. Alipoingia nyumbani alimkuta mkewe anasuka ukili. Huko jikoni hakukuwa na shughuli yo yote ya mipango ya chakula, maana jiko lilikuwa hata moto haukuwa umewashwa. Jivu la jana lilikuwa hali ile ile ya jana. Kuni zilizowaka katika upikaji wa jana zilibaki katika kukaa kwake huko huko baada ya kuzimika. Bwana mwenye njaa alimwuliza mkewe aliyokuwa akifanya wakati wote hata hakukuwa na dalili yo yote ya chakula. Mke alisisitiza kuwa chakula kitakuwa tayari mara tu. Bwana kusikia hivyo alisema kwa chiki, wewe unadhihaki, unasema kuwa chakula kitakuwa sasa hivi na jiko limelala paka.

A man had been digging for five hours since the morning. When the time for his return came he realized that he was very tired, from hunger. He went straight home. When he went into the house he found his wife plaiting palm strips. In the kitchen there was no sign of cooking, as the stove wasn't even lit. The yesterday's ash was as it had been yesterday. The wood burned in yesterday's cooking was just as it was after burning out. The hungry husband asked his wife what she'd been up to that there was no sign of food. The wife insisted that the food would be ready in a moment. Hearing this her husband retorted acidly, you're having me on, you say the food is just about ready and the cat's on the stove.

-shuk-
    Eiii *mti umeshuka nyoka sasa.*
    J.D.M. gives the following explanation:

Palikuwa na wazee waliokuwa wakikaa chini ya mti uliokuwa katika shamba. Basi walipokuwa wakipumzika hapo kivulini mara kwa ghafla akashuka nyoka kutoka mtini akaanguka chini kwa kishindo kikubwa. Walijaribu kumwua lakini walishindwa akatoroka. Walipokuwa wakiendelea na mazungumzo yao mara alifika mtoto mmoja ambaye alitaka kupanda katika ule mti acheze, mzee mmoja katika wale akamwambia, wewe mtoto mti huo umeshuka nyoka sasa hivi.

There was a group of elders sitting under a tree in a field. While they were resting in the shade a snake suddenly came out of the tree and fell with a loud thud. They tried to kill it but failed and it got away. While they were going on with their talking, a child came who wanted to climb the tree to play, so one of the elders said to him, look, sonny, a snake has just dropped out of that tree! (*or* That's the tree a snake has just dropped from).

In some cases the verb in Piii appears to have a quite different connotation from that of Piv:

    Piv *msichana yule alikimbia sokoni,*
        That girl ran off to the market.

    Piii *msichana yule alikimbia soko,*
        That girl ran *from* the market.

    Eiii *soko lilikimbia msichana yule,*
        The market was the scene of the girl's running away.

Verbs like *-ham-* and *-tok-* may also be grouped here, and remind one of the sharply divergent connotations of certain extended radicals, e.g. *-nuk-/-nuki-*; *-sem-/-seme-*.

Group B
-pepe-
    Piii *bendera inapepea mlingoti.*
        A flag is flying on the mast (one that is generally known, talked about; perhaps one which is not usually thought of as having a flag flying from it).

Eiii *mlingoti unapepea bendera,*
: The mast has a flag flying on it. There is almost a sense here of the mast being a special flag-flying variety.

-*nywe*-
Piii *maji yamenywea shamba,*
: The 'shamba' is sodden with water. Here there appears to be less focus on 'shamba'.

Eiii *shamba limenywea maji,*
: The 'shamba' is soaked with water. Here the implication is that is has been soaked for a purpose, and one might expect some such comment as, *nitapanda mpunga kesho,* I shall sow rice tomorrow.

-*ele*-
Piii *chombo kinaelea bahari,*
: The vessel floats on the sea, i.e. it is strong enough even to cope with the open sea. One might compare here the proverb, *ukiona vinaelea vinaundwa,* If you see them (vessels) floating they're well made. This is more commonly used in a figurative sense, if you see that things are well-organized or that someone is well turned out it means that a lot of work has been done behind the scenes. It appears here that the focus on *bahari* is of a paradigmatic rather than a syntagmatic kind.

Eiii *bahari inaelea chombo,*
: The sea is calm enough for a vessel to float on it (there had previously been a good deal of bad weather, but at last someone noticed a vessel out at sea, hence the comment).

-*zam*-
Piii *watu wengi walizama bahari,*
: Many people drowned in the sea. It was, at the time, very rough, and this point had previously been made.

Eiii *bahari ilizama watu wengi,*
: The sea in question—a particular bay—was very dangerous, many people having drowned there.

-*me*-
Piii *Kumbe, maboga yanamea shamba,*
: Goodness, vegetables are growing in the 'shamba'! Surprise that an area previously thought to be unsuitable was now growing vegetables.

Eiii *Kumbe, shamba linamea maboga,*
: Goodness, this is a 'shamba' that is suitable for growing vegetables (but not for sweet potatoes, cassava, etc.).

III. *Cases where Eiii/Piii is the major pattern.*

There are a very small number of radicals in which this situation obtains: they include *-ja-*, Become full; *-ene-*, Be spread over, be diffused over; and perhaps *-kauk-*, Become dry. The most important respect in which they differ from the radicals discussed up to now—especially those participating in Pi/Ei as a major pattern—is that the extra-linguistic status of Eiii is experiential, and there is little discernable difference of meaning between Piii and Eiii beyond the weak paradigmatic focus associated with transposition of S and O. Such radicals have been referred to in the earlier study as bi-valent, and this seems a useful term to keep:

Piii *maji yameenea nchi*
Eiii *nchi imeenea maji*   The country is covered with water

Piii *watu wamejaa nyumba*
Eiii *nyumba imejaa watu*   The house is full of people

Piii *maji yamekauka mto*
Eiii *mto umekauka maji*   The river is dry of water

Bi-valency appears to be linked with the acceptability of Eiii as experiential and with the consequent diminution of focus on S. Verbs to which the term can be applied may be seen as occurring towards the end of a scale, towards the other end of which are those verbs which participate in Pi/Ei as a major pattern, and whose uni-valency is evidenced by the fact that transposition of S and O is associated with an extra-linguistic status which is clearly recognized by the native speaker as contra-experiential. It is tempting to see those radicals which participate in Piv/Eiv as a major pattern as lying somewhere midway along this scale of 'valency', but it is very difficult to provide unequivocal evidence of this. What is clear, is that Group A of these verbs, with a minor pattern Ei, leans towards the Pi/Ei end of the scale, while Group B, with a minor pattern Piii/Eiii leans towards the other end, and in some cases at least, one can note a diminution of S-focus.

IV. *Cases where Piii/Eiii occurs as one of a number of patterns.*

In the earlier study (see especially Section F, pp. 44–55) a number of radicals were noted as participating in several P/E patterns in such a way as to make it difficult to assert which were major and which minor. They were, in addition, found to be characterized by a number of unusual features which forced some modification of the P/E numbering, notably Pii and Eii (for the radical *-ka-*). The redefinition of Piii/Eiii has rendered such modifications unnecessary and generally simplifies the presentation. These Piii/Eiii sentences conform to the patterns already discussed, but are exemplified here for ease of reference:

(i) *-chemk-, -bubujik-, -fok-, -fur-*

   Piii *maji yanachemka birika*,
      Water is boiling in the kettle (some special kettle, one usually used for ceremonial display only).

   Eiii *birika inachemka maji*,
      The kettle is boiling as to water (with retrospective focus on 'kettle').

(ii) *-ingi-*

The distinction noted in the earlier study between the two connotations of this radical, 'enter' and 'be permeated with', can now be located in the Piv/Eiv, Pi/Ei patterns on the one hand, and the Piii/Eiii patterns on the other. Thus

   Piii *watu wameingia vumbi*,
      People are covered in the dust.

   Eiii *vumbi limeingia watu*

The fact, however, that there is this distinction in connotation seems also to be correlated with a lack of focus on *vumbi*, and to this extent *-ingi-* differs from the other radicals participating in Piv/Eiv (sub-group A).

(iii) *-ka-*

With this radical there is no need to postulate a Pii/Eii- or Pii:

   Piii *watu wali(i)kaa nyumba moja*,
      People lived in the house (some special house, one previously mentioned).

   Eiii *nyumba moja ilikaa watu*,
      Here the implication seems to be that the one house being referred to was large enough to accommodate a number of people.

   J.D.M. supplies the following examples:

   Baada ya wageni kufika nyumba ya mzee Mchelo, bwana huyo alimwambia mtoto wake aende barazani akalete viti kwa ajili ya wageni ambao walifika, lakini mtotowe alipofika barazani alikuta viti vyote havina nafasi kwa ajili ya watu waliovikalia, basi alirudi bila kiti cho chote, baba yake alimwuliza. Mtoto viti viko wapi? Naye mtoto akamjibu baba yake akisema, Baba, viti vyote vimekalia watu.

   After the guests had arrived at Mzee Mchelo's house, he told his son to go on to the verandah and bring chairs for the guests who had come, but his son, when he went to the verandah found that all the chairs were occupied by people sitting on them, so he came back without one, and his father asked him, Where are the chairs? And he replied, Dad, all the chairs have someone on them.

Wanawake wawili waliingia katika chumba cha mtu mmoja mwenyewe alipokuwa hayupo. Basi aliporudi hakuwakuta walikuwa wamekwisha kwenda bali alisikia harufu ya marashi na hakujua harufu hiyo ilikotoka. Alipokuwa akishangaa alifika rafiki yake akamwambia chumba chake kilikaa wanawake.

Two women went into a chap's house when he wasn't there. When he came back he didn't find them there, they's gone, but he noticed a smell of perfume, and didn't know where it came from. While he was wondering a friend came and told him that his room had had two women in it.

(iv) *-wak-*

Piii *moto unawaka nyumba,*

Fire is burning in the house (already referred to).

Eiii *nyumba inawaka moto.*

A summary of the transitivity patterns of these verbs is given in Table I, where four groups of verbs are listed. Of these Group 2 can probably be subsumed under Group A of the Piv/Eiv verbs of 'motion', while Group 3 might be regarded as a sub-group of Group B of the Piv/Eiv verbs of 'areal dispersion'. Both Groups 1 and 4 might be regarded as constituting sub-groups of the category of verbs whose characteristic pattern is Pi/Ei.

TABLE I

	P_0	Pi/Ei	Pii/Eii	Piii/Eiii	Piv/Eiv
1. *-chemk-, -fok-, -bubujik-, -fur-*		x	x	x	x
2. *-ingi-, -kaz-, -paki-*		x		x	x
3. *-wak-, -kauk-, -tapaka-*			x	x	x
4. *-wak-, -zib-*	x	x		x	x

CONCLUSIONS

In the 1968 study, already referred to, an attempt was made to set up a framework within which problems of transitivity could be stated. Transitivity is here conceived in terms of the nature and range of certain relationships within a clause, especially those between a verb and an associated subject and object. More recent work has suggested that this framework requires modification, but that once this is effected it remains a useful device with which to codify information relating to this general area of syntax.

However, this recent work has also forced us to look again at the relationship between P sentences and their entailments, in terms other than the simple transposition of their constituent lexical items. It is recognized, for example, that P/E sentences may be located on a scale of 'focus' or 'marking', and hence that the choice of Ei, rather than Pi, is largely a function of the type of focus required by the speaker. The same appears to be true for Pii/Eii and for Piv/Eiv. The case of Piii/Eiii, with which we have been mainly concerned, is rather different: not only is the strength of the expounded focus variable, but, in the case of Eiii, its extra-linguistic status is variably contra-experiential; the variability being dependent in both cases on the participating verb. Piii, being iso-morphic with Pi, cannot be selected by those verbs whose characteristic pattern is Pi/Ei, but only by those whose characteristic pattern is Piv/Eiv, where it expounds a strong retrospective focus. What we have, in effect, is a particular pattern whose distribution is complementary with respect to Pi/Ei and Piv/Eiv verbs. Eiii, by contrast, may be selected by a wider range of verbs. With Pi/Ei verbs it expounds the strong retrospective focus associated with Piii as selected by Piv/Eiv verbs, and again there is complementarity. But here we are dealing with a particular focus, the distribution of whose patterns is complementary with respect to Pi/Ei and Piv/Eiv verbs, with the added complication that the extra-linguistic status of one pattern, Eiii, is contra-experiential. With Piv/Eiv verbs, Eiii is, as it were 'freed' to expound strong prospective focus, though it is not always easy to establish the precise location of the focus. Again, its extra-linguistic status is contra-experiential.

The whole question of contra-experientiality is an extremely interesting one, and it seems possible that a scale for this feature could be set up which could also be directly correlated with focus. Those patterns whose extra-linguistic status are recognized by the native speaker as being most markedly contra-experiential, seem also to be associated with a particularly strong focus. Those whose extra-linguistic status is recognized as being minimally contra-experiential, seem to be associated with particularly weak focus. At one end of the scale, therefore, one might place the Pi/Ei verbs like -*pig*-, -*pik*-, -*on*-, and at the other end the Piii/Eiii verbs like -*ja*-, -*ene*-. The Piv/Eiv, Group A verbs, like -*kimbi*-, -*fik*-, seem to lie somewhat closer to the -*pig*- group, while the Group B verbs, like -*ele*-, -*pa*-, seem to be somewhat closer to the -*ja*- end of the scale. Clearly such placings are somewhat arbitrary in the present state of our knowledge, and much more work needs to be done, but so far the results appear to be suggestive, providing an insight into the intuitions that native speakers may have about particular lexical items and the relationships in which they participate.

NOTES

1. W. H. WHITELEY, *Some Problems of Transitivity in Swahili*, S.O.A.S., London, 1968, p. 110.
2. Mr. Mganga's first language is Zigua, but he does not use this outside his home unless he meets someone whom he knows to be fluent in the language. His language of communication at work is Swahili, and he has been a teacher of the language for twenty-three years. Swahili is also the language of recreation wherever the company is mixed, i.e. contains non-Zigua. English is used whenever Europeans or non-Swahili speakers are present.
3. I (W.H.W.) have to admit to having used sentences of this pattern extensively in my own work, and have only recently come to recognize that patterns characterized by an SSN_S and SSN_O are much less common than I had assumed.
4. But cf. László DEZSÖ, 'Typological Questions of Swahili Word Order', being a revised version of a paper read at the 2nd International Congress of Africanists held in Dakar in December 1967 (to be published?).
5. One wonders why these patterns have for so long remained unnoticed in Swahili, when there is increasing evidence of their occurrence in other Bantu languages. I (W.H.W.) noticed them occurring in Yao for a restricted range of radicals; Professor Van den Eynde has drawn my attention to their occurrence in Lingala; Mrs. K. Sommerfelt has reported their occurrence in Konzo and Mr. Mganga has commented on their occurrence in Zigua. One might suggest that his use of the patterns in Swahili owes something to his first-language habits in Zigua were it not for the ready acceptance of the patterns among those for whom Swahili is a first language. It seems much more likely on present evidence that the phenomenon will be attested very widely over the Bantu field once one is conscious that it occurs at all. Contra-experiential sentences do not, after all, usually form the subject of discussion between investigator and informant and they are easily missed in conversation or assumed to be errors!
6. The grammatical status of *mgeni wetu* raises problems. It probably cannot be regarded as an O, since in this pattern the occurrence of an object-prefix is precluded. It cannot be an adjunct, since it will, after all, transpose to occur at S. Can it then be regarded as a second S, and recessive to the extent that it does not participate in grammatical control?

APPENDIX

Synopsis of major and minor patterns acceptable to J. D. Mganga

P_O AS MAJOR PATTERN: NO MINOR PATTERN

-ch-, Dawn; *-chach-*, Ferment; *-f-*, Die; *-kimw-*, Be disgruntled; *-ku-*, Mature; *-law-*, Get up early in the morning; *-pe-*, Be fully mature; *-pw-*, Ebb (of the tide); *-sa-* (rare in minimal form), Remain over; *-tot-*, Be soaked; *-w-*, Become; *-wang-*, Practise witchcraft; *-zind-*, Stick fast; *-duwa-*, Be speechless; *-koma-*, Be fully developed; *-pumba-*, Be retarded (mentally); *-shanga-*, Be amazed; *-kunya-*, Be withered, crumpled; *-duma-*, Be stunted.

P_O AS MAJOR PATTERN: MINOR PATTERN Pii/Eii

-bop-, Be dented; *-chaka-*, Be worn out; *-changamk-*, Be cheerful; *-fa-*, Be of use; *-ish-*, Come to an end; *-iv-*, Become ripe; *-kalamk-*, Be alert; *-kom-*, Be fully developed, mature; *-kond-*, Become thin; *-kong-*, Become old; *-leg-*, Become slack; *-lema-*, Be disfigured; *-low-*, Become wet; *-nuk-*, Give out a smell (generally bad); *-nyeg-*, Make itch; *-nyok-*, Become straight; *-pap-*, Tremble, be anxious; *-pay-*, Talk nonsense, indiscreetly; *-po-*, Become cool; *-pooz-*, Become useless, paralysed; *-pum-*, Throb; *-shupa-*, Be stiff; *-sinzi-*, Doze; *-tap-*, Tremble; *-terem-*, Be at ease, happy; *-tetem-*, Shake, quiver; *-tumbuk-*, Burst out; *-tutuk-*, Swell up; *-tutum-*, Swell up; *-ugu-*, Be ill; *-vimb-*, Swell; *-vund-*, Become decomposed.

P0 AS MAJOR PATTERN: MINOR PATTERN Piv/Eiv

-*chamb*-, Clean oneself after defecation; -*chuchuma*-, Squat on the haunches; -*j*-, Come; -*kawi*-, Delay; -*met*-, Shine; -*vi*-, Fail to mature; -*amk*-, Awake.

P0 AS MAJOR PATTERN: MINOR PATTERNS Pi/Ei; Piv/Eiv

-*charuk*-, Take hold of (fig.); -*chechem*-, Limp; -*gom*-, Strike (of workers); -*kojo*-, Urinate; -*korom*-, Snore; -*lal*-, Fall asleep; -*lew*-, Become drunk; -*ny*-, Drip; -*nyeny*-/-*nyeng*-, Nag, worry with questions; -*ambaz*-, Apply lightly; -*rash*-, Apply lightly, skimpily, freshen up; -*ton*-, Fall by drops; -*towe*-/-*towele*-, Use relish on.

P0 AS MINOR PATTERN: MAJOR PATTERN Pi/Ei

-*ban*-, Press on, clamp together; -*kom*-, Bring to an end; -*chuj*-, Sieve, filter; -*fung*-, Close, fasten; -*fyat*-, Press between two surfaces; -*chong*-, Sharpen; -*pamb*-, Decorate; -*pind*-, Bend, change direction; -*remb*-, Beautify; -*teg*-, Set a trap; -*tung*-, Compose, make up; -*ung*-, Join; -*zing*-, Block, put in the way of.

Pi/Ei AS MAJOR PATTERN: MINOR PATTERN Eiii

The radicals listed in Appendix A (1968) together with -*bong'o*-, Bend over; -*og*-, Bathe; -*sap*-, Break into pieces (for some reason or other); -*taga*-, Avoid something that is in the way.

Pi/Ei AS MAJOR PATTERN: MINOR PATTERN P0

Vid. Sup.

Pi/Ei AS MINOR PATTERN: MAJOR PATTERN Piv/siv

Vid. Inf.

Pii/Eii AS MINOR PATTERN: P0 AS MAJOR PATTERN

Vid. Sup.

Piii/Eiii AS MAJOR PATTERN: Piv/Eiv AS MINOR PATTERN

-*ene*-, Spread over; -*ja*-, Be full; -*kauk*-, Become dry.

Eiii AS MINOR PATTERN: Pi/Ei AS MAJOR PATTERN

Vid. Sup.

Eiii AS MINOR PATTERN: Piv/Eiv AS MAJOR PATTERN

Vid. Inf.

Piv/Eiv AS MAJOR PATTERN: Pi/Ei AS MINOR PATTERN

-*chipu*-, Sprout; -*end*-, Go; -*fifi*-, Disappear; -*fik*-, Arrive; -*gand*- (Also Piii/Eiii), Adhere to; -*kimbi*-, Run off; -*ruk*-, Jump; -*shuk*-, Descend; -*simam*-, Stand; -*tand*-, Spread over; -*tangatang*-, Wander about; -*tanga*-, Be dispersed; -*tembe*-, Walk around; -*telemk*-, Descend; -*tu*-, Descend; -*vum*-, Blow (of wind); -*zuba*-, Loiter; -*mulik*-, Flicker; -*ogele*-, Swim.

For all the above Eiii also occurs as a Minor pattern.

Piv/Eiv AS MAJOR PATTERN: Piii/Eiii AS MINOR PATTERN

-*chururik*-, Trickle; -*ele*-, Float; -*gaaga*-, Be prostrate (with grief, anger, etc.); -*me*-, Grow; -*ning'ini*-, Be suspended; -*ng'a*-, Shine; -*nywe*-, Be sodden; -*pepe*-, Sway, flutter, wave about; -*pa*-, Rise into the air (but also on land); -*tamba*-, Crawl, stretch over, out; -*tanda*-, -*tiririk*-, Trickle, glide; -*vuj*-, Leak-; -*yeyuk*-, Melt; -*zam*-, Sink.

Piv/Eiv AS MAJOR PATTERN: Eiii AS MINOR PATTERN

-*tikisik*-, Shake.

Piv/Eiv AS MINOR PATTERN: P0 AS MAJOR PATTERN

Vid. Sup.

Some Lexical Differences Among Verbs in Kenya Coastal Swahili Dialects

CAROL M. EASTMAN

INTRODUCTION

Swahili scholars have long been concerned with phonological and morphological differences among Swahili dialects but have accorded slight attention to comparative lexical analysis. Polomé stressed in a recent paper that a 'thorough word-geographical examination of the Swahili dialectal lexicon'[1] is urgently needed. Polomé's paper pointed out that a good deal of preliminary work has already been done, consisting principally of lists of dialectal contrasts in lexical items appended to grammatical sketches of different dialects, but that no 'systematical dialectal survey of the Swahili lexicon' is available.[2] Such a survey, it is felt, would have many historical, cultural and socio-linguistic implications: 'It would also put the discussion on the origin of Swahili and its dialects on more solid bases, as it would make valid comparisons possible with the neighbouring Bantu dialects all along the coast. Besides, taking into consideration the spread of Swahili inland, it would give valuable hints as to the area of the Swahili territory from which the upcountry dialects have derived their vocabulary. . . . important also will be the tracking of the replacement of Bantu words by local synonyms or the choice between semantically closely related lexical items of the word resembling a local Bantu term. . . .'[3]

In my study of extended verbs in five Kenya coastal Swahili dialects,[4] dialectal information both relevant and extraneous to verbal extension was brought to light. My corpus consisted of fifty standard Swahili (or dictionary-entry) verbs chosen for their freedom to combine with extension suffixes. Even with such a limited corpus it was possible to make some generalizations about the dialects in relation to each other. The following is a presentation of the lexical differences found among my corpus verbs in the Bajuni (Gunya, Tikuu), Amu, Mvita, Jomvu and Vumba dialects, all spoken on the Kenya coast. It is a small-scale survey of a controlled portion of the Swahili lexicon and has implications for a larger survey.

Most striking from the very start was the need to isolate lexical items from simple verb roots before a dialectal comparison could be made. It was therefore necessary to set forth a working definition of a lexical item. In the dialects I have investigated certain forms may be termed *fixed stems*, and although they share one or more morphemes with the lexical-entry (or corpus verb), they may have a different function and meaning that are not deducible from a knowledge of the verb in the lexicon. Indeed, in some cases, the lexical (Standard) entry is not known in one or more, or any dialects. Each dialect, then, has its own lexicon. It shares some entries with some dialects, some with all dialects, and it has some entries with a specialized meaning peculiar to itself. As used here, a lexical item is a fixed stem which has inherently an independent meaning or has acquired one.

I. A STATEMENT OF LEXICAL DIFFERENCES AMONG THE DIALECTS

The following lists comprise a statement of a common lexicon and a lexicon for each dialect based on the corpus verb forms used. Zeroes (ø) in the common lexicon indicate that there is no common form similar to the corpus item which has a form and function and meaning common to *all* dialects. Zeroes in the dialect lexicons indicate that only the common form (or forms) is used. Double-starred (**) forms in the common lexicon represent lexical items which are the same in form and function/meaning in *all* the dialects (therefore, the corresponding number slot in each dialect lexicon will contain ø).

The numbers in the lists correspond to the verbs of the corpus[5] which are:

1. *-amb-* to adhere, be in contact
2. *-chang* to collect together for a special purpose
3. *-ep-* to get out of the way
4. *-fa-* to be of use
5. *-fik-* to arrive (at)
6. *-gand-* to coagulate, stick to
7. *-in-* ~ *-inam-* to stoop, bend down (tr. & intr.)
8. *-it-* to call, summon, invite
9. *-kam-* ~ *-kamat-* to squeeze (milk), to take forcible hold of, seize with the hands
10. *-kimbi-* to run away, fly (from)
11. *-king-* act as a screen against
12. *-kunj-* to fold, wrap up
13. *-kut-* to meet
14. *-ling-* to make equal, be like, fit
15. *-nyeny-* to talk a person into telling, extort admission from
16. *-o-* to take a wife
17. *-omb-* to beg for, request
18. *-on-* to see, smell (sense), think
19. *-ondo-* to start off, take away, abolish
20. *-pang-* to arrange, hire, rent
21. *-pat-* to get

22. *-pekech- ~ -pek-* to drill, produce fire, excite ill will, gnaw, ache
23. *-pend-* to like, love, wish, choose
24. *-pep-* to sway, stagger
25. *-pet-* to bend
26. *-pig-* to strike, beat, hit
27. *-pind-* to bend, twist, make tense
28. *-ping-* to cause an obstruction, oppose, wager
29. *-pit-* to pass
30. *-po-* to become cool, be cured
31. *-pot-* to twist
32. *-pu-* to wipe the face with the palm of the hand
33. *-remb-* to adorn, decorate, make beautiful
34. *-shind-* to overcome, surpass
35. *-shik-* to grasp, hold fast, resolve
36. *-siki-* to hear, perceive, notice, heed, obey, understand
37. *-simam- ~ -sim-* to stand, rise, be erect
38. *-song-* to press together, squeeze, overwhelm
39. *-tand-* to extend, spread out
40. *-tat-* to tangle, complicate, confuse
41. *-to-* to put out
42. *-tum-* to employ, send (a person)
43. *-tumbu-* to disembowel, perforate, lay open, display
44. *-tung-* to put together (in order), compose
45. *-vum-* to roar, growl, buzz
46. *-vumbik-* to pile up, cover up
47. *-vurug-* to stir up, mix
48. *-zib-* to fill up a hole
49. *-zim-* to repress, quench, rub out
50. *-zing-* to move in a circle (tr. & intr.)

1.1. COMMON LEXICAL ITEMS

1. *ambat-* to adhere, be in contact; *ambu-* to remove; *ambukiz-* to infect, be contagious
2. *chang-* to collect together for a special purpose (money); *changany-* to mix
3. *epuk-* to avoid
4. *fa-* to be of use; *fanan-* to resemble; *fany-* to do, make
5. ø 6. *gand-* to coagulate, stick to
7. *inam-* to bend, to stoop
8. *itik-* to reply
9. *kam-* to milk, squeeze; *kamu-* wring
.**10. *kimbi-* to run away, run (from)
11. *king-* to act as a screen against (protect)
**12. *kunj-* to fold, wrap up; *kunju-* to unfold, unwrap

13. *kut-* to meet
14. ø 15. ø **16. *o-* to take a wife 17. ø
18. *on-* to see; *one-* to tease, bully; *onyesh-* to show
19. *ondo-* to take away, remove
20. *pang-* to arrange
21. *pat-* to get; *patan-* to agree
22. ø **23. *pend-* to love 24. ø
25. *pet-* to bend
**26. *pig-* to strike, beat, hit; *pigan-* to fight
27. *pindu-* to overturn
28. *ping-* to cause an obstruction, oppose
29. *pit-* to pass
30. *ponyok-* to drop, slip out of grasp, escape
31. *poto-* to bend, pervert (words, plans, etc.); *pote-* to lose, be lost 32. ø
**33. *remb-* to adorn, decorate, make beautiful
34. *shind-* to overcome, surpass; *shindan-* to compete; *shindikiz-* to show one to the door; *shindili-* to press down, in 35. ø
**36. *siki-* to hear, perceive, notice, heed, obey, understand (generally 'sense')
37. *simam-* to stand, rise
38. *songaman-* ∼ *songan-* to crowd together
39. ø 40. ø 41. ø
**42. *tum-* to employ, send (a person); *tumi-* to use, employ (a person)
**43. *tumbu-* to perforate, lay open; *tumbuki-* ∼ *tumbukiz-* to throw forcibly, fig. in Mvita; to entertain
44. *tung-* to put together (in order), compose
45. *vum-* to roar, growl, buzz; *vumili-* to tolerate, persevere
46. *vumbik-* to pile up, cover up
47. *vurug-* to stir up, mix
**48. *zib-* to fill up a hole; *zibu-* to make a hole
49. *zim-* to extinguish
50. *zingir-* to surround

1.2. BAJUNI

1. *ambis-* to be in contact
2. *tangu-* to disconnect; *tangaman-* to collect together for a special purpose (not money, i.e. things)
3. *epu-* to lift off
4. *fanyiz-* to manufacture
5. *fik-* to arrive (at)
6. *gandram-* to coagulate, stick to; *gandru-* to remove
7. *inyik-* to slant, pour

8. *ich-* to call, summon, invite
9. *kamach-* to seize, take forcible hold of
10. ø 11. *kingam-* to act as a screen against (obstruct)
12. ø 13. ø
14. *lingan-* ~ *lingaman-* ~ *lingany-* to make equal
15. *nyenyeke-* to defer to, to act with submission toward; *nyeny-* ~ *nyenyele-* to talk a person into telling, extort admission (from)
16. ø 17. *omb-* to beg (for), request; *ombow-* to comfort
18. (*w*)*ony-* to warn, to show
19. *ondo*(*w*)- to send away, start off; *ondoke-* to worsen, recontact a disease
20. *pangus-* to sweep
21. ø 22. ø 23. ø
24. *pep-* to sway, stagger; *pepe-* to fan, wave; *peperuk-* to be blown away; *pepes-* to blink; *pepet-* to sift
25. *pechu-* to overturn
26. ø 27. *pindr-* to bend, twist, make tense
28. ø 29. ø 30. *po-* to be cured; *pon-* to rescue
31. *poch-* to twist
32. *puapu-* to slice 33. ø
34. *shindu-* to open; *shindi-* to visit, remain as a guest
35. *shik-* to grasp, hold fast, resolve
36. ø 37. *simik-* to erect, be erect
38. *song-* to grab by the neck; *songe-* to approach, come near; *songomedh-* to roll over, roll together; *songo* ~ *songonyo-* to strangle
39. *chandr-* to decorate, dress lavishly, neatly; *chandra-* to spread out, extend; *chandru-* to remove
40. *chach-* to tangle, complicate, confuse; *chachu-* to unravel
41. *to-* to put out, give, present; *tok-* to go out, come, appear
42. ø 43. ø
44. *chungaman-* to bring together, follow along; *chungik-* to hang up
45. *vumish-* to win at cards
46. *vumbu-* to take by surprise, discover, rebuild
47. *vuruju-* to soften, make soft
48. ø 49. *dhumu-* to revive, rekindle
50. *dhing-* ~ *dhungu-* to move in a circle, to turn around; *dhingi-* to jilt

1.3. AMU

1. *ambik-* to be in contact
2. *tangu-* to disconnect
3. *epu-* to lift off 4. ø 5. ø

6. *gandam-* to coagulate, stick to; *gandu-* to remove
7. *inik-* to slant, pour
8. ø   9. *kamat-* to seize, take forcible hold of
10. ø   11. *kingam-* to act as a screen against (obstruct)
12. ø   13. ø
14. *lingan-* ~ *lingaman-* to make equal, arbitrate
15. *nyenyeke-* to defer to, act with submission toward
16. ø   17. *omb-* to beg (for), request
18. *ony-* to show
19. *ondok-* to send away, start off
20. *pangus-* to sweep; *bangat-* to pick up and carry on one's back
21. *patik-* to put or place under
22. *peket-* to produce fire by friction, cause trouble between friends; *peku-* to pry, try to find out a secret   23. ø
24. *pep-* to sway, stagger; *pepe-* to fan, to wave; *peperuk-* to be blown away; *pepes-* to blink; *pepet-* to sift; *pepetuk-* to stagger from lack of strength
25. ø   26. ø
27. *pind-* to bend, twist, make tense; *pindaman-* to sink, to drown
28. *pingam-* to cause an obstruction, oppose   29. ø
30. *po-* to become cool; *pon-* to be cured; *pony-* to rescue
31. ø   32. ø   33. ø
34. *shindu-* to open; *shindi-* to visit, remain as a guest
35. *shik-* to grasp, hold fast, resolve
36. ø   37. *simik-* to erect, be erect
38. *song-* to mix (food); *songe-* to approach, come near to; *songomez-* to roll over, roll together
39. *tand-* to spread out; *tandik-* to arrange neatly; *tandu-* to remove
40. *tatiz-* to tangle, complicate, confuse; *tatan-* to tie, wind; *tatu-* to unravel
41. *to-* to put out, give, present; *tok-* to go out, come, appear
42. ø   43. ø
44. *tungaman-* to bring together, follow along; *tungik-* to hang up
45. ø   46. ø   47. ø   48. ø   49. ø
50. *zing-* ~ *zungu-* to move in a circle, turn around

1.4. MVITA

1. ø   2. ø   3. *epu-* to lift off
4. *fan-* to be successful; *fanyiz-* to manufacture
5. *fik-* to arrive (at)
6. *gandam-* to coagulate, stick to
7. *inik-* to slant, pour; *inuki-* to grow up
8. *it-* to call, summon, invite

9. *kamat-* to seize, take forcible hold of; *kami-* to crave
10. ø   11. *kingiz-* to act as a screen against (obstruct)
12. ø   13. ø   14. ø   15. ø   16. ø
17. *omb-* to beg (for), request; *ombolez-* to mourn, bewail
18. *ony-* to warn
19. *ondok-* to set out, start off
20. *pangus-* to sweep; *pangish-* (*nyumba*) to rent
21. *pash-* (*moto*) to heat up, put on the fire; *pas-* to pass (exam)
22. ø   23. ø
24. *pepe-* to wave; *peperuk-* to be blown away; *pepes-* to blink; *pepet-* to sift
25. ø   26. ø
27. *pind-* to bend, twist, make tense, hem, fold over; *pindan-* to roll over and over
28. ø   29. ø
30. *po-* to become cool; *pon-* to be cured
31. ø   32. *pun-* to scratch, scrape, skin   33. ø
34. *shindi-* to visit, remain as a guest; *shindik-* to close, fill a container
35. *shik-* to grasp, hold fast, resolve
36. ø   37. ø
38. *song-* to plait; *songe-* to approach, come near; *songo-* ~ *songonyo-* to strangle
39. *tand-* to cover the head; *tandik-* to arrange neatly; *tanda-* to spread out, extend; *tandu-* to remove
40. *tatiz-* to tangle, complicate, confuse
41. *to-* to put out, give, present; *tok-* to go out, come appear
42. ø   43. ø   44. ø   45. ø
46. *vumbu-* to take by surprise, discover
47. *vuruju-* to soften, make soft
48. ø   49. *zimu-* to reduce intensity; *zimi-* to faint
50. *zungu-* to exorcise, treat by local means

1.5. JOMVU

1. ø   2. *tangu-* to disconnect
3. *ep-* to lift off   4. ø   5. *fik-* to arrive (at)
6. *gandam-* to coagulate, stick to
7. ø   8. *it-* to call, summon, invite
9. ø   10. ø   11. *kingam-* to act as a screen against (obstruct)
12. ø   13. ø   14. ø
15. *nyenyeke-* to defer to, act with submission toward; *nyenyele-* to slip in or out unheeded
16. ø   17. *omb-* to borrow; *ombolez-* to beseech
18. *ony-* to warn
19. *ondok-* to send away, start off

20. *pangus-* to rub; *pangish-* (*nyumba*) to rent (a house)
21. ø   22. *pekech-* to produce fire by friction   23. ø
24. *pep-* to sway, stagger; *pepe-* to fan, wave; *peperuk-* to be blown away; *pepes-* to blink; *pepet-* to sift
25. *petaman-* to be turned over and over, to roll
26. ø   27. *pind-* to hem, fold over
28. ø   29. *piti-* to greet
30. *po-* to become cool; *pon-* ~ *pony-* to rescue; *poz-* to be cured
31. ø   32. *pun-* to scratch, scrape, skin
33. ø   34. *sindu-* to open
35. ø   36. ø   37. ø
38. *song-* to plait; *songan-* to help each other; *songo-* ~ *songonyo-* to strangle
39. *tand-* to catch fish with a net; *tandik-* to arrange neatly; *tandu-* to remove
40. *tatu-* to unravel
41. *to-* to put out, give, present; *tok-* to go out, come, appear
42. ø   43. ø
44. *tungaman-* to bring together, follow along   45. ø
46. *vumbu-* to take by surprise, discover; *vumbi-* to be constipated (passive)
47. *vuruju-* to soften, make soft   48. ø
49. *zimu-* to reduce intensity; *zimi-* to faint
50. *zingi-* to jilt; *zungu-* to exorcise, treat by local means

1.6. VUMBA

1. *ambik-* to set fish traps; *ambish-* to suckle
2. *changu-* to disconnect; *changaman-* to become friends; *changamiz-* to incite, perplex
3. *epu-* to lift off
4. *fanyiki-* to improve bit by bit; *fanyiz-* to manufacture
5. *fik-* to arrive (at)
6. *gandam-* to lean against, depend (on); *gandu-* to remove
7. *inik-* to slant, pour
8. *ir-* to call, summon, invite
9. ø   10. ø
11. *kingam-* to act as a screen against (obstruct)   12. ø
13. *kutik-* (*maji*) to be damp (water)
14. *lingan-* ~ *lingaman-* to resemble, seem, appear; *lingamanish-* ~ *lingamanis-* to make equal; *lingany-* to make, do
15. *nyenyeke-* to defer to, act with submission toward   16. ø
17. *omb-* to beg (for), request; *ombolez-* to comfort; *ombo-* to bore; *ombole-* to mourn, bewail

18. *onele-* to intend; *ony-* to warn
19. *ondok-* to send away, start off
20. *pangus-* to sweep; *pangu-* to scatter
21. ø   22. *pekech-* to produce fire by friction
23. ø   24. w̱er- to sift; w̱ew- to wave; w̱ewele- to fan
25. *petu-* to overturn   26. ø
27. *pind-* to hem, fold over; *pindan-* to be cramped; *pinduki-* to climb from one side to another
28. ø   29. ø   30. w̱o- to become cool, be cured   31. ø
32. *pun-* to scratch, scrape, skin, wipe face with palm of hand
33. ø   34. *sindu-* to open
35. *shik-* to grasp, hold fast, resolve
36. ø   37. *simik* to erect
38. *song-* to mix (food); *songe-* to approach, come near; *zongomez-* to roll over, roll together; *songo-* ~ *songonyo-* to strangle
39. *rand-* to catch fish with a net, spread out; *randik-* to arrange neatly; *randaga-* to spread out, extend; *ranzu-* to split
40. *tatiz-* to tangle, complicate, confuse; *tati-* to wind, tie; *tatu-* to unravel   41. ø   42. ø
43. ø   44. *rung-* ~ *rungik-* to hang up   45. ø
46. *vumbu-* to take by surprise, discover; *vumburuk-* to remove quickly
47. *vuruju-* to soften, make soft
48. ø   49. *zimu-* to reduce intensity
50. *zing-* ~ *zungu-* to turn around, move in a circle; *zungu-* to exorcise, treat by local means

II. DIALECT GEOGRAPHY

On p. 144 ff. are lexical maps that show the distribution of shared items in the dialects. Sound changes that are consonantal are more or less regular from dialect to dialect; accordingly, pronunciation maps are not exhibited. The following table indicates correspondences that are necessary for interpretation by a person unfamiliar with the dialects. ṯ is dental *t*; w̱ is a bilabial voiceless fricative; *dh* is a voiced dental fricative.

The items on the maps are normalized (rather than in phonetic notation). The form of a particular verb may be deduced from the correspondence table.

At the end of this section are lists of fixed stems which occur only in one dialect—these are stems which have a specialized and restricted meaning in one dialect area.

All my informants were 'uncultured' in terms of criteria in the *Linguistic Atlas of New England* (Providence, R.I., 1939): these people had 'little formal education, little reading and restricted social contacts' and were 'aged, and/or regarded by the field worker as old-fashioned'. For this reason symbols are not required on the maps to distinguish informants.

Some Phonetic Correspondences in Kenya Coastal Swahili Dialects

Bajuni	Amu	Mvita	Jomvu	Vumba
ch	t̠	t ~ t̠	t ~ t̠	r
ndr	nd	nd	nd	nd
dh	z	z	z	z
shi	zi	vi	vi	vi
t̠	ch	ch	ch	ch
w	— ~ w̠	—	—	—
j̠ ~ i	j ~ i	j	j	j
nd	nd	nj	nj ~ nd	nj
ki	ki	ki	chi	ki
p	p	p	p	w̠ ~ p
sh	sh	sh	sh	s ~ sh

In a sense, all responses were suggested. Elicitation involved asking for sentences using each of the corpus verbs from the dictionary in combination with suggested possible extension suffixes. All responses are, I believe, current forms accepted and used by informants in everyday speech.

II.1. LEXICAL ITEMS COMMON TO FOUR DIALECTS (cf. Map 1)

A dialect not using the common item may have an identical form with a different meaning, or the meaning of the common item may be expressed in that dialect by a different form or by a circumlocution.

Thus, *nyenyeke-* 'to defer, act with submission toward' does not occur in Mvita. This concept is expressed by a phrase in Mvita rather than by *one* verb form, and the phrase varies according to context. *It-* 'to call, summon, invite' in all dialects but Amu is expressed by *amku-* in that dialect. *Po-* 'to become cool' in all dialects but Bajuni occurs with the meaning 'to be cured' in that dialect.

If a same form (i.e. as *po-* above), or meaning (i.e. as 'to call, summon, invite' above) occurs in the dialect which does not have a common lexical item (i.e. with common form *and* meaning) with the other four, it appears under that dialect at the end of this section in the lists of stems with a specialized and restricted meaning for each dialect. Here, a lexical item marked + indicates that the item corresponds to an item which has the same shape in the other dialect(s) with a different meaning (e.g. +*po-*); a lexical item marked — indicates that the item corresponds to one with a different shape in the other dialect(s) but which has the same meaning (e.g. *-it-*).

A lexical item unmarked (i.e. X on the map) has no *one word* counterpart in the other dialect(s) (e.g. *nyenyeke-*). *Items common to four dialects are listed below, and the items on map 1 represent the uncommon items per dialect.* The numbers again correspond to the corpus and thus, too, to the lists in 1.1–1.6 above. The latter lists may be referred to for the meaning of the forms cited here.

3. —*epu-*	18. +*ony-*	38. *songo-* (*songonyo-*)
5. —*fik-*	19. —*ondok-*	39. *tandik-*
6. +*gandam-*	20. +*pangus-*	39. +*tandu-*
7. *inik-*	24a. *peperuk-*	40. *tatu-*
8. —*it-*	24b. *pepes-*	41. —*to-*
11. —*kingam-*	24c. —*pepet-*	41a. *tok-*
15. *nyenyeke-*	30. +*po-*	46. *vumbu-*
17. +*omb-*	35. —*shik-*	47. *vuruju-*

II.2. LEXICAL ITEMS COMMON TO THREE DIALECTS (cf. Map 2)

Items marked ± represent synonyms in all dialects. Thus, ±*ambu-* which occurs in Jomvu and Mvita instead of *gandu-* 'to remove' also means 'to remove' in Vumba, Bajuni and Amu. In Jomvu and Mvita ±*ambu-* is used where the other dialects sometimes use *gandu-* and sometimes *ambu-*.

Items 27 and 50 on map 2 require comment. +*pind-* (27a) in Bajuni and Amu means 'to bend, twist, make tense'. In the other three dialects, +*pind-* (27a) means 'to hem, fold over'. +*pind-* (27b) in Jomvu and Vumba means 'to hem, fold over' and 'to bend, twist, make tense' in the other three dialects. In other words, Mvita *pind-* means both 'to bend, twist, make tense' and 'to hem, fold over'. The same situation occurs in item 50, *zungu-* meaning both 'to exorcise, treat by local means' and 'to move in a circle, to turn round' in Vumba; with regard to this item, however, see the discussion below in section III.

Items common to three dialects are listed below and the items on map 2 represent the relevant items in the two other dialects.

2. *tangu-* (*changu*)	27a. +*pind-*	40. *tatiz-*
4. *fanyiz-*	27b. +*pind-*	44. *tungik-*
6. *gandu-*	32. *pun-*	49. *zimu-*
9. *kamat-*	34. *shindi-*	50a. *zing-* (*zungu-*)
22. *pekech-*	37. *simik-*	50b. *zungu-*
24. +*pepe-*	38. *songomez-*	

II.3. LEXICAL ITEMS COMMON TO TWO DIALECTS (cf. Maps 3 and 4)

Map 3 shows items shared by two dialects, and corresponding items where they occur in the other dialects are listed below.

30. -pon-	50. X	20. X
49. X	17. X	25. ±pendu

Some other roots/stems are common to two dialects and are more clearly seen on a map showing distribution of the particular item on the whole coast (*map 4*), with the situation in the other dialects displayed on the map as well. Meanings are included on the map for clarity, therefore, whereas + and − forms need not be, and are not, indicated. As above, a ± form here indicates a form (and meaning) used in all five dialects.

II.4. FIXED STEMS WITH A SPECIALIZED AND RESTRICTED MEANING, PECULIAR TO A SINGLE DIALECT

BAJUNI

puapu- to slice
vumish- to win at cards
dhumu- to revive, rekindle
tangaman- to collect together for a special purpose (not money, i.e. things)
ondow- to send away, start off
nyeny- ~ *nyenyele-* to talk a person into telling, extort admission (from)
ombow- to comfort
poch- to twist

tand- to decorate, dress lavishly
vumbu- to rebuild
ambis- to be in contact

po- to be cured

ondoke- to worsen, recontact a disease

AMU

ambik- to be in contact
tatan- to tie, wind
amku- to call, summon, invite
amki- to arrive
ony- to show
peket- to cause trouble between friends
pepetuk- to stagger from lack of strength
pindaman- to sink, to drown

tand- to spread out
lingan- to arbitrate
aziw- to warn
nend- to arrive (at)
patik- to put or place under
peku- to pry, try to find out a secret

pangam- to cause an obstruction, oppose

MVITA

shindik- to close, fill a container
fan- to be successful

tand- to cover the head
king- to act as a screen against (obstruct)

changi- to collect together for a special purpose (i.e. things rather than money)
tangu- to take back, revoke, annul
kami- to crave
pas- to pass (exam)
inuki- to grow up
pash- (*moto*) to heat up, put on the (fire)
pindan- to roll over and over

JOMVU

songan- to help each other
omb- to borrow
fut- to sweep
vumbi- to be constipated (passive)
ombolez- to beseech
piti- to greet
ep- to lift off
pangus- to rub
bwi- to grasp, hold fast, resolve
nyenyele- to slip in or out unheeded
petaman- to be turned over and over, to roll
poz- to be cured

VUMBA

avy- to put out, give, present
kutik- (*maji*) to be damp (lit. to be in the state of being wet—from water)
ombolez- to comfort
onele- to intend
pindan- to be cramped
pun- to wipe the face with palm of hand
randaga- to spread out, extend
tat- to tie, wind
ambik- to set fish traps
changamiz- to incite, perplex
lingan- to resemble, seem, appear
ombo- to bore
pangu- to scatter
pinduki- to climb from one side to another
ranzu- to split
vumburuk- to remove quickly
changaman- to become friends
fanyiki- to improve bit by bit
lingany- to make, do

III. DISCUSSION

All the dialects in respect to the lexical items found to be in use share approximately the same number of items with each other in addition to the items found to be common to all. Amu and Jomvu have thirty-two items in common; Amu and Bajuni forty-two; Amu and Vumbu thirty-five; Amu and Mvita thirty-three; Mvita and Jomvu thirty-four; Mvita and Bajuni thirty-seven; Mvita and Vumba thirty-three; Jomvu and Bajuni thirty-five; Jomvu and Vumba thirty-eight; Bajuni and Vumba thirty-seven.[6] Of course, as the preceding map-charts have shown, the particular shared items vary from dialect to dialect.

Any conclusions that may be drawn from the geographical distribution of lexical features in this study will be necessarily biased in favour of unborrowed forms since the study has been primarily concerned with certain or probable Bantu roots, stems, and their derivatives or extended forms.

Even with this inherent restriction, one example of borrowing appeared—*pas-* 'to pass (exam)' in Mvita. This is an interesting example since it seems to have been borrowed from English and then to have become associated with the Swahili *pit-*, also meaning 'to pass' but in the sense of 'to go by'.[7] Generally, though, no estimate of the influence of borrowing on the Kenya coastal dialects can be made here.

That Amu and Bajuni have the greatest number of lexical items in common is probably due to their geographical proximity. Today, many Bajuni speakers live on the island of Lamu itself and, due to the then current border dispute between Kenya and Somalia, Bajunis can be now found as far south as Malindi. These migrant Bajunis have, for the most part, kept to their traditional trade of fishing and continue to identify themselves as Bajunis rather than as Swahilis. This socio-cultural situation may help account for the fact that despite lexical mixture, Amu and Bajuni continue to remain distinct phonologically, with syntactic differences also being apparently preserved. Amu speakers find Bajuni amusing to the ear (all Bajuni speakers, at first, to the unitiated, sound as if they are afflicted with a serious lisp!) and regard it as inferior to their own dialect.

Much the same situation occurs in Mvita and Jomvu—where the sophisticated Mombasans nod knowingly when they hear Jomvu spoken. Amu speakers in the Jomvu area regard it in much the same way as 'country' Swahili. There seems to be a certain amount of mutual respect between Mvita and Amu speakers, with Mvita considered a cosmopolitan dialect and Amu a literary one.

Jomvu, Mvita, Amu and Bajuni are familiar to Swahili speakers from south of Mombasa all the way north to the Bajun Islands. Vumba, on the other hand, is relatively unknown outside the south-eastern coastal area in Kenya. Its phonological and syntactic diversity seems to be greater than that among the other dialects.

These general observations, the contact I have had with speakers of these dialects, and some work done with Swahili as spoken in the town of Siu on Pate Island, north of Lamu, and with Standard Swahili in the classroom has led me to postulate, if somewhat subjectively, that the dialect situation today on the Kenya Coast breaks down most probably in this way:

1. Dialect: Vumba
   Area: Tanzania and Southern Coastal Kenya
   (Further research might show that Vumba is, rather, a sub-dialect of Standard Swahili or a Tanzanian dialect)

2. Dialect: Mvita–Amu
   Area: Central Kenya Coast, incl.
               Mombasa–Mvita
               Malindi–Amu and Mvita
               Lamu–Amu and Bajuni (see below)
   Sub-Dialect: Jomvu
   Area: Mainland off Mombasa Island *only*

3. Dialect: Bajuni
   Sub-Dialect: Siu
   Area: Northern Kenya Coast, Bajun islands, and now also many speakers on Lamu Island; there is a trend for Bajuni speakers to migrate further south along the Coast.

It is interesting to note that most of my informants (except the Vumba speakers) regarded Standard Swahili as the language of Tanzania and not Kenya. There was also a certain amount of feeling that Standard Swahili is for tribal Africans to learn in school. Swahili children who are also taught Standard Swahili in school tend to run into difficulty at home if they adopt it too readily. In Mombasa, there is some quite heated feeling that Swahilis should not be forced to learn 'Dar es Salaam Swahili'.

Some cautionary remarks must be made here as to conclusions which may be drawn from statements of shared items or features among dialects as pointed out above. It is to be taken for granted here that all five dialects are genetically related and belong to the same language family—specifically, the Bantu group of the Benue–Congo branch of the Niger–Congo sub-family of the Congo–Kordofanian family of languages.[8] This is the current genetic classification of Swahili and its dialects based on the criterion of Common Origin. However,

> There are three methods of language classification which are of major significance: the genetic, the typological, and the areal. Of these, the genetic is the only one which is at once non-arbitrary, exhaustive, and unique. By 'non-arbitrary' is here meant that there is no choice of criteria leading to different and equally legitimate results. This is because genetic classification reflects historical events which must have occurred or not occurred. If the classification is correct, it implies events which did occur. By 'exhaustiveness' of a classification is meant that all languages are put into some class, and by 'uniqueness' that no language is put into more than one class.[9]

Since the genetic classification is regarded as 'given' here and since it is the *only* classification where there may be no arbitrary choice of criteria, it follows that any other generalizations made here on a different basis (typological or areal) will be arbitrary and thus inconclusive. For this reason, few generalizations are made, and the treatment of areal features (based on the 'effects of languages upon one another whether they are related or unrelated')[10] and typological features ('based on criteria of sound without meaning, meaning without sound, or both')[11] is restricted to a presentation of the data.

Also, since the subject matter of this study involved dialects rather than different languages it would be necessary before being able to make any conclusive areal or typological statements to solve the problem of genetic sub-grouping among the dialects and

> The problem of genetic sub-grouping is ... one which is methodologically distinct, though related, to that of the establishment of genetic relationship.[12]

Further, sub-grouping involves

> ... the recognition of the existence of a set of changes common to a particular subgroup which has occurred between the period of divergences of the family as a whole and that of the subgroup in question. It is a dynamic problem of the detection of changes. Even when phrased as though it employed criteria based on the synchronic sharing of features, a historical analysis is implied.[13]

The data here do show extensive synchronic sharing of features but do not reflect or distinguish sufficiently certain factors, necessary to establish sub-grouping, such as 'chance, symbolism, borrowing [not reflected here at all], and genetic inheritance from the period of common development of the language ancestral to the subbranch'.[14]

Also, the data do not permit any generalizations to be made as to which dialect acts as an innovator if an item is new, or as to whether or not items such as those with a specialized and restricted meaning are obsolete in the other dialects or innovations in the particular dialect where they occur. The data presented in this study would be useful and necessary in an investigation into the factors mentioned above. As it stands here, however, the prime significance of the data is that material has been gathered and is available to supplement a larger dialectological study. Such a study would more accurately determine the dialect groupings postulated above.

Since this was a language-specific synchronic study of only one Bantu language, Swahili, it lacks the historical perspective which might point up some of the reasons for the occurrence of semantically distinct homonyms and, conversely, of semantically similar noncognates. The appearance of the first volume of Malcolm Guthrie's *Comparative Bantu*[15] has made available data which seem to shed light on some of what has been said above.

To illustrate the effect of comparative-historical data, let us examine corpus verbs 3, 9 and 50: i.e. 3. *-ep-* 'to get out of the way';

9. *-kam-* 'to squeeze (milk)'/*-kamat-* 'to take forcible hold of, seize with the hands'; 50. *-zing-* 'to move in a circle (tr. and intr.)'. The starred form of verb 3. *-ep-* is *-*yèp-* 'avoid'. It has been suggested to me by Miss M. A. Bryan that the *-ep-* ~ *-epu-* 'to lift off' forms found in the dialects are actually a conflation of two forms *-*yèp-* 'avoid' and *-*yįpud-* 'dish up'.

To link the roots *-kam-* and *-kamat-* semantically as was done implicitly in my analysis goes against the proposed historical reconstruction in which there are starred forms for each, *-*kám-*, *-*kámud-* 'to squeeze, wring' and *-*kàmat-* 'to seize'. Even though there is both formal and semantic evidence of one root *-kam-* in Swahili, the reconstructed Bantu forms show different tones on the two roots, an indication that they are originally distinct.

With regard to corpus verb 50. *-zing-* 'to move in a circle (tr. and intr.)' which has two meanings and apparently interchangeable alternate forms in Amu and Bajuni (i.e. *-zungu-* and *zing-*, both meaning 'to turn around' and 'to move in a circle'), it would appear that two starred forms may be posited: *-*dįŋg-* 'wind round, surround' and *-*dįuŋg-* 'wander about, turn'. Their confusion in these two dialects apparently has to do with chance sound and meaning correspondences rather than with a common historical origin.

As more and more comparative-historical Bantu data are made available, it will be possible to make more definitive statements regarding dialect differences within single languages such as Swahili.

NOTES

1. Edgar C. POLOMÉ, 'Geographical Differences in Lexical Usage in Swahili', paper for the *Second International Congress of Dialectologists* (Section VIII, Word Geography), Marburg, 1965, p. 11.
2. Ibid., p. 4. Some of the previous works of comparative lexical relevance cited by Polomé include: H. E. LAMBERT and Haji CHUM, 'A Vocabulary of the Kikae (KiMakunduchi, KiHadimu) Dialect', *Swahili*, 33/1, 1962–63; H. H. JOHNSTON, *A Comparative Study of the Bantu and Semi-Bantu Languages*, Oxford, 1922; J. T. LAST, *Polyglotta Africana Orientalis*, London, 1885; C. SACLEUX, *Grammaire des Dialectes Swahilis*, Paris, 1909, and *Dictionnaire Swahili–Francais*, 2 vols., Paris, 1939; C. H. STIGAND, *Grammar of Dialectic Changes in the KiSwahili Language*, C.U.P., 1915; *Studies in Swahili Dialect*, all vols., Kampala, East African Swahili Committee, 1956–58. A more complete bibliography may be found in Edgar C. POLOMÉ, *Swahili Language Handbook*, Center for Applied Linguistics, 1967 (pp. 30–31), and in M. VAN SPAANDONCK, *Practical and Systematical Swahili Bibliography*, Leiden, 1965 (esp. pp. 17–18). One may look forward to a new comprehensive dictionary of Swahili, which will consider dialect and colloquial usage, currently being prepared by the Institute of Swahili Research of the University College, Dar es Salaam.
3. Ibid., p. 12.
4. Carol M. EASTMAN, *An Investigation of Verbal Extension in Kenya Coastal Dialects of Swahili with Special Emphasis on KiMvita*, Ph.D. thesis, University of Wisconsin, 1967.
5. One is urged to keep in mind that these verbs are taken from the *Standard Swahili–English Dictionary*, Oxford, 1939, and for the most part contain or are Bantu roots. The corpus was selected with a view to apparent productivity of extensions.
6. The shared items are as follows:

Mvita and Bajuni:
  epu-; *fanyiz-*; *fik-*; *gandam-*; *inik-*; *it-*; *kamat-*; *omb-*; *ony-*; *pangus-*; *pepe-*; *peperuk-*; *pepes-*; *pepet-*; *pind-*; *shindi-*; *shik-*; *songe-*; *songo-* (*songonyo-*); *tanda-*; *tandu-*; *to-*; *tok-*; *vumbu-*; *vuruju-*.

Amu and Jomvu:
  tangu-; *gandam-*; *kingam-*; *nyenyeke-*; *ondok-*; *pekech-*; *pep-*; *pepe-*; *peperuk-*; *pepes-*; *pepet-*; *po-*; *pony-*; *shindu-*; *tandik-*; *tandu-*; *tatu-*; *to-*; *tok-*; *tungaman-*.

Amu and Bajuni:
  tangu-; *epu-*; *gandam-*; *gandu-*; *inik-*; *kamat-*; *kingam-*; *lingan-*; *nyenyeke-*; *omb-*; *ony-*; *pangus-*; *pep-*; *pepe-*; *peperuk-*; *pepes-*; *pepet-*; *pind-*; *shindu-*; *shindi-*; *shik-*; *simik-*; *songe-*; *songomez-*; *tandu-*; *to-*; *tok-*; *tungaman-*; *tungik-*; *zing-*; *zungu-*.

Amu and Vumba:
  tangu-; *epu-*; *gandam-*; *gandu-*; *inik-*; *kingam-*; *nyenyeke-*; *omb-*; *ondok-*; *pangus-*; *pekech-*; *pepe-*; *po-*; *shindu-*; *shik-*; *simik-*; *song-*; *songe-*; *songomez-*; *tandik-*; *tatiz-*; *tatu-*; *zing-*; *zungu-*.

Mvita and Amu:
  epu-; *gandam-*; *inik-*; *kamat-*; *omb-*; *ondok-*; *pangus-*; *pepet-*; *pepes-*; *peperuk-*; *pind-*; *po-*; *pon-*; *shindi-*; *shik-*; *songe-*; *tandik-*; *tandu-*; *tatiz-*; *to-*; *tok-*.

Mvita and Jomvu:
  gik-; *gandam-*; *ony-*; *ondok-*; *pangish-* (*nyumba*); *pepe-*; *peperuk-*; *pepes-*; *pepet-*; *pind-*; *po-*; *pun-*; *song-*; *songo* (*songonyo-*); *tandu-*; *to-*; *tok-*; *vumbu-*; *vuruju-*; *zimu-*; *zimi-*; *zungu-*.

Mvita and Vumba:
  epu-; *fanyiz-*; *fik-*; *inik-*; *it-*; *omb-*; *ony-*; *ondok-*; *pangus-*; *pepe-*; *pind-*; *po-*; *pun-*; *shik-*; *songe-*; *songo-* (*songonyo-*); *tandik-*; *tatiz-*; *vuruju-*; *zimu-*; *zungu-*.

Jomvu and Bajuni:
  tangu-; *gandam-*; *it-*; *kingam-*; *nyenkeke-*; *ony-*; *ondok-*; *pep-*; *pepe-*; *peperuk-*; *pepes-*; *pepet-*; *pon-*; *shindu-*; *songo-* (*songonyo-*); *tandu-*; *tatu-*; *to-*; *tok-*; *tungaman-*; *vumbu-*; *vuruju-*; *zingi-*.

Jomvu and Vumba:
  tangu-; *epu-*; *fanyiz-*; *fik-*; *gandu-*; *inik-*; *it-*; *kingam-*; *nyenyeke-*; *omb-*; *ony-*; *pangus-*; *pepe-*; *petu-*; *po-*; *shindu-*; *shik-*; *simik-*; *songe-*; *songomez-*; *songo-* (*songonyo-*); *tatu-*; *vumbu-*; *vuruju-*; *zimu-*; *zungu-*.

Bajuni and Vumba:
  tangu-; *epu-*; *fanyiz-*; *fik-*; *gandu-*; *inik-*; *it-*; *kingam-*; *nyenyeke-*; *omb-*; *ony-*; *pangus-*; *pepe-*; *petu-*; *po-*; *shindu-*; *shik-*; *simik-*; *songe-*; *songomez-*; *songo-* (*songonyo-*); *tatu-*; *vumbu-*; *vuruju-*; *zing-*; *zungu-*.

7. Miss M. A. Bryan has kindly pointed out that in Tanzania *ku-pasi* is used for 'to pass an exam', rather than *ku-pasa* as I found in Mvita, where the verb is homonymous with *ku-pasa* 'to behove' and synonymous with *ku-pita*. In the form *ku-pasi* we are of course dealing with a direct loan from English 'pass'.

8. Joseph H. Greenberg, *The Languages of Africa*, Indiana University, 1963, p. 153.

9. Joseph H. Greenberg, 'Language, Diffusion, and Migration' in *Essays in Linguistics*, University of Chicago Press, 1957, p. 66.

10. Ibid., p. 67.

11. Ibid., p. 66.

12. Joseph H. Greenberg, 'The Problem of Linguistic Subgroupings' in *Essays in Linguistics*, pp. 47–8.

13. Ibid., p. 49.

14. Ibid.

15. Malcolm Guthrie, *Comparative Bantu*, Vol. I, Farnborough, 1967.

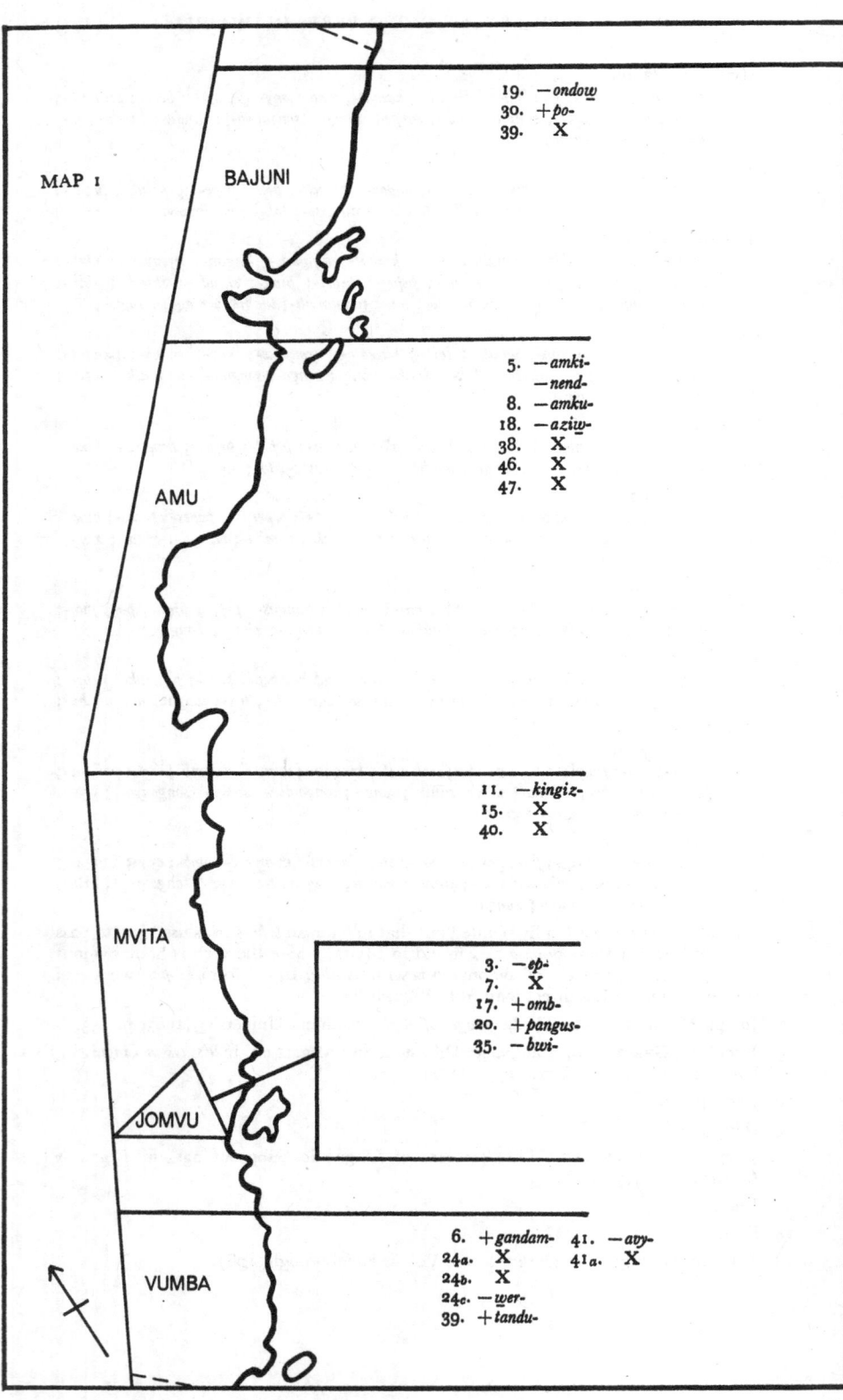

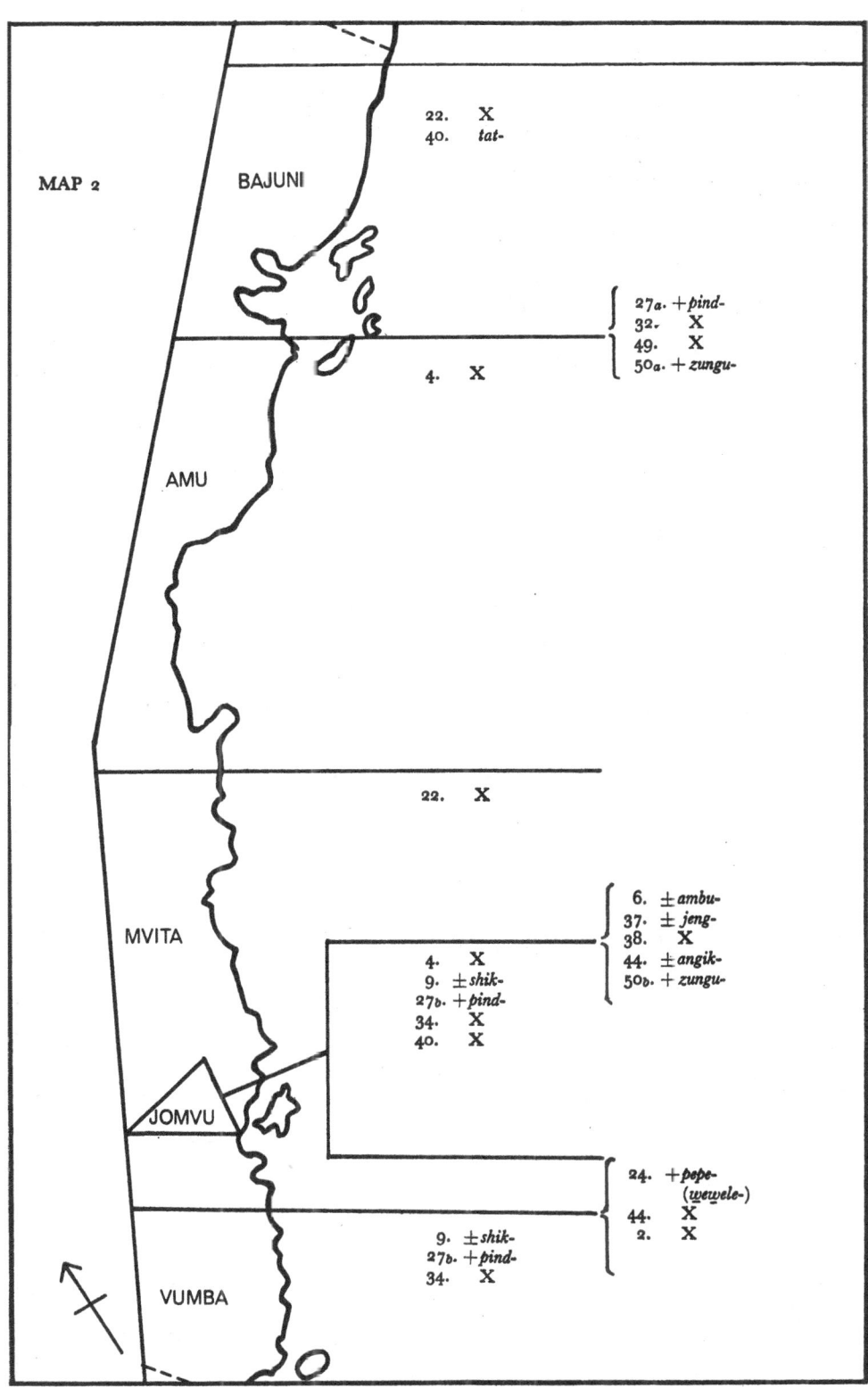

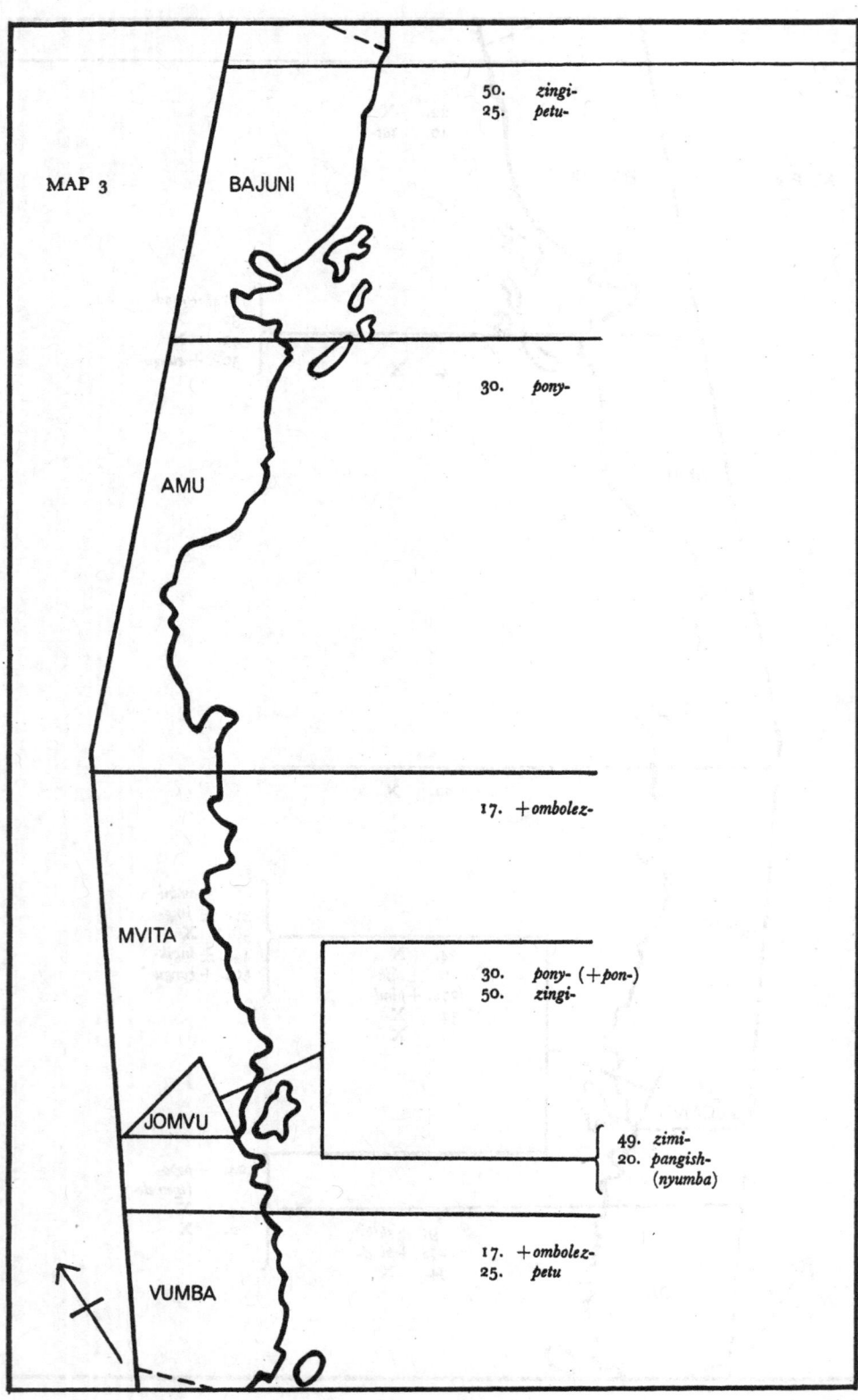

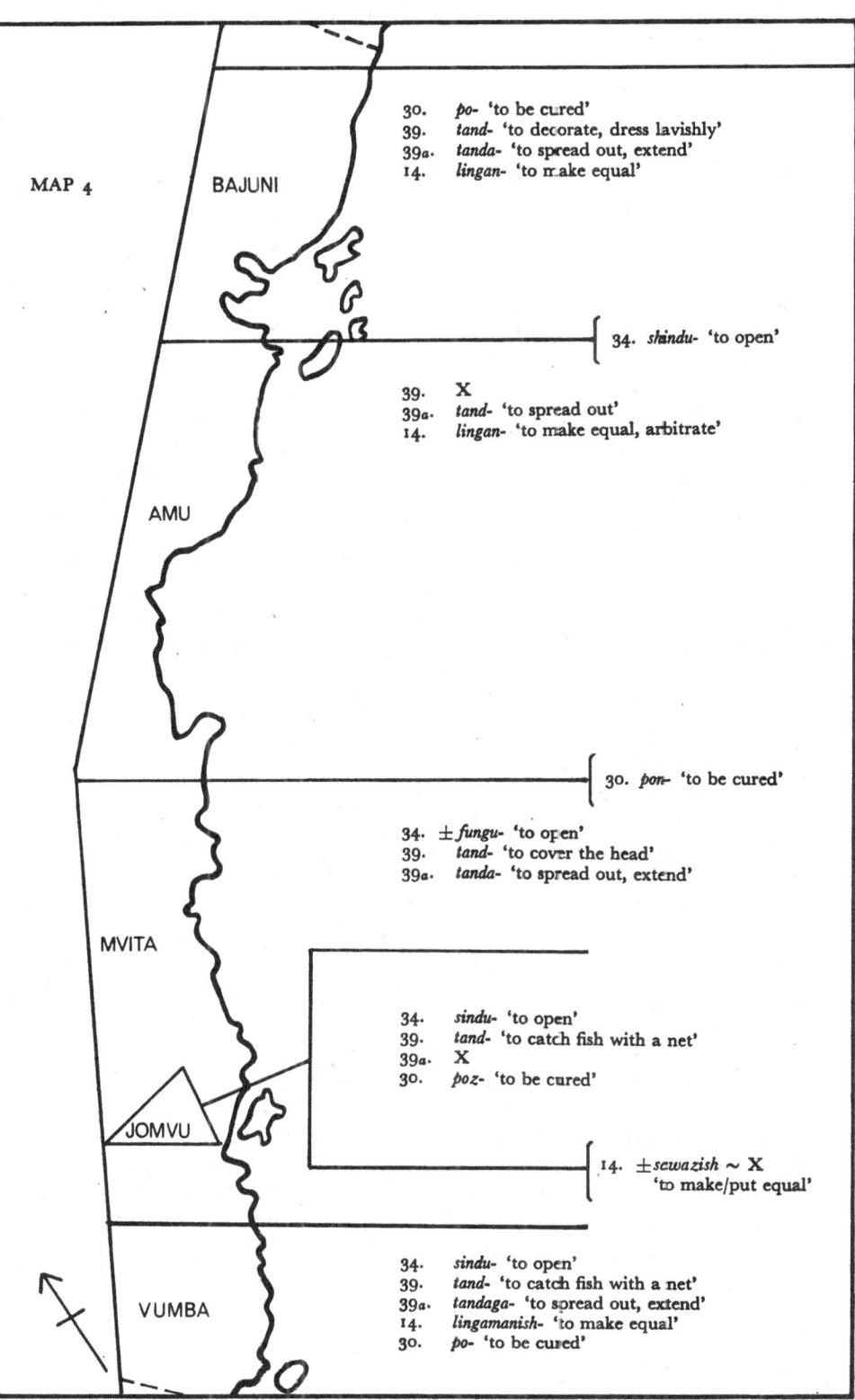

MAP 4

Sanye and Sandawe: a Common Substratum?

ERIC TEN RAA

THE term *Wa-Sanye* is a name which Swahili-speaking Kenyans apply to the speakers of at least two different languages or dialects in the north-eastern part of their country; it is with only one of these two languages that I am concerned in this article, and that is the language of a small tribe who refer to themselves as *Dahalo*. The other language with which I am concerned here is the one which is spoken by the click-speaking Sandawe of central Tanzania.

The language of the Sanye (Dahalo) appears to be a *Mischsprache* in which Galla, Bantu and Somali provide the principal constituent elements as far as the vocabulary is concerned; structurally it may perhaps be equally mixed—recent investigations by Tucker and Andrzejewski appear to show that Sanye (Dahalo) is more divergent from Galla than either Waat[a] or Aweera (Boni), two other languages which Tucker has recently investigated.[1] Sanye (Dahalo) has also retained in its vocabulary a small number of items which are neither Galla, Bantu nor Somali and which, apart from being unrelated, stand out clearly from the remainder of the vocabulary because they begin with click sounds. The number of these click items is very small yet it is to these that I would like to draw attention here.

The Dahalo-speaking Sanye live along the lower reaches of the Tana River in north-eastern Kenya. Physically they appear to be virtually indistinguishable from the Galla populations nearby, but, if the click element in their language is any indication at all, one might suspect that they could be partly descended from an ancient click-speaking population. Although most click languages are associated with peoples of Capoid racial stock, there appear to be no physical traces of this stock among the Sanye (Dahalo), and culturally they seem to stand closer to their neighbours than to the Khoisan peoples. In itself this does not amount to certain evidence against a possible link: the two modern click-speaking peoples who live closest to the Sanye, i.e. the Sandawe and the Hadza of Tanzania, are of entirely different racial stock from each other, their cultures are dissimilar, and their languages are also unrelated to each other.

Literature on the Sanye (Dahalo) language is scant. Until the recent publication of Professor Tucker's investigations, one of the most important sources was a short paper by Professor Dammann which provides us with some general impressions, a summary of other published sources, and a brief vocabulary. Some years ago I attempted to compare this vocabulary with Sandawe, but without success. The majority of apparent similarities seemed to be due to borrowing from common sources, foreign to both languages. Even for the three click items contained in Dammann's list I could not find, at the time, any correspondence with Sandawe, nor with any other language.² This situation was radically changed by the list of vocabulary items collected by Tucker which is included in his recent paper (1969: 79). Professor Tucker asked me whether these items showed any similarity with comparable items of Sandawe vocabulary; he had already established that they showed no resemblance to Hadza. Tucker's list contains the three click items of Dammann's vocabulary (but with modifications in the orthography), plus three new click items not shown in Dammann's list. This time a quick look convinced me that a fruitful comparison might indeed be possible, and since then I have been urged to make these findings available for public scrutiny. This I am now doing, in the hope that further material may turn up which will either validate the proposition of a Sandawe (or Hottentot)-like substratum in Sanye, or disprove it.³

The click material discussed in this paper consists of no more than the six items referred to; the non-click part of Sanye vocabulary will not be considered. In a personal communication Professor Tucker has noted that 'the non-click vocabulary does not live up to the promising start of the click-vocabulary'—a view with which I entirely agree—and he asks, 'are we perhaps dealing with two vocabularies?' It would seem so. The click vocabulary of Sanye seems to be clearly divorced from its non-click vocabulary, and my suggestion in the following pages, that the former may be related to Sandawe, appears to answer Tucker's question in the affirmative.⁴

Before discussing the material we have to consider an apparent discrepancy between Dammann's and Tucker's lists. In two of the three click items which they have in common, Tucker's orthography shows a dental click (/) where Dammann writes an alveolar one (≠). This may be explained by differences in articulation between their informants. If this is accepted, then we must assume a tendency, among some Sanye, to alveolarize their dental clicks or, alternatively, a tendency to place the front releases of alveolar clicks further forward, near the teeth. A Sandawe analogy suggests that this would by no means be impossible. Among the Sandawe individual variations are heard in which a click sound may range from alveolar (≠) to post-alveolar and retroflex (!). It is even possible to recognize regional patterns in this variation.⁵

The material under consideration is the following:

	SANYE (DAHALO)		SANDAWE		
				v.d.	
	Dammann	Tucker	Dempwolff	Kimmenade	ten Raa
1. Breast	≠one	/óónɛ	/'ina	/'ina	/'ina
2. Forest	—	n/aba	/ne	n/ᶜè	n/ee (n/ɛɛ)
3. Saliva	—	/ááni	tuk'a	tuk'a	thuk'a
4. Star	≠ingelie	/ɛŋkìlìᶜɛ̀	/nowan̈	n/ᶜowã	n/ooã
5. To run	—	/éani	thá, plur. giribe	tha, plur. giribé	tha(a), plur. girĭbé
6. To lick	a/a	á/'ɛ	man̈!'o	ma!'o	mã!'o

Except perhaps in the case of the second item of this list, no direct word-comparison would seem to be possible and, in a comparative exercise of this kind, finding only one correspondence out of six could hardly be called satisfactory. Indeed, the temptation would be strong to attribute a single correspondence to mere coincidence.

If, then, we cannot satisfactorily compare our two series by means of direct correspondence, we may try to see whether the Sanye items can be shown to cohere with their Sandawe equivalents by analogy. Fortunately, Sandawe is better known than Sanye and, by employing this knowledge in the investigation of analogies between the languages, we shall see that we can indeed expand our single correspondence into a more general pattern of similarity. As a method of validation this must be regarded as less satisfactory than the establishment of similarities by direct correspondence, yet the method is not entirely without advantage. It forces us to make a few structural propositions which can be tested, and later, in the light of new material, either confirmed or disproved. If they are found correct they will be of some value, and may perhaps be useful in further linguistic analysis. Let us then examine the material item by item.

1. *Breast (both the Sanye and Sandawe terms denote the female breast)*

Dammann had to collect his material under very unfavourable conditions: he had only a single informant at his disposal with whom he could converse. He had discovered him among a few Sanye in a coastal hospital, not in Sanye country itself. Tucker, too, had only one informant, a refugee in Malindi from the Shifta, but in a private communication he describes her as 'a very intelligent old lady'. As already suggested, the differences between Dammann's and Tucker's click items may be due to free variation in speech, but the quality of their informants may have contributed further to the differences in the two presentations. Under the circumstances I assume that Tucker's orthography is likely to give us a better reflection of average Sanye (Dahalo) speech than Dammann's. And it is Tucker's list which makes it possible to compare the Sanye terms with Sandawe analogues.

If, then, we view the Sanye click phoneme in the word for 'breast' as a dental rather than an alveolar click, a correspondence between Sanye /óó ('sucking') and Sandawe /'i ('the state of sucking') becomes plausible from a Sandawe point of view. Sandawe is an agglutinative language in which monosyllabic word elements combine to form words. Comparison of a large number of such Sandawe word elements which are often used in a variety of combinations, shows us that differences in vowels correspond consistently with differences in the meanings which can be attributed to them. I am not suggesting that a precise meaning can be attributed to a vowel, nor to other dependent word-elements, for that matter: the choice of vowels corresponds rather with general meaning-associations, and no more. Yet these associations are significant and can be used to discover the meanings, however vague, of many exclamatory words and similar speech items which make up the texts of story-songs, riddles, and ritual songs of the kind which are too often dismissed by scholars as having no meaning. Once the meanings of the words have been discovered, the meanings of the songs follow, and in this manner song meanings can be clarified even in cases where they had seemed to be lost beyond recovery. This, in turn, may lead to the clearing up of a considerable amount of contextual detail (including punning, ritual, etc.) which would otherwise have remained obscure.

The principal meaning-correspondences found for Sandawe vowels are as follows:[6]

- *a* implies 'there', something which can be pointed out, remoteness, urgency.
- *e* implies 'here', something taken for granted, presence and steadiness or continuity.
- *i* implies a general condition, a neutral state, existence, *esse*.
- *o* implies action, the act itself or the condition of action, and the result of action.
- *u* is the vaguest of all. It seems to imply generality of purpose or condition, and a movement away from something.

In accordance with this theory of Sandawe vowel values we can construe the word /'ina (breast) as consisting of the element /'i (the *general condition* of sucking with spittle), plus an affix -*na* which means 'there'. /'i corresponds well with /'ú (the *vague generality* of producing spittle in sucking, munching, or spitting) which we shall encounter later in the discussion of item No. 3. Sandawe /'ó (the *act itself* of producing spittle) corresponds equally well with the Sanye element /óó of /óó-nɛ (breast). The presence of a glottal stop (') in the Sandawe series of equivalents need not deter us, because the presence of a stop can often be correlated in Sandawe with emphatic meaning. Also the affixes -*na* and -*nɛ* of the Sandawe and Sanye words for 'breast' appear to be homologous and to fit equally well into our vowel schema.

2. *Forest*

Here the case for direct correspondence is a good one, as Sanye *n/aba* may be compared with the Sandawe *n/ee* plus an affix -*we*. Greenberg is probably right when he compares the Sandawe wordending -*we* (as in the personal pronoun *hewé*, 'he') with the Hottentot and Naron -*b* masculine gender affix (1963: 74). Thus Sandawe **n/ee-we* appears to be a form-equivalent of the Sanye *n/aba*, which incorporates a masculine gender affix no longer grammatically exploited in Sandawe.

3. *Saliva*

In our list we have presented the Sandawe word for saliva as *thuk'a*, which is the general term and shown also in Dempwolff's and van de Kimmenade's vocabularies. For the verbal action of spitting the form *thuk'é* is used. But in a more specific sense *thuk'é* means only one particular method of spitting, and the Sandawe language has a number of other words for describing other methods:

> *thuk/é* refers in particular to the alveolar ejection of spittle.
> *pú'um'sé* describes bilabial spitting, as done in sacrifices and other situations of respect.
> *aχinté* is to produce velar spittle (phlegm).
> *ǀ'eketé* is to eject denti-alveolar saliva with a well-directed squirt.
> *ǀ'ú'é* describes the ejection of tobacco or sugar-cane sap, or any other frothy chewed matter from the denti-alveolar region, with curved lips.

Verbal spitting thus reflects actual spitting, but the Sandawe avoid physical ejection of saliva from the dental and alveolar regions by the use of *injectives* (clicks) instead of *ejectives*. Possibly this is done in order to avoid being offensive or too imitative, but more probably because it simply fits more naturally into the whole Sandawe system of verbal expression. Other languages, too, use imitative verbs. English *spitting*, German *spucken*, Spanish *escupir*, Polish *pluć*, and French *cracher* all appear to imitate ejections from various oral regions, but their techniques of imitation differ from one another as well as from the Sandawe forms. The Sanye word */ááni* (saliva) may well reflect also an imitative process, and the technique involved would then be similar to the one which we have observed in the case of the Sandawe.

The vowel *u* of the Sandawe verb *ǀ'ú'é* may be the result of imitation of the rounded position of the mouth in tobacco-spitting, but it can also be explained from the process of vowel changes described above. This explanation would enable us to relate the Sanye root

/áá with Sandawe /'ú in the same manner as we have done in the case of item No. 1. In respect of the meaning of the word we have to note that it reflects not only the *ejection* of spittle, but also the *production* of spittle and the frothy associations of the process, so that the root /'ú describes 'the production of froth in the denti-alveolar region', no matter whether this is done in spitting, munching or sucking the mother's breast.

The /áá- part of the Sanye word for 'saliva' thus corresponds well enough with Sandawe /'ú, and we are left with the second word element -ni. This could be an affix of the same order as the affixes -ke- (vaguely causative), -k'é (to cause forcibly), -sé (having the action of), and -té (place denoting, and a directive with an association of closeness), which appear in the Sandawe spitting vocabulary. Analogy with the Sandawe vowel-value system suggests that the Sanye -ni may originally have had a neutral-state connotation, but in the absence of comparative Sanye material it is impossible to substantiate this.

4. *Star*

Sanye /éŋkìlì^cὲ and Sandawe n/ooã show no direct correspondence but the Sanye term is very similar to a Sandawe construction which, although not normally used of stars, is a perfectly feasible expression: /'ánki-le in Sandawe means 'that which is always above', from /'ánkì, 'up' or 'above', and -le, indicating habitual action or condition. It is common practice in Sandawe to repeat the last vowel of a noun to stress its essence, or to personify it. /'ánki-le-'e would thus mean something like 'The One Which Is Always Above'. It is worthy of note that the Sanye word for 'star' should resemble so closely this Sandawe construction.

5. *To run*

As in the previous case, the Sanye word /éani cannot be compared with its Sandawe equivalent *tha* (pl. *giribé*), but we may consider the following: Sandawe *tha* means 'to run', and *thán'* or *thánì* means 'to run up to me' (i.e. to the speaker). The Sandawe verb /i means 'to come' (in the plural n/atí is used), and in accordance with what we have seen in the case of running, /in or /iní would mean 'to come up quickly to me' (i.e. to the speaker). Although this verb is not normally used by the majority of Sandawe it is actually used in the Bisa dialect of Sandawe. If we now compare Sanye /éani with Sandawe /iní we have of course to bridge the gap in meaning; nevertheless, the phonological resemblance is a close one.

6. *To lick*

The Sanye verb á/'ὲ and the Sandawe mã!'o are clearly not comparable, but let us consider the specific meanings of some Sandawe verbs which describe various methods of licking:

mã!'o	to lick, i.e. ordinary licking.
hlak'hlak'	to lap up, to lick like a cat or a dog.
k'o	to lick off or to suck off, like the flesh of a soft fruit off its kernel.
ǀ'úku	to lick with the sound of spittle being sucked in.
ǀ'úkum'sé	to lick at something, or to lick up something, with the sound of spittle being sucked in.

The last two verbs are based on the word element *ǀ'ú* which has already been discussed. We have seen that the basic idea which underlies it is the production of froth, no matter whether this is done in licking, sucking, munching, or spitting. It is this element which we have to consider once more, this time in relation to the Sanye verb *ɑ̂ǀ'ɛ̀*. A typical feature of Sandawe is that it likes to place verbs in apposition to form a new speech element with a combined meaning. The process is exactly the same as that of combining word elements into words.

The Sandawe verb *há* or *háã* means 'to open the mouth' or 'to gape', and the combination *háã ǀ'úku* is a perfectly legitimate one which can be used to convey the process of opening the mouth in order to lick up something. Sandawe does not use the word element *ǀ'ú* in isolation, as we have seen, and therefore employs the combination *háã ǀ'úku* instead of **háã ǀ'ú* (*-ku* is a vaguely causative affix with an even more general meaning than *-ke*, which we have already mentioned). We may note, in this context, that one of the verbs of the Sandawe spitting vocabulary, *aχinté* ('to produce velar spittle', see item No. 3), has a structure which runs parallel with that of our combination *háã ǀ'úku*. Among the speakers of the Bisa dialect of Sandawe *aχinté* may be heard as *há-χinté* and even as *háã χinté*, i.e. as two separate verbs which are placed in apposition. The second verb, *χinté*, describes the clearing of the throat.

We are now in a position to compare the Sandawe verb construct *háã- ǀ'ú(ku)* with the Sanye verb *ɑ̂ǀ'ɛ̀*; in the light of our scheme of vowel values this is perfectly feasible.

What, if anything, are we to conclude from the analysis of our material? It has provided us with only a single instance of direct correspondence (item No. 2), but we have been able, nevertheless, to explain several Sanye words in terms of Sandawe constructions. As a method this is of course less satisfactory than direct word comparison. Moreover, the levels of satisfaction which we have derived from each comparison are not the same, and they are not all equally convincing. Nevertheless, one may feel that a rate of six positive results out of six sets of comparative data is in itself not unsatisfactory, in particular when it concerns the kind of 'basic' words which are to be preferred in linguistic comparisons.[7] I would suggest, therefore, that we should admit at least the possibility that Sanye and Sandawe may share a common substratum.

NOTES

1. Dammann calls the language *Sanye*, but Tucker identifies the term *Dahalo* as its proper vernacular name. In his recent paper 'Sanye and Boni' Tucker also gives us, for the first time, a clear statement on the distribution of 'Sanye' languages (1969: 66), and points out that what Dammann calls Sanye is in fact Dahalo. Therefore, it might perhaps have been formally more correct for me to break with tradition and use *Dahalo* instead of *Sanye* in the title of this article, although the latter term is widely used by Swahili speakers to denote Dahalo, while the term *Dahalo* may actually be quite unknown to them. However, they use the term *Sanye* indiscriminately for both Dahalo and Waat[a], while my discussion deals *only* with Dahalo and not with Waat[a]. It is largely in deference to the Swahili tradition and to Dammann's pioneering work that I continue to use the term *Sanye* which, in the context of the present discussion, also has the merit of being suggestively alliterative with *Sandawe*. Where it is necessary for clarity I qualify my use of the term *Sanye* by adding *Dahalo* in parentheses: 'Sanye (Dahalo)'.
2. Dammann (1950: 677) compares two non-click words: Sanye *yayo* (mother) with Sandawe *'iyo* (same meaning), and Sanye *buru* (maize) with Sandawe *buruku* (to winnow).
3. Tucker (1967: 677) has kindly credited me with 'having found some interesting correspondences in Sandawe', but I would like to stress the point that the conclusion drawn from my analysis must remain strictly tentative for the time being.
4. More recently, Professor Tucker has drawn my attention to the Sanye non-click words for 'bird', 'boy', 'egg', 'hair', 'hill', 'nail', 'stomach' and 'tongue', for possible Sandawe cognates, urging me not to come to any firm conclusions on the possible separate origin of non-click words (private communication). This I gratefully acknowledge. On second thoughts, it may indeed be possible also to find correspondences in that part of the vocabulary, and more investigation is needed in this direction.
5. TEN RAA, 'The Couth and the Uncouth'.
6. TEN RAA, *Society and Symbolism*. The second chapter of this volume discusses some details of the language. Applications of the vowel theory are found throughout the book.
7. Breast, forest ('woods'), saliva, star and to lick ('suck') are included in the Swadesh Test Lists, cf. Hymes (1960: 3–36). The verb 'to run' is equally basic, although the Swadesh lists include only 'walk' and 'come'. All six words of our material appear in the S.O.A.S. *Outline Vocabulary for African Languages*.

REFERENCES

Ernst DAMMANN, 'Einige Notizen über die Sprache der Sanye (Kenya)', *Z. f. Eingeb. Spr.*, XXXV, 3/4, 1950, pp. 227–34.
Otto DEMPWOLFF, *Die Sandawe: Linguistisches und ethnographisches Material aus Deutsch-Ostafrika* (Abh. hbg. Kol. Inst., XXXIV, Reihe B, Bd. 19), Hamburg, 1916.
Joseph H. GREENBERG, *Languages of Africa*, Indiana University, 1963.
D. H. HYMES, 'Lexicostatistics So Far', *Current Anthropology*, 1, pp. 3–36, 1960.
Eric TEN RAA, *A Descriptive Sandawe–English Dictionary*, M/S.
———, 'The Couth and the Uncouth: Ethnic, Social, and Linguistic Divisions Among the Sandawe of Central Tanzania', *Anthropos*, 65 (1970, forthcoming).
———, *Society and Symbolism in Sandawe Oral Literature*, Frank Cass, London (forthcoming).
SCHOOL OF ORIENTAL AND AFRICAN STUDIES, *Outline Vocabulary for African Languages*, n.d.
A. N. TUCKER, 'Fringe Cushitic: An Experiment in Typological Comparison', *Bull. S.O.A.S.*, XXX, 3, 1967, pp. 655–80.
———, 'Erythraic Elements and Patternings: Some East African Findings', *A.L.R.*, 6, 1967, pp. 17–25.
———, 'Sanye and Boni', *Wort und Religion* (Ernst Dammann zum 65. Geburtstag), Stuttgart, 1969, pp. 66–81.
M. VAN DE KIMMENADE, *Essai de grammaire et de vocabulaire de la langue Sandawé* (M/S), *M.B.A.*, IX (Microfilm).

Hausa *nàà*:
'To be' or not 'to be'?

CARLETON T. HODGE

THE basic types of Hausa sentence are few in number. They include 1. N N (*suunaanaa Audù* 'my name is Audu'), 2. N *nee* (*niinèè* 'it is I'), 3. N *nàà* N (*yanàà zuwà* 'he's coming'), 4. V-s (*baatà nan̲* 'she's not here'), 5. p-V (*yaa tàfi* 'he went'). Of these 1, 2, 4 and 5 have close parallels in other Afroasiatic (hereinafter AAs) languages: 1 = N N, the nominal equational sentence. This is normally atemporal. See Brockelmann 1961.2.41–102 for Semitic, Edel 1964.476–489 for Egyptian. 2 = N d, noun plus demonstrative. This is discussed as an AAs phenomenon by Hodge 1969.[1] 4 = V-s, the common AAs 'verb' forms with suffix pronouns. These were apparently originally stative, and this is reflected in the usage of such forms as the Akkadian permansive, the Egyptian Old Perfective (Diakonoff 1965.78–79, 86–90) and the Hausa forms (Parsons 1960.5, quoted below). Diakonoff fails to recognize the Hausa statives (90). 5 = p-V, the familiar verb prefix forms of AAs, found in some form in all branches (Diakonoff 1965.79–84). There remains 3, which is the subject of the present paper.

The N *nàà* N construction is that sometimes known as the continuative. The second N may be (with some verbs) a verb form identical to that following a perfect prefix (cf. Parsons 1960.4), a verbal noun, a noun, or an adverb (cf. Kraft 1964.233), thus differing greatly from other verb forms. The crux is how to classify *nàà*. This a number of Hausa grammars have not bothered to do, treating the pronouns plus *nàà* as formatives for the present or continuous verb forms (e.g. Westermann 1911, Mischlich 1911, Taylor 1923, Abraham 1941, 1959). Schön refers to it as a 'verbal affix' (1862.64, quoted by Kraft 1964.231). One may also note that Mischlich does not include *nàà* in his discussion of 'to be'.

Other scholars have shown more interest, or perhaps curiosity. Migeod has a rather obscure discussion and then suggests: 'It might, therefore, be assumed that the syllable "na" of the pronoun is no other than the preposition "of", not readily translatable, however, uniformly into "of", as indeed it is not in many other cases also' (1914.134). Robinson recognizes that there is a problem of identification but avoids discussion (1925.28). In his early work Abraham remarks, 'This na. is low and unstressed and was originally a preposition meaning "in the act of", cognate languages using the words "in the head of" to denote the same idea' (1934.52). One wishes that he had given examples of some of the forms in related languages. Kraft comments, 'This suggestion does not seem to have been taken seriously, however, even by Abraham and it is missing from his later grammars' (1964b.232 fn. 1).

At the same time we have two other statements. Westermann, in writing of the grammar says, 'The progressive has *na*, to be in a place, as its formative element' (apud Bargery 1934.xviii). In the dictionary Bargery calls it a 'particle suffixed to personal and impersonal pronouns to form the continuous tense' (1934.809), which was no more informative than the grammars noted earlier.

In 1945 the present writer connected *nàà* with the *n* of the N*n*N construction, repeating this analysis in 1947 (32–33).[2] In 1963 he treated *nàà* as some kind of verbal particle translatable as 'is/are in a given state or position' (157). This was not the result of a fresh analysis, just the abandonment of the earlier one. However, Kraft (1964b) gave careful consideration to the 1945 view, being kinder to it than its author. In the discussion he made a perceptive observation: 'Should this view be further developed it would be possible to describe the Hausa continuative aspect construction as differing fundamentally from the other aspect constructions in that it is completely nominal whereas the others are verbal' (1964b.234). The relevance of this statement will appear below.

Parsons, fully aware of the problems which not only *nàà*, but *kèè*, *baa* and other forms present, says, 'Verbs indeed they are, but of a special defective sort' (1960.4–5). The historical linguist might well look twice at this, suspecting as he does the defective to be a remnant of an earlier pattern. Parsons goes on to say 'in the case of all of them, the combination of verb and pronoun signifies, not an action, but a state' (5). This should be kept in mind when considering Gregersen's aspect theory below.

Kraft has made several statements on *nàà*, reflecting successive analyses. In 1963 he treated it as an aspect particle (1.128–129; 2.12; 1964a.70). In his full discussion of the matter he concludes with Parsons that *nàà* is a specialized verbal, a single aspect verb, grouping it with *kèè*, and, less closely, with others (1964b; see his summary of verb types 237–238).

Brauner also considers it a verb: 'Zum Ausdruck des lokativen Seins (des sich Befindens) verwendet das Hausa das Verb *na* sich befinden, vorhanden sein' (Brauner-Ashiwaju 1965.39).

Diakonoff (1965) has a brief discussion, mentioning but rejecting the idea of associating *nàà* with the genitive *n(a)* and concluding that 'It is more probable that *n(a)* is a relic of the auxiliary verb "to be"' (84).

Gregersen treats *nàà* as a realization of continuous aspect, transformationally related to *-nee* (1967). Some features of this treatment are discussed below.[3]

Curiously enough, the most stimulating of the above suggestions and formulations would appear to be that of Abraham in 1934, that *nàà* is a kind of preposition and has parallels in related languages. This is hardly justifiable on a descriptive basis, and there is also no other 'preposition' in Hausa which takes pronominal prefixes. Is there, however, anything to be said for the suggestion historically?

Such a question raises the whole issue of the propriety of historical or comparative evidence in descriptive work. As long as linguistics was primarily concerned with phonology and morphology, it was easy to rule out historical considerations. As soon, however, as linguistics took the other tack and made analyses primarily of syntax and the motivations of syntax, issues were raised which must inevitably involve historical considerations where these are known. It would appear that, if universals have a place in descriptive analysis, then historical and comparative work is of even more importance. Universals (if known) may be taken for granted. It is precisely the non-universals which establish the peculiar nature of each language. Comparative work, where emphasizing non-universals, may lead to insights concerning shared features. The present writer is well aware of the heretical nature of this suggestion but feels that it is forced upon any analyst who would propose a general theory of language.

The primary area which must be studied comparatively and historically before full descriptive use may be made of it is semantics. Weinrich has pointed up some of the desiderata in this field (1966.142–143), one of which is directly relevant to our problem: 'Despite the basically arbitrary quality of semantic "mapping" displayed by languages, there are nevertheless remarkable parallelisms between both related and unrelated languages. How are these parallelisms to be formulated and quantified?' Treatment of these parallelisms must follow that of any others in language, i.e. they may be '*generic* (inherent in all units within the frame of analysis) or *convergent* (due to chance . . .)' or 'due to historical connection . . . genetic . . . or *diffusional*' (Hymes 1964.567). In other words, we must begin to treat semantic motifs in the same way in which we have hitherto dealt with forms.

This may not justify the present proposal to utilize comparative data, as the desideratum of a comprehensive semantics is hardly begun, let alone realized, and it is therefore impossible to ascertain which of the points being discussed are universal and therefore irrelevant. However, the linguist working on a language not his own is at a great semantic disadvantage. One way of meeting this, at least partially, is by the use of comparative and historical data.

After this historico-semantic digression (a species of *apologia pro opere suo*) we return to the problem at hand. Is there within the AAs family a morphosyntactic parallel which would assist us in the analysis of the *nàà* construction? (Parallels are necessarily partial, given the fragmentary state of our knowledge of AAs.) Three possibilities have been raised by the literature.

The first of these is that *nàà* is indeed a verb. There is in AAs a number of words associated with the idea of existence or equation and which contain *n* as a root consonant. Within Hausa we may mention *-nee* as well as *nàà*. Egyptian has *wnn* 'be, exist', associated with Amharic *na-* (copula), Saho-Afar *na* 'to be' and other Semitic and Cushitic items by Cohen (1947.185–186 #445). It may be noted that Cohen earlier proposed a demonstrative origin for this set (1924.75–106; 1947: 'n'est pas prouvée'). Another set is Semitic (e.g. Arabic) *kwn* 'to be' Agau-Bilin *kŭn*, etc. (Cohen 1947.117 #196). Diakonoff selects from both groups, setting up Egyptian *wnn*, Saho *na* and Hausa *nàà* as related (1965.47).

The second possibility is that raised by the association of *-nee* and *nàà*. This would at first glance garb these in even more definite verbal robes, but the implication is really the opposite. Gregersen (1967) is the main advocate of such a view. He points out the complementarity of the constructions X Y-*nee* and W *nàà* Z and draws the conclusion that these are both expressions of imperfective aspect (cf. Kraft's identification of *nàà* as an aspect particle) and hence are in some underlying fashion the same. He therefore derives *-nee* from *yanàà* by a transformational rule.

One may question the attribution of aspect to a form such as *-nee*, which is used in statements of being X, being in X place, etc. to which there is no perfective counterpart. In the case of *nàà* the aspect is rather a feature of the construction, associated with or inherent in the 'state' described (see above).

Regardless of the matter of aspect, the association of *-nee* with *nàà* has other implications. It has been shown to be likely that *-nee* is the equivalent of the demonstrative in the N d construction of other AAs languages (Hodge 1969). The association of *-nee* with the masculine particle *na* and *-cee* with feminine *ta* in Sokoto (Bargery 1934.xxvi) is further confirming evidence. The present theory to associate *-nee* and *nàà* would thus result in reviving the theory that *nàà* is related to *na* (Hodge 1945). In thus arguing for a demonstrative origin of *nàà*, the nominal nature of the construction would be asserted, a result which I feel sure Gregersen did not intend.

The third possibility is that suggested by Abraham, a nominal construction: N prep N or N A. Use of a verb 'to be' as an auxiliary is found in other languages, e.g. *kaana* in Arabic (Brockelmann 1961.2. 509–510), *al-* in Ethiopic languages (Leslau in Tucker–Bryan 1966.610), etc. These are structurally very different from what we have in Hausa, being the addition of verbs 'to be' to forms already conjugated for person, number, etc.

The closest formal parallel which has come to my attention is in

Cushitic, where the construction Person -*n*- Verb-stem occurs as an imperfect: Bedauye *e-n-diir* 'he kills', *k-an-hiin* 'he loves' (Tucker–Bryan 1966.501, 530). Whether this is (1) a form of the verb 'to be' in Cushitic and/or (2) related to the Hausa under discussion are both matters for which I feel there is insufficient evidence.

There are two constructions in ancient Egyptian, both of them nominal, which should be considered. The first of these involves the preposition *n* 'to'. In Egyptian a prepositional phrase may be nominalized, so that *n rʿ* 'to (the god) Re' may have the nominalizing affix -*y*: *ny rʿ* 'one belonging to Re'. This in turn may serve as N in an N N construction. Should the other N be a pronoun, it follows *ny*: *ny sw rʿ* 'he (*sw*) belongs to Re' ('he [is] one belonging to Re'). With metathesis of the pronominal element **sw ny rʿ* one might compare Hausa *šinàà zuwà* (dial.) 'he's coming' ('he [is] one who pertains to coming'). Without more evidence, however, this equivalence seems strained.

The second construction in Egyptian is one which is of far greater frequency. This is N *ḥr* N, a construction of Nominal Preposition Nominal which is parallel to others with different prepositions. It functions as a nominal sentence with adverbial predicate. An example is *dqrw nb ḥr xtwf* 'all (*nb*) [kinds of] fruits (*dqrw*) [were] on (*ḥr*) its (*f*) trees (*xtw*)' Gardiner 1957.93). This might be compared with Hausa *yanàà gida* 'he is at home', where an ordinary noun follows *nàà*.

Early in the history of Egyptian there are found sentences of the type N *ḥr* N where the second N is a verbal noun. The first N may be a noun or one of a number of nominal substitutes, including particle plus pronoun. Examples are: *xtw ḥr gmgm* 'the trees were breaking up' (Sander-Hansen 1963.123) with N *ḥr* N. *mk w' ḥr 'rt r ḥztk* 'see (*mk*) I (*w'*) am ('upon'—*ḥr*) doing (*'rt*) so that (*r*) you will praise ('your praising'—*ḥztk*), particle plus pronoun *ḥr* verbal noun; *'(w)s ḥr 'čt xtw nbw nw ḥmk* 'she (*s*) is taking ('upon taking'—*ḥr 'čt*) all your worship's menials'. (OEg. exx. Edel 1964.472–473; a full discussion of MEg. in Gardiner 1957.243–255.) One may also mention, as a close parallel in construction, the use of *r* 'to' in N *r* N. When the second N is a verbal noun, one has such a sentence as: *'ws r 'rt mrrt'* 'she will do ('to doing'—*r 'rt*) what I want' (Edel 1964.474–475).

Interestingly, the Egyptian construction includes as one of the replacements of the first N the verb 'to be' with noun or pronoun (*wnnf ḥr sǧm* 'he hears' Edel 1964.473–474). This is of considerable interest in the total picture, considering the many conjectures about *nàà*. One interpretation might be that such a verb, when it occurs, does not affect the essentially nominal character of the construction. In any case, the role of 'to be' vis-à-vis other verbs must be clarified. It would not appear to the present writer that it affects the significance of the parallelism of structure and meaning which are found between the Hausa and Egyptian.[4]

Although it does not have the formal similarity found with *ny* : *nàà*, the structural and semantic parallels of N *ḥr* N : N *nàà* N appear to be very close. Even the hieroglyph for *ḥr* is a full face head, which makes Abraham's remark all the more interesting. Both constructions have like meaning, both may have either an ordinary noun or a verbal noun as second N, both may have a pronoun as first N. The attachment of the pronoun is different, and Egyptian shows considerable variety compared to the Hausa.

In all fairness one must also note that the *ḥr* was lost in the Coptic survivals of this construction: *efsōtm* 'he hears' on one side of a merger is from '*wf ḥr sǵm* 'he is upon hearing' (Steindorff 1951.148; cf. Edgerton 1935). The fact that the construction did survive is, on the other hand, a very important factor from the time perspective point of view.

On the basis of the above evidence it would appear highly probable that N *nàà* N is to be interpreted as a N A (nominal adverbial) type of sentence, the *nàà* N being originally a prepositional phrase. As such it is atemporal but indicates a state. This interpretation also fills a gap in the list of syntactic correspondences between Hausa and other AAs languages with which this article began.

NOTES

1. The occurrence of both N N and N d / N d N in both Semitic and Egyptian militates very strongly against setting up N d as 'basic' (i.e. d as obligatory) and deriving N N from N d N, as does Schachter for Hausa (1966.37–38).
2. There is now no recollection of influence from Migeod or Abraham, as Kraft thought might have been the case (1964b.232). It was a purely formal analysis, with *nà* heard short and the resulting construction having P *n* N as a parallel to N *n* P under this interpretation, with noun or pronoun occurring on either side of the *n*.
3. Schachter's use of N *nàà dà* N in forming modifiers (1965.37) is of no relevance to the present analysis.
4. The generative grammarian's urge to posit a verb where no verb is (e.g. Warotama-sikkhadit 1969 on Thai) rests upon a failure to recognize that a semantic motif, such as equivalence, may be realized by a construction rather than a morpheme. The creation of a verb 'to be', later deleted, is merely a device to avoid making the proper assignment of meaning to form. It shows, in fact, a morpheme-bound mentality rather than a syntactic outlook.

REFERENCES

R. C. ABRAHAM, *A Modern Grammar of Spoken Hausa*, London, 1941.

———, *The Language of the Hausa People*, London, 1959.

G. P. BARGERY, *A Hausa–English Dictionary and English–Hausa Vocabulary*, O.U.P., 1934.

Siegmund BRAUNER and Michael ASHIWAJU, *Lehrbuch der Hausa-Sprache*, Lehrbücher für das Studium der Orientalischen und Afrikanischen Sprachen, 10, Leipzig, 1965.

Carl BROCKELMANN, *Grundriss der vergleichenden Grammatik der semitischen Sprachen*, 2 vols., Hildesheim, 1908–13 (repr. 1961).

Marcel COHEN, *Le système verbal sémitique et l'expression du temps*, Paris, 1924.

———, *Essai comparatif sur le vocabulaire et la phonétique du chamito-sémitique*, Paris, 1947.

I. M. DIAKONOFF, *Semito-Hamitic Languages*, Moscow, 1965.

E. EDEL, *Altägyptische Grammatik*, 2 vols., Rome, 1955/1965.

William F. EDGERTON, 'On the Origin of Certain Coptic Verbal Forms', *JAOS*, 55, pp. 257–67, 1935.

Alan GARDINER, *Egyptian Grammar*, 3rd edn., O.U.P., 1957.

Edgar A. GREGERSEN, 'Some Competing Analyses in Hausa', *JAL*, 6, pp. 42–57, 1967.

Carleton T. HODGE, 'Morpheme Alternants and the Noun Phrase in Hausa', *Language*, 21, pp. 87–91.

——, *An Outline of Hausa Grammar*, Lang. Diss. 41, Ling. Soc. of America, Baltimore, 1947.

—— and Ibrahim UMARU, *Hausa Basic Course*, F.S.I., Washington, 1963.

——, 'Afroasiatic Pronoun Problems', *IJAL*, 35, pp. 366–76, 1969.

Dell HYMES, *Language in Culture and Society*, New York, 1964.

Charles H. KRAFT, *A Study of Hausa Syntax*, 3 vols., Hartford, 1963.

——, 'A New Study of Hausa Syntax', *JAL*, 3, pp. 66–74, 1964a.

——, 'The Morpheme nā in Relation to a Broader Classification of Hausa Verbals', *JAL*, 3, pp. 231–40, 1964b.

Frederick William Hugh MIGEOD, *A Grammar of the Hausa Language*, London, 1914.

A. MISCHLICH, *Lehrbuch der Hausa-Sprache*, Berlin, 1911.

F. W. PARSONS, 'The Verbal System in Hausa', *AuÜ*, 44, pp. 1–36, 1960.

Charles H. ROBINSON, *Hausa Grammar*, 5th edn., London, 1942 (1st edn. 1925).

C. E. SANDER-HANSEN, *Ägyptische Grammatik*, Wiesbaden, 1963.

Paul SCHACHTER, 'A Generative Account of *NE/CE*', *JAL*, 5, pp. 34–53, 1966.

Georg STEINDORFF, *Lehrbuch der Koptischen Grammatik*, Chicago, 1951.

F. W. TAYLOR, *A Practical Hausa Grammar*, Oxford, 1923.

A. N. TUCKER and M. A. BRYAN, *Linguistic Analyses: the non-Bantu Languages of North-Eastern Africa*, I.A.I., London, 1966.

Uriel WEINREICH, 'On the Semantic Structure of Language' in Joseph Greenberg, ed., *Universals of Language*, 2nd edn., pp. 142–216, Cambridge (Mass.) and London, 1966.

Diedrich WESTERMANN, *Die Sprache der Haussa in Zentralafrika*, Deutche Kolonialsprachen, III, Berlin, 1911.

A Hausa Poet in Lighter Vein
NEIL SKINNER

PROBABLY the leading Hausa poet alive today is Malam Aliyu na Mangi. Descended from a branch of the ruling family of the town of Jibiya in Katsina Emirate, domiciled since the days of his grandfather, Abdullahi, in the village of Mangi ten miles south of Zaria, he was born in 1895. Before he was two, he lost his sight through the combined attack of measles and smallpox. In spite of this—one would have thought—overwhelming handicap, he pursued the normal education of a Hausa malam and, though of course being unable to write, over the years studied and learnt by heart the Arabic texts proper to that education, moving from one specialized teacher to another. He wrote his first poem in Hausa at the age of 21. This, he says, was a translation from Arabic of Malam Shi'tu's *Jiddul ᶜaajizi*, which he fitted to the tune of *Kanzul ᶜadhiimi*. Since then he has composed and recited a large number of poems but, despite his knowledge of Arabic, always in Hausa. Of these the most famous are the several parts of his *Waaƙàr Imfiraajìi*, 'Song of Comfort', of which some eight have appeared in print, published in Zaria at various dates since 1949. This poem, of which there remain several hundred verses still to be published, is of the traditional Hausa genre, primarily religious: Praise of the Prophet, Exhortation to Correct Worship, Meditations on the Vanity of the World, etc., etc. But its vocabulary and style, far from being slavishly Arabic, are vividly Hausa and full of everyday metaphors and images.

Before the coming of radio—and to a lesser degree since—Aliyu, like other Hausa poets, relied on giving performances to groups of the pious, who would bestow alms on him for his virtuosity or, as they would put it, 'for the sake of God and the Prophet'. Since the coming of radio, of course, he has been able to reach a much wider audience and is now very well known indeed. In spite of the publication of *Imfiraajìi* (or perhaps because of his early struggle to get royalties for it), Malam Aliyu is on the whole adverse to having his work written down, for fear of having it pirated. It remains in his head, which, from the world's point of view, as he is now 74 years old, seems a pity. His only other published poem, on the doctrine of *tauḥiid* (the unity of God), is entitled *Waaƙàr Tàkàndaa*, 'Song of Sugar-Cane' (i.e. metaphorically, of that which is sweet).

The concern of Hausa poets with things religious led, in accordance with the traditional patterns of Islam, to a concern with the reform of social evils and, latterly for some of them, to a vehement interest in politics. So in the days of the NPC–NEPU struggle, some poets were not backward in speaking out with great vigour. Malam Aliyu, as befits an older man and a teacher of traditionalist outlook, took no part in the political battle of words but, as a good Muslim, he has been concerned with social evils. It is in the criticism of these, often through the medium of satire and usually involving cynical comment on human nature, that perhaps the genius of Hausa flourishes best. Traditionally such cynicism is to be found especially in proverbs. So we have *in kaa ga kùuraa nàa taashìi, àlheerìi nee a kèe raamàawaa*, 'If you see dust rising, someone is repaying a kindness' (i.e. if you see a fight, someone is returning evil for good); and *koomee ka dasàa kanàa shañ inuwàrsà, ban dà baki mài 'yan kunnuwàa*, 'Whatever you plant, you'll enjoy its shade—except for the black thing with the small ears' (i.e. everything will repay time and trouble spent on it, except for man).

Apart from cynicism, another common element in Hausa humour (and indeed in humour universally?) is the deflating of what society normally over-inflates, or the toppling of what society normally places on a pedestal; the deflation or toppling preferably to be sudden, surprising and shocking. So in the traditional tales we have the situation where the Lion (i.e. the chief) is digging away to get at his prey in a hole in the ground, when the Hyena comes up behind him and removes his testicles, which he sees swinging so temptingly. Malam Aliyu, too, for all his piety and earnest social purpose, has more than his share of such humour, and I was lucky enough to be able to record in the summer of 1968, two short poems that he chanted for me, one a satire on a slatternly wife, *Waakàr Kàzaamaa*, and the other ridiculing the folly of the dignified malam in his large, flapping gown who attempts to ride that emblem of the hurrying, modern age that the Europeans have brought—the bicycle. This latter is entitled *Waakàr Kèekee*, 'Song of the Bicycle' and it is the text of this that follows. It is worth reiterating that its creator has been without sight since the age of one and a half.

The poem is said to have been composed in 1959, the year the Northern Region of Nigeria became independent. I recorded[1] it during a morning spent with Malam Aliyu in the entrance-hut (*zaurèe*) of his home in Tudun Nufawa, Zaria City, in August 1968. Present were Malam Salihu Kontagora, a younger poet and respected man of Islamic learning; a representative of Turaki, District Head of the City, and a number of boys who dropped in to enjoy the recital. Malam Salihu, in particular, was convulsed with laughter during much of the performance. The humour must have appealed very strongly to him, for it is not usual for a Hausa of standing to allow his emotions to appear so readily and openly in public. The other adults were also much amused. Malam Aliyu sat cross-legged, very upright, on a mat and chanted with great force and marked rhythm, and—as with all that he recorded for me except on one brief occasion during several hours—without any hesitation or memory lapses.

FORM

One has difficulties discussing form with the poets, for Hausa does not yet have a widely accepted vocabulary of its own for the purpose. Talking with some of them, I arrived tentatively at the following equivalents (some based on the relevant Arabic terms) which served for purposes of discussion, but by some 'tune' and 'rhythm' were felt to be one concept and they seemed to dislike the idea of divorcing pitch pattern from rhythmic pattern:

'to chant'	reerà
'couplet'	'yar biyu
'hemistich'	dangoo (but Malam Salihu prefers to apply this only to the one that bears the running rhyme)
'poem, song'	waakàa (wàakee tends to imply that the content is religious)
'quatrain'	'yar hudu
'rhyme'	kaafiyàa
'rhythm, metre'	(?) rhythm karìi; metre ma'cunin waakàa, mazubin waakaa
'takhmiis'	'yar bìyar
'tune'	karìi (this interpretation differs from that given in the dictionaries); perhaps launìi or labdìi. Cf. karyà waakàa 'to vary or embroider a tune'
'verse', i.e. the span from one running rhyme to the next	baitìi

I found no one word the equivalent of 'foot', the poet usually preferring to use the Arabic version of the specific foot in question. Thus the foot – ∪ – – would be described as faaᶜilaatun; the foot ∪ – – as faᶜuulun, etc., according to the standard Arabic method of indicating a particular combination of long and short syllables. But more usually the poet himself didn't appear to think in terms of feet at all. He was just composing a poem 'to fit the shape' of such and such a well-known waakàa.

Ba seems to be a favourite *kaafiyàa* with Malam Aliyu, as he also chose it for the hundreds of verses of his *Imfiraajìi*. The Hausa negative, it is forceful and easy to fit in, for—the negative being of such frequent occurrence even in ordinary speech—it does not give too much appearance of being artificially introduced to meet the exigencies of rhyme. As it usually, in standard Kano speech at least, ends a sentence, it further helps to synchronize the conclusion of a segment of discourse with the end of the couplet—which, in Arabic poetry at any rate, is almost obligatory. Moreover, though Malam Salihu holds that it is a weakness if a poet is forced too soon to repeat a whole word in order to get his rhyme, *ba* as a functional particle may perhaps be exempt from this criticism. Indeed, constantly repeated negatives seem especially suitable to the moralizing nature of *Imfiraajii*. However, in the present poem, unlike *Imfiraajii*, the poet chooses to rhyme every second hemistich rather than every fifth. These two alternatives, the couplet and the *takhmiis*, are those usually chosen by Hausa poets, the quatrain being much rarer—unlike Swahili verse. In fact, Malam Aliyu himself says that he has never used a quatrain form.

The metre of this poem is the Arabic *waafir*, which consists of ∪ – ∪̄ ∪ –, usually repeated three times for the hemistich; it is always catalectic (i.e. short of the last syllable) and has the—now—last syllable obligatorily realized as a long. So we should get:
∪ – ∪ ∪ –|∪ – ∪ ∪ –|∪ – –||∪ – ∪ ∪ –|∪ – ∪ ∪ –|∪ – –
but, in fact, the final syllable of the *baitii*, *ba*, is always short, both in normal speech and in this recitation (except at the end of the first hemistich of 30). M. Aliyu avails himself of the possibility of substituting one long for the two shorts as marked above quite often; but in addition he uses two shorts for one long in the following:

1. 2nd hemistich   ∪ – – –|∪ ∪ ∪ ∪ ∪ –|∪ – ∪
2. 2nd hemistich   ∪ – ∪ ∪ ∪ ∪|∪ – ∪ ∪ ∪ ∪|∪ – ∪
4. 1st hemistich   ∪ ∪ ∪ ∪ ∪ –| ∪ – ∪ ∪ – |∪ – –

It is noteworthy that the first three involve the verb *yii/yi*, which in poetry often becomes *y*, suffixed to the preceding pronoun. So here, he might have said *yai*, *sukai* and *tai*, in order to avoid the resolution. That he did not do so makes the rhythm trip along faster and, perhaps, preserves a more natural speech rhythm. In the third case, the resolution could have been avoided, if he had pronounced the word as in the Arabic *ṣarf*, from which Hausa *zaràfii* seems to derive. On one occasion (31) a short occurs at the end of the first hemistich, while on a number of occasions, syllables are omitted at the beginning of the hemistiches. By Hausa listeners knowledgeable in poetry this is felt to be a distinct weakness in the poem, but to the writer it seemed to add a measure of pleasant variation. These omissions are 8, 17, 23, 27, 33: 1st syllable of first hemistich in each case; 36: 1st syllable of second hemistich. On the other hand, an extra syllable is inserted as follows: *short* in 6: 2nd foot of second hemistich (here again, the poet might have used poetic licence and said *ba kui* but didn't); *long* in 11: 1st foot of second hemistich (he also altered the length of the second syllable of *kèekee* from long, as it is elsewhere in the poem [and in the dictionaries—wrongly according to M. Kabiru Galadanci], and made it short); *long* also in 20, 26, 27: 1st foot of second hemistich (in 26 and 27 the word *wai* 'it is said' is the redundancy, which is, semantically speaking, parenthetical).

The last foot, ∪ - ∪, is completely uniform throughout and chanted with especial emphasis, as it is strongly characterized in tune (see below).

Apart from the variation in *kèekee* already mentioned, the poet takes poetic licence on several occasions to vary syllable length from what it would be in normal speech. Examples are *kamarkaa* for *kàmarkà* in 28; and *kulaa* for *kulà* in 17 and 35. Another interesting feature in vowel length is the occurrence of syllabic *n* as a short syllable whenever the 1st person singular subjunctive is used (e.g. twice in 19); and *n* also occurs once at the end of the first hemistich— the only consonant to do so—instead of vowel length (32). However, if such licence is rare, what is not unusual is the exaggeration of what would have been the spoken rhythm by the regular increase of the length of the long vowels. *kurumbooo* in 16 is a good example of much exaggerated vowel length, usually coupled with a fall in pitch—as if to reach the pitch with which he wishes to begin the 2nd hemistich. The caesura between the two hemistiches is not usually marked by pause, but occasionally pause occurs, perhaps only to enable the reciter to draw breath. I have marked such pauses by || in the text. It is noteworthy that they do not occur after the extra long vowel discussed above.

As for the melodic line, which is an essential—perhaps *the* essential —element for the average Hausa listener, Malam Aliyu said that for this poem he employed a common, well-known tune. Cf. his *Imfìraajìi*, where at the end of Part I, he states explicitly that he wrote the poem to go with the *caajì waakàa*. Most Hausa poets seem to fit their words to an already existing tune. It was my observation that few of them compose their own tunes, preferring rather to use one that is traditional, one that they have heard from a popular singer or one that they have heard used by another poet—perhaps a rival. One exception appears to be Mudi Sipikin who claims to compose his own, and, in fact, gave me some examples of those he had composed. As an illustration of the indivisibility of words and tune, one may put a printed poem into the hands of a literate Hausa and ask him to read it aloud. In my experience, he will always chant rather than read in a normal speaking voice. I made several attempts to get poets further to identify tunes for me. One method I tried was to ask them to hum one for me; but I found some difficulty in making my request clear, as I failed to identify a Hausa word for 'hum'!

Speaking of a Hausa song, Wängler[2] has made a distinction between motifs sung in recitative style and those of the tune proper. In the former, the full intervals of lexical pitch, which tend to get blurred in the falling sentence contours of the spoken language, are restored, so that the tones of words chanted in recitative style are closer to the lexical patterns than when the same words are used in normal speech. Where, however, the tune proper predominates, the lexical tones will tend to be lost. If we define recitative as a vocal style designed to imitate and to emphasize the natural inflections of speech, on the whole this is not employed in *Waakàr Kèekee*, where the melodic line predominates. The following, with approximate pitches, is the pitch outline for a complete couplet:

As can be seen, this tends to emphasize five or six main pitches in the order given, with 4 (A′) occurring for the last four syllables of that couplet. Thus—as with the rhythm—it is at the end of that couplet that the most regular characteristic of the tune occurs. Normally the last metrical foot is sung on pitch 4. If we add the recurrence of rhyme—the main criterion of Hausa learned poetry—in the same area of the couplet, we can appreciate the importance of this last foot for the *waakàa* as a whole.

I have numbered the pitches from 1 to 6, 1 being approximately D″ and 6 D′, and over the text I have marked the most noticeable points at which a higher pitch begins (but not where it ends, for it tends to change with each syllable or within a single long syllable). In general, the melody consists of three main areas of pitch range, marked with horizontal square brackets, which usually occur in the same order in each couplet, each one beginning at more or less the same point, but with considerable variation in detail. As has been said, the second hemistich is much more regular in this respect. The first hemistich, on the other hand, shows much variety, its highest note sometimes being 1, sometimes 2, and sometimes 3; and the number of peaks also varies from zero (e.g. couplet 20, which is mainly a *piano* line) to five (i.e. c. 11, which is a *fortissimo* line). The pitch area of the first part of the hemistich includes pitches 1 or 2, 3 and 4, beginning usually with pitch 4, going to pitch 1 and then back to pitch 4. Towards the end of the first hemistich and the beginning of the second the range includes pitches 5, 6 and often pitches from the lower octave (below pitch 6). The third range goes from pitch 6 to the repeated pitch 4s at the end of each line.

As for the lexical tones, in general the sung intervals of the pitch pattern take precedence over these, and they have not been marked, except where a grave accent has been used to mark a fall when it occurs on the second (or third) component of a long vowel. It will be noted that there is a tendency to fall thus on the last syllable of the first hemistich, where such occurs, in e.g. couplet 3 *faifaaà*. Otherwise the main effect of the underlying lexical tone patterns may be to influence the reciter in his choice of the exact syllable on which he will make the next main pitch change. It is, for example, noteworthy that the biggest jump up, from 6 to 4, nearly always occurs where there is a lexical low-high, so that in fact the exact point of its occurrence in the metrical framework varies slightly.

An attempt has been made to indicate the volume. This appears to rise to some four climaxes. Artistically speaking, those at 39 and 11 are well justified, the former by its position at the end; and the latter by the sense (underlined by the use of the ideophone *tirmis*) of the poet's indignation at the bicycle's refusing to lower its charges. That at 33 also is the punchline of a joke—see Notes on Text. The marking pp—which does not occur—would indicate the volume and resonance of normal, loud speech. It is noticeable that a reduction of volume seems to occur between c. 20 and c. 27, coinciding with two of the examples of irregular rhythm cited above and with a marked absence of peak pitches. Summing up the features of this tune then, we may say that there are three pitch areas, the high range occurs at the beginning of the first hemistich; the low range—the most ornamented—at the end of the first and beginning of the second; and the medium at the end of the second hemistich.

Malam Aliyu, like many traditional-style Hausa performers, has great volume at his control and can achieve loudness comparable to that of a man reciting the *kiraarìi* ('praise-song') of an important chief. On the other hand, from time to time, he—as other poets—will simplify the melody for a number of lines, perhaps for variety, perhaps merely to rest his voice. He usually slightly speeds his delivery when he does this, with the text assuming prime importance. The punctuation is, of course, my own and intended to help the reader to understand syntax and meaning.

f 1. *Munaa shukuraa ga Rabbal 'aalamiinaa da 'alhairin da ya yi mana baa kaḍan ba.*

2. *Munaa murnaa da mulkin 'ingiliishii—zuwad da suka yi, ƙasarmu ta ta yi tsiyaa ba.*

3. *Zamaa zamanirsu nee 'aka zoo da faifaaà kuḍii baa maasu nauyaya 'aljiƙuu ba.*

4. *Daḍa 'a zarafinsu nee 'aka zoo da jirgiii, ka jee Maka baa da taashin ƙanƙalii ba.*

5. Sa'an nan gaa su baabur, gaa su maatooo, da farkoo daa 'acan ba mu san da suu ba.

6. 'izan tafiyaa ta faaru, ka neemi maatoo 'izan jirgii ba ku yi daidai da shii ba.

7. 'izan kau baabu jirgin, baabu maatoo, ka jee da kafarka, baa keekee tsiyaa ba.

8. Ban ni da baasukur! Hoo dan jidaalii shakiyii, baa 'abin babbaa ya hau ba!

9. 'a dam-Mahawaayi nih hau, sai ya bar ni || Tudun Yaakaaji, ban kaawoo garii ba.

10. Ya bar ni da jin jikii da zamaa 'a turbaa, || da bai koo Jumma'aa ba 'a jee da nii ba.

ff 11. Kudii tirmis na baa shi sulee da siisii; keeke bai mini rangwamen koo daa darii ba.

12. Na cee masa 'Baasukur, rika sauwakeewaa.' Ya cee 'Maalam, halaa ba ka san ni nee ba.

13. Inaa da tsiyaa biyar: farkonsu fancaa, || na kan buga bindigaa baa mai wutaa ba.

f 14. 'n babbake zuuciyaa 'n tafii da saawuu cikin daajii kamar ba 'a jee da nii ba.

15. Munaa tafiyaa, na kan kuma fizge kainaaa mu faada kwazazza-boo, nii ban kulaa ba.

16. Inaa da cikii 'anaa cee mai 'kurumbood'—karambaanin hawa baa kaa sayaa ba!

ff 17. Hanjinaa kacaa mai kaama riigaa, mu fizgoo mai hawaa, nii ban kulaa ba.

mf 18. *Tsiyan naa can, mu jee bisa kan kadarkooo madaidaicii 'n cee baa zaa mu hau ba.*

f 19. *'n hau bisa kaafadar mahayi 'n zaunaa kamar mahayin dadai bai hau ni shai ba.'*

mf>p 20. *Sukai kaddaa da Saale 'a kan kadarko, sai ya cee 'Haba Saale! Baa zan yaa da kai ba.'*

21. *Garin suka wantsalaa haka, kan ya kwaacèe—* || ᵖ*'ashee baa Saale nee 'a cikin ruwaa ba?*

22. *Ya bii shi, ya bangajee, ya bugee, yanaa cee ''a zoo 'a ganii 'izan ban yaa da kai ba!'*

mf 23. *Maalan Saale sai da ya tuuɓe riigaaa ya saa ka ga Saale har bai shaa ruwaa ba.*

24. *Ya taashi ya hau tuduu, keekee ya bii shii,* || *da riigar Saale keekee bai sakoo ba.*

25. *Su Maalan Sanda duk suka tar ma keekeee da ban maganaa. Ya cee baa zai sakoo ba.*

26. *Ya maa ranısee da jirgii, har da maatoo wai ba zaa shi sakoo 'izan ba 'a saa wukaa ba.*

f 27. *Maalan Sanda sun shiryaa da keekee, wai yanaa kaunarsa baa doomin tsiyaa ba!*

mf 28. *Ya cee 'Haba! Maalamii babbaa kamarkaaa ba zan iya yaa da babban maalamii ba.*

f 29. *'izan dai zac ka hau ni, ka taara riigaca da wandoo, baa ka hau ni hawan 'isaa ba.'*

30. *Ya taashi hawaa, 'ashee bai tattaraa kaa.* ᵐᶠ *Ya fizgoo maalamin ba 'a jinjimaa ba.*

p 31. *Ya yaasai nandanan 'a tsakar gidansa* || *cikin maatansa tun ba 'a kai daɓee ba.*

p 32. *Ya cee 'Bari, nai kuren yaashee ka, maalan,* || *zamaa ban kai ka baakin kaasuwaa ba.*

ff 33. *Ban naa soo 'n yaa da mutun na kirkii 'izan baa 'inda zaa 'a yi daariyaa ba.*

f 34. *Da mootsa ƙararrawarka da kaama burkii ba zaa su hanaa ni 'in jeefad da kai ba.'*

mf 35. *Ya cee 'Too, baa ni ƙaara hawanka, keekee.' Ya cee masa koo ''adankiya, ban kulaa ba.'*

mf 36. *Hawan da rashin hawaa 'a garee ni ɗai naa, ban ga 'abin da zai cuutad da nii ba.*

f 37. *Kamar tafiyaa na saurii koo na fizgeeè, ba kaa jee 'inda kaa soo nandanan ba.*

f 38. *'izan koo zaa ka hau ni, ka baa ni 'iskaaà na shaa, baa 'inda baa zan jee da kai ba.'*

ff 39. *'asheeè baa mai hawaa keekee ya mooree, 'izan baa wanda yaa iya zanzaroo ba.*

1. We give thanks to the Lord of the Worlds for the bounty bestowed on us in no small measure.
2. We rejoice in the rule of the English, for since they came our country has not known poverty;
3. for in their time we have been brought paper money, which does not weigh down the pocket.
4. So too through their kindness we have received the aeroplane, so that you go to Mecca without trouble.
5. Then there are motor-cycles, cars and the rest, which in the old days were unknown to us.
6. If you have to travel, look for a lorry if you don't coincide with a railway.
7. But if there's neither train nor motor, then go on your feet and not on a shameless bicycle.

8. Just leave the bicycle to me! You wicked troublemaker, you! Thing not fit for an adult to ride!
9. It was at Dan Mahawayi that I got on, but it left me at Tudun Yakaji and I never reached town.
10. It left me sore all over, sitting on the road, and afterwards the Friday mosque took place without my presence!
11. Money I gave it, hard cash aplenty, one and six, for the bicycle wouldn't allow me a reduction of even a halfpenny.
12. Yes, for I said to it 'Bicycle, please be lenient' but it said 'Malam, it seems then that you don't know me.
13. I have vices five: the first is a puncture, when I fire a gun but not with flame
14. and sear the heart and cause the feet to go off into the bush, as if I was not making the journey;
15. or else, as we go along, I wrench my head away, so we fall into the ditch—but I don't care!
16. My stomach is called 'gear-case'—impertinence to ride something you haven't bought!
17. My guts are a chain that grabs hold of a gown and we snatch off the rider—I don't care!
18. Yet another trouble comes when we reach a plank bridge—a rickety one—and I decide that we won't go across,
19. but that I'll get up on the shoulders of my rider and sit there, as if *he* had never mounted on *me*.'
20. Bicycle and Sale disputed on the bridge and it said 'For shame, Sale! Of course I won't throw you!'
21. But as they tipped over, it jerked its head free and—dear me, isn't that Sale down in the water there?
22. It followed him, pushing and hitting, saying 'Now anyone can come and see whether I haven't thrown you!'
23. And it was only when Malam Sale had managed to strip off his gown that he escaped getting a bellyful of water.
24. He got up and climbed on the bank. The bicycle followed him, for it hadn't let go of his gown.
25. Then Malam Sanda and the others gathered round the bicycle coaxing it, but it refused to let go,
26. swearing by Train and Motorcar that it wouldn't let go, unless they used a knife.
27. Then Malam Sanda came to an agreement with the bicycle, professing to like it but apprehensive of its tricks,
28. saying 'Absurd! A leading malam like you—why, I couldn't throw an important malam!
29. But if you mount me, you must gather together your gown and trousers and not ride with the voluminous flamboyance of rank.'
30. So he got on, but still failed to gather in his clothes, and before many minutes had passed, it whipped the malam off,

31. almost immediately threw him down in the middle of his compound in front of his wives, before he could reach the *daɓe*.
32. Says the bicycle 'Wait, I've made a mistake in throwing you off, malam, since I didn't take you to the outskirts of the market.
33. For I don't like to throw off an honest citizen except where people can have a good laugh.
34. And all your bell-ringing and brake-grabbing won't stop me chucking you off either!'
35. The other replied 'Well, I'm not riding you again, bicycle', but the bicycle answered 'San fairy ann, what do I care?
36. Whether you ride me or don't ride me is all one to me—neither will do me any harm that I can see.
37. Hasty riding or wrenching me about won't take you immediately where you would be,
38. But if you mount me, first giving me air to drink, there is nowhere where I won't take you.'
39. So you see, no one will have a comfortable ride on a bicycle who can't bring himself to wear his shirt tucked into his trousers!'

NOTES ON TEXT AND TRANSLATION

1. The traditional invocation is cut very short, as is fitting in such a light-hearted genre.
2. *faifàa* (< paper) is an English loan-word, well-suited to this context, not yet commonly used in Hausa. *Takàrdaa* would not have served the metre in any case.
4. *zaràfinsù* is usually 'opportunity' or 'wealth' but is here used with the sense of 'that which includes or makes possible'. *jirgii* could, of course, be other sorts of vehicle, but the reference to Mecca makes the present translation probable.
6. *'ìzan*, which is the scholarly version of *'ìdan*, approaching more closely the Arabic *'idhan*, is the poet's favourite word for line-initial position in this work.
7. *tsiyaa* is another word that occurs several times. It is a favourite with another poet, Aƙilu Aliyu. In this poem it is used with at least two different connotations.
9. These are two villages close to Zaria City.
15. *kainaa, cikì, hanjiinaa* all underline the personification of the bicycle, which is one of the main points of the poem.
16. *kurumbòo—karàmbàanin*. The break in the construction is perhaps compensated for by the assonance.
18. *madàidaicii* is unusual in this sense of 'peculiar' in a pejorative way.
19. Because mount and rider end up so far apart!
20. *Saalè* is the rider's name.
22. It is boasting of its prowess.

26. It swore by its parents, its most solemn oath!

31. *daɓee* is the area that is beaten hard in front of the householder's *tùraakaa* (part of the compound reserved for himself).

32-33. The humour here lies in concluding what is apparently a normal statement with something unexpected and, incidentally, somewhat aggressive. Apparently the bicycle is about to apologize for throwing him off, but goes on to add 'where your fall caused minimal public mirth'.

39. *zànzaroo* is the narrow-waisted wasp, and also describes a slim or 'wasp-waisted' person. In particular it is applied to the European-introduced style of tucking shirt into trousers. This was felt at first to be a mark of deviance when adopted by young Hausas. So in Mu'azu Hadeja's *Waakàr Giyà*[3] at v. 73, we have *Hakà mài taayè dà mài zànzaroo,/baa nàa yàrdaa dà suu, 'yan giyàa*, 'So too those who wear ties and affect *zanzaro* style, I don't trust them, topers all'. European clothes and unshaven heads have now achieved a status of respectability among Hausa intellectuals such as was unknown twenty years ago.

NOTES

1. Acknowledgements are due, and I gratefully make them, to the Social Science Research Council, which enabled me to make this visit to Nigeria; to Malam Aliyu for putting his time and talent at my disposal; to my colleague, Lois Anderson, who guided my ear, helped me analyse the tune and much mitigated my musical ignorance; to Malam Salihu and Malam Isa Kurawa who have helped me in preparing the text and translation; to the Nigerian Broadcasting Corporation for letting me have the tape of a previously recorded interview with Malam Aliyu; and to Professor D. W. Arnott, Mr. M. Besmer and Dr. Kabiru Galadanci for invaluable guidance.
2. H. H. WÄNGLER, 'Singen und Sprachen in einer Tonsprache' in *Zeitschrift für Phonetik*, XI, 1958, pp. 23-4.
3. Mu'azu HADEJA, *Waƙoƙi*, Zaria, ?1955.

There is a short bibliography of Hausa poetry in John PADEN, 'Kano Poetry', *Kano Studies*, 1, 1965.

Diola-Fogny Funeral Songs and the Native Critic

J. DAVID SAPIR

THIS paper gives a brief preliminary description of one type of Diola-Fogny funeral song called *buñansaŋ*. The description is based on recordings that were made in 1960–61, and later in 1964–66, as well as on commentary given by *buñansaŋ* singers responding to a number of questions about the songs.[1] The most important inquiries concerned textual exegesis and criteria for excellence in solo singing. I want to emphasize at the outset that reliance on this informant commentary or 'ethno-criticism' was absolutely central to an adequate description of the genre; and this was as true for the seemingly obvious mechanical aspects of the songs as it was for their meaningful content.

BACKGROUND

The Fogny make up one subgroup of the Diola, a people living in the Basse-Casamance region of Sénégal. The *buñansaŋ* songs are restricted to one small area of the Fogny region located in the *arrondissement* of Sindian (to the north of Bignona). The area is bounded on the north by the village of Sitoukène, on the west by Téloum, on the south by Kagnarou and Guimel, and on the east by Ouniok (where, according to some informants, the genre is said to have originated).

The overall form of the *buñansaŋ* consists of an ensemble–solo alternation with the solo section being an extemporaneous verse. This form is shared by songs sung at a secular dance called *bugɔɔr*, a type of dance popular throughout the entire Fogny region and extending down into the so-called Buluf area to the south of Bignona. Such extemporaneous versification contrasts with songs made up of ensemble–solo alternation based on fixed verses and with songs consisting of an alternation of fixed verses between two ensembles. The latter antiphonal type of song, because of its almost pan-Diola distribution, is, in all probability, the traditional form. By contrast, extemporaneous singing seems to be a rather recent innovation. At least Diola informants would have it this way. Also, unlike antiphonal singing, it is restricted to one continuous area, the Fogny, which borders, to the north and east, extensive Manding and Fula populations. Perhaps the original stimulus for the form came from the extemporaneous praise songs of these neighbours.

The *buñansaŋ* are sung only at the funerals of elder male Diola who are traditional, i.e. who are neither Moslem nor Catholic converts. They are never sung out of context.[2] As one singer put it:

'If we are just here, as we are now, I would not be able to sing anything. But if there were a funeral and I began to sing, no matter what, I would be able to go through with it and sing about whomever I would like.'

The sing takes place throughout the night after death and then the following afternoon at the time of burial. If the death is abrupt, catching the family of the deceased unprepared and without immediate means to feed the funeral guests, or if it occurs at the height of the rains when agricultural work is at full pitch, the sing, as well as the rest of the funeral celebration, will be postponed.

The personnel involved in the *buñansaŋ* are always men: soloists, called 'singers' (*ǝcịmǝ*, pl. *kụcịmǝ*) and an ensemble or 'those who follow'. There are usually from two to four soloists. They stand next to each other in a row with the ensemble gathered behind. Any one singer will have several friends in the ensemble from his own village or ward who will stand directly behind him. They encourage his singing with shouts of approval, anticipate some of his lines, and sometimes help him terminate his verse.

If there is a particularly large crowd two groups will be formed. No matter how many are present, however, there will always be a crowd of bystanders who listen but do not participate in the ensemble singing. They too are men; women are otherwise occupied.

The entire group walk, while singing, with very short, slow and rhythmic steps around a hut, usually located in the centre of the compound, where the deceased, in the role of compound elder, lived his last years and under which he is to be buried.

Anyone capable and so inclined may be a soloist. Aside from sex there are no restrictions on singing determined by status, as there are, for example, with the Manding and Wolof praise singers. Rewards come from the sheer pleasure of singing and from the prestige of being a good singer. They also come in payment of meat. The family of the deceased is required to kill a cow—or at least several goats—for the singers, who divide the meat amongst themselves, eating it *sur place* and sharing it with members of the ensemble.

THE SONGS

Inquiries about singing excellence brought out three essential criteria which were, in order of importance: 1. mastery of song mechanics, i.e. control of the onward flow of the singing, 2. clearness of voice, and 3. correctness in versification.

SONG MECHANICS

The *buñansaŋ* consists of an interchange between chorus and verse, with the entire ensemble (or part of it) singing the chorus and the soloists singing both the chorus and the verse. The soloists sing in turn. The chorus, which is melodious, is usually no more than *oo-ee-oo* ..., or in some songs *oo-ee* plus a verbal phrase such as *sankɛn manugama*, 'speak so we may judge'. The verses, which are best described as 'recitatives', are composed almost entirely of meaningful words. Closer hearing reveals that they terminate with a melodious cadence.

Discussion with singers (and with one in particular) about these mechanics allowed a more elaborate and precise description. Informants use four terms which serve to define the song's structure; these are: *fɔñ* 'to sing out the melody' (literally 'to resound'); *kit* 'to begin'; *sankɛn*, 'to speak, or *salɛn*, 'to praise', both referring to the solo's verse; and *buj* 'to kill' or *nɛn* 'to place', both meaning in this context 'to terminate the solo section'.

Control of the on-going movement is completely in the hands of the soloist who is singing at the time, with the crucial manipulation being the *buj*, i.e. 'kill' or termination. It is here that the soloist, by pre-figuring the melodic line, announces that he has completed his verse. If the *buj* is executed correctly the ensemble will *fɔñ*, i.e. sing the melody, without pause and in unison; otherwise there will be confusion. It is exactly here that an inexperienced singer will fall down, and as far as the singers' judgements are concerned the *buj* is the acid test for correct performance:

'Now in order to kill the song he will turn and lead to where the song is (i.e. to the *fɔñ*). When he is finished speaking he will kill. When he kills they (the ensemble) will know this very song, the one that he kills. But when you hear the song without precision (any old way) and the singer becomes quiet without killing (then the ensemble is lost) ... Should you speed up and forego the killing it will not be good. The singer ... looks for the road by which he is to kill so that everyone in the ensemble will hear the song and remember it.'

To 'hear the song' refers to the *buj* passage. The singer reinforces his *buj* kinesically during the cadence by turning his head towards the next singer, or back towards the ensemble.

The *buj* signals the chorus. In some songs the chorus consists simply of the ensemble singing the melody through once (Type A song: see Appendix). In others it consists of a more complicated sequence (Type B song) involving a choral 'interjection', followed by a two-section melody with the first section being sung by the soloist and the second by the ensemble.

With either type of song, when the ensemble terminates the next singer must begin (k̞it) his section; otherwise there will be complete silence. The new singer is given two major options: he may go on immediately to his verse (sankɛn) or he may demand a repetition of the chorus. In Type A song he will do this by singing the melody (fɔñ)—usually with a certain amount of embellishment—and in Type B song he will sing a special verbal phrase. In both cases the chorus will then be restated. The entire k̞it may, at the discretion of the soloist, be repeated several times.

Type A song can also k̞it with a verbal phrase instead of the soloist's melodic fɔñ. This is subject to further elaboration in a variant popular with singers from the village of Djakoye Banga. Here the soloist starts with a phrase that is then completed by his friends, gathered directly behind him and acting as his 'sub-ensemble'. These variants are terminated, as expected, with the ensemble singing the regular chorus.

A third song (Type C) differs significantly from both Types A and B by making the k̞it the central part of the song. The k̞it here consists of a two part solo-ensemble phrase that is obligatorily repeated at least ten times, with the solo verse (sankɛn) becoming correspondingly short. The chorus is similar to that of Type A: the melody is stated in its entirety by the ensemble.

A song may be changed by terminating (buj) a verse with a new melody, or more precisely with a buj line that pre-figures a new melody. This does not seem to happen very frequently, for it takes a particularly good singer and a very alert ensemble to perform it successfully. The more common practice is to change the melody during the k̞it section. We have the following pattern: At the end of a verse the preceding singer kills the song, the ensemble follows and the next singer introduces the new song in his k̞it; the ensemble immediately responds. The singer then re-cycles the k̞it a number of times until he is sure that the chorus are sure of it: 'that they have taken it well, and are not singing *jagum-jagum* or *gut gut gut!* He then proceeds with his verse.

That these mechanics are important to the singers was made amply clear to me when I asked my principal informant for his opinion of one particular singer whom I had felt was rather good. My informant demurred. I insisted, saying that this singer's verses were very amusing. The reply to this was ' 'ã'ã, have you *heard* him sing?'. On replaying the tapes of the discredited singer it became immediately apparent what was wrong. He would always k̞it by going directly to his verse and would seldom bother with the buj. As a result the ensemble was usually in discord and often completely confused. This kind of confusion is contrary to the whole idea of what buñansaŋ is basically about: the smooth and harmonious interchange between solo and ensemble, between individual and group.

FORMAL 'GRAMMAR' OF THE *Buñansaŋ*

The following 'grammar' summarizes in formal terms the *buñansaŋ* mechanics described above. The presentation adopted here is based on techniques developed by the 'transformational' or 'generative' school of linguistics.[3] Anyone familiar with this school will immediately notice that the presentation is rather out of date and—what is worse—that it is subject to one or two heretical *legerdemains*. Nevertheless, it serves our present needs, which are simply to illustrate that on a general level *buñansaŋ* song-phrasing can be subject, without much difficulty, to formal statement. Obviously, other techniques of formal representation could serve equally well.

I. *Conventions:*

The subscripts indicate who sings: s = soloist, e = ensemble and s–e = sub-ensemble. The superscripts 1 and 2 (as in T.4, 5 and 6) indicate respectively the first and second section of a given phrase or melody (*fɔñ*). In T.6 the expression: ... N reads: 'the operation is performed at least N times (N being equal to or greater than 10). Phrase structure rules 1 and 3 are recursive rules: thus 1 reads 'A *buñansaŋ* consists of a sequence or a series of sequences' and 3 reads 'a *kit* consists of a *kit* or a series of *kit*s'. The abbreviation (opt.) in T.1 and T.4 indicates that the transformation is optional. A slash (/) reads 'in the environment of': thus in T.1 *kit* optionally becomes zero in the environment of continuous singing, i.e. where there is no change of melody.

II. *Phrase Structure Rules:*
  1. $Buñ \to S(Buñ)$
  2. $S \to kit + V + fɔñ_e$
  3. $kit \to kit(kit)$
  4. $V \to sankɛn + buj$

III. *Transformation Rules:*
  T.1 (opt.) $kit \Rightarrow \emptyset$/continuous singing
  T.2 $kit \Rightarrow fɔñ_s + fɔñ_e$
  T.3 $fɔñ_s \Rightarrow phrase_s$
  T.4 (opt.) $phrase_s \Rightarrow phrase_s^1 + phrase_{s-e}^2$
  T.5 $fɔñ_e \Rightarrow interjection_e + fɔñ_e^1 + fɔñ_e^2$
  T.6 $kit \Rightarrow fɔñ_s^1 + fɔñ_e^2 \ldots N, N \geqslant 10$

IV. *Order Rules for generating Song Types:*
  Type A = PS + T.1 + T.2
  Type A' = PS + T.1 + T.2 + T.3 + T.4
  Type B = PS + T.1 + T.2 + T.3 + T.5
  Type C = PS + T.6

Explanation: The Phrase Structure Rules indicate the basic structure common to all song types. The Transformation Rules indicate the possible operations that may be performed on the basic structure. And the Order Rules indicate the steps that must be taken in order to 'generate' any particular song type. For example, to produce Type A' songs (the phrase $+f\tilde{o}\tilde{n}_e$ alternate of the regular Type A) we must perform, in the order indicated, the Phrase Structure Rules 1 through 4 followed by the Transformations 1 through 4. If the optional T.1 is performed, we must stop there, for it zeroes the *kit*. If T.1 is by-passed we must perform T.2 (which gives us the regular Type A) and then T.3. We may then optionally perform T.4 giving the Djakoye Banga variant.

CLARITY OF VOICE

The next most important criterion of good singing is for the soloist to sing with a clear full voice that is not scratchy or 'shrill and hard (like unripened fruit)', i.e. that sounds ŋaŋaŋaŋ. A singer should have good diction so that he can be heard clearly by all who might be present.

Although informants offer no particular commentary, all verses (*sankɛn*) have prosodic features. These vary from singer to singer and, with good singers, from song to song. The exact nature of these features has yet to be determined.

VERSIFICATION

The ability to 'speak' well, though second to control of mechanics and clarity of voice, remains central to 'good' singing. On exploring this topic informants made clear two points: First, the songs 'call' people, individuals, groups, character types, etc. Further, those who are called must be outstanding; they must be noticeable people who get talked about. This may include not only warriors and rich men but also thieves, drunkards, scandal-mongers and fools. Natural forces may also be included, especially death. Secondly, if someone is named, something must be said about him. A minimal statement must therefore have a subject and a predicate, with the subject naming and (optionally) 'placing' someone and the predicate describing him and/or his actions. A statement like 'Alassane (who is) tall' would be acceptable (though hardly exciting) while 'I go to Sindian and I call Alassane' would be unacceptable, because nothing is said about Alassane. Mediocre singers excel at lengthy subjects with minimal predicates. They will name a locality, such as a particular compound, list off its head and principal occupants and then terminate with a rather uninformative predicate such as 'why do I call them?'.

As is almost universal with extemporaneous versification, singers rely heavily on stock words, phrases, formulae and the like, combining, enlarging and altering them to suit their immediate needs. The *buñansaŋ* offers three general types: Firstly, there are interjections and 'fillers' such as *ñam* 'my mother!', *mɔbɛtɛ* 'that's why', *digɔl* 'de Gaulle', *ujuk nɔn* 'see and you'll say' or simply *oo-ee*, these serving primarily as prosodic devices that separate, round out and punctuate calls. Secondly, there are subject 'praise' terms that permit disguise and variety. They are not necessarily complimentary: *jirigɔraj* 'noise maker', *jibambukan* 'finisher of people (death)', *kanɛnkuñinɛnkuñ* 'flat-buttocked one'. And finally, there are predicate phrases which are often complex in shape and elaborate in their meaningful allusions. Thus the phrase *bakɔlɔŋ balɛ ro lɛtari* 'if there are no condiments he won't eat' indicates that the person referred to is a great thief. Diola thieves, or at least the ones who are sung about, only steal livestock and do so solely for the meat. Thus a thief is accustomed to having meat sauces with his rice (the staple food) at every meal, something normally unheard of. The phrase *lɔnka yan kufule ri yɔ, ban lɛ kugonk* 'the Dane gun which they are dragging, and it is not a vine' would apply to a great warrior or fighter, i.e. his gun is so big and heavy that others must drag it along the ground.

Any one verse will consist of a series of calls. They might all be addressed to one subject or, at the other extreme, each to a different subject. As a general rule most, though by no means all, verses of worth focus on one subject. For example, such a verse might start with a short introductory call referring perhaps to the bystanders, the ensemble, or the preceding singer (*wanurɛgum jɔŋɔjɔŋɔr* 'what you say is good'). This is followed by the main section made up of several calls addressed to the central subject. The verse is then terminated via a number of stock phrases leading to the final *buj*. These may or may not refer to the main subject.

A *buj* should, in order to be clearly made and properly understood, coincide exactly with a common predicate phrase. This permits the spoken words to reinforce the musical line. For instance, in the musical illustration given at the end of this paper the first singer accomplishes this perfectly with: *atiikɔrɔl eñab ɛbujɛ*, 'the elephant killed his enemy' (enemy-his elephant killed). The subject which precedes the *buj*, is *Jɛmɛ Musa*, a man's name: 'If it is only an elephant that can kill your enemy, then it is only an elephant that can kill you. A man is always equal to his enemy'. The second singer was not so successful, for the terminal predicate started before the *buj*: *bulɛkab ɛput rubandaw*, with the *buj* starting at *ɛput*. This translates 'poverty rots on the shoulders' (A poor man wears his shirt until it rots). The subject, in this case the addressee, is *ɔyonini* 'the difficult one', and is separated from the predicate by the filler *mɔbɛtum* 'that's why'. A free translation would be: 'My difficult friend, it is for that reason that poverty rots on the shoulders'.

TEXTUAL EXAMPLES

The following are the texts of three complete verses. Each one is accompanied by an explication derived from informant commentary.

I. (Sung by Sitafa Djediou (*chef de village*) of Niankite; at Niankite, August 7, 1961.)[4]

1. *Karamɔ manurεgum   jɔŋɔjɔŋɔr, buñansaŋ bati kunifan niñesε ri*
   teacher what you said is good   „   of elders I look and
   bɔ ɔɔεε, mɔbεmi   uraampεnɔm.
   it   that's why you help me.
   Teacher, what you said is good, it is the elder's *buñansaŋ* that I am always looking for, and that is why you help me.

2. *ɔε Wεnεŋa, ulɔka ɔ   bilen.*
   W.   we cry him last time.
   Wεnεŋa, we cry for him for the last time.

3. *Jikuŋgo, taŋ siñayɔ   bεy   sijε?   simama*
   J.   and mothers his where? they go they left for
   kumandiŋay.
   Manding country.
   Jikuŋgo, where have his mothers gone? They have gone off to Manding country.

4. *kuriŋul   man fɔk   εban.*
   they arrive hither and burial finish.
   They arrive here and the burial is over.

5. *kulinten   kapɔr kujum, Jɔinɔ,   egutum   εju   εmuruutεn.*
   they dance dust stops   big man vulture sees smiles.
   They dance and the dust rises, Big man, the vulture sees this and smiles.

1. Refers to the previous singer, who was an elder. The word *karamɔ* is a term of respect borrowed from Manding (cf. *kara-mòrò*, 'one who can read, who knows the Koran by heart'[5]). The phrase: *karamɔ manurεgum jɔŋɔjɔŋɔr* is very frequently used as an initial call.

2. *Wεnεŋa* was the deceased for whom the sing was being performed. *-lɔk* has the meaning 'to cry out (in full voice), wail' and here connotes singing (cf. also Kasa-Diola: *εlɔka* 'rooster').

3. *Jikuŋgo* is a general praise term and probably refers to the deceased. 'His mothers/mother's sisters', that is all female agnates of his mother (regardless of age) as well as his mother's brothers' wives. This group of kin have strong obligations to care for a sick, especially dying, sister's or husband's sister's child. They are also expected to attend his funeral.

4. The suffix *-ay* in *kumandiŋay* is an abstract marker and refers not only to the region and population of the Manding, but also to their way of life. This implies that they have become careless in fulfilling their traditional Diola obligations: they arrive after the burial, and this represents a general criticism of modern women and their mobility (cf. text III, below).

5. Emphasis shifts, for here they have arrived for the women's funeral dance, *kəlinten*, or *windiken*. They have come in great numbers, hence all the dust.

6. The vulture is associated with the *buñansaŋ* singers, for vultures are considered to be the original singers of the *buñansaŋ*, from whom the Diola learned the art. Great singers are said to transform themselves directly into vultures in order to perfect their singing abilities. The vulture and thus the singer smiles, for the dust implies the large crowd and hence the large number of cattle that are to be killed and eaten.

II. (Sung by Abdoulay Diongoume Djemé, Kagnarou; at Niankite, August 7, 1961.)

1. *gam   manutɛy.*
   judge so you may run.
   Judge so that you may go.
2. *Landiŋ umu manakanaam   falamat naŋaŋar ɛgundakɛy yɛti*
   L.   this and he did me silly act he took A's apple of
   yɔn   aja   fumat sịbe.
   crocodile he went herd cows.
   This Landing here did me a silly thing, he took the Adam's apple of a crocodile and went off to herd cows.
3. *Jịriyon nəgolụm   di (aim)ban.*
   J.   he depends on whom?
   On whom does *Jịriyon* depend?
4. *kubujɔ   kunɔnɔmɔr   kuŋar   ɛjawɔ.*
   they kill him they have greasy hands they take walk his.
   They killed him, their hands became greasy, they took his walk.
5. *Gəngụn,   ka(t) bəlamụk naŋɔɔlɛn.*
   good man leave back   he is able.
   Good man, he is able to turn (his) back.

   1. You, the deceased, judge, give an opinion, tell us the cause of your death; then you may leave, run (from this life). The dying may, if the cause of their illness is witchcraft, reveal the source before death. The Diola also, though infrequently in the Fogny, question a corpse before it is buried.

   2. Landing is the deceased. 'If you die and you leave me crying, you have done a silly thing' (cf. 5 below). The translation of the rest of this call follows the text with the 'he' of *naŋaŋar* referring back to Landing. The explanation (given by the singer) has it otherwise: '(if you die) I will say that you father's father has come and taken you, a crocodile (strong man), by the Adam's apple and has lead you off to herd his cattle': Death, it is said, is situated in the Adam's apple. The dead (*kati tɛntam* 'those of below') live as people do on earth and like the living they have cattle. When they are in need of a herdsman they will take one of their living agnates. When a man dies he becomes a young boy in the 'underworld' where, as in the world of the living, it is usually the youths who do the herding. With this explanation (which fits the Diola's notion of death) the 'he' becomes a deceased ancestor and the 'crocodile' refers to Landing.

   3. *Jịri yon* refers back to Landing. The call is rhetorical and implies that Landing has no need to depend on anyone (cf. 4) for he is a strong and rich man.

   4. They, Landing's kin, kill him in order to take his goods, wives, cattle, etc. As it was explained: 'If you happen to have a wife, or wives; we will look at you and have desire for them. We will kill you and people will say that perhaps we took your wives, and if we did, won't we take your manner of walking (of living), the way it was? The verb *kanɔnɔmɔr* may be translated 'to get hands greasy, stained with grease'. The grease is wasted, for once it has been smeared on the hands or spilt into the fire it cannot be eaten. The person killed is likened to this wasted grease. Thus to kill a rich man is wasteful, for if he is dead, on whom is one to depend? (cf. 3). (The allusion here is not very different from that of the Western proverb about the Goose and the Golden Eggs.)

5. A very common *buj* call. Like 2 it reprimands Landing (here *Gəngua*) for dying: 'You really are someone exceptional if you can turn your back like this on your kin and your responsibilities! (cf. the common call: *nɛn nimanjɛɛn lɛtuwɔɔgal* 'if I had known (that you were to die and leave me crying) we wouldn't have been kin (i.e. I would have renounced kinship with you)'.

III. (Sung by Souleymane Agnara Djemé of Djilakunda; at Djireme, July 26, 1965.)

1. *manjiyabɛn   nɛn jikolikoli.*
   and you take as   you afraid.
   And you sing the chorus as if you were afraid.
2. *muyul jimanjut   kunarak   kati iñe, kulalañ   siganar*
   you you know not women the of now they become crows
   iñɛ kumamal   bɛ tilibɔ.
   now they left for to 'east'.
   Don't you know the women of today? They've now become crows and have gone off to the east.
3. *daru   bɔbu kufəlumək   wɔ-wɔ-wɔ ɛjaw sɛnɛgal,*
   other little there old women the   go S.
   (w)amban bɛ kanɔ   uyəməjut.
   why?   to put on brassieres.
   The old women, w-o-o-o!, have gone off to Sénégal. Why? In order to put on brassieres.
4. *imanjut   urɛmpunəw   utɛy kabuŋɔ*
   I don't know one with little hair runs hairdressing.
   I don't know, but the one with hardly any hair goes for hairdressing.
5. *ajanɛni   nɛn kawɔnk ebeo.*
   he made known as call   cow his.
   He, like his cow's call, is heard about.
6. *jirigɔrajɛ   Fandiŋ kanɔkɛn nan di kɔ.*
   noise maker this F.   enter   he is and it.
   This noise maker, Fanding, is entering.
7. *bu narɛbɔ   ajanɔray.*
   how? he stops there who is known.
   How is it that he is so well known?

1. Refers to the ensemble. 'So you sing as if you were afraid. When you are singing and you are afraid of something you won't sing clearly. But if you sing without fear then you'll perform well.'

2. General comment on the mobility of women (cf. I above). The *siganar* is a white-necked pied-crow that, according to the Diola, leaves the Casamance for the north during the rains in order to eat fish' in the St. Louis area. It then returns south in November, for the peanuts. Thus the insult is addressed to the women who go away during the work period to eat and live better and who come back only when times are easy. Although things do not actually happen in quite this way, the *siganar* metaphor does express the common belief (especially among men) that the 'women of today' (the young women in particular) avoid many of their traditional obligations by migrating out for long periods of time. The actual tendency is for young unmarried girls to go north to the large cities of Bathurst, Kaolack and Dakar to seek work as maids, etc., returning home only

when absolutely necessary, as for funerals of kin and during the heaviest part of the work cycle. At marriage this 'going and coming' usually stops, when the girls settle down. There are, however, notable and much talked about exceptions. For *tilibɔ* cf. Manding *tele-bò* 'sun come out' (Delafosse, 1955).

3. The attack on women's mobility becomes particularly pointed with the incongruous and very humorous shift from *kunarak* 'women' to *kufɔlymɔk* 'old women'. What could be more absurd than old women with 'wrinkled dugs' hurrying off *w-o-o-o* (the sound of birds flying in a flock) to the big cities to put on one of the prize symbols of modern femininity: brassieres? (Sénégal here refers to the region north of the Gambia.) The phrase *daru bɔbu* 'other tiny little thing there' emphasizes this humorous shift from the very start. The *d-* class (restricted to a small circle of villages centered on Niankite) is an 'augmentive' diminutive and contrasts with the standard diminutive *ji-* (pl. *mu-*) class (contrast *jiliba* 'knife' with *diliba* 'pen-knife'). When it is applied to persons it becomes, as it is here, strongly pejorative, translating as something like 'puny', whereas the standard diminutive tends to be complimentary. (Contrast *dinarɛ* 'puny woman' with *jinarɛ* 'good little woman'.)

4. Though Añara uses this call in other contexts as a general comment it does, by its very placement, refer to 'old women'. They, among women, are most likely to have lost their hair. Further, *kabuŋɔ* is a pan-Sénégal hair-style popular with 'modern women'. Thus the metaphor of old women acting like the young continues: they run off to be 'modern'.

5. (The calls 5–7 are general and do not refer to the main subject.) Each Diola cow has a name and (like each male Diola) a whistle-call (*kawɔnk*). The latter can be heard and recognized at a considerable distance. Like his cow's call the subject (here not identified) is heard (i.e. known) about at a distance. He is a troublemaker who causes gossip to spread beyond his immediate surroundings. Gossip is likened to the resounding of a cow's call, since both spread out in all directions. This call is a condensation of *utyngynɔw jiliba ajanɛn nɛn kawɔnk ebeo* 'short legged one tries (his) knife as his cow's call'. The metaphor becomes complex, for the verb *-janɛn* 'to try out, make known' has a precise meaning of 'trying out by tossing up and down' (as one would toss up and down a small bag of something to judge its weight). We now have a synaesthetic parallel: tossing the knife around is like the up and down melody of the cow's call. And both, one through gossip and the other through sound, are heard (about). Such a 'short legged one' fits a type of person who is bothersome to his kin. He is small and cowardly (he 'is not a complete person') but he nevertheless likes to pick fights with people, thereby forcing his kin ('the true men') to come to his aid, for he—when the chips are down—is unable to defend himself. One informant summed up the entire metaphor a little differently, but in the same vein: 'they talk of him the way he talks about his cow, they consider him no better than a cow'.

6. The extended version of 5 implies 6. 'Entering' here means 'being buried'. As Añara described it: 'Fanding of Téloum was killed with knives by the people of Téloum. (He was) a man, but he went to the ward which they call Bassene-Futa. There he followed (the occupants) with anger and they chopped him up till they killed him. Now it is this that the singers took: "you who were quick to get angry, now what? Today you are entering" '.

7. A common rhetorical *buj*.

CONCLUSION

Let me conclude by reiterating my initial remark about ethno-criticism. This preliminary description of the *buñansaŋ* is based on informant commentary. Although the 'grammatical' analysis of the mechanics goes considerably beyond what any informant suggested, it is nevertheless entirely dependent upon the Diola terms: *kit*, *sankɛn*, *buj* and *foñ*. Further, and perhaps more importantly, the informants' insistence that the success of the songs rests primarily on the soloist's ability to control the 'onward flow of the singing' provides a criterion for evaluating the entire corpus of recordings, something that would have otherwise been rather risky. There is good singing, and there is bad singing, and the native critic has indicated how the choices are to be made. This is equally true for voice clarity and versification, especially the latter. Verses call and describe people. Knowledge of this simple fact, a fact that is not at all immediately obvious to the outsider, makes it possible to unravel and to evaluate the structure of particular verses. As far as the textual exegesis is concerned, little can be said other than that without adequate native commentary all explication would have been, at best, trivial.

More generally, and as a final point, all ventures of this nature that endeavour to penetrate folklore material, especially 'verbal art', must actively create a dialogue between informant and investigator. This is not to say that any informant will do. Quite the contrary. The average Diola can no more explicate the nuances of the *buñansaŋ* than can the average college student the nuances of English poetry (cf. I. A. Richard's *Practical Criticism* for that!). However, there are those who can, and in the case of the Diola it proved to be the performers themselves. With other peoples and with other genres, the 'native critic' might not be among the performers but instead among interested bystanders, patrons or religious priests. Whoever he may be, it is the investigator's task to find him.

NOTES

1. An earlier draft of this paper was presented at the 1967 meeting of the African Studies Association in New York. For this present version I should like to thank Dr. Joel Sherzer for his help in working out the *buñansaŋ* 'grammar' and Mrs. Judith Irvine for transcribing the musical example. Excerpts of these songs can be heard on the Ethnic Folkways Library record FE 4323 (Folkways Records and Service Corp., New York, 1965), side two, Band 4–6.

   The 1960–61 field period was made possible by a grant from the West African Languages Survey and that of 1964–66 by Public Health Service fellowships 1-F2-MH-21, 745-01 and 5-F2-MH-21, 745-02 from the National Institute of Mental Health, Public Health Service. During my entire stay in Sénégal I worked under the local auspices of the Institut Fondamental d'Afrique Noire. Their kind welcome and continuous support is deeply appreciated.

2. Especially true for the *buñaasaŋ* and generally true for almost all other genres of Diola singing. For example, I completely failed to persuade Diola youths to sing wrestling songs out of season. The songs belong in context and to sing them at other times does not make sense.

3. Cf. N. Chomsky, *Syntactic Structures*, The Hague, 1957; E. Bach, *An Introduction to Transformational Grammars*, New York, 1964; and A. Koutsoudas, *Writing Transformational Grammars*, New York, 1966.

4. For a description of Diola-Fogny grammar and phonology cf. J. D. Sapir, *A Grammar of Diola-Fogny*, Cambridge, 1965 and 'Temps et Langage' (notes linguistiques par J. D. Sapir) in L. V. Thomas, 'Le Diola et le temps', *Bull. de l'I.F.A.N.*, série B, nos. 1–2, 1967, pp. 340–58.

5. Cf. M. Delafosse, *La Langue Mandingue*, II, Paris, 1955.

APPENDIX I: SONG STRUCTURE

Basic phrase structure:

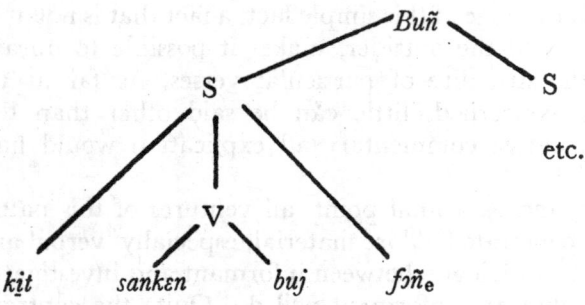

Type A:

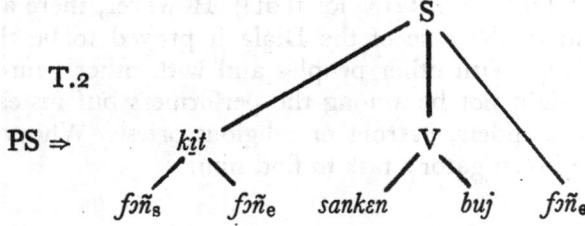

Type A':

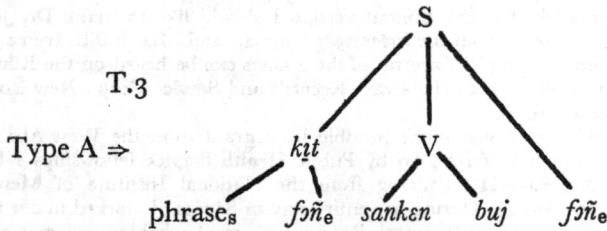

Type A' (Djakoye Banga variant):

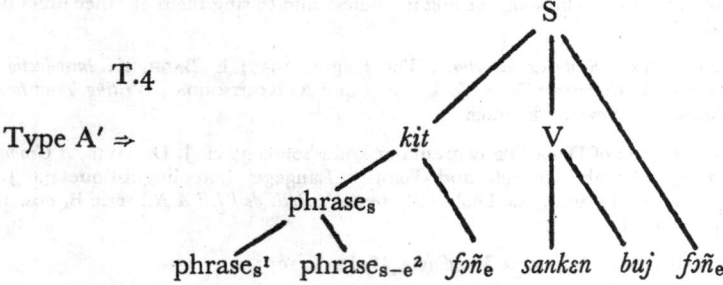

Type B:

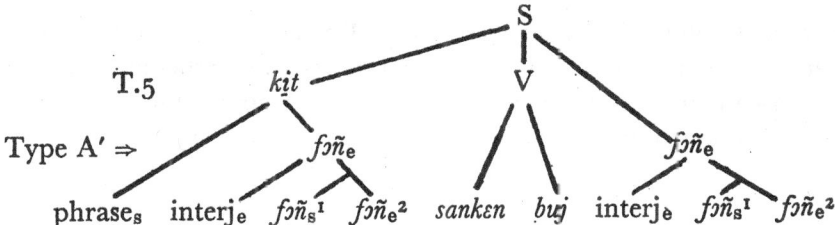

Type C:

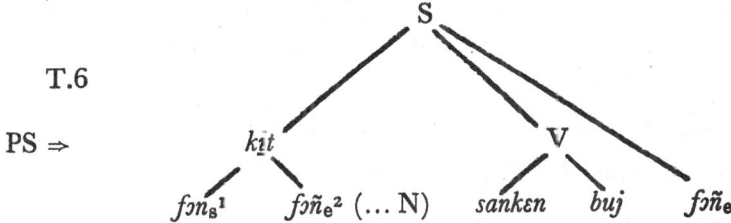

Types A, A', A' (Dj.B. variant)—T.1 performed:

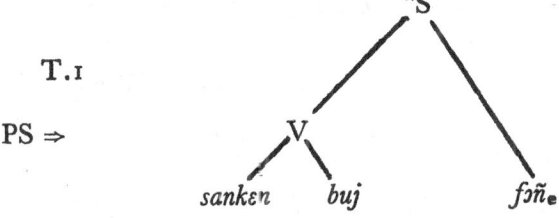

Type B—T.1 performed:

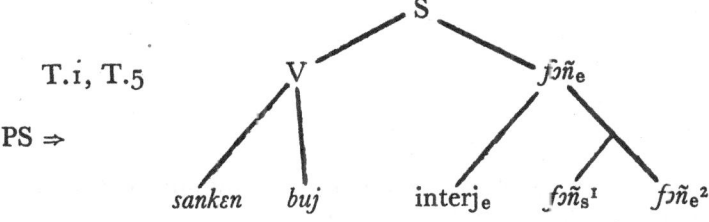

African Language Review 9, 1970

The next volume of African Language Review will contain a wide range of papers on cultural, historical and descriptive themes relating to African and Afro-American languages. Among almost twenty separate contributions will be the following:

Towards Comparative Edo by John Kelly

Future Prospects in Azayr Studies by H. T. Norris

Jukunoid Languages in the Polyglotta Africana—Part I, Eregba by Kiyoshi Shimuzu

Inalienable Possession in Swahili by Lyndon Harries

Mende and Maninka Tonal Correspondences by Richard A. Spears

African Language Material in Arabic Sources—The Case of Sonrai by J. O. Hunwick

Sonrai Relative Clauses by Martha B. Kendall

Problems of Toponymy in Post-Independence Africa by A. N. Tucker

Les Badiaranké et leur Environnement Linguistique by Gisèle Ducos

The Phonology of Mahas Nubian by Herman Bell

The Place of Africa and Afro-America in the History of the English Language by David Dalby

Some Applications to English Teaching of Current Research in Black American English by Burr Angle

Bedik and Binarity by N. V. Smith

Orders for African Language Review 9, and standing orders for subsequent volumes, should be directed to:

FRANK CASS & CO. LTD.,
67 Great Russell Street, London WC1B 3BT

La Langue Manjaku et l'Alternance Consonantique Initiale

J. L. DONEUX

Le Pr. J. H. Greenberg a récemment consacré un article, dans la *Language Review*,[1] à des phénomènes d'alternance consonantique initiale relevés dans la langue manjaku sur la *Polyglotta Africana* de Koelle.

J'avais évoqué rapidement ce même problème au Colloque de Linguistique d'Aix-en-Provence sur la Classification nominale dans les langues négro-africaines.[2]

Il n'est pas sûr que nous tenions, dans ces phénomènes d'alternance consonantique initiale dans les langues africaines une piste fructueuse de recherche. Il se peut qu'il y ait là un simple problème d'évolution intéressant plus les phonéticiens que les linguistes, problème d'ailleurs déjà largement étudié dans d'autres domaines linguistiques. Il se peut aussi, par contre, que des investigations précises sur ce sujet apportent quelques lumières intéressantes pour notre connaissance des langues africaines.

On verra suffisamment ici que mon hypothèse reconduit purement et simplement la position habituellement tenue voulant que l'alternance prend d'ordinaire sa source dans des évolutions phonétiques. Il n'empêche que, lorsqu'un phénomène d'alternance se généralise dans une langue, il peut amener des conséquences où la phonétique cesse d'être explicative. Des nivellements peuvent se produire qui atteindront finalement tous les thèmes; en outre, comme M.-P. Ferry l'a bien mis en relief dans sa thèse sur le bedik[3], l'alternance peut être soumise à des contextes grammaticaux très précis.

Il semble donc qu'une bonne connaissance de la genèse, de l'évolution, des aboutissements des phénomènes de mutation dans une zone linguistique donnée ne puisse qu'éclairer la recherche comparative, ne serait-ce que parce qu'actuellement des faits de mutation mal connus ou mal interprétés voilent provisoirement dans le domaine du lexique comme dans celui de la grammaire des reconstructions qui pourront s'avérer possibles lorsqu'une analyse plus précise du phénomène aura été faite.

L'intention de l'étude, trop rapide, qui suit est d'une part de livrer aux linguistes africanistes des éléments d'information sur les faits manjaku actuels, d'autre part d'attirer l'attention sur les possibilités d'une double réduction du phénomène d'alternance, réduction phonologique et réduction morpho-phonologique, dont la réussite est évidemment variable d'une langue à l'autre, mais qui a l'avantage, me semble-t-il, de mettre les linguistes comparatistes en face d'autres hypothèses que celle de l'alternance comme phénomène primaire dans un groupe donné.

1. LES DONNÉES DU DIALECTE BƆK

1.1. *Phonématique*. Pour élaborer, à partir du matériau phonétique recueilli, la phonématique des consonnes en bɔk, nous devons tenir compte des faits suivants:

1.1.1. Des paires oppositionnelles de morphèmes permettent d'établir sans grande difficulté l'existence des consonnes: m, n, ɲ, ŋ, b, d, j, g, p, t, ts, c, k, f, s, l. Selon qu'on est influencé par la linguistique américaine ou par les thèses du Pr. Martinet, on ajoutera ou non w, y.

1.1.2. Des séquences NC, dont le second élément est toujours une occlusive orale (y compris *ts*), se trouvent en grand nombre dans les thèmes substantifs à l'initiale ou à la finale d'une suite de type CVC, et dans les thèmes verbaux à la finale seule, si on prend comme référence la 3e p.s. d'un énonciatif: *a-tap* « il a piqué », mais **a-NCVC* est exclu.

Quelques exemples: *-mbaŋ* « coin »; *-ndiamt* « langue »; *-ɲjëk* « rat de forêt »; *-ŋgari* « fusil »; *-mpëli* « jeune fille »; *-ntɨŋ* « corne »; *-ɲcɛnc* « anneau »; *-ŋkuël* « crépuscule »; *-pamb* « pousser »; *-tsɛnd* « donner »; *-lɨɲj* « nase »; *-liŋg* « suffire »; *-lɛmp* « travail(ler) »; *-gɔnts* « silure »; *-tɛɲc* « eczéma »; *-lëŋk* « mur ».

A la seule lecture de ces exemples, on peut se rendre compte qu'il n'y a ni harmonisation ni assimilation consonantique entre C et C¹ du thème CVC¹. Il importe de remarquer en outre que l'ensemble des thèmes cités introduit la combinaison avec tous les préfixes de classes nominaux, exception faite des deux préfixes locatifs.

Poser ou non neuf phonèmes qui soient des occlusives prénasalisées dépend donc du choix du linguiste. En bɔk, une raison milite en faveur de l'interprétation biphonématique des séquences phoniques NC: les séquences homorganiques, dans la syntagmation des morphèmes, reproduisent exactement le comportement du phonème /n/ devant occlusive orale. Ceci demande explicitation.

Le phonème /n/ en finale CVC (ex: *-pën* « sortir de ») a les réalisations suivantes:

— En finale absolue, il est, selon les locuteurs, réalisé à l'ordinaire, ou implosé, ou supprimé, ou considéré comme réalisé par une légère nasalisation de la voyelle précédente (*apën, apëŋ, apë, apë˜*, « il est sorti »).

— Devant une voyelle, il est réalisé normalement (*apëni* « il est sorti de »).

— Devant une occlusive orale, il est homorganique (*apën takël* « il est sorti hier »; *apëm bu̧ts* « il est sorti aussi »; *apëŋ kak* « il est encore sorti »).

— Devant une nasale, une constrictive, une semi-voyelle il est supprimé (*ka pë fan* « il sortira demain »; *ka pë na pënak* « il sortira à midi »).

En résumé, le phonème /n/ n'apparaît, hors le cas de la finale absolue largement marquée par des variantes libres, que devant occlusive ou voyelle. Il est tronqué devant nasales, constrictives ou semi-voyelles. Les séquences NC à l'intérieur du corps du morphème présentent donc la même suite phonétique que /n/+occlusive dans un syntagme, il y a économie à définir toutes les séquences NC comme étant des séquences phonologiques /n/+/C/.

1.1.3. Une variante [r] du phonème /d/ se présente à l'intervocalique et en finale. La réalisation [d] se maintient à l'initiale absolue, à l'initiale d'un syntagme grammatical, après nasale homorganique, et en certains cas par emphase:

dɛɛn « mange », vs: a rɛ « il a mangé », vs: a dɛ mak! « il a mangé (vraiment) beaucoup »;

anɔr « il est fatigué »; rɐdɔ « tu as fait », vs: arɔ « il a fait ».

Il n'y a aucune amorce de disjonction en deux phonèmes de ces variantes combinatoires, pas même par l'introduction de termes étrangers, qui sont soumis à la réalisation phonétique du bɔk:

dapas « jeune homme » (créole: rapaz); kara « chaque » (créole: kada);

man tɛn dɛk « je regarde seulement » (wolof: rɛk), arɔ rɛk « il a fait seulement ».

1.1.4. En prononciation très relâchée, on peut saisir une ouverture des autres occlusives sonores à l'intervocalique et en finale: $b > v$; $j > dy$; $g > \gamma$. Mais le phénomène n'est que peu perceptible et se trouve loin d'être le fait de l'ensemble des locuteurs.

1.1.5. Il faut probablement établir un morpho-phonème /ɦ/, difficile à repérer dans la synchronie du bɔk, mais dont on ne peut guère se passer pour rendre compte de manière satisfaisante de certains faits de syntagmation. Ainsi, on a:

[bi̭:s] « nez », yi̭s « nez (pl.) »; [pi̭ël] « sein ».

On peut considérer toute suite ië, iä, uë, uä comme réalisations de i̭:, i:, ṷ:, u:, ou de i̭+i̭, etc. ... Dès lors, si [bi̭:s] est à la rigueur explicable comme |bë-i̭s| > [bi:s], il n'en est pas de même du pluriel, qui devrait être |i-i̭s| > [yës]. La solution paraît se trouver dans la restitution des formes de base suivantes:

|bë-ɦi̭s, i-ɦi̭s| « nez », |pë-i̭:l| « sein ».

1.1.6. En fonction de ces faits, on peut tenter de donner pour le système consonantique du bɔk le tableau suivant:

m	n	ɲ	ŋ
b	d(r)	j	g
p	t	c	k
	ts		
f	s		
	l		ɦ
w		y	

Note : suivant la tolérance de l'I.A.I., nous continuerons dans la suite de cet article à employer *d* et *r* selon leur apparition comme variantes combinatoires.

1.2. *Morpho-phonologie.* Le système phonématique retenu ci-dessus paraît avoir valeur opératoire dans la chaîne de l'énoncé, à condition d'introduire les deux règles de morpho-phonologie suivantes :

1.2.1. Un morphème *m*V qui est outil grammatical est représenté par *m*V*n* devant les occlusives orales. Cette règle explique clairement deux cas de syntagmation dans le système verbal et suffisamment les représentations diverses de la 1e p.s. des indépendantes affirmatives.

1.2.2. Un morphème outil grammatical (1e p.s. négatif) qui est zéro ou *i̧-*, selon le jeu des aspects verbaux, devant nasales, constrictives, semi-voyelles est représenté par *n-* ou *i̧n-* devant occlusives.

1.3. *Le bɔk et l'alternance consonantique.* En présentant le système phonématique complété de ces deux règles de morpho-phonologie on propose donc un traitement du bɔk qui ne fait nulle part appel à l'alternance consonantique initiale. Mais est-ce à raison ? Certains faits pouvaient en effet inciter à traiter le dialecte en termes d'alternances.

1.3.1. La présence dans les thèmes nominaux de séquences NCV(N)C. Le bɔk comportant des préfixes de classes, on aurait pu, en recourant par exemple à la dérivation, tenter de définir des classes préfixielles différentes, selon que le préfixe nominal est suivi d'une occlusive ou d'une prénasalisée; ainsi pouvait-on espérer obtenir un système d'alternances à deux degrés (occlusives, prénasalisées).

Mais, d'une part cela équivaudrait à multiplier par deux l'ensemble des classes nominales du bɔk, car les thèmes des deux types CVC et NVCV se trouvent liés à toutes et chacune des classes, locatifs exceptés :

	degré d'occlusive	*degré de prénasalisée*
cl. 1.	*na-tiëm* « gd-parent »	*na-~pëli* « jeune filles »
2.	*ba-tiëm* « gds-parents »	*ba-~pëli* « jeunes filles »
3.	*u-jëku* « perdrix »	*u-~jëk* « rat de forêt »
4.	*ngë-pi* « chèvres »	*ngë-~kämbɛ* « porcs »
5.	*bë-cäm* « palmier »	*bë-~tiën* « caïlcédrat »
6.	*m-dungël* « baobabs »	*m-~tiën* « caïlcédrats »
7.	*ka-bats* « oreille »	*ka-~baŋ* « coin »
8.	*i̧-bats* « oreilles »	*i̧-~baŋ* « coins »
9.	*pë-kës* « œil »	*pë-~tiŋ* « corne »
10.	*kë-kës* « yeux »	*kë-~tiŋ* « qqs cornes »
11.	*ndë-kɔ* « machin »	*ndë-~pëli* « gamine »

(Le système des classes nominales du bɔk se trouve ici simplifié, l'échantillon étant suffisamment représentatif pour les points qui nous préoccupent. Dans la suite du texte, les chiffres accompagnant un thème lexical renvoient à l'indice de classe tel qu'il est noté ci-dessus.)

D'autre part, si on compare ces thèmes nominaux aux thèmes nomino-verbaux, on fait une double constatation :

a) La plupart de ces thèmes nominaux n'ont pas de correspondant sémantique repérable dans les thèmes nomino-verbaux. De tous les thèmes cités ci-dessus, aucun ne paraît lié à un thème verbal soit similaire, soit décelable en évoquant les alternances consonantiques les plus diverses (*nd/d*; *nd/t*; *nd/l*, etc. ...). Ceci, à l'exception de -*kës* 9,10 « œil » qu'on pourrait rapprocher du verbe -*kës* « suffire », avec un peu d'imagination sémantique.

b) Par contre, certains thèmes nominaux sont manifestement liés à des thèmes conjugables, soit qu'ils en dérivent par le jeu du préfixe, soit qu'en outre ils requièrent l'intervention du suffixe substantivant -*i* :

-*lɛmp* « travailler »   -*lɛmp* 3,4 « travail »
-*tsuär* « s'asseoir »   -*tsuär-i* 9,8 « siège »

Or, dans cette dérivation nominale à partir d'un thème verbal, il y a parfois apparition d'une nasale homorganique à l'initiale du thème. Mais dans l'état actuel de mes recherches je ne trouve aucune règle apparente permettant de prédire le comportement du thème. Ce n'est ni le préfixe nominal, ni la consonne initiale du thème, ni l'intervention du suffixe -*i* qui expliquent l'apparition de cette nasale :

-*rɛ* « manger »   -*rɛ* 9 « nourriture »
-*rjts* « être lourd »   -*ndjts* 9 « charge »
-*tɔr* « verser »   -*tɔr-i* 7 « entonnoir »
-*tan* « se ceindre »   -*ntan-i* 7 « boucle à grimper »

Si enfin on considère la permutation des préfixes de classes devant le thème nominal, on notera deux faits :

a) L'appariement singulier/pluriel ne détermine jamais de changement à l'initiale du thème. Si l'on a, comme c'est le cas, *na-mpëli* « jeune fille », au singulier, on aura *ba-mpëli* au pluriel. Une mutation du type *ba-pëli est introuvable.

b) Par contre, dans une permutation qu'on pourrait appeler de dérivation, un cas unique a été relevé dans l'ensemble du lexique disponible dans mes documents :

   ba-tsiën 5a « navire »   *ka-ntsiën* 7 « navette de tisserand »

c) Enfin, on notera l'alternance *r/d* : *bë-rungël* « baobab », *m-dungël* « pain de singe, baobabs »; mais la solution est de l'ordre de la phonologie combinatoire (1.1.3).

1.3.2. Les paradigmes verbaux. Il apparaît, dès les premières informations fournies par l'enquête, qu'il serait tentant de les traiter en termes d'alternances consonantiques. Faisant permuter aux personnes un verbe comme dɔ « faire », on obtient le paradigme suivant:

[mandɔ] « j'ai fait », [mdɔ] « tu as fait », [arɔ] « il a fait ».

Apparemment, on trouverait une formulation très satisfaisante de la valeur des éléments de ce paradigme en dégageant: ma- « 1e p.s. »; m- « 2e p.s. »; a- « 3e p.s. », et nd/d/r « alternance initiale au thème ». Prenons le verbe -gac « vomir ». Nous obtenons:

[mangac] « j'ai vomi », [mgac] « tu as vomi », [agac] « il a vomi ».

Le degré constrictif de l'alternance disparaît, et nous sommes ramenés pour le cas précédent à la règle de combinatoire énoncée plus haut pour le seul phonème /d ~ r/.

Il paraît donc pertinent de se demander si l'élément « 1e p.s. » est bien /ma/ et non /man/, qu'on attribue à cette seconde forme une valeur purement phonologique, ou un caractère de représentation morpho-phonologique. Etablissons encore un paradigme:

mangac « j'ai vomi » -gac; manɔr « je suis fatigué » -nɔr; mafal « j'ai coupé » -fal; mawaap « j'ai acheté » -waap; mayɔr « j'ai avalé » -yɔr; mañi̯s « j'ai partagé » -ñi̯s [i̯s].

Donc, devant nasale, constrictive, glide l'élément nasal présent devant une occlusive orale disparaît. Le dernier item pose un problème: on a dit plus haut que /n/ est représenté devant une voyelle. Il faut donc discuter toute solution en tenant compte de ce cas.

Il y a deux solutions possibles. Ou bien on donne /ma/ comme thème « 1e p.s. » et l'apparition du segment N comme un phénomène morpho-phonologique. Dans ce cas, on peut admettre ma i̯s « j'ai partagé ». Cette solution serait hasardeuse si le phénomène était isolé dans la grammaire du bɔk. Il ne l'est pas. Dans une construction conditionnelle, on constate l'apparition claire du phénomène $mV > mVn$:

na rɔts tsëp « s'il n'était pas parti (cl. 1) »
ba rɔts yër « s'ils n'étaient pas tombés (cl. 2) »
ba rɔts yër « s'il n'était pas tombé, arbre (cl. 5) »
vs: mandɔts yër « s'ils n'étaient pas tombés, arbres, (cl. 6) »

On voit qu'il y a également apparition du segment nasal après et seulement après un élément mV, la classe 1 montrant qu'on ne peut étendre la règle à un élément NV. C'est la justification, avec d'autres cas sur lesquels on ne s'attardera pas ici, de la règle donnée plus haut en 1.2.1. Il s'agit d'une règle de morpho-phonologie, non de phonologie, car dans les thèmes lexicaux, on trouve des séquences mV : -mɛ « savoir »; -muä « os ».

La seconde solution consisterait à admettre /man/ comme thème de « 1e p.s. ». Dans ce cas, il faut décider qu'il n'y a pas de verbe à structure VC, car on n'a jamais : man VC. Ici encore la décision peut paraître audacieuse, bien qu'elle trouve sa justification dans une phonématique du bɔk admettant un /ɦ/ et dans la comparative dialectale où apparaît un /h/ sourd à l'initiale des verbes. Si elle est admise, la forme /maɦi̯s/ s'explique par le comportement de /n/ devant les glides.

Cette position une fois prise, qui consiste à réduire l'alternance consonantique dans le système verbal comme dans le système nominal, devra être poussée jusqu'à ses dernières conséquences. Elle implique, par exemple, qu'on traite la 1e p.s. dans la construction conditionnelle ci-dessus comme étant représentée par /n/ : (uci) n dɔts « si je ne fais pas »; elle implique aussi qu'on définisse l'élément relatif comme /n/ : wëli̯n ka n ci ki di p̈ɛtsɛfi « donne-moi celle (ka-rafi 7 « bouteille ») qui est sur le siège ».

1.4. En conclusion, il semble bien que, dans la description phonologique et morpho-phonologique du bɔk, on puisse faire l'économie d'un appel à l'alternance consonantique mais, on doit le reconnaître, en admettant un double résidu : dans la dérivation de rares substantifs à partir d'un thème verbal (ri̯ts/ndi̯ts) et dans la permutation aux préfixes d'au moins un thème substantif (-tsiën/-ntsiën). Il faut remarquer que l'alternance consonantique latente est entre occlusive et prénasalisée.

S'agissant ensuite de questions comparatives et diachroniques, on s'attardera au fait de la présence massive en bɔk de thèmes nominaux présentant une structure NCVC.

2. LES FAITS DANS LE DIALECTE CUR[4]

2.1. *Phonématique.* On peut proposer pour le cur le tableau phonologique suivant, comparativement au dialecte bɔk :

2.1.1. Le phonème /ts/ a une variante [h] à l'initiale, à l'intervocalique, en finale après voyelle. En fait, la réalisation [ts] n'est plus assurée qu'avec prénasalisation.

2.1.2. Le (morpho-)phonème /ɦ/ du bɔk est ici une sourde. Il y a donc équivalence avec la réalisation du phonème /ts ~ h/, mais une étude précise, encore à faire, montrerait sans doute qu'il faut, même au plan synchronique, distinguer en cur h_1 et h_2.

2.1.3. Excepté, semble-t-il, à l'initiale absolue, une variante combinatoire des occlusives sonores apparaît en toute autre position que post-nasale : *v, r, z̧, γ*. En bɔk, on l'a indiqué, ceci n'est possible qu'en discours très relâché. En cur, il s'agit d'une habitude articulatoire qui a un caractère contraignant pour les locuteurs.

2.1.4. Le phonème /m/ est homorganique devant toute consonne, tout comme /n/ l'est en bɔk devant les seules occlusives orales. Les deux autres nasales, /ɲ/ et /ŋ/ résistent mieux mais certains locuteurs tendent à les réaliser également homorganiques.

2.2. *Le cur et l'alternance consonantique.* Abordons à partir de quelques paradigmes la possibilité de contrôler des phénomènes d'alternances en cur, en prenant le passé affirmatif indépendant aux trois personnes du singulier de quelques verbes, et en y adjoignant l'impératif affirmatif de deuxième personne du singulier:

-bandi « arriver »: 1. *mambandi*, 2. *mbandi*, 3. *avandi*, imp. *bandi*.
-pĕni « sortir de »: 1. *mampĕni*, 2. *mpĕni*, 3. *apĕni*, imp. *pĕni*.
-dɔ « faire »: 1. *mandɔ*, 2. *ndɔ*, 3. *arɔ*, imp. *dɔl-an* (irrég.).
-tɛ « entendre »: 1. *mantɛ*, 2. *ntɛ*, 3. *atɛ*, imp. *tɛ-an* > *tɛɛn*.
-jɔn « durer »: 1. *maɲjɔn*, 2. *ɲjɔn*, 3. *aʑɔn*, 4. *jɔn-an*.
-cisa « être pressé »: 1. *maɲcisa*, 2. *ɲcisa*, 3. *acisa*, imp. *cisa-an*.
-gac « vomir »: 1. *maŋgac*, 2. *ŋgac*, 3. *aɣac*, imp. *gac-an*.
-ka « avoir »: 1. *maŋka*, 2. *ŋka*, 3. *aka*, imp. *ka-an*.
-fal « couper »: 1. *ma~fal*, 2. *~fal*, 3. *afal*, imp. *fal-an*.
-hĕp « partir »: 1. *mantsĕp/ma~hĕp*, 2. *ntsĕp*, 3. *ahĕp*, imp. *hĕp-an*.
-sis « rentrer chez soi »: 1. *mantsis/ma~sis*, 2. *ntsis*, 3. *asis*, imp. *sis-an*.
-lilan « être content »: 1. *ma~lilan*, 2. *nilan*, 3. *alilan*, imp. *lilan-an*.

Si l'on veut bien oublier un moment les indications données plus haut sur la phonologie du cur, on est immédiatement tenté de définir à partir de ces paradigmes un complexe d'alternances consonantiques à trois degrés:

3.	~b	~d	~j	~g	~p	~t	~c	~k	~f	~ts	~ts	~l, n
2.	b	d	j	g	p	t	c	k	f	s	h	l
1.	v	r	ʑ	ɣ	p	t	c	k	f	s	h	l

Le degré 1 est présent à la 3e p.s., le degré 2 à l'impératif, le degré 3 aux 1e et 2e p.s. Sauf dans la dernière case, au degré 3, les nasales simples ne sont pas représentées dans ce tableau.

Il faut cependant examiner l'ensemble point par point. Ma position est que le phénomène d'alternance, ici comme en bɔk est réductible par un double appel à la phonologie et à la morpho-phonologie. Traiter le dialecte en termes d'alternances ne serait probablement pas contradictoire, mais plus dispendieux que le traitement que je préconise.

2.2.1. *Les réalisations occlusives et constrictives sonores.* Alors qu'en dialecte bɔk seul le phonème /d/ a une variante essentiellement combinatoire [r], on a vu qu'en cur la variante constrictive est combinatoire pour chacune des consonnes sonores. Il n'y a pas d'alternance consonantique articulable sur le fait qu'à un phonème constrictif on puisse opposer, pour un autre thème, un phonème occlusif (type: *vuk « mortier » vs.* buk « champ ») tandis que certains thèmes comporteraient à l'initiale tantôt la constrictive, tantôt l'occlusive (type: *vak « il marcha » vs. *bak « il marche »). Or, ce test me paraît constituer la pierre de touche d'une alternance consonantique non réductible phonologiquement.

2.2.2. La série des occlusives sourdes ne manifeste que deux degrés apparents d'alternance. En cur comme en bok, il n'y a pas relâchement des occlusives sourdes en certains contextes et ce, probablement, parce qu'il s'agit de parlers où une série de phonèmes constrictifs sourds s'oppose aux occlusives sourdes, interdisant leur relâchement (p et f restent bien distincts).

2.2.3. C'est la série où le degré 1 est représenté par des constrictives sourdes qui présente le profil le plus tourmenté. Il faut l'examiner en détail :

- a) $f/f/\sim f$. On aurait pu s'attendre à $f/p/\sim p$. On en est loin : il y a apparition d'une prénasalisation du /f/ au seul degré 3. La solution peut être fournie par la morpho-phonologie : la loi du bok ($mV > mV\tilde{~}$) joue aussi en cur, et même devant constrictive. On posera donc comme forme de base : |man fal|, ou |ma fal| +intervention de la règle : man fal.

- b) $s/s/\sim ts$. Cas intéressant. Cependant, ne nous laissons pas influencer par un exemple unique, et alignons un autre paradigme face à celui qui a été découvert (-sis) :

    ma~sac « j'ai fixé », nsac « tu as fixé », asac « il a fixé », sacan « fixe ! »

    Face à des verbes qui présentent à la 2e p.s. (plus intéressante à retenir que la 1e p.s. car elle n'admet pas de variante libre) une initiale [~ts], nous en trouvons d'autres qui présentent [~s]. La solution dépend d'un examen recouvrant également les cas suivants.

- c) $h/h/\sim ts$. Ici aussi, on peut tenter la contre-épreuve d'un autre paradigme (face à -hëp) :

    ma~hɛp « j'ai demandé », ntsɛp « tu as demandé », ahɛp « il a demandé », ɑɛpan « demande ! »

- d) $l/l/n$. Représentation curieuse. Nous l'examinerons plus bas. Il faut dire tout de suite qu'on ne peut lui opposer comme paradigme que celui d'un verbe à initiale /n/ inaltérable :

    ma nɔr « je suis fatigué », n nɔr « tu es fatigué », anɔr « il est fatigué », nɔran « sois fatigué (inus.) ».

Peut-on proposer pour ces faits une explication qui fasse l'économie de l'alternance consonantique ? Il semble que oui, et il semble qu'un examen attentif du dialecte nous achemine nécessairement vers cette explication.

2.2.4. S'il existe des verbes qui présentent une alternance phonique *s*/*s*/~*s* face à d'autres qui comportent *s*/*s*/~*ts*, c'est parce que la forme de base n'est pas la même. Si l'on propose |*sac*| pour « fixer », on peut donner pour la 1e p.s. la même réponse que plus haut pour *f*/*f*/~*f*, et pour la 2e p.s. dire qu'il y a prénasalisation parce que le thème verbal est précédé du morphème |*m*| « tu », et que le /*m*/ est homorganique en cur.

Si on propose |*tsis*| pour « rentrer », il faut expliquer /*sis*/ à l'impératif et à la 3e p.s.; on attendrait en effet [*his*] puisque c'est la variante combinatoire dans ces positions de /*ts* ~ *h*/. Cependant l'existence d'au moins un autre verbe présentant le même paradigme: *mantsas*, *asas* « je cherche, il cherche » permet d'énoncer la règle suivante: il y a assimilation régressive de /*ts*/ par /*s*/ lorsque /*ts*/ n'est pas préservé par une nasale antécédente. (Des règles similaires pourraient être posées pour quelques éléments du lexique nomino-verbal en cur. Il faut attendre une documentation très large sur la langue pour voir se profiler une règle générale. A titre d'indication, on notera la correspondance bɔk *a-suëts*, cur *a-huuh* « il est rassasié », et le maintien en cur de *a-tsiats* « il a emprunté » qui permettent d'envisager la piste pour l'énoncé de cette règle).

Une fois ceci admis, la forme [~*tsis*] s'explique comme |*m-tsis*|, avec une application de règles identiques à celles données pour -*fal* et -*sac*; quant aux deux formes en variantes libres, [*mantsis*] et [*ma*~*sis*], elles s'expliquent l'une et l'autre au mieux à partir de la règle morpho-phonologique déjà évoquée; pour [*ma*~*tsis*], il y a application de la nasalisation sur la forme |*tsis*|, et l'initiale est considérée comme apparition normale de la variante combinatoire après nasale, tandis que pour [*ma*~*sis*], il y a application de la nasale sur la forme reprise à l'intervocalique suivant la règle *ts* — *s* > *s* — *s*.

2.2.5. Examen de l'alternance apparente *h*/*h*/~*ts*. Pour le paradigme de -*hëp*, nous posons une forme de base |*tsëp*|. Les formes /*hëpan*/ et /*ahëp*/ s'expliquent par la phonologie de /*ts*/. La forme [~*tsëp*] doit être reconstruite comme |*m-tsëp*|, avec application de la règle de phonologie de /*m*/ homorganique. Les variantes [*mantsëp*] et [*ma*~*hëp*] s'analysent comme les variantes similaires de [~*tsis*], avec la différence que dans la forme 2 ci-dessus la règle particulière *ts* — *s* > *s* — *s* ne joue évidemment pas, et c'est [*h*] qui est conservé.

Face à ce paradigme se trouve celui de -*hɛp*. Il n'y a pas de variante *[*mantsɛp*] admise pour la 1e p.s. La raison en est que nous avons ici le phonème h_2 (cf. 2.1.2). La comparative éclaire le fait:

	bɔk		cur
	tsëp	« partir »	*tsëp*, *hëp*
	ɦɛp	« demander »	*tsɛp*, *hɛp*

Dès lors, nous donnerons comme forme de base |*hɛp*|. La forme [*ahɛp*] s'impose sans examen. La forme [~*tsɛp*] s'explique si nous posons comme règle phonologique: « il y a neutralisation des phonèmes /ts ~ h/ et h_2 après nasale au profit de [ts]. La forme [ma~hɛp] se comprend et ne se comprend bien que si l'élément nasal devant h n'est pas phonologique, mais morpho-phonologique. S'il était phonologique, il détermineirait obligatoirement [mantsɛp]. Etant encore senti en cur comme représentation morpho-phonologique de |ma|, il détermine un régime différent de celui qu'impose |m| de 2e p.s. Il faut dire brièvement que tous les cas d'initiale verbale où [h] initial du cur correspond à /ñ/ du bɔk, et non à /ts/, fonctionnent sur ce modèle.

2.2.6. Le groupe l/i,'n. Ce n'est pas une alternance. C'est l'application de deux règles phonologiques du cur. La première est déjà connue: /m/ est homorganique (donc ici: $m-l > n+l$); la seconde dira: $n+l > n$. On peut vérifier qu'on n'introduit pas une règle particulière pour les besoins de la cause (éviter le recours à un système d'alternances) en recourant à un paradigme. Le préfixe de classe 6 en cur a comme forme de base |m|. Le phonème /m/ étant homorganique devant toutes consonnes, on ne peut y contrôler le niveau d'articulation de ce préfixe nasal. Mais devant les voyelles, la forme de base apparaît:

m-iil 6 « seins »; *m-ɔm* 6 « cadavres ».

La règle ici relevée à propos des thèmes verbaux se trouve donc aussi applicable à des thèmes nominaux:

pë-lik 9 « puits », *m-lik* 6 « eau » $>nik$.

Une confirmation supplémentaire serait donnée par l'accord au démonstratif: *nik mini* « cette eau-ci »; *nir mumun* « voilà de la graisse là ». On peut donc reconstruire: $nilan < |m\text{-}lilan|$.

2.3. On peut donc en cur faire l'économie d'un traitement par alternances consonantiques, en faisant jouer les règles suivantes:

a) *règles phonologiques :*
— /m/ et /n/ ont des réalisations homorganiques devant consonnes.
— il faut poser un phonème /ts ~ h/ et un phonème /h ~ ts/.
— occlusives sonores et constrictives sonores sont des variantes combinatoires.

b) *règles morpho-phonologiques :*
— une séquence nasale+constrictive ne se présentant pas dans le corps d'un morphème, une règle dira que pour certains éléments grammaticaux, il y a maintien du segment nasal.
— une règle différente dira que *m*V outil grammatical est représenté par *m*VN (et non *m*V*n*, comme en bɔk) devant toute consonne.

Apparemment, cela fait beaucoup de règles à intégrer pour dévoiler le système. Mais une analyse en termes d'alternances aurait le désavantage de ne pas rendre compte du système, car elle devrait expliquer:

— pourquoi *asis* ne commute pas comme *asac*, ni *ahëp* comme *ahɛp*.
— pourquoi on admet trois degrés d'alternances, alors qu'on ne peut en cur opposer par paires minimales les constrictives et les occlusives.

3. QUELQUES FAITS DE LA LANGUE PƐPƐL

La langue pɛpɛl appartient à l'ensemble *Manjaku. Il n'y a plus aujourd'hui intercompréhension entre ses locuteurs et les Manjaku, peut-être pour des raisons qui tiennent plus à l'ethnologie qu'a la linguistique, car il y a moins d'écarts entre le pɛpɛl et un dialecte manjaku tel que le yu qu'entre le cur et le bɔk, dont les locuteurs se « comprennent ».

Contrairement aux deux dialectes précédents, je ne peux proposer pour le pɛpɛl d'évaluation d'ensemble de la phonématique, et me bornerai donc à souligner certains faits.

3.1. *Les rapports occlusives/prénasalisées*. En premier lieu, il apparaît qu'en pɛpɛl comme en bɔk ou en cur un thème nominal possède une initiale inaltérable. L'omniclasse « petit », à thème *-ntiëk* en fournit une bonne illustration:

nimpili a-ntiëk 1 « une petite jeune fille », *butiëm bu-ntiëk* 5 « un petit caïlcédrat », *muntiëm mu-ntiëk* 6 « des petits caïlcédrats ».

Quelle que soit la classe, le thème est invariable. La règle de morphophonologie qui fonctionne en bɔk et en cur doit être élargie: dans les outils grammaticaux, toute séquence NV, toute nasale deviennent NVN devant une consonne, à l'exception de la liquide:

pɛpɛl		bɔk
num-buur̥s	« pêcheur »	*na-buëts* 1
nun-kiiga	« voleur »	*na-kiëj* 1
ŋën-sar̥sa	« singes »	*ngë-catsa* 4
ŋën-fɔnts	« tortues »	*ngë-fɔnts* 4
muŋ-kiɛm	« palmiers »	*m-cäm* 6
mun-tum	« bouche »	*m-tum* 6

Ceci provoque deux représentations différentes de ces préfixes de classes à nasale, devant consonne d'une part, devant voyelle et liquide de l'autre:

pɛpɛl
nuŋ-gɔ:ŋar 1 « chasseur », *n-lir* 1 « tisserand ».
ŋëm-pulɔ 4 « serpents », *ŋ-lala* 4 « araignées », *ŋ-iit* 4 « vaches ».
mun-tɔu 6 « lait », *m-iila* 6 « seins ».

J. H. Greenberg dans son article cité semble s'y être trompé, qui dit: 'that it is not merely that the prefix is *nun*- can be seen from such instances as Sarar *pi:al/mi:al* "breast" in which *n* does not occur ». Evidemment, la règle morpho-phonologique ne peut apparaître qu'après un examen minutieux de l'ensemble de la grammaire manjaku, mais ceci acquis, il est difficile de prétendre que l'élément nasal appartient au thème nominal et non au préfixe de classe. On pourrait vouloir à tout prix obtenir des alternances au thème, mais en pepel comme en bɔk, cela reviendrait à dédoubler toutes les classes nominales. Un examen rapide de l'appariement 3/4 où entrent tous les lexèmes désignant des animaux le montrerait bien:

Préfixe 3 à degré d'alternance 2 (occlusive):

-*tifër* « scorpion », -*tapërs* « fourmi blanche », -*kɔmël* « buffle », -*taka* « lézard », -*guka* « poule ».

Préfixe 3 à degré d'alternance 3 (prénasalisée):

-*nsinka* « léopard », -*nfɔnts* « tortue », -*mpalalu* « brebis », -*nsumpëlis* « cheval ».

Pour les autres classes, on obtiendrait les mêmes dédoublements: *bi-mpili* « jeunes filles » 2 (degré 3), *bɔ-pɔrs* « jeunes enfants » 2 (degré 2).

Il nous semble plus opérant d'admettre que certains thèmes ont une initiale C et d'autres une initiale NC, la règle de morpho-phonologie intervenant en outre lorsqu'un thème est uni aux préfixes à nasale. Les substitutions sont toujours possibles qui permettent de décider si la nasale appartient au préfixe ou au thème:

ɔkɔmël, ŋëŋkɔmël 3,4 « buffle » -*kɔmël*
vs: ɔmpalalu, ŋëmpalalu 3,4 « brebis » -*mpalalu*
nɔmpɔrs, bɔpɔrs 1,2 « enfant » -*pɔrs*
vs: mimpili, bimpili 1,2 « j. fille » -*mpili*.

3.2. *Les rapports constrictives/occlusives*. Le pepel se caractérise par un relâchement plus net encore qu'en cur des sonores dans les thèmes nominaux, et par un renforcement des mêmes dans les thèmes verbaux. Comparer:

pepel		bɔk	
k-wars	« oreille »	ka-bats	7
ɔ-wuls	« chien »	u-bus	3
ɔ-wale	« colombe »	u-bal	3
a-wuk	« enfant »	a-buk	1a
ɔ-reu	« foie »	u-räb	3
ɔ-fou	« cendre »	u-fäb	3
adɛ	« il a mangé »	arɛ	
adaani	« il a bu »	aran	
adɔli	« il a fait »	arɔ	

Mais pour le relâchement, les faits restent susceptibles d'interprétations phonologiques différentes. Un même énoncé pris chez un même locuteur à des moments distincts donne: *baars vukun, baars wukun, baars ukun* « voilà des femmes ». On sait que /w/ peut être posé en bɔk. Si en pɛpɛl on avait de manière sûre les correspondances lexicales avec ce phonème maintenu, et d'autre part un relâchement de certains /b/ en /w/, il y aurait lieu sans doute de distinguer des thèmes ayant alternance w/b et d'autres qui maintiendraient w en toute position. Ce peut être le cas, mais les documents en ma possession ne dévoilent pas ce phénomène. Les rares points clairement comparables montrent au contraire une disparition de /w/ du bɔk en pɛpɛl:

bɔk *waap* « acheter », pɛpɛl *aap*.

Il me semblerait dangereux de vouloir, sans examen suffisant, décréter quelle est la meilleure approche du pɛpɛl. Plus qu'en bɔk et en cur peut-être un traitement par alternances consonantiques pourrait se révéler correct. Je doute pourtant qu'il soit plus élégant et plus simple qu'un traitement par règles morpho-phonologiques.

4. L'ÉTUDE DE J. H. GREENBERG SUR LES DONNÉES DE KOELLE

En nous appuyant sur les faits analysés plus haut, qui relèvent de la synchronie de certaines unités linguistiques provenant de *Manjaku, nous pouvons désormais tenter un lecture critique de l'article de J. H. Greenberg. (Les données de Koelle sont citées ici en vedette, selon la convention de la *Language Review*.)

Il faut d'abord fixer un point d'ethno-linguistique. Les Manjaku qui se nomment eux-mêmes *Särär* aujourd'hui sont un groupe étroitement apparenté, y compris dans les usages linguistiques, aux Bɔk et aux Tsaam. C'est à de rares écarts lexicaux par rapport au dialecte bɔk qu'un locuteur särär peut être reconnu. Suivant les données de Koelle reprises par Greenberg, les faits linguistiques attribués au **saraːr** nous sembleraient à chercher, s'ils sont encore vérifiables aujourd'hui, du côté de groupes apparentés aux Mankaɲ et aux Diɔl, le *gi* comme 1e p.s. affirmatif (*Polyglotta*, p. 158 sq) est typique de ces groupes. C'est donc avec raison que Greenberg voit un sous-groupe sarar-bola (donc mankaɲ), avec cette réserve qu'à ma connaissance il n'y a pas de groupe mankaɲ qui se dise aujourd'hui sarar. Dès lors, nous pouvons émettre plusieurs hypothèses, toutes plausibles: 1) l'informateur **saraːr** de Koelle n'était pas un Särär, du moins il n'en parlait pas le dialecte; 2) un groupe dit **saraːr,** apparenté aux Mankaɲ existait au dix-neuvième siècle, qui n'était pas constitué par les ancêtres des Särär actuels, lesquels seraient plotôt les **Bashɛːrɛd** de Koelle (*Polyglotta*, Intr. 1); 3) le groupe särär a changé ses usages linguistiques depuis le dix-neuvième siècle, passant d'un parler proche du mankaɲ à un parler bɔk.

Ces précisions apportées, relevons quelques points dans l'étude de Greenberg, en essayant d'éliminer les faits explicables par l'analyse esquissée plus haut.

4.1. Une grande partie des données recueillies par Koelle concerne l'alternance occlusive/prénasalisée et répond en fait à la règle de morpho-phonologie telle qu'elle se manifeste en pepel: N(V) se présente comme NVN devant toute consonne, liquides et nasales exceptées. Ceci vaut pour les faits **pεpε:l** comme pour les faits **sara:r** de Koelle. Ainsi:

sara:r **poti:/mun-ti:** « saison des pluies »; **bu-kia:m/muŋ-kia:m** « palmier »; **mon-tum/i-tum** « bouche »

pεpε:l **mon-tu:n/i-tu:n** « bouche »; **be-ki:amε/meŋ-ki:amε** « palmier »; **nin-djo:k/ba-djo:k** « esclave »; **niŋ-ka:nya/bɔ-ka:nya** « docteur »; **min-tau** « lait »; **mun-sop** « eau »; **miŋ-kir** « huile de palme »; **muŋ-kilh** « visage »

bo:la **min-tunk** « bouche »; **bu-keε:m/muŋ-keε:m** « palmier »

4.2. Restent par contre inexpliquées sous cet angle les formes suivantes:

sara:r **kadja:ghεn/indja:ghεn** « côte »; **pundia:mont/india:mont** « langue (organe) »; **o:nshimna/ŋge:simna** « perroquet »

pεpε:l **punshu:ntoŋ/inshu:ntoŋ** « nombril »

bo:la **pndε:mnt** « langue »; **nsa:gan** « côte »

On peut proposer à leur sujet les traitements suivants:

4.2.1. Les items **pundia:mont/india:mont** « langue » et **punshu:ntoŋ/inshu:ton** « nombril » nous renvoient à ces nombreux thèmes nominaux manjaku pourvus d'une nasale initale. On peut délimiter: **pu-ndia:mont/i-ndia:mont** et **pu-nshu:ntoŋ/i-nshu:nton** car il a été montré plus haut que, contrairement à ce que semble indiquer Greenberg dans les conclusions de son article, les thèmes de ce type sont susceptibles d'apparaître à toutes les classes nominales. Mais il faut admettre aussi qu'on peut toujours s'attendre à trouver ces mêmes thèmes sans nasale initiale dans une autre partie du domaine manjaku:

    pundia:mont/india:mont « langue » (**sara:r** de Koelle)
vs: *prεmte/irεmte* (cur actuel)
    punshu:ntoŋ/inshu:ntoŋ « nombril » (**pεpε:l** de Koelle)
vs: *pëcintan/icintan* (bɔk actuel)

Faut-il pour autant en appeler à des classes d'alternances occlusive/prénasalisée imputables à la reconstruction du groupe ouest-atlantique, conclusion à laquelle Greenberg se rallie, ce ne semble pas certain à partir de ces seules données. Il y a au moins deux pistes qu'il semble nécessaire d'envisager au préalable.

En premier lieu, considérer l'interaction possible d'une nasale du préfixe sur le thème nominal et vice-versa. Des documents montrent qu'on observe les mêmes variantes occlusive/prénasalisée dans le corps du thème nominal. Une seule illustration de ce fait suffira. Dans un court article de D. Dalby et P. E. H. Hair,[6] on trouve les données suivantes :

	myonga	« eléphants (?) » (texte portugais de 1456)
mankaɲ	*u-loŋge*/**u-loːnk**	« éléphant »
pɛpɛl	*a-yogan*/**o-yoːga**	« éléphant »
manjaku	*u-loŋge*/**u-lɔːnga**	« éléphant »

Le préfixe de classe 4, pluriel des noms d'animaux et autres thèmes, pourra probablement être reconstitué pour *Manjaku comme *N- ou même *ng(ë)-. On peut penser ici que cette nasale a réagi sur la finale d'un thème *log pour donner les items à prénasalisée ci-dessus, le pɛpɛl conservant jusqu'à nos jours (-*yug*) la forme sans prénasalisation.

Le même phénomène, mais appliqué à l'initiale du thème expliquerait probablement pourquoi on trouve plus de thèmes à prénasalisée initiale dans les noms d'animaux que dans les autres nominaux. Quant à **-ndɛːmnt, -ndiaːmont, -rɛmte** « langue » et **-cintan, -nshuːntoŋ, -shindɛːn, -suntaːn** « nombril », on constate que ces deux thèmes comportant également une séquence NC au thème, qui a pu réagir dans certains dialects sur l'initiale, le préfixe (*pë-*) étant ici hors cause.

Ensuite, il faudrait examiner la possibilité de l'existence d'une classe *n-* perdue, ou le passage d'un thème verbal à une classe nominale par l'intermédiaire d'une relative (cf. 1.3 dernier paragraphe). La forme **nsaːgan** « côte » recueillie par Koelle en **boːla** nous incite à envisager cette hypothèse. En cur actuel, on a *ka-cag-an*, et *-cag* est « clôturer ». Bien que le cur n'ait pas retenu cette forme à nasale, on peut se demander si une locution : *ka-n-cagan-ki* « qui fait clôture » ne serait pas à l'origine du substantif en bola. Cette classe *n-*, ou ce passage par la relative expliquerait cur actuel *-bɔp* « sucer », *ka-m-bɔp* « écorce de citron ». Il y aurait donc réinsertion dans 7,8 à partir d'une classe disparue, ou par la relative. On notera dans le même sens : *pë-li* « lune »; *ka-pë-li* « jeune homme »; *u-pë-li* « nom de femme »; *na-m-pë-li* « jeune fille » (bɔk).

4.2.2. Une forme reste inanalysée : **oːnshimna/ŋgeːsimna** « perroquet ». Dans une liste cur, on trouve : *uncima/ŋgëncima*. Un phénomène inverse de celui relevé par Koelle (prénasalisée au pluriel, à cause du préfixe) n'aurait pas surpris. L'alternance ici évoquée, par contre, laisse perplexe.

4.3. *Les cas d'alternance sans prénasalisée.* Avec Greenberg qui a vu clair pour chacun des cas, nous pouvons écarter **piːal/miːal, keŋ/iheːŋ, bɛːne/eːhɛnɛ, wiːbal/ŋgushoːwal**. Il ne s'agit pas d'alternances, mais pour trois spécimens, de la représentation du préfixe devant voyelle ou *h* (voisé?). Quant à la dernière paire, il est exact qu'il y a deux radicaux sous-jacents, d'ailleurs apparentés. En bɔk : *u-ḟbël, u-subël* « pluie ».

Les dernières formes à traiter sont donc les suivantes :

kewaːt/ibaːt « oreille »; **kɛdjaːk/ishaːk** « épaule »; **kaguːp/ikuːp** « maison »; **kawasaŋ/ibasaŋ** « natte »

et, mais à part :

uboːz/ŋgiwoːz « chien »

Elles sont incontestablement intéressantes. Les quatre premières en particulier offrent les mêmes appariements singulier/pluriel.

ke-waːt (7 sing)/**i-baːt** (8 plur); **ka-wasaŋ** (7 sing)/**i-basaŋ** (8 plur); **kɛ-djaːk** (7 sing)/**i-shaːk** (8 plur); **ka-guːp** (7 sing)/**i-kuːp** (8 plur).

Deux traitements sont possibles, selon qu'on décide ou non de faire confiance à la phonétique et à la graphie de Koelle.

4.3.1. Dans le premier cas, et à condition d'admettre cependant que **ishaːk** constitue un écart graphique, et qu'il faut restituer *icaːk, nous aurions l'ébauche d'une règle d'alternance :

classe 7	*classe* 8
constrictive	occlusive sonore
occlusive sonore	occlusive sourde

Remarquons en passant que nous ne sommes pas là dans un type d'alternance consonantique en degrés seuls, tels qu'ils apparaissent, par exemple, dans le bedik traité par M.-P. Ferry, mais dans un type qui rappelle les phénomènes venda.[7] Or, l'origine des alternances consonantiques en venda est connue, il s'agit du résultat d'une évolution des préfixes de classes bantous 5 *i-*, 9 *n-*, 10 *n-*. Il faut d'ailleurs souligner qu'un traitement du venda qui réduirait l'alternance consonantique est encore aujourd'hui possible.

Retenons le préfixe 5, qui est une voyelle très fermée. Les bantouistes savent que dans plusieurs langues son évolution donne des aboutissements divers. La voyelle peut disparaître en laissant une trace dans l'initiale des thèmes nominaux (ganda, venda, certains dialectes swahili). En lega, langue du Congo (D.25), le préfixe est bien conservé, mais il faut établir une règle phonétique qui veut que la consonne initiale du thème est géminée :[8]

mu-kazi̧ 1 « femme »
vs: *i̧-kkazi̧* 5 « gauche »
mu-lume 1 « homme »
vs: *i̧-ddume* 5 « droite »

Or, ci-dessus les exemples relevés par Greenberg manifestent tous le préfixe i̯- au pluriel, et c'est précisément là qu'apparaît à l'initiale du thème un renforcement de la consonne. La situation est donc très similaire à celle du lega, et l'étude faite plus haut du pepel ne nous incitera guère à accorder aux réalisations *w* et *b* d'autre valeur que celle de variantes combinatoires ou libres. On objectera qu'il en va à l'inverse dans **uboːz, ŋgiwoːz**. Ce n'est pas sûr. Le *u*-, voyelle fermée, est bien attesté comme préfixe de la classe 3, alors que -*i*- de **ŋgi-** apparaît soit comme une voyelle épenthétique (Wilson),[9] soit comme une centrale (mon interprétation). Il est donc normal que pour ce thème le renforcement de l'initiale ait lieu au singulier, non au pluriel.

Je pense donc qu'ici encore il faut examiner de très près les réalités phonétiques et phonologiques avant de conclure à l'existence d'une alternance non réductible.

4.3.2. On peut aussi mettre en doute la valeur de certaines notations de Koelle. Sans vouloir enlever nul mérite à ce pionnier de la linguistique africaine, il faut remarquer des faiblesses dans son écoute et sa transcription. La différence entre sourdes et sonores n'est pas toujours perçue par lui en contexte intervocalique ou final, et il n'a donné qu'un signe (**dj**) pour rendre compte des occlusives palatales sonore et sourde et des affriquées.

Ainsi, pour le domaine manjaku, je relève les confusions suivantes (en tablant sur le fait que dans l'ouest-atlantique les consonnes se maintiennent beaucoup plus fermement que les voyelles) :

p pour *b*
  mɔːp « prendre » ('catch') -*mɔb*
d pour *t*
  priːamd « langue » -*ndiamt*
g pour *k*
  amaːg « malade » -*maak*; **ugoːg** « poule » -*guk*; **punaːg** « jour » -*nak*; **pulaːg** « pierre » -*laak*; **mleːg** « eau » -*lik*; **pidjug** « front » -*ju̯k*

Quant à la notation **dj**, elle vaut parfois pour *j*, d'autres fois pour *c* :

dj pour *j*
  djõː « cuire » -*jun*; **neːdj** « se laver » -*nij*; **djeː** « rire » -*ji*
dj pour *c*
  tuːdja « fustiger » -*tu̯can*; **djat** « mourir » -*cäts*; **adjɔːl** « ê. droit » -*cɔɔl*; **afaːdj** « ê. blanc » -*faac*; **udjai** « esprit » -*cay*; **bidjeːndj** « poitrine » -*jinc*; **kadjaːg** « bras » -*cak* (« épaule »)

S'il en est ainsi, on peut suspecter les oppositions sonore/sourde que Koelle décèle dans certains mots de l'ensemble manjaku. Il en va de même pour les oppositions constrictive/occlusive. Pour la même langue bantoue **ntɛghe** (**X.A.6**) Koelle donne :

kuːmi ŋa biteːt « treize »; **kuːmi ŋa wina** « quatorze »; **kuːmi ŋa witaːn** « quinze »; **kuːmi ŋa wiseːmini** « seize »

Il est plus que douteux qu'il y ait dans cette langue bantoue une alternance *w/b* à l'initiale du préfixe 8. Ce qui ne signifie pas nécessairement que Koelle entendait mal, mais les degrés de relâchement peuvent être plus ou moins accusés chez un même locuteur, les exemples relevés plus haut en pepel le montrent. Quoi qu'il en soit de la phonétique, dans le domaine ouest-atlantique une étude structurale de l'appareil phonologique semble bien s'imposer, en même temps que le recours à la morpho-phonologie, pour juger exactement de phénomènes susceptibles de décider s'il faut ou non recourir à un traitement en termes d'alternances consonantiques.

4.4. Je crois qu'il faut conclure provisoirement par une position de prudence. L'alternance à l'initiale des thèmes ne se manifeste comme irréductible en manjaku que dans de rares éléments hors système. Cette présence et le nombre impressionnant de thèmes à initiale NC posent certainement un problème diachronique. Avant d'aboutir, comme semble le faire J. H. Greenberg, à une reconstruction d'ensemble du groupe ouest-atlantique comme comportant l'usage de l'alternance consonantique initiale, d'autres pistes sont à explorer soigneusement. Si une langue comme le manjaku peut être aujourd'hui traitée de telle sorte que le phénomène d'alternance s'y trouve réduit par l'appel à la phonologie et à la morpho-phonologie, cela implique peut-être que dans la reconstruction du groupe ouest-atlantique nous nous trouverons devant un tableau où les divers phénomènes de différenciations phonétiques, de transphonologisation et de contamination n'auront pas encore commencé à jouer.

NOTES

1. J. H. GREENBERG, '*Polyglotta* Evidence for Consonant Mutation in the Mandyak Languages', *Sierra Leone Language Review*, 5, 1966, pp. 106–10.
2. C.N.R.S., *La classification nominale dans les langues négro-africaines*, Colloque d'Aix-en-Provence 1967, pp. 261–76.
3. M.-P. FERRY, *L'alternance consonantique et son utilisation dans la grammaire bedik*, 1967, polycopié (thèse).
4. A. Akoka étudie actuellement les faits cur d'une manière approfondie, spécialement les phénomènes d'accentuation, qui peuvent se révéler importants pour notre débat.
5. Il y a dans certains dialectes pepel une latérale fricative, correspondante de *s* dans la majorité des dialectes manjaku. Mon informateur la réduisait à *l*.
6. D. DALBY et P. E. H. HAIR, 'A West African Word of 1456', *Journal of West African Languages*, IV, 1, 1967, pp. 13–14.
7. D. ZIERVOGEL et R. S. DAU, *A Handbook of the Venda Language*, Pretoria, 1961, 239 (cyclo).
8. Je remercie le Pr. M. G. GUTHRIE d'avoir attiré mon attention sur ce point au Colloque d'Aix-en-Provence.
9. W. A. A. WILSON, « Diola et langues de Guinée », in *Actes du 2ème Colloque international de linguistique négro-africaine*, 1963, pp. 280–90.

L'étude ci-dessus a été rendue possible par un subside de recherches sur la langue manjaku attribué à l'auteur par le C.N.R.S.

Language, Script and Vernacular Literature in West Africa

PETR ZIMA

0. In recent years, the problems of script, orthographies and subsequently of the written form of vernacular languages in West Africa have attracted considerable attention from linguists. Interest has been shown in the analysis of hitherto unknown or little known indigenous scripts, including the problems of their origin, occurrence and usage and the history of their discovery (cf. Klingenheben,[1] Dalby,[2] etc.). Problems of applied character have arisen, on the other hand, in connection with mass literacy campaigns, involving the introduction of new written forms of languages as well as putting existing written forms on a new quantitative basis, where these have existed hitherto in restricted functions and quality.[3] In a third category are scholars interested in the creation or description of literature in West African vernaculars, who obviously approach this complex of problems from another methodological point of view.[4]

This paper is an attempt to analyse some problems of the existence (or absence) of written forms for West African vernaculars. The existence of written forms is considered here not only in relation to the usage of individual scripts and orthographies, but also as an intermediary stage between the emergence of scripts and the creation of written vernacular literature. Particular and general aspects of the relation between spoken/oral and written/printed forms of languages are also taken into consideration (cf. Vachek,[5] Ferguson[6]).

1.0. If we consider the western part of sub-Saharan Africa as a whole, then we may, very roughly, say that three major types of script have been introduced in the area, and that written forms of vernacular languages have arisen in these respective types of scripts. These are the Arabic script, the Latin script and a group of mostly syllabic, and probably local, indigenous scripts. The Arabic and the Latin scripts have definitely come here from areas outside this zone and from usages for other types of languages; there is enough historical non-linguistic evidence on this point. As far as the third type of scripts is concerned, most facts known by contemporary scholars—mainly of non-historical character—seem to present them as products of local, West African origin, even though some degree of distant foreign influence or at least inspiration cannot be excluded. It might be of value to make some remarks briefly about the zones where the respective scripts are used for writing vernaculars.

1.1. Although recent research shows that the zone of influence of the indigenous vernacular West African scripts is much broader than previously supposed, this area is still the most restricted of the three types. It is represented first of all by a group of languages, including Vai, Mende, Loma, Kpelle and Bassa, covering adjacent areas of Sierra Leone and Liberia. There are further languages with scripts of their own scattered to the north, including Manding, Wolof and Fula, and further south along the Atlantic Coast, including Bete in Ivory Coast and Bamum and Bagam in the Cameroons, etc. (A map of the distribution of most of these scripts is included in Dalby, op. cit., 1967.) Some other restricted areas where pictographic symbols are used could be added perhaps, if we accept that they are script-like in character (cf. Dieterlen and Griaule[7]). Owing to the fact that so little has been done in the search for indigenous scripts in relatively vast areas of West Africa until quite recent times, surprises cannot be altogether excluded.

1.2. The problem of vernacular texts written in Arabic script in West Africa is also complicated. No clear-cut identity can be established between the language areas where this form of written vernacular exists, and the Islamic zone of West Africa, including the zone of occurrence of Arabic texts, although definite ties between these factors obviously exist. It is true that the languages of such nations as the Hausa and the Fulani, who have been relatively long in contact with Islam, have developed a comparatively large number of vernacular texts in Arabic script (called *ajamiya*, from Arabic 'foreign, non-Arabic'). Apart from the use of Arabic script for vernacular texts in these two important West African languages, as known at an early stage,[8] recent research has revealed that vernacular texts written in Arabic script do occur in a surprisingly vast, but rather incoherent zone of other languages as well. Apart from such important languages as Kanuri,[9] these texts occur also in Dagbani, Mamprule, Guang, Dyula and others.[10] It is not yet clear how many languages in the zone of Islamic influence in West Africa have actually developed vernacular literature in the Arabic script, for apart from Fula and Hausa this kind of research is still in its initial stages and there is much exploration to be done. It seems that although the influence of Islam was an essential factor, other—probably local—factors may have been decisive for the development or non-development of this type of written vernacular text.

1.3. The usage of Latin script for writing West African vernaculars obviously came as a result of cultural, religious and—last but not least—administrative contacts with Europeans. The early stimulus for using the Latin script for vernaculars came from Christian missions, but later the colonial administrations joined the missions in their effort to introduce written forms of vernaculars in Latin script, at least in some areas and in some functions. The missions aimed to reach the average African primarily with religious texts, but their effort was never limited to the presentation of religious texts.[11] Owing to the fact that they started their activity long before the definitive creation of colonial administrative units, they never limited their activities to these artificial territorial areas, but were mostly oriented towards certain genuine African language communities or groups of closely related language communities. Later efforts by the administrative organs of the newly formed territorial units took the form of what were called language and literature (or translation) bureaux, committees, etc. These activities were mostly limited to certain territories only, and they overstepped the politico-administrative frontiers of these territories very rarely, even where the language communities they were serving extended beyond the limits of a single territory.

There were fundamental differences, however, between the language policies of different colonial administrations in West Africa. In the British zone the vernaculars, or at least some vernaculars, were accepted in their basic written usage for the purposes of education, mass communication and public life. In the French zone, however, only the French language was accepted even for the basic purposes of all these areas of communication, and written vernacular usage was neither sponsored nor even generally tolerated.

The final result of these and other local factors was that although by the middle of this century the zone of influence of Latin characters theoretically extended over the whole of West Africa, this did not mean, as in the case of the Islamic zone and the vernacular texts in Arabic script, that vernacular texts in Latin script existed in all language communities. The activity of the missions seems to have covered the largest linguistic areas, but did not involve some language communities in West Africa, either because of their affinity with Islam or because of their small size and relative unimportance in trade and communication. On the other hand, the administrative language and literature bureaux and committees covered the zone of British influence only,[12] although they penetrated the zone of Islam with some success and established written usage in Latin script even for some languages which had previously employed the Arabic script.[13]

1.4. The result of the historical coexistence of these zones of influence of three main types of scripts in West Africa seems to be a certain measure of interference and interaction: the usage of Arabic script and Latin script seems to penetrate into the zones of languages where indigenous, vernacular scripts exist, but not vice versa; the marginal exception in this direction, noted by Stewart, could be mentioned perhaps as a curiosity,[14] which we may put aside for the moment. Schematically, all possible and all realized combinations of the three main language types of West Africa (Indo-European, Arabic and West African vernacular) with the three types of script (Latin, Arabic and indigenous) are expressed on the table below.

If we take into consideration the fact that despite the influence of all three types of script there are still many languages without any written form, we may conclude that theoretically the number of written forms of any West African vernacular may vary from three to zero. As the upper extreme is rare, and the lower extreme of little value for our subject, our attention is attracted by the fact that the existence of two different types of a written form of a vernacular language provides us with an interesting case of *digraphia*[15] in West Africa, especially in those language communities where both types of the written form of the language show tendencies to develop into a literature in the true sense of this term. But before we proceed to this problem, the question of mutual analogies between the system of a script and that of the language for which it is used must be dealt with.

2. The problem of the mutual relationship between the graphic systems of scripts and the language systems for which these scripts are used is obviously a complex one. Generally speaking, this relationship may take a different form when a given script is created for a given language, or at least for a language typologically or genetically close to it, and when a foreign and structurally different system of script is applied to another language.

2.1. Most linguists who have studied the so-called indigenous, vernacular scripts of West Africa have based their arguments about the probability of local origin on certain parallels between the

REALIZATION OF POSSIBLE COMBINATIONS OF LANGUAGE AND SCRIPT IN WEST AFRICA

script / language	Latin	Arabic	Indigenous
Indo-European	yes	no	no
Arabic	no	yes	rarely
Vernacular	yes	yes	yes

graphic systems and their respective language systems. If older papers showed that the Vai script reflects some features distinctive in the Vai language system, the most recent contribution (Dalby, op. cit., 1967) shows that this script might reflect features redundant in the present Vai language, but relevant in other languages, genetically related to Vai. This parallelism between the graphic systems and language systems shows at least that there is a rather close relationship between the two systems which probably cannot be entirely arbitrary.

2.2. If, however, a graphic system is applied to a foreign language system because of linguistically arbitrary factors, such as factors of historical, cultural and other importance, then—obviously—the necessity for adaptation of one of the systems arises, if at least some degree of suitability for communication is to be reached in the script-language relationship. As the arbitrary system of a script can be modified much more readily and with less harm for communication, the problem of the adaptation of the script arises. This particular problem obviously arose when both Arabic and Latin scripts become used for West African vernaculars, and two factors seem to have played different roles in the process of their adaptation. The spontaneous, traditional factor in this process seems to have been much stronger in the case of Arabic script, although even the arbitrary factor was not completely absent in this case. The reverse seems to be valid for the process of adaptation of the Latin script.

2.2.1. The degree to which Arabic script has been adapted for writing various vernaculars seems to vary considerably.

In the case of Hausa and Fula, a certain traditional norm, though vague and inconsistent, had developed at least in some areas and probably for some traditional schools of scribes only. The importance of this type of script and its long establishment, as well as the large number of occurring texts, especially at certain historically pertinent periods,[16] seem to be the cause of this relative stabilization of a written norm. It was established probably more by tradition than by arbitrary decision. Some more general rules for the adaptation of the graphic system of the Arabic script to these two languages have been established on the basis of the analysis of relatively large corpuses of texts (cf. Robinson,[17] Taylor,[18] Mischlich,[19] Na'ibi Wali[20]). They include the principle of more of less consistent vocalization, based on a triadic system of notation of vowels. This system gave way in some areas and scribes' schools to a four-vowel marking system, both for Hausa and Fula. The distinction of vowel quantity seems to have been much more respected and marked, especially for Hausa, than that of tonality. There is considerable variation in the usage of symbols for diphthongs and the same is true of the notation of consonants non-existent in classical Arabic, especially where these have no similarity to analogous sounds in that language. If at least some kind of traditional norm had developed for the use of Arabic script in Hausa and Fula, however vague, traditional, spontaneous and inconsistent it may have been, vernacular texts using Arabic script in other languages seem to be much less adapted and even less consistent. As these texts are more restricted in function, their number being no more in some cases than a token minimum, and their tradition much shorter, the development towards the establishment of traditional rules of adaptation seems hardly to have begun: Manding is a possible exception.[21]

2.2.2. As has already been pointed out, the adaptation of Latin script to West African vernaculars was much more a matter of arbitrary decision than of traditionally developing norms. Three approaches characterized this process: the varied application of Lepsius' standard alphabet,[22] the application of the orthographical rules valid for the various Indo-European (IE) languages of the missionary and administrative centers, and the application of the phonetic principles of the IPA. The use of Lepsius' alphabet and orthographical rules, proper to an IE language (especially English and French) were characteristic of the earlier vernacular texts in Latin script; the IPA phonetic principles penetrated into usage relatively recently. Even the application of the orthographical rules of a single IE language sometimes introduced the element of division, where the vernacular language community was divided into zones of influence under different missions or administrations. This situation was a considerable help, however, in the process of transition from writing in the vernaculars to writing in the European lingua franca. The application of IPA rules which was realized by D. Westermann and I. C. Ward and by a group of phoneticians and linguists associated with the International African Institute,[23] helped to express particular features of African vernaculars, especially phonetic features; the too detailed reflection of phonetic features at the language and dialect level, however, brought difficulties with it. Where linguistic norms were not clearly defined, the system led to disintegration rather than to integration of the written norm, introducing—or in some cases petrifying—different dialectal written usage. This was, for example, the case of Ibo and Akan. The stress on special characters rather than on diacritics for expressing sounds non-existent in Latin and other IE languages, on the one hand, and the acceptance of diacritics for marking tones also brought difficulties. 'Exotic' characters were difficult to find, type and print; consequently, various practical measures have been taken since their introduction in the thirties, in an attempt to avoid them (Swadesh[24]). Linguistically as well as psychologically interesting is the problem of the use of diacritics for marking tones. Although linguistically in most cases perfectly justified, the marking of tones in West African vernaculars of such widely differing structures, ranging from Gã to

Hausa, became the subject of earnest discussion, grouping most linguists on one side and the practical language users—readers, writers, editors, teachers, etc.—on the other. The latter are in their vast majority against this usage, the former obviously in favour of it.[25] Generally speaking, no adaptations of Latin script to the written usage of West African vernaculars complies entirely with both the theoretical and practical principles of a good orthography in this area. Two such principles were established by Hans Wolff in his attempt to unify the adaptations of Latin script for various vernaculars in Northern Nigeria.[26] The first principle is to unify the orthography of the local vernacular and the area vernacular in order to facilitate educational transition in literacy projects. The second principle is then to unify principles of all vernacular orthographies with the main principles of the respective European lingua franca of the given area, in order to facilitate the transition from basic to higher levels of education. A third problem arises, however, in the case of the so-called 'divided' language communities. By 'divided' in this sense we mean language communities divided either between zones with different IE administrative languages (Hausa in Nigeria and Niger, Yoruba in Nigeria and Dahomey/Togo, Manding in Gambia and the adjacent French-speaking territories, etc.) or language communities divided between different areas of missionary or administrative language policy (as with the different 'standards' adopted for Ibo and Akan, etc.). In the case of these divided language communities a third principle must be added: to unify the principles of adaptation and usage of Latin script for the whole language community. Such attempts at unification are not always easy, especially since—in the case of language communities divided between zones with different European lingue franche—the third principle may contradict the two preceding ones. Recent adult literacy campaigns on a mass-scale, based on areal vernaculars—at least for the first stage in rural areas, have been undertaken with the assistance of UNESCO in several West African states, and have had to tackle some of these interesting problems. Problems of these 'divided' language communities are, however, not limited to the level of the adaptation of Latin script and orthographic rules.[27]

Alongside all these arbitrary, official attempts to adapt Latin script to the needs of vernacular written usage in West Africa a certain amount of spontaneous adaptation developed as well. Bad and inconsistent teaching, as well as no teaching at all, always left room for such spontaneity. The interesting extreme effects of such spontaneous adaptation are reflected not only in individual written usage in the vernacular of people who have not been taught the official adaptation systems, but who know something about Latin characters or know how to write in the European lingua franca. Examples are provided not only by particular correspondence-models, wall-inscriptions, lorry-inscriptions and slogans, but also frequently public announcements, warnings, traffic directions, etc. A particularly interesting case is the written usage of a vernacular in a country where it is not taught, although existing in an 'official' adaptation in another, not too distant West African country: this is the case, for instance, of written Hausa in Ghana, at least in Latin characters.[28]

3. So far the corpuses of written texts in West African vernaculars have been assumed to be homogeneous. If we proceed, however, to analyse the functions of the respective texts and their quantitative occurrence, the situation looks different.

3.1. The situation is relatively simple with texts in indigenous, vernacular West African scripts. Although the functions and quantity of texts in such languages as Vai, Bamum, etc., are far from being so restricted as might have appeared some years ago, the corpus of written texts in these is still somehow different from what might be called 'normal' written usage according to Ferguson.[29] Basic epistolary usage and written records do exist. Occasional efforts to record oral literature or even attempts at mass distribution remain, as far as we know, only marginal. We can thus speak about basic written usage, but only on an individual and not a mass scale. It is difficult to speak about the necessary conditions for further development in these scripts of a literature in the true sense.

3.2. The vernacular texts written in Arabic script can be divided basically into two groups, according to their main function and quantitative basis.

3.2.1. The texts written in such languages as Guang, Mamprule, Dagbani, but also texts in such relatively important West African languages as Dyula (Manding) and Kanuri seem to fulfil only a limited function, similar to that of texts in indigenous, vernacular scripts. Correspondence, historical records, etc., do exist, but few other types of texts. Possibly many other written documents in various West African vernaculars, hitherto perhaps scientifically unrecorded, would fall into this category. The quantity of texts in each language seems limited.

3.2.2. In the case of Hausa and Fula, however, texts written in Arabic script are much more numerous and cannot be limited to basic epistolary and recording functions. In the case of Hausa not only local chronicles, lists of chiefs, local histories, etc., exist, but there are also attempts to record traditional oral literature, especially poetry and efforts to paraphrase Arabic classical poetry.[30] These two types of written texts in particular present rather important features of the transition towards a genuine Hausa literature. We believe that true popular Hausa literature could have developed from the previous recording of oral literature in much the same way as the so-called 'classical' or 'Islamic' Hausa literature—and poetry in particular—developed from long coexistence with analogous forms in the Arabic language: we must of course assume a continuing influence from Arabic in the process of growth of Hausa literature, using the Ajami variant of the Arabic script. In any case, the character of Hausa texts written in Arabic script has not been limited to usage by individuals only, even though relatively little printing in Ajami has been undertaken so far. Copying by hand and reciting in public places have helped to strengthen the mass basis of the written usage in Hausa, and in many aspects this would seem to be valid for Fula as well, although with some special features (cf. Lacroix[31]).

3.3. The difference between various West African vernaculars written in Latin script, from the point of view of their functions and quantitative occurrence, are even greater than among those written in Arabic script. The scale of transitional features seems even broader. Languages with no or very little written usage, limited mostly to basic individual or restricted educational, religious and epistolary functions obviously include numerically small and unimportant language communities, such as some of the Jos Plateau languages in Nigeria, the so-called Togo remnant languages in Ghana and Togo, etc.[32] But not all numerically minor languages have failed to develop larger written usage, while on the other hand some numerically important language communities do belong to this group. Various transitions from the restricted, almost individual written usage towards the full 'basic' written usage on a mass scale obviously do exist in this zone. There are communities with a restricted, but rather stable corpus of texts, distributed on a mass scale (Gã, Nupe, etc.), although the distribution of written texts may have been limited to certain periods of time only. There are also large language communities with considerable corpuses of written texts with many literary functions, distributed on a mass scale, and this seems to be the case of Yoruba, Ewe, Akan, etc. All these communities represent perhaps tendencies towards the development of a vernacular literature in a modern sense. Curiously enough, the intersections of zones of the two major scripts, Latin and Arabic, created interesting cases of digraphia, especially in the case of Hausa and Fula, where two corpuses of written texts exist, one using the Arabic script, the other the Latin script. Since these differences of script seem parallel to other, functional differences between the texts in style, form, content and even language, especially at the lexical level, the problem arises of the amalgamation of two literatures, virtually coexisting within one language community.[33]

4. The problems of the co-existence of the oral and written forms of vernaculars have interesting repercussions as far as the relationship and coexistence of vernaculars with IE administrative languages are concerned. As we stated above, the language policies of the two main administrations in West Africa differed in the past in respect of their attitude towards the written form of vernaculars using Latin script, and towards its functions in individual as well as mass communication. In the British zone the administration favoured and to some extent encouraged the introduction of written forms of vernaculars in at least some basic functions in education and public life. In the French zone, however, this was not so (cf. para. 1.3) and official language policy involved the use of French only in the written form. These two different attitudes resulted in a slightly different form of coexistence between vernaculars and the respective IE lingua franca, especially from the point of view of their oral-written stratification. Whereas English coexisted with vernaculars both in their oral and written form, French coexisted with them in the oral form only, the written language being the exclusive domain of the official language. Some marginal cases of missionary and other vernacular written usage apart, this fact has had one very interesting consequence: the contact of the respective IE languages with the vernaculars in the oral forms of these languages resulted in various types of mutual interference in their respective systems, especially at their lexical levels. Pidginization or creolization of English and French, though in various degrees and differing in form according to areas, periods and other criteria, has been an immediate result of the coexistence of the IE languages with African vernaculars in their spoken form.

If the process of mutual interference and influence in the oral form developed both in the English and the French zone, in the written form it occurred only in the English zone, however, because here the coexistence was realized not only in the oral form, but also to some extent in the written form. Various forms of 'African English' are documented in West Africa by the unofficial 'market literature', showing various forms of influence on English of the vernaculars, although the degree of pidginization of English is much lower in the written than in the oral form. Some authors of such texts even insist on the 'correctness' of their English.[34] It may be that even the language of Amos Tutuola can be taken as evidence of this process, if we accept the thesis that his work belongs—although with some reservations—in the category of 'market-literature'. The other interesting fact which should be mentioned in this context is the occurrence of some literature in the most classical example of 'mixed' language in West Africa—in Krio.[35] The coexistence of English and the vernaculars both in their oral and written forms clearly has great importance for the further development of West African vernacular literature.

5. In conclusion, we should like to say that the complex interrelationships of scripts, languages and vernacular written texts of various function offer an extremely interesting picture in West Africa. Study of the relationships between script and language, the functions of written texts and the mutual relations of the oral and written forms of languages are likely to produce interesting results, at least in two aspects. First of all, new light might be thrown on the analogies and differences between the systems of scripts and the systems of languages for which these scripts are being used. The same can be said about the analogies and differences between the functions of oral and written forms of languages. This in turn might throw new light on the problems of the creation and growth of a vernacular literature as a process of the fixation of a written form of the vernacular in certain specific functions. A script is obviously the basic precondition for the existence of a written form of a language, just as the written form of a language is a precondition for the development of a literature. A developing literature is then a precondition for a literature in the classical sense of this term.

In this modest contribution we have tried to draw attention to the fact that West Africa offers a very interesting choice of transitional features from pictographic forms of written language to a literature in the classical sense. An interdisciplinary approach to this problem between linguistics—or even sociolinguistics—and literary theory appears most promising.

NOTES

1. A. KLINGENHEBEN, 'The Vai Script', *Africa*, 6, 1933, 158–71.
2. David DALBY, 'A Survey of the Indigenous Scripts of Liberia and Sierra Leone: Vai, Mende, Loma, Kpelle and Bassa', *African Language Studies*, 8, 1967, 1–51; 'The Indigenous Scripts of West Africa and Surinam: Their Inspiration and Design', ibid., 9, 1968, 156–97; 'Further Indigenous Scripts of West Africa: Manding, Wolof and Fula Alphabets and Yoruba "Holy" Writing', ibid., 10, 1969, 161–81.
3. As in the case of the recent alphabetization campaign, sponsored by UNESCO in several French-speaking West African states in such languages as Hausa, Fula, Songhay-Djerma, Kanuri, Tamasheq and Manding.
4. As in J. A. RAMSARAN, *New Approaches to African Literature*, Ibadan, 1965, esp. 5–12.
5. J. VACHEK, 'Zum Problem der geschriebenen Sprache', *TCLP*, 8, 1939, 95–104; 'Written Language and Printed Language', *Recueil Linguistique de Bratislava*, 1, 1948, 67–75 (both these papers have been recently reprinted in Vachek's *Prague School Reader in Linguistics*, Bloomington, 1964). See also by the same author: 'Two Chapters on Written English', *Brno Studies in English*, 3, 1961, p. 9–78.
6. Charles A. FERGUSON, 'The Language Factor in National Development', *Anthropological Linguistics*, 4, 1962, 23–27; reprinted also in *Study of the Role of Second Languages*, ed. by Frank A. Rice, Washington, 1962, p. 8–15.
7. See M. GRIAULE-G. DIETERLEN, *Signes graphiques soudanaises*, Paris, 1951.
8. Cf. C. H. ROBINSON, *Specimens of Hausa Literature*, London, 1896.
9. On Kanuri literature see, e.g.: P. A. BENTON, *Kanuri Readings*, including facsimiles of MSS., London, 1911 (repr. in Benton, *The Languages and Peoples of Bornu*, II, London, 1968); Rudolf PRIETZE, 'Bornu-Texte, mit MS in arabischer Schrift', *Mitt. Sem.*

Orientforschung, 33, 1930, 82–159; Jean-Paul LEBEUF et Maxime RODINSON *Les mosquées de Fort-Lamy* (manuscrit kanouri avec traduction), *Bull. IFAN*, 14, 1952, 970–4.

10. See a report on such 'Arabic' manuscripts in some languages, in *Ghanaian Research Review*, Inst. of Afr. Studies, Univ. of Ghana, 1, 1965, pp. 15 ff.

11. Cf. F. ROWLING and C. E. WILSON, *Bibliography of African Christian Literature*, London, 1923 (with Supplement publ. 1927).
Cf. also *Books for Africa, Bibliography of Books in the Vernacular*, publ. quarterly by the International Committee on Christian Literature, London, 1931 onwards.

12. On the activity of such institutions see, e.g.: R. M. EAST, *A Vernacular Bibliography for the Languages of Nigeria*, Zaria, Literature Bureau, 1941; *Bibliography of Works in Ghana Languages*, Compiled by the Bureau of Ghana Languages, Accra, 1967.

13. See, e.g.: P. ALEXANDRE, 'Les problèmes linguistiques africains vus de Paris', in J. SPENCER, ed., *Language in Africa*, Cambridge, 1963, p. 53 ff.

14. Gail STEWART, 'Notes on the Present-day Usage of the Vai Script in Liberia', *African Language Review*, 6, 1967, 71–4. According to Mrs. Stewart's findings the Vai script has been used also to record Arabic texts.

15. I am using *digraphia* in a sense parallel to Ferguson's term and understanding of *diglossia*; cf. Charles A. FERGUSON, 'Diglossia', in Dell HYMES, ed., *Language and Culture in Society*, New York, 1964, 429–39.

16. M. HISKETT, 'Hausa Literature', *The Encyclopaedia of Islam*, p. 280 ff., explains his opinion on the historical reasons for the occurrence of texts in Hausa language in certain historic periods, especially in the *djihad* time.

17. C. ROBINSON, *Hausa Grammar*, 5th edn., London, 1953, p. 172–91.

18. F. W. TAYLOR, 'Fulani–Hausa Readings', in the *Native Scripts, with Transliterations and Translations*, Oxford, 1929.

19. A. MISCHLICH, *Wörterbuch der Haussa-Sprach*, Berlin, 1906, *passim*.

20. The Gaskiya company has published a popular booklet under the title *Mu Koyi Ajami da Larabci*, by M. Na'ibi S. WALI and M. Haliru BINJI.

21. R. T. ADDIS, *A Study on the Writing of Mandinka in Arabic Script*, duplicated, [Bathurst], 1963.

22. R. LEPSIUS, *Nubische Grammatik, mit Einleitung über die Völker und die Sprachen Afrikas*, Berlin, 1880.

23. The concrete realization of these principles was the so-called *Practical Orthography of African Languages*, Memorandum I, I.A.I., London, 1927. A later edition (1930) gives a selected bibliography of other contributions in this direction, esp. pp. 7–8.

24. M. Swadesh's proposals in this area were presented as a contribution to the 5th West African Languages Congress in Accra, 1965.

25. On the problem of marking tones in a phonemic script see my opinion in P. ZIMA, 'On the Function of Tones in African Languages', *Travaux Linguistiques de Prague*, 2, Prague, 1966, p. 153.

26. H. WOLFF, *Nigerian Orthography*, Zaria, 1954.

27. Serious problems arise in the lexicon as well, owing to the fact that the particular language coexists with two official languages and cultural systems, each introducing new concepts and terms: this sometimes results in the double borrowing of words. My earlier paper (P. ZIMA, 'Some Remarks on Loanwords in Modern Hausa', *Archives Orientales*, 32, 1964, pp. 522–8) exemplified some of these problems in the case of Hausa.

28. On the problems of Hausa written in Ghana, see in P. ZIMA, 'Hausa in West Africa: Remarks on Contemporary Role and Functions', in J. A. FISHMAN, C. A. FERGUSON and J. DAS GUPTA, eds., *Language Problems of the Developing Nations*, New York, 1968, pp. 365–77.

29. Op. cit., p. 9.

30. Several works analyse Hausa literature and poetry in particular. Apart from Robinson's work (note 8 above), we should mention as examples R. PRIETZE, 'Dichtung der Haussa', *Africa*, 4, 1931, pp. 86–95, and J. H. GREENBERG, 'Hausa Verse Prosody', *Journ. Amer. Oriental Soc.*, 69, 1949, pp. 125–35. Recently John N. PADEN devoted special attention to this topic, in 'A Survey of Kano Hausa Poetry', *Kano Studies*, I, 1965, pp. 33–9; a discussion of this author with M. Liman Muhammad is published in *Kano Studies*, II, pp. 44–55. The most recent contributions arising from scholarly research on Hausa literature are by M. HISKETT. Apart from his survey (op. cit., note 16), see also 'The Song of Bagauda: A Hausa King List and Homily in Verse, I–III', *Bull. SOAS*, 27, 1964, pp. 540–67; ibid., 28, 1965, pp. 112–35 and 363–85.

31. P. F. LACROIX, *Poésie Peule de l'Adamawa*, I–II, Paris, 1965.

32. See R. M. EAST, Bibliography (op. cit., note 12) and the Christian literature bibliography (op. cit., note 11).

33. Cf. my paper on Hausa (op. cit., note 28). Also in Paden (op. cit., note 30).

34. Recorded by U. BEIER, 'Public Opinion on Lovers, Popular Nigerian Literature sold in Onitsha Market', *Black Orpheus*, 14.

35. See, e.g. Eldred JONES, 'Krio in Sierra Leone Journalism', *S.L.L.R.*, 3, 1964, pp. 24–31; Thomas DECKER, 'Three Krio Poems', ibid., 3, 1964, pp. 32–4.

An Ethnolinguistic Inventory of the Lower Guinea Coast before 1700: Part II

[The first part of this article appeared in *African Language Review*, 7, 1968, pp. 47–73.]

P. E. H. HAIR

'KRU', GIBI-BASSA, KRA, GREBO

We considered earlier whether the 'Karou' in the Kquoja account were speakers of a 'Kru' language: if they were, then this is the earliest documented use of the term in an ethnolinguistic sense. Before their conquest of Kquoja, the Karou lived in part of 'Folgia', on the twin streams of the Junk River 'ten to twelve' Dutch miles inland, and neighbouring the Folgia people.[1] Folgia itself was separated by the Junk River from its overlordship, the kingdom of Manou.[2] Finally (according to the Kquoja account), to the immediate West of the Karou–Folgia–Manou complex, around Cape Mesurado and on the East bank of the St. Paul River—and therefore the Eastern coastal neighbours of the Vai—lived the Gebbe.[3]

The Cape Mount viewpoint of Dapper's account led to great emphasis being put on the political supremacy of the Folgia and Manou, but very little information was supplied which would enable us to discover their ethnolinguistic identity.[4] It is difficult to know the precise meaning, or trustworthiness, of the statement that 'the peoples of Gebbe and Folgia differ in language a little from each other', but we may begin by supposing that it means that the languages were inter-intelligible dialects.[5] Gebbe can be identified with fair certainty, for in much the same location today (inland from Cape Mesurado and between the St. Paul and the Junk rivers) the Gibi dialect of Bassa is spoken.[6] A vernacular name for the Junk River (or part of it) is Dukwia.[7] Nineteenth-century sources referred to a people behind Cape Mesurado, that is up the Dukwia River, known as Queahs, and it appears that this people too was Bassa-speaking.[8] Thus, there are some grounds for accepting Dapper's statement at its face value: the Folgia may have been the ancestors of the Queah/Kwia and, like the Gebbe, Bassa-speaking.[9] But the possibility cannot be excluded that our equation is incorrect and that Dapper's statement did not mean what we supposed it to mean. In this case, it is likely that the Folgia were a section of one of the two peoples who today occupy, with the Bassa, the region around the middle St. Paul and the upper Junk, the Gola or the Kpelle.[10] Identification of the Manou is also difficult. The name (in the variant form, Manoe) fits exactly the name of a modern Mande language of Liberia, Mano: but whereas the Manou/Manoe were found on the upper Junk River, the modern Mano live nearly one hundred miles to the East, separated from the Bassa by a wide stretch of Kpelle.[11] Since Dapper tells us virtually nothing about the Manou except that they were at one time powerful enough to dominate their neighbours,[12] and since there are no other references to this people in early sources, it seems pointless to speculate further.

The location of the Gebbe and Folgia in the seventeenth century approximates to the present-day location of the north-western limit of the Kru language group—apart from the following exception. Today, a very small group, speaking an unstudied language, the De or Dewoi, occupy an area on the North side of the lower St. Paul River, in the immediate interior.[13] Nineteenth-century sources asserted that the De, before the foundation of Liberia, had occupied a much larger area, including the coast from the Lofa (Half Cape Mount) River to the St. Paul River.[14] Since this coast was in the possession of the Vai in the early seventeenth century, and is in the possession of the Vai today, and if the assertions about a larger De domain are correct, then there must have been some shifting back and forward of the ethnolinguistic frontier during the eighteenth century. Furthermore, there appear to be no references to the De in the pre-1700 sources. It may therefore be that the De provide an exception, previously overlooked, to our generalization about ethnolinguistic continuity on the coast. On the other hand, the nineteenth-century sources are not altogether trustworthy and may have exaggerated the extent of De territory in the eighteenth century. It is also possible that the De are not a separate ethnolinguistic unit, but merely an overflow of the Bassa across the St. Paul River,[15] in which case their omission from our previous scheme would be less significant.

The most southern people mentioned in the Kquoja account were the Quaabe, who lived on the River Sess, but little was said about them.[16] Barbot visited the River Sess about 1680 and collected a vocabulary of this people, but later lost it—or so he said.[17] It is likely that Quaabe is a version of *Krao-be*, a Kra man.[18] This appears to be the earliest documentation of the name Kra (the relationship, if any, to the name 'Karou' is, as we have seen, obscure), but two fairly extensive vocabularies of much earlier date have been identified as being of the Kra.16 language. The earlier was collected, probably in the 1540s, at an unstated location probably near the River Sess, by a Frenchman: the second was collected in 1555, probably on the River Sangwin, by an Englishman.[19] Two words collected probably just before 1500 South of River Sess cannot be identified decisively in terms of Kra, possibly owing to defects in recording, but certainly resemble equivalent terms in the western Kru languages.[20] Pacheco Pereira, who supplied these two words, also stated that from River Sess for '25 leagues or more' to the South—30 leagues of his reckoning would bring one to the Grand Sess River—lived a people called Zeguebos.²¹ Modern sources record Segleo as the vernacular name for the Grand Sess River and Sikrɛkpo as the name of the local people, the most southern section of the Kra.²² The resemblance between Zeguebo and Sikrɛkpo is close. But if Pacheco Pereira's information was correct, the term originally had a wider connotation, applying apparently to the Kra as a whole.²³

Pacheco Pereira also supplied the name of the coastal people around Cape Palmas; and his 'Eguorebo' resembles the name of the modern ethnolinguistic unit in that area, Grebo.²⁴ A French author of the mid-sixteenth century reported the vernacular name of Cape Palmas,²⁵ while a German source of 1624 spoke of 'Gruvo'—though this may have been a local toponym rather than a version of the ethnonym.²⁶ Very little vocabulary was collected before 1700 from Cape Palmas, or from the coast further east where the Eastern Kru languages are now found. But a few words collected near Cape Palmas can probably be identified in terms of modern Grebo. As for the further coast, the Englishman Towerson remarked in 1555 after visiting a river 'thirteen leagues' beyond Cape Palmas, that 'the language of the people of this place, as far as I could perceive, differeth not much from the language of those which dwel where we watered before'.²⁷ The vocabulary collected at the earlier place was Kra.16, and the river visited beyond Cape Palmas almost certainly lay within the coast where the Kru language, Abri, is today spoken.²⁸ Towerson may therefore have been right in detecting a similarity between the two languages.

Western Kru: Bassa, Kra, Grebo²⁹

acoty begitoutou 'apresche toy baille moy ton pennyer' French MS. *c.* 1540, f. 51r: ——— Kra *a koti, be je tutu* 'sit down, let see basket' Informant.

aquio 'Par toute cette coste [of Malaguetta and up to Cape Palmas] quand ils nous saluent, ils prennent nostre grand doigt et l'indice avec les leurs, et les tirant de force les font claquer, disant *Aquio* comme qui diroit Serviteur' Villault 1669 (p. 137): *aqui-o* (probably plagiarized, but now said to be a women's greeting, at River Sess) 'a good day to you'; *macro* (the same) Barbot 1680 (p. 131) ——— cf. Grebo *nahwio*, pl. *ahwio* 'a form of greeting equivalent to "how do you do"' Payne; *na* 'my', *a* 'our', *wio* 'greeting' Innes.³⁰

dabo 'their Captaine' (probably collected near River Sangwin) Towerson 1555 (p. 102); *tabe* (king, chief, on River Sess) Dutch MS. 1598 (cited in Brun, op. cit., p. 39); *thaba* (title of king at Cape Mount—possibly an error of location, since River Sess was also visited) Brun 1623 (p. 51/39); *tabo* '... Grein-Kust ... Het lant wort bestiert door eenen Koning Tabo Seyle genaemt' Dapper 1668 (p. 430/60) ——— Kra *dɔbo*, 'head, leader' Informant.

guybo 'la mer' French MS. *c.* 1540, f. 51v; *guipo* 'Die Einwohner der gantzen Grein-Küst sind grosse Fischer/fuhren mit ihren kleinen Canoen 3 bis 4 Meilen in die offenbare See/denen dahin kommenden Schiffen entgegen/zu welcher mann sie kommen ... schreuende: Guipo!' Gröben 1682 (p. 33): —— Bassa *kuipu*, Kra *kuipi* 'white man' Koelle: Kra *kwi-bo* 'white man place' Informant.[31]

toma, toua, enfa nemate 'S'il arrive à bord [apparently near Cape Palmas], deux amis de differens lieux, ils se prennent par le haut du bras, les étendent l'un contre l'autre, et disent *Toma*, descendant ensuite au coude qu'ils se serrent, ils disent *Toua*; et enfin se pressant les deux doigts ... se les faisant claquer, disent *Enfa Nemate, Enfa Nemate*. Ce More qui parloit Hollandois nous explique ce salut, et nous dit que c'estoit la mesme chose que amy, comment vous portez-vous? tout ce que j'ay est à vous, et ma vie mesme...':[32] (plagiarized) Barbot 1680 (p. 138); —— cf. Grebo? *to nɔ* 'touch', ? *tɔ̃ã* 'begin', ? *tuɛ* 'honour, respect': ? *na fɛ de* 'how are you?': ? *nenatimiɛ* 'friend, companion' Innes: Port. *toma* 'take'.

waizanzag '... Guinea pepper ... the Blacks of Sestro call it *Waizanzag* ...' Barbot 1680 (p. 132) ——? (not the word for 'pepper' in any Kru language).

'QUAQUA'

Between Cape Palmas and Cape Three Points, Pacheco Pereira named only one people—and that by a Portuguese nickname—and he described the inhabitants as 'bad people'.[33] Part of this coast continued up to the eighteenth century to be known as the Coast of Bad People;[34] but this abusive nomenclature mainly reflected the fact that the region was much less well known to Europeans than were the regions to West and East, the Pepper and Gold Coasts. Moreover, the coastal peoples were less easy to know, or at least to distinguish: in the Ivory Coast section, the modern ethnolinguistic units are tiny and crowd in on one another—there are almost a dozen units on the shores of the lagoons[35]—and if anything like this confusion existed in the earlier period, it must have discouraged European visitors from close inquiry. In fact, few ethnolinguistic references occur in the early sources, and since we have dealt with most of these in our first (*Journal of African History*) paper, we here add only explanatory notes.

The Dutch named part of the coast the Quaqua Coast—the term probably derived from a local greeting[36]—and this produced some amusing comment from the ignorant.[37] Portuguese references to the 'Alares' living on this coast may refer (we have suggested) to the Aladyã: an additional early reference where the name appears as 'alandes' strengthens the suggestion.[38] The very limited knowledge of the peoples and languages of this coast shown by writers before 1700 was not improved on until the later nineteenth century: even Koelle's *Polyglotta Africana* (1854) failed to include a vocabulary of any one of the coastal languages between Cape Palmas and Cape Three Points.[39]

AKAN, GÃ-ADANGME, EWE

For the next part of the Guinea coast, we are moderately well supplied with ethnolinguistic information, and even with vocabularies. The short vocabulary collected at Elmina in 1480 has been re-examined, and although the items are poorly recorded, many can be identified in terms of modern Twi.[40] Additional to the vocabularies mentioned in our earlier paper,[41] the Frenchman Thevet included in his muddled account of Guinea a small number of words and phrases allegedly employed at Mina. It is clear that Thevet obtained the information through Arabic (which he claimed to speak) and little if any of the vocabulary is Akan.[42] It is of interest that a few Akan terms appeared in the first (and last?) global dictionary, published by Hieronymus Megiser in 1603.[43] The longest word-list published before 1700 was by the Danish chaplain Müller in 1673; Barbot's slightly shorter vocabulary was collected around 1680, but was not published till 1732.[44] Müller's 400 words and phrases in the 'Fetu' language, though collected at Afutu, are not in the modern Afutu/Guan language, but in Twi, the major language of the district: had they been in Afutu, they would have provided possibly decisive evidence on the historical relationship between Twi and the Guan group of languages, a point much under discussion today.[45] It is to be noted that opinion in this discussion appears to be moving towards a view confirmatory of our general thesis, the view that there is no evidence of Guan migrations in recent times.

The history of the interior units of Gold Coast is difficult to sort out, not least to decide which units named in early sources are ethnolinguistic and which are merely political.[46] Pre-1700 sources failed to indicate the language spoken in each unit, but Dapper (1668) made it clear that the language spoken between Shama and Kormantin, i.e. Twi, was also spoken in the interior for a considerable distance.[47] The western coastal boundary of Twi was indicated by a Dutch source of 1629 which remarked that the state of Guaffo or Great Comendo had a different language from that spoken in its western neighbour Anta (i.e. Ahanta/Anyi).[48] As for the eastern coastal boundary, Dutch sources knew that between Kormantin, and Berku, the chief town of the state to the east, the language changed, but they failed to state exactly where the language boundary fell in this forty or so miles: today, Akan (i.e. Twi/Akan) extends to just beyond Beraku.[49] However, on this same stretch of coast (in pockets around Apam, Winneba and Beraku), the Guan language Afutu is spoken today, and probably this was one of the four languages which Dapper asserted was spoken between Kormantin and Accra.[50] To sum up the evidence regarding the Akan languages and to repeat the conclusion of our first paper: there is nothing in the early sources to suggest either that these were spoken outside of the area in which they are spoken today, or that other languages were in the earlier period spoken within the Akan area; and the broad divisions within Akan, between Twi (including Fante), Guan and Anyi-Baule (including Ahanta), can be faintly detected in the early sources. This conclusion may be compared with recent statements by scholars working from a Ghana base. Dr. Goody, commenting on an affinity alleged to exist between the language families of this region ('Kwa, Guan, Gur and Togo Remnant'), remarks that 'in this area we seem to have no major ethnographical problems arising from radical discontinuities between the larger linguistic groups. ... What relatively complete linguistic continuity does show is that there were no wholesale invasions from outside, mass invasions of the kind which destroy the tongue of the indigenes and substitute a completely different language'.[51] And Dr. Stewart writes—'Apart from a few isolated pockets, all the Volta-Comoe languages [i.e. Akan in the wider sense] are spoken in a continuous area, and within this area all the languages of each sub-group with the exception of the Guan sub-group are also spoken in a continuous area. This orderly arrangement almost certainly means that Proto-Volta-Comoe was spoken somewhere in the region of the present main area and that there has not been a great deal of movement since.'[52]

Pacheco Pereira (1500) stated that the 'Mina' language was spoken in the Kormantin area, but implied that another language was spoken beyond, to the East:[53] De Marees and Dapper knew that 'another language' was spoken at Accra.[54] The latter called this new language a 'varying tongue' and said that the peoples of Accra, of Ningo, and of Sinko who spoke it could not understand each other: the former said that Ackra and Chinka spoke different tongues. These statements apparently referred to the related Gã and Adangme dialects.[55] Unlike Akan, Gã-Adangme had very little vocabulary in print before 1700.[56] The next language to the East, Ewe, did much better, with the publication of a translation of a standard missionary handbook in 1658, and a fairly extensive vocabulary was also collected around 1680 (published 1732).[57] Its coastal boundaries to West and East were not, however, exactly indicated in the early sources.[58] Much information was collected about the political units on the Ewe coast, and some of these units seem to correspond to ethnolinguistic sub-units.[59]

ETHNOLINGUISTIC INVENTORY—LOWER GUINEA COAST 231

Akan (Twi)[60]

barbero blaa 'ung blanc enffant' De la Fosse 1480 (almost certainly a miscopying for *barbero baa*) —— *aburo-ba* 'European child' Christaller. For the early use of *aburo-* 'foreign, imported, European',[61] cf. *abrobensi* 'Trompete' Müller 1673, *abbourbenn* 'trompette' Barbot 1680 —— *aborɔ-bɛŋ* 'European horn' Christaller; *abrenba* 'Oranje appelen' De Marees 1602 —— *aborɔbɛ* 'pine-apple' Christaller; *broddi* 'Banansen' Müller 1673, *obourady* 'banana' Barbot 1680 —— *oborɔ-de* 'plantain' Christaller; *abbrouhouâ* 'du suif' Barbot 1680 —— *aborongua* 'tallow' Berry; *brouhoumacatra* 'livres à ecrire' Barbot 1680 —— *borɔ-hōma* 'paper' Christaller; *brodjo* 'Patattas' Müller 1673, *boraguiho* 'patates' Barbot 1680 —— *ndwo* 'root' Christaller (not the modern term for 'potatoes', which is *borɔfo-ntommo* Christaller, i.e. 'foreigner's sweet-potato'); *bramba* 'Limonien' —— *aba/amba* 'fruit/s' Christaller (not the modern word for 'lemons' or 'limes'); *abronama* 'duyvven' De Marees 1602, Dapper 1668 (p. 464/92), *abronnuma* 'Taube' Müller 1673, *abbronouma* 'pigion' Barbot 1680 —— *aborɔnōmã* 'dove, domestic pigeon' Christaller; *abbrochéhanquabâ* 'orange' Barbot 1680 —— *aboraŋkaa* 'sweet orange', *aba* 'fruit' Christaller; ? *brouckou* 'haut-de-chausses' Barbot 1680 ——? *kuw* 'to pull off' (not one of the modern words for 'trousers'); ? *broto* 'pain' Barbot 1680 ——? *too* 'corn-pap' Christaller (but cf. the modern word for 'bread' *abodoo*: possibly a mis-hearing); ? *abrobra* 'quaetaerdige koortsen' Dapper 1668 (p. 95) —— (not the modern words for 'fever', 'malaria') ? *bra* 'menses' Christaller, i.e. the white man's periodical sickness; ? *abrakree* 'hoeren' Dapper 1668 (p. 479/106) ——? *a-kraa* 'female slaves' Christaller (not the modern word for 'prostitute').

berre bere 'vous soyez les bien venus' De la Fosse 1480; *bere bere* 'pax, pax' De Barros, Decada 1, liv. 3, cap. 1, 1552; ? *berá* 'comt hier' De Marees 1602 ——? *bĕrà* 'come' Christaller.

bruy 'milho grande' Brasio, op. cit., 3, item 15, Informação da Mina 1572; *abrui* 'Grosse Mielie, Türckischer Weissen' Müller 1673; *abbrouann* 'gros mil' Barbot 1680 —— *aburo* 'maize, Indian corn' Christaller, but the older term appears to have been *oburɔ-wi*, from *awi* 'grain' Christaller, thus linking it with the words listed above under *barbero blaa*.

dade 'Yser' De Marees 1602; *dabàn* 'Eisen' Müller 1673; *d'abban* 'barre de fer' Barbot 1680 —— *daa-de* 'iron', *ɔ-dabaŋ* 'bar of iron' Christaller.

dassee 'I thanke you' Towerson 1555 in Hakluyt 1589; *mame dasche* 'schenckt my wat' De Marees 1602; *daché* 'quelque present' Villault 1669 (p. 322); *midassi* 'grand merci' Barbot 1680 —— *da ase* 'to thank, lit. to lie down', *me ti da ase* 'thank you!' Christaller (and there may have been some convergence with the Portuguese *dar* 'to give', *das* 'you give'): information from Dr. Dalby.

elquethan 'toile blanche' Thevet, op. cit., 1575, f. 67r (allegedly in a language spoken at Mina) ——? Arabic *al-quṭn* 'cotton'; probably no connection with *kent/ŋ* 'country cloth/s' Christaller.

enchou 'leaue' De la Fosse 1480; *enchion* 'water', *fa inchon bera* 'brengt versch water' De Marees 1602; *ensù* 'Wasser' Müller 1673; *insou* 'de l'eau' Barbot 1680 —— *nsu* 'water' Christaller.

eninsan 'du coste du bras droit' Villault 1669 (p. 323) (apparently a misprint: *s* for *f*) —— *nifa/enyifa* 'the right side' Christaller.

foco, foco 'cloth' Towerson 1555 in Hakluyt 1589; *ensocó dasso* 'Türckische Tapetten' Müller 1673 (possibly a misprint for *enfoco*) —— *ɔ-daso* 'blanket' Christaller; if *foco* is a common element, cf. (?) *fukuu/fukufuku* 'villous, shaggy with long hairs' Christaller (but in the first item *foco* may be a misprint for *fofo*, on which see the next entry).

fouffe 'toile' De la Fosse 1480; *foufou* 'Linnewaet' De Marees 1602: *fúfu* 'Leinward' Müller 1673; *foufou* 'linen cloth' Barbot 1680 —— ? *e-fufu* 'a white thing' Christaller (but not one of the modern words for 'cloth' or 'linen').

henna 'König, Oberherr' Brun, op. cit., pp. 64/47, 76/56 (at Sabu, 1617); *aene* 'Capiteyn' De Marees 1602; *ohinne* 'König' Müller 1673 —— *ɔ-hene* 'king, chief' Christaller; possibly derived from this is: *bohen* 'tiger' Dapper 1668 (p. 464/91); *bohèn* 'ein Tigerthier' Müller 1673 —— *aboa* 'animal', *ɔ-hene/ɔ-hen* (Fanti) 'king' Christaller, cf. *aboa-fufu* 'a name of the leopard' Christaller.

[*sika*] *vyqua* (misprint for *syqua*) 'ouro' Pacheco Pereira, op. cit. (1500), p. 128: *sheke* 'golde' Towerson 1555 in Halkuyt 1589; *chika* 'gout' De Marees 1602; *scheke* 'aurum' Megiser, op. cit., 1603; *sicka Fouttou* '... mit dem besten Gold' (i.e. Futu gold) Brun, op. cit. (voyage of 1617), p. 67/50; *chika* Dapper 1668 (p. 466/93); *sica* Müller 1673; *chika* Barbot 1680 —— *sika* 'gold' Christaller.

tacous 'certains grains rouges, se servent au lieu de poids' Villault 1669 (p. 254); *taku* 'ein Gewächs, gleich hiesigen Erbsen, mit welchem auff dem Marckt das Gold gewogen wird' Müller 1673 —— *taku* 'seed of plant, formerly used as gold-weight' Christaller.

Adangme[62]

kackie, ennio, ette, ebbie, ennom (numerals 1–5) De Marees 1602 —— *kake* (Gã *eko*), *enyõ, etẽ, ewie* (*edfe*), *enuõ* (*enumo*) Migeod.

eppa, paou, pannie, neva, nomma (numerals 6–10) De Marees 1602 —— *ekpa, kpako* (*kpawo*), *kpanyõ* (*kponyõ*), *nẽ* (*nehũ*), *nyôn ma* Migeod.

YORUBA, 'BENIN', 'WARRI', URHOBO

Neither the Portuguese nor the Dutch had vigorous contacts with Yorubaland—and no vocabulary of Yoruba was published until

1819.[63] But Pacheco Pereira (1500) knew of Ijebu and recorded three Yoruba titles from the interior;[64] Dapper (1668) referred to the kingdom of Ulkami—probably an Ewe name for the Oyo Yoruba[65]—as 'a mighty territory, lying between Arder and Benin', much as today the whole Yoruba unit lies between Eweland and the Bini/Edo district. Though Dapper here seems to mean by 'Ulkami' all the Yoruba-speaking states, he later spoke of 'Ulkami, Jaboe, Isago and Oedobo' lying North of Benin, Jaboe being certainly Ijebu, and Oedobo, if not Owo, then (in error) a second name, Oyo, for Oyo/Ulkami.[66]

Benin, kingdom and town, was visited fairly frequently by the Portuguese and Dutch and occasionally by the English, and much information concerning the state and its trade was published before 1700.[67] But surprisingly little vocabulary was included in the accounts. Missionaries reached Benin town in 1515 and were soon teaching the royal household to read; by 1539, missionaries were offering the king 'cartilhas', little books of Christian doctrine. These were apparently in Portuguese; but since we know that by 1556 missionaries further South were producing 'cartilhas' in the Kongo language, the possibility that the missionaries in Benin began work on the vernacular is a strong one, and vocabularies of Edo may yet be discovered in missionary archives.[68] The interior boundaries of Benin were not known, but Dapper named neighbouring states: apart from the Yoruba states mentioned above, he referred to Isago, a land first said to be North West, then later West, of Benin, and to Istanna, to the East—both recently conquered by Benin.[69] These names resemble those of two modern peripheral Edo-speaking areas, Etsako and Ishan, but in the case of Isago, the geographical particulars cited do not fit.[70] No comment on the languages of these interior states was offered and no vernacular terms were cited.

To the South of Benin, Pacheco Pereira (1500) knew two peoples on the Forcados River, the Huela on the lower part, the Subou further inland.[71] These we take to correspond to the Iwere/Itsekiri and Sobo/Urhobo who occupy roughly these positions today.[72] The Iwere kingdom of 'Warri' was documented by Europeans from the 1570s, but not a single item of vocabulary is to be found in the published or unpublished accounts so far known.[73]

EDO[74]

akalles 'mensch-etende vogels' Dapper 1668 (p. 503/129) ——?
ahĩaṽɛ 'bird' Melzian.
ambasis 'kleine kleden' Dapper 1668 (p. 500/126) ——?
gore 'mensch-etende vogels ... en slagh' Dapper 1668 (p. 503/129) ——? *oghohɔ̃* 'fish eagle' Melzian.
iguou '... husam huũs buzios por moeda ...' Pacheco Pereira, op. cit. (1500), liv. 3, cap. 2, p. 135 of 1905 Lisbon edition; *iguos*

'buzeos' Ryder, op. cit. (1959), p. 308 (from the accounts of a ship trading in the Forcados River, 1522) —— *igho* 'money' Melzian.

mouponoqua 'katoene kleetjes' Dapper 1668 (p. 499/126) ——? *ukpõ* 'cloth' Melzian.

onegwa (chief who supervises on king's death) Dapper 1668 (pp. 503-4/130) —— *unwagwɛ* (chief who supervises on king's death) Melzian, Bradbury (pp. 25, 39).

oosaa 'huus homeẽs salvajens que abitam nos montes e arvoredos . . . e sam cubertos de sedas como porcos; tudo teem de criatura humana, se nam que em luguar de falar, gritam . . .' Pacheco Pereira, op. cit. (1500), liv. 2, cap. 7, p. 134 of 1956 edition —— *ɔsa* 'big ape, chimpanzee' Melzian.

orisa, owiorisa 'Godt, God's kint' Dapper 1668 (p. 505/131) —— *osa* 'High God' Melzian, Bradbury (p. 52); and cf. Yoruba *orişa* = *oòsa* 'any deity other than the High God' R. C. Abraham, *Dictionary of Modern Yoruba*—despite the semantic difference, suggesting that *orisa* may have been an older form of *osa* in Edo; plus *ovi* [*oβi*] 'child' Melzian (see Bradbury (p. 26) for the cult of Oloku, senior son of Osa).

ossade, arribo, ongogue 'Opper-rijxraden, d'oppersten des lants naest den Koningh' (and they rule parts of the town) Dapper 1668 (pp. 501-2/128) —— *osodi, ɛribo* 'town chiefs' Melzian, Bradbury (pp. 25, 38); the third title may be another version of *unwagwɛ*, see under *onegwa* above.

sjasseere or *owe-assery* 'de Velt-marschalk' Dapper 1668 (p. 500/127) —— *iyasɛ* 'war-captain' Melzian, Bradbury (p. 36): ? *ovi-iyasɛ* from *ovi* 'child' Melzian.

veeljes 'Koopluiden' Dapper 1668 (p. 499/125): *veilles* 'the Mercadors or Merchants; . . . the Veilles or Elders' Bosman, *Description of Guinea*, 1705, p. 437 —— Portuguese *velho* 'old'.

IJƆ,[75] IBIBIO, IGBO, DUALA-BANTU

According to Pacheco Pereira (1500), 'cannibals called Jos' lived in the rivers following Forcados River, up to Bonny River.[76] The earlier rivers were seldom visited by Portuguese or Dutch, but Bonny River became an important centre for Dutch trade in the 1640s.[77] Pacheco Pereira quoted one vernacular term which might be an earlier form of an Ijɔ.20 word; Dapper supplied the Ijɔ numerals 1–5, in connection with a language apparently spoken near Bonny and around Okrika.[78] The name Calabar began to appear in early seventeenth-century sources, and was applied to the Bonny River region, particularly to the port later known as New Calabar.[79] In 1627, Father Sandoval, a priest working among African slaves in the Caribbean, distinguished between 'Caravalies naturales e puros' and

'Caravalies particulares', without unfortunately making it clear who the former were: the latter traded with the native-Calabars (at New Calabar?) but did not speak the native-Calabar language, and were from 'innumerable' tribes and nations speaking non-interintelligible languages. Sandoval then listed some names of the 'innumerable', and about a dozen appear to be the same as those of modern settlements or peoples within thirty miles of New Calabar.[80] We cannot of course be sure that the toponyms of the early seventeenth century represented the same places as the same toponyms represent today; but it is significant that almost all the modern toponyms relate to Ijɔ settlements and the names appear to be Ijɔ in origin. It would seem therefore that a large proportion of the 'Caravalies particulares' were speakers of Ijɔ dialects, and it is perfectly possible—though there is no definite evidence—that Ijɔ was also spoken by the native-Calabars. This would however mean that Sandoval's statement about non-interintelligibility was exaggerated: while some of the 'particulares' would certainly not understand the Ijɔ-speaking 'puros' and 'particulares', it is not likely, judging by the range of the modern dialects, that at this date speakers of the various Ijɔ dialects would find it impossible to communicate. The non-Ijɔ 'particulares' are indicated by the other names on Sandoval's list, which turn out to be the same as those of the ethnolinguistic units neighbouring the Ijɔ today, i.e. the Evo-Sobo, neighbours on the Forcados River to the North West, the Ibo/Igbo to the North, the Andoni and the Ibibio to the East.

Sandoval's Done was most probably the same as the 'Odone' shown near Bonny on a map of 1665, and the 'Dony' visited near Bonny by a Frenchman in 1699: today, the Andoni, usually considered the most westward section of the Ibibio, though they count themselves distinct, meet the Ijɔ just East of Bonny.[81] The Moco/Moko referred to by Sandoval and Dapper were probably the remaining Ibibio, but no Moko vocabularies were printed before 1700.[82] Around 1640, the name 'Calabar' also appeared on the Cross River, which Dapper called, probably in error, the Old Calabar River.[83] A vocabulary of 'the Old Calabar language' collected probably around 1680 is mainly pidgin Portuguese but has traces of Ibibio in it.[84] Apart from Sandoval's inclusion of 'Ibo' in his list of 'Caravalies particulares', the only reference in this period to the modern northern neighbours of the Ijɔ and Ibibio came when a visitor to the coast between Bonny and Old Calabar referred, casually and without indicating a precise location ('The Hackbous country is some Leagues above New Calabar town'), to the interior 'Hackbous', apparently a mis-hearing or misprint for 'Hickbous', i.e. Igbo.[85] No Igbo vocabulary appeared in print.

We now reach the final unit of our ethnolinguistic survey. Information on the pre-1700 disposition of units is markedly less full for Lower

Guinea than for Upper Guinea; for two sections of the Lower Guinea coast—between Cape Palmas and Axim, and between the Bonny River and the Cameroons River—we have very little exact information, and the boundaries of units in other sections are often not very clearly defined. Vocabularies are too often fragmentary. It is pleasing therefore to conclude with the notice that, since writing our first paper, we have come upon additional evidence relating to the final unit, Duala-Bantu—evidence, moreover, of a linguistic nature, and therefore a further demonstration of the value of the method of inquiry. An extensive vocabulary of 'Words from the Cameroons, Rio del Rey and the Highland of Ambosus', previously overlooked in a printed source of 1665,[86] is closely identifiable in terms of the modern languages of the Duala group (A.20) of North Western Bantu—in practice, in terms of the best known language of the group, Duala itself. This group is today located around the Cameroons estuary and on the South and West slopes of Mount Cameroons: it thus falls wholly within, but occupies only a part of, the area between the Rio del Rey and the Cameroons estuary (including Mount Cameroons) to which the somewhat imprecise title of the vocabulary refers. In 1668, Dapper printed the numerals 1–5 in 'Kalbongo', stated to be spoken between Rio del Rey and the Cameroons River:[87] these numerals appear to belong to the same language as the vocabulary of 1665.[88]

The name 'Ambo', frequently stated in early sources to be an ethnonym from this part of the coast, usually with reference to the inhabitants of Mount Cameroons, remains a mystery. Was it only a pseudo-ethnonym—a corruption, perhaps, of a misplaced Portuguese toponym, or, conceivably, of a wandering Abyssinian toponym—or was it a genuine ethnonym, related perhaps to the (at least coincidental) name of a modern Bantu language-group of the Cameroons near-interior, the Mbo?[89] No Ambo vocabulary is available:[90] only if one is discovered is the mystery likely to be solved.

Ijɔ[91]

bozy 'ho carneiro' Pacheco Pereira, op. cit. (1500), liv. 2, cap. 9, p. 146 of 1956 edition —— *oḅori* 'goat' (but sometimes used as a cover-term for both 'sheep' and 'goat'): a mis-reading of the second consonant? or a sound-shift?

barre 'een' Dapper 1668 (p. 509/135) —— (not the modern word in any dialect: perhaps an informant's wrong answer) cf. *ḅara* 'hand' (reply when one finger held up?), or *ḅari* 'again'.

ma, terre, ni, sonny (2–5) Dapper 1668 (p. 509/135) —— (in the Bonny dialect) *ma* (qualifying, not counting form), *tɛrɛ, ini, sɔno/sɔnɔ* (perhaps combined with *-ye*, short form *- i* 'thing'?).

Duala[92]

moo/mo, meba/ba, melelle/melella, menaey/meleɟ, metany/matan (1–5) Woorden 1665/Dapper 1668 (p. 512/138) —— *mo, maba, malalo, manei, matanu* (1–5, in one set of prefix variants) Dinkelacker.

metoba, 's Jamba, lomba, sieyte [an error?], *d'Jon* (6–10) Woorden 1665 —— *mutoba, samba, iombi, dibua, dom* Dinkelacker.

corea 'hoenders' Woorden 1665 —— not *uba* 'fowl/s', but cf. Isuwu *kuba* 'fowl', *na gbi kuwa* 'I kill a fowl' Koelle.

fyne ''t is goet' Woorden 1665—not Duala ('F in Duala selbst nur in Fremdwörtern' Christaller), but cf. Portuguese *fino* 'thin, clever, excellent'; also cf. *fino* 'goet' in the language of Cap Lopez (according to P. de Marees, *Beschryvinghe* . . ., 1602, 1912 edn., p. 251). The appearance of this term in these vocabularies tends to confirm the Portuguese derivation suggested for modern Temne *finɔ*, in A. T. von S. Bradshaw, 'Portuguese in the Languages of Sierra Leone', *Sierra Leone Language Review*, 4, 1965, pp. 5–38, on p. 21.

gayombo 'ein tranck von etlichen Wurtzen' Brun, op. cit., voyage of 1614 (p. 40/32); ? *gajanlas* 'zekere wortelen . . . dia zy in water koken en daer eenen drank von maken' Dapper 1668 (p. 512/138) —— ?

kende 'gaat' Woorden 1665—not *ala* 'go', but cf. Mokpe *kende* 'go' Johnston.

lobbesje 'een vrou' Woorden 1665, *labouche* 'a woman' Barbot 1680 (p. 383) (supposedly in the Old Calabar language)—possibly an orthographic influence from Dutch *lobbes* 'big, good-natured person'; not *mutɔ, bito* 'woman, wife', but conceivably derived from Isuwu and Mokpe *libɛ* 'woman's breast' Koelle, Johnston.

longe 'kopere staven' Woorden 1665 —— *wɔngo/lɔngo* 'pot/s' Christaller (the gloss is wrong: both copper bars and copper pots were traded in the Cameroons).

makonsje 'iniames' Woorden 1665—not *mba* 'yam', perhaps confusion with *mukanjo* 'branch' Christaller, or (better) Isuwu *mokaŋga* 'root' Koelle.

macrale 'blancke' Woorden 1665 —— *mukala* 'white man' Dinkelacker.

mareba 'water' Woorden 1665 —— *madiba* 'water' Christaller, and cf. Isuwu *maliwa* 'water' Koelle.

moeye 'vuur' Woorden 1665—not *wea* 'fire' Dinkelacker (which has no other forms), but cf. Isuwu *moya* 'fire' Koelle.

myse 'oogen' Woorden 1665 —— *di-sɔ/mi-* 'eye/s' Christaller.

nanga 'slapen' Woorden 1665, *kinde* [see *kende* above] *nongue-nongue* 'go sleep' Barbot 1680 (p. 383) (supposedly in the Old Calabar language) —— *nanga* 'to lie down, to sleep' Christaller.

singa 'komt'—not *ya* 'come', perhaps *seŋga* 'to hear, listen!' Christaller, i.e. a command which would have much the same effect.

tocke tocke 'kleyn' —— *tiki-tiki* 'small, very diminutive' Saker.

NOTES

[Cf. bibliography in the Notes to Part I, incl. reference to our first paper on this subject: P. E. H. Hair, 'Ethnolinguistic Continuity on the Guinea Coast', *Journal of African History*, 8, 1967, pp. 247–68.]

1. O. Dapper, *Naukeurige Beschrijvinge der Afrikaensche Gewesten* ..., Amsterdam, 1668 and 1676 (in the latter, second pagination), p. 386/17: 'Het lant Karou ... is een byzonder landschap in Folgia, wel eer een woon-stede der volken Karous, die heden het Koningrijk van Kquoja te leen van de Folgias bezitten: want de Karous, gelijk te voore staet aengeroert, eer zy door de Folgias overwonnen waeren, woonden mede aen de reviertjens Rio Junk en Arveredo, tien of twalef mijlen recht op te lande in, nevens, om en by de Folgias'.

2. Dapper, op. cit., p. 386/17: 'De landen of Koningrijk van Folgia en Manou of Manoe, (welk laeste een machtigh Koningrijk is, en byna al d'omleggende landen onder zijn gebiedt heeft,) leggen aen twee klene reviertjes, in 't Portugeesch genaemt Rio Junk en Arveredo; te weten, Folgia Oost en Noorden boven Rio Junk, die beide tien mijlen bezuiden de Caep van Mesurado ... in zee storten, en scheiden dezen twee landen van elkandre ...'.

3. Dapper, op. cit., p. 426/56 ('Het lant ontrent kaep de Mesurado wort Gebbe genaemt, en de volken Gebbe-monou ...') and again p. 425/55, p. 386/17 ('... eveneens gelijk door de reviere van Sinte Paul het Vy-berkoma of Kquoja-berkoma van het lant Gebbe gescheiden wort') and also p. 384/14. On the Dutch MS. map (cited in Part I of this paper, n. 24), the 'Gebba' are shown on the edge of the map, South of the Lofa River; this is at variance with Dapper and was perhaps the map-maker's error.

4. Apart from personal (dynastic) names, no words in the Folgia or Manou languages were supplied. The only Folgia name was *Flangire*, a king: the first part might be *farā* 'chief', a term from Malinke found in Kquoja titles, but this might only indicate that in the Kquoja account alien names were given a Mande flavour. The Manou names were *Mendymo*, a king, *Manimassah*, his son, *Mimynique*, his grandson, *Kquwawoe*, a later king: the first two have a marked and perhaps inherent Mande resemblance—*mendi* ('lord' in Kquoja), *mo* ('man' in Vai, S.W. Koelle, *Vei Grammar*, 1853), *mani* (the ethnonym), *mansa* ('king' in Malinke, M. Delafosse, *La langue mandingue*, vol. 2, 1955). The names are to be found in Dapper, op. cit., pp. 412/42, 420/51, 423/53.

5. Dapper, op. cit., p. 406/36 ('De volken van Gebbe en Folgias verschillen in tale een weinigh van elkandre'), repeated p. 411/42. The quotation follows another statement about the local languages which we consider to be an example of European misreading of the situation: 'De Kquojas spreken niet alleen hun eigen en de Timmasche, Hondische, Mendische of Folgiasche tale, maer ook die van Gala en Gebbe.' While there may have been a fair number of Vai-speakers who also spoke some Temne or Gola or one of the Kru languages or one of the 'Hondo' languages, we do not believe that many Kquoja spoke all these languages or that multilingualism was any more general than it is today.

6. D. Westermann and M. A. Bryan, *Languages of West Africa*, 1952, p. 51 (*gibi*, spoken not around Monrovia but 'in the west'); De Tressan, *Inventaire linguistique de l'AOF*, 1953, p. 142 and carte 7: if this map is to be trusted, 'Givi' occupies the whole northern section of the Bassa-speaking area, i.e. from Monrovia inland some 20–30 miles. However, Gibi Mountain, Gibi Ridge and Gibi district are shown on the 1 : 500,000 map of East Liberia (U.S. Coast and Geodetic Survey, 1957) in the extreme North East of the Bassa area, on the upper Farmington (Junk) River, 40–50 miles inland.

7. J. Büttikofer, *Reisebilder aus Liberia*, Leiden, 1890, 1, p. 184, 2, map; De Tressan, op. cit., 'Duqueah'.

8. '... the Queahs, a small and quiet people whose country lies to the East of Cape Mesurado'; J. Ashmun, *History of the American Colony in Liberia*, Washington, 1826, p. 6 (the same statement was repeated in many later works on Liberia); Büttikofer, op. cit., 2, pp. 187, 326 n. 1.

9. Folgia may be *fo-k(w)ia*, in which case we note that *fɔ* in modern Gola means 'country' (Westermann and Bryan, op. cit., p. 23), hence *fɔ-kwia*, 'country of the Kwia': or

fol-k(w)ia, in which case there might conceivably be a connection with *fela*, the modern Kpelle name for the Bassa (ibid., p. 51).

10. The Gola, having been mentioned previously in the Kquoja account (as 'Gala'), may be thought to be less likely, but Gola *fɔ̃-gola* 'country of the Gola' bears a slight resemblance to Folgia. The name Kpelle does not seem to be documented before the late eighteenth century (see P. E. H. HAIR, 'An Account of the Liberian Hinterland *c.* 1780', *Sierra Leone Studies*, 16, 1962, pp. 218–26, on p. 220). But the 1957 map of Liberia shows a district North of Gibi, apparently in Kpelle country, named Nyafokole, a name which also has some resemblance to Folgia.

11. *Cartes Ethno-démographiques*, 2, IFAN, Dakar; WESTERMANN and BRYAN, op. cit., p. 39. Note however that Mano is apparently not the self-name of the people, and the latter source does not state which neighbouring language employs Mano. That the earlier Manou were located on the upper Junk River tends to be confirmed by the casual comment that a prince from Manou fled 'een weinigh noortwaerd op, in the lant van Gala' (DAPPER, op. cit., p. 421/51).

12. DAPPER, op. cit., p. 386/16: '. . . Galas, die onder het gebiet des Koningrijks van Manoe staen, en tot overste eenen Gallafally hebben' (Gallafally is perhaps *gola-fari*, Gola chief or governor, another Mande-ism); p. 411/42: 'Gelijk de Kquojas onder de Folgias staen, op een zelve wijze staen de Folgias onder den Keizer van Manou of Manoe, een machtigh Vorst, en geweldigh heerscher over verscheide meer andere landen en volken' (the Folgia and Gala send annual tribute to Monou and the former call the Monou 'Lords'—curiously, though, the Folgia language is the 'noblest speech' and called Lordly Speech, while the Monou language is not mentioned).

13. *Cartes Ethno-démographiques*, 2 note however that DE TRESSAN, op. cit., carte 7, and *The Tribes of the Western Province and the Denwoin People*, Bureau of Folkways, Monrovia, 1955, p. 37, both indicate a wider contemporary De territory than that shown on the *Cartes*, reaching at some points to the Lofa River. Relying on the *Cartes*, we previously assumed that De was not a modern coastal unit. A century ago, it was said of the De that 'this tribe will probably soon cease to exist . . . it being already confined to five hamlets in the vicinity of Monrovia' (KOELLE, *Polyglotta Africana*, 1854, p. 4). But this view must have been an exaggerated one.

14. '. . . Deys, who inhabit from 25 miles to the North of Montserado to the Junk, about 36 miles to the South', ASHMUN, op. cit., p. 6; but it must be doubtful if even in 1826 the De extended South of the St. Paul River—possibly Ashmun was confusing them with Bassa groups—and this doubt reflects on the reliability of his other information. Later sources on Liberia were often quoting Ashmun. An 1860 map (*Spirit of Missions*, Boston, 25, 1860, p. 366) shows 'Dey Country' running between the Lofa and the St. Paul rivers but marked 'Almost depopulated by slave trade'. It is possible that this area has never supported a large population (unlike the areas to North and South, around Capes Mount and Mesurado), for natural reasons, and that therefore the ethnic ownership of all or part of it has often been in doubt, or at least has often been not obvious.

15. De is also, and may have been originally only, a toponym, the vernacular name for the St. Paul River (according to KOELLE, *Polyglotta Africana*, p. 4). It may be noted that 'many Dei and Bassa elders state that the two groups are one people' (*Tribes of the Western Province*, p. 39)—not that much weight can be given to this sort of assertion.

16. DAPPER, op. cit., p. 419/50: '. . . de volken Quaabe-Monou, te weten, de volken die aen Rio-Cestes woonen': the Folgia and the Quaabe fought. In the section of his book after the Kquoja account, Dapper discusses the River Sess area, but his information is conventional and unoriginal—and the Quaabe are not mentioned.

17. 'I would have added [the vocabulary] of the Quabes-Monou, who inhabit the banks of Rio Sestro, and the circumjacent territories, but that I have lost that paper', J. BARBOT, *A Description of the Coasts of Guinea*, 1732, p. 414. The use of the term 'Quabes-Monou' proves that Barbot derived the ethnonym from Dapper, and is not therefore independent testimony to 'Quaabe'. Elsewhere Barbot said, 'The languages of the Blacks of this coast cannot be understood at all, and 'tis by signs and gestures that trade is carried on with them' (p. 137): he did however supply two original terms.

18. D. DALBY and P. E. H. HAIR, ' "Le langaige de Guynee": A Sixteenth Century Vocabulary from the Pepper Coast', *African Language Studies*, V, 1964, pp. 174-91, on p. 191, n. 5 to p. 190.
19. The vocabularies, to be found in Bibliothèque Nationale MS. Fr.24269, f. 51r-52r, and in R. HAKLUYT, *Principall Navigations*, 1589, p. 102 (in 'The First Voyage Made by Mr. William Towrson ... 1555'), are examined in detail in DALBY and HAIR, op. cit.
20. DALBY and HAIR, op. cit., p. 187, n. 1.
21. PACHECO PEREIRA, *Esmeraldo de situ orbis*, liv. 2, cap. 2, p. 102 of 1956 Bissau edition ('... este Rio dos Cestos ... e a jente d'esta terra e d'aly por diante vinte e sinco leguoas ou mais se chamam Zeguebos').
22. 'Ségleō' (KOELLE, *Polyglotta Africana*, 1854, p. 4): 'Sigli, the Kru Tribe at Grand Cestos' (CLARKE, op. cit., 1848/9, p. 95): 'Sikrɛkpo', i.e. Sikrɛ men (M. J. HERSKOVITS and S. TAGBWE, 'Kru Proverbs', *Journal of American Folk-lore*, 43, 1930, pp. 225-93, on p. 225). The southern boundaries of Kra are shown on *Cartes Ethno-démographiques*, no. 2, and map 7 of DE TRESSAN, op. cit., as just south of the Grand Sess River.
23. However, in a personal communication, Mr. Ronald W. Davis, of the Department of History, Western Michigan University, who has carried out field-work in the Grand Sess area, has questioned the equation of Zeguebo and Sikrɛkpo, on the grounds that local oral traditions suggest that the Sikrɛkpo only migrated into the area c. 1800, probably from the East.
24. PACHECO PEREIRA, op. cit., liv. 2, cap. 3, p. 110 of Bissau edition: '... e a gente d'este cabo das Palmas se chama Eguorebo'. *Goêdbo* is the more correct form of the self-name of the modern Grebo: see the references in DALBY and HAIR, op. cit., p. 190, n. 5. When a slightly revised version of Pacheco Pereira's roteiro of Guinea was published in 1608 (with subsequent editions and further versions up to the nineteenth century), mention of the Zequebo at River Sess was omitted, and the Eguorebo of Cape Palmas were renamed 'Siguerebo', probably a conflation of the earlier names (Manoel DE FIGUEIREDO, *Hydrographia ... com os roteiros ...*, Lisbon, 1608, 1614, etc., f. 40r). A Dutch source which leaned heavily on Figueiredo (Pacheco Pereira of course remained unpublished) reprinted the name as 'Signorebo' (D. RUITERS, *Toortse der Zee-vaert*, Vlissinghen, 1623, and edited 1913, pp. 340, 361/71 and n. 1).
25. A. THEVET, *La Cosmographie*, 1575, I, p. 68: Thevet, normally an unreliable source on Guinea, though he claimed to have visited there in the 1550s, stated that Cape Palmas was 'nommé Bourich en la langue des villains du pais'. A much later French source, who may however have been quoting Thevet, asserted that slaves from the Malaguetta Coast were known in the West Indies as 'Bouriquis' (MOREAU DE SAINT MÉRY, *Description de l'île de Saint-Dominique*, 1797-98, 1958 edn., I p. 49). A nineteenth-century missionary-linguist reported the Grebo tradition that 'directed by an oracle, the scattered fragments of the Tribe collected and built a large town, on Cape Palmas, called Bwine, or Bwimle' (J. PAYNE, *Dictionary of the Grebo Language*, New York, 1860, p. 4). The resemblance between 'Bwi-ne' and 'Bourich' suggests that Thevet's information was correct.
26. S. BRUN, *Schiffarten*, Basel, 1624, and edited 1913, p. 54/41: '... haben wir unser Raisz auff de Rio de Sesto und Palma [probably Pacheco Pereira's 'ilha da Palma', a little South of River Sess], wie auch gehn Gruvo fürgenommen. Seind sehr lustig anzusehen, ligen ohngefahr 30 meil van einander [30 German = 135 English miles: River Sess to Garraway is 120 miles], und hat jedes sein eigne sprach'. Brun's modern editor identifies Gruvo as Grebo, but it is probably the village of 'Goayva' (in P. de MAREES, *Beschryvinge ... vant Gout Koninckrijk*, 1602) or 'Gravay' (in JANSEN's *Atlas*, 1641), modern Garraway. The reference to 'each his speech' presumably indicates the difference between the Kra of Sess and Palma, and the Grebo of Gruvo. Brun had earlier observed (in a section on Cape Mount, but apparently in reference to the whole Liberian coast, along which he had sailed before reaching Cape Mount from the East)—'Doch hab ich gespeuret, dasz sich jhr spraach auff 20. oder 30. meil [100-130 English miles] schon änderet, wie bey uns Teutschen auch beschicht' (p. 53/40). The last phrase probably means that he was judging in terms of obvious interintelligibility whether of dialects or languages. Compare the remark of an Englishman: 'I have

observed that hence [near Cape Mesurado] along the coast to Cape Tres Puntas [at the beginning of Gold Coast], they have a different dialect every twenty leagues' (T. PHILLIPS (1693–94) in *Churchill's Voyages*, 6, p. 208).

27. HAKLUYT, op. cit., p. 104.

28. DE TRESSAN, op. cit., carte 7. The earliest vocabularies of Eastern Kru languages to be published were those in J. CLARKE, *Specimens of Dialects*, 1848/9; on which, see P. E. H. HAIR, 'Collections of Vocabularies of Western Africa before the *Polyglotta*: A Key', *Journal of African Languages*, 1966, pp. 208–17, and P. E. H. HAIR, 'An Introduction to John Clarke's "Specimens of Dialects" 1848/9', *Sierra Leone Language Review*, 5, 1966, pp. 72–82, on pp. 77–8.

29. The vocabulary is drawn from the French MS. in DALBY and HAIR, op. cit.; TOWERSON in HAKLUYT, op. cit.; BRUN, op. cit.; DAPPER, op. cit.; VILLAULT, sieur de Bellefond, *Relation des costes d'Afrique, appellées Guinée*, Paris, 1669; O. F. VON DER GRÖBEN, *Orientalische Reise-Beschreibung*..., Marienwerder, 1694, 'Guineische Reise-Beschreibung', 1682; BARBOT, op. cit., his original information dated to 1680. Unfortunately these sources are generally vague about the exact location at which vocabulary was collected, and tend to assume that there was more uniformity of language than was most probably the case. It has to be remembered that the authors of most of these sources were voyagers who visited the coast only once or twice. Further early vocabulary in Kra can be found in DALBY and HAIR, op. cit., 1964. Modern lexical works cited are KOELLE, *Polyglotta Africana*; PAYNE, op. cit.; Gordon INNES, *A Grebo–English Dictionary*, 1967. The material available on Kra and Bassa is clearly very inadequate, and modern dictionaries of these languages are desperately needed.

30. It is not known whether a similar greeting exists in Kra or Bassa. If not, it will be necessary to explain how a Grebo term came to be collected on River Sess. However the sources may be responsible: Villault is vague about the point of collection, and Barbot may be just copying (though it must be admitted that his version *macro* seems to be original).

31. DALBY and HAIR, op. cit., p. 186, suggest that the semantic confusion evident in the first entry arose because the French inquirer pointed out to sea ('la mer') and received the reply *kwi-bo* ('white man place, i.e. white man's home country).

32. This long gloss is included partly to illustrate the failure of many early sources to provide accurate and clear translations of African language material. The text continues—'ce qui fait bien voir que qui sçauroit cette langue la trouveroit plus belle qu'elle ne paroist', VILLAULT, op. cit., pp. 160–1.

33. Pacheco PEREIRA, op. cit., liv. 2, cap. 4, p. 114 of Bissau edition: 'Do Rio d'Alaguoa adiante sete leguoas sam achadas sete aldeas ... e duraram estas aldeas do principio atee o fim d'ellas sete ou oyto leguoas ... E os negros d'esta costa sam grandes pescadores ... e ha estes chamamos "Beiçudos" e aqui nam ha comercio e sam maa gente'. In the Bissau edition, R. Mauny identifies 'Lagoon River' as the mouth of the Bandama River at Grand Lahou, and adds that A. TEIXEIRA DA MOTA, *Topónimos de origem Portuguesa na costa ocidental de África*, Bissau, 1950, p. 295 'admet cette identification': in fact, on p. 259 (sic), Teixeira da Mota remarks 'notamos, porém, que de ... D. Pacheco, se deduz ser o actual R. Fresco' (and see p. 262). We agree with Teixeira da Mota that the coast (of the Seven Towns) is that just beyond Grand Lahou where the people today are Aladyã. A note in a nineteenth-century compilation is puzzling: it states that the people near Assinie—on the next stretch of coast—were known as 'Ecudo', a term not noted again but bearing some resemblance to 'Beiçudo' (which we suppose to be from Port. *beiço* 'lip')—A. TARDIEU, 'Sénégambie et Guinée', in *L'Univers: histoire et description de tous les peuples*, 1847, page not noted.

34. E.g. DAPPER, op. cit., 1668, p. 430, and in the second edition, 1676, second pagination, p. 60: '... de Tant-kust ... die andere ook de kust van Mala Gens noemen, dat is, van het quaed volk. Zy neemt haer begin van het dorp Gruwa, twee mijlen beoosten kaep de Palm gelegen, en eindight aen de kaep van Lohoe of Lahou ...'; 'Côte des Male-gens', on maps by and after D'Anville, e.g. 'Guinee entre Serre-Lione et le passage de la ligne', 1775.

35. See DE TRESSAN, op. cit., cartes 6, 7.

36. HAIR, op. cit., 1967, pp. 257–8 and footnote 37. The examination of 'Quaqua' history in Y. PERSON, 'En quête d'une chronologie ivoirienne', in J. VANSINA, R. MAUNY and L. V. THOMAS, *The Historian in Tropical Africa*, 1964, pp. 322–8, is disappointingly thin.

37. Material additional to references in footnote 37 of the first paper: BRUN, op. cit., pp. 32–3 of original/25–7 of reprint (voyage of 1614): '... kommen seind auff die Quaquase Kuste. Die Völcker daselbsten werden von uns Quaqua genennt, von wegen ihrer spraach, in deren sie uns also gepflegt anzureden und heissen willkomm seyn: Quaqua', 'Assine ligt bey 80. meilen von Quaqua' [this shows that 'Quaqua' did not extend to Assinie, but the distance is greatly exaggerated: from Assinie to Cape Palmas is only 300 English = 70 German miles, from Assinie to Cape Lahou 150 English = 35 German miles]; RUITERS, op. cit., pp. 304–05 of original/71 of reprint: '... en van de 7. mylen beoosten Cabo das Palmas, begint een Cust, al waer de Negros een seltsame sprake hebben, en schijnt datse anders niet als queeck, queeck, en spreken, en wat oostelijcker langhs die Cust, gaet haer sprake min noch meer, al ofte men de Ravenen hoorde roepen ... Dese Cust werdt ... ontrent 30. mylen lanck, tot een plaetse genaemt As sete Aldeas, al waer de Queeck, queeck-Cust zijn eynde heeft ...' [the reference to 'As sete Aldeas' shows that Ruiters is borrowing from Figueiredo (i.e. ultimately from Pacheco Pereira): his suggestion that from just beyond Cape Palmas to just beyond Cape Lahou only one language was spoken was almost certainly a misunderstanding of his sources]; A. BRASIO, *Monumenta missionaria Africana: Africa Ocidental*, 8, 1960, item 67, letter of Columbine de Nantes, 20.6.1634, on p. 279: 'les habitants de cette coste [beyond Malaguetta] quand ils viennent nous voir dans nos navires pour demander asseurance s'ils y seront bien venus, ils mettent le doigt dans l'eau et le portant à l'oeil en disant Coaqua'; VILLAULT, op. cit., p. 180: 'En abordant [apparently near Drewin], ils disent Qua, Qua, Qua, qui est comme bon jour et bien venu. C'est aussi la raison pourquoi les Hollandois appellent une partie de cette coste, la coste des Quaqua'; DAPPER, op. cit., p. 431/61: '... de kaep van La Hou, het uitterste van de Tant-kust en begin van de Quaqua-kust, die haer strekt tot aen Assine'; LOYER 1702, in P. ROUSSIER, *L'établissement de l'Issiny*, 1935, p. 154: '... Quaqua parcque les peuples qui l'habitent ont souvent cette parole à la bouche, qui signifie serviteur'; W. BOSMAN, *A New Description of the Coast of Guinea*, 1705, p. 491: 'The land from below, or a little Westward of Cape Lahoe to Jacque Lahoe is distinguished in the Maps and Charts by the name of the Quaqua Coast: but wherefore so called I cannot determine, unless it be that some compare the Speech of the Negroes to the Noise of Ducks, which I cannot confirm to you, because I could not observe so remarkable a difference between their Language and that of other Negroes, as should make it sound like Quacking. The Natives call their country Adaouw'; BARBOT, op. cit., pp. 138–9, 143: 'The Dutch and French reckon ... that of Quaqua from Rio Lagos [? River Fresco] to Rio de Sweiro da Costa [River Comoe] ... Cape La Hoe is ... the most trading place of all the coast ... Their language is barbarous, and altogether unintelligible, and they speak hastily and by starts. When they meet one another, either ashore or aboard, they use this word Quaqua, quaqua, each laying one hand on the other's shoulder, and then taking hold of their fore-fingers, repeating the same Quaqua very low; for which reason I suppose the name Quaqua was given to the ivory coast'; W. SMITH, *A New Voyage* ..., 1744, p. 113: 'Mr. Bosman seems mighty puzzled to know why this is call'd the Quaqua Coast ... the truth of this right Mistery is, that the word Quaqua in their Language signifies a Tooth ...'. We have suggested in our first paper (p. 258) that 'quaqua' derives from a greeting in the Avikam and Aladyā languages. Today these languages are spoken along the sea-coast and the inner lagoon from just East of Fresco River (where they neighbour Kru languages) to the Abidjan area, West of River Comoe: that is, in the older terminology, they are spoken around Cap Lahou and Grand Lahou and for some distance to the East. This part of the coast was the one most frequently visited in the seventeenth century, and was probably intended to be included in any definition of Quaqua. But the earlier definitions (Brun and Ruiters) include the coast West towards Cape Palmas, and Dapper includes the coast East to Assinie, and in neither of these additional sections are the two languages spoken today. This may indicate that the languages were spoken on a longer section of the coast in earlier centuries, or that a greeting resembling 'quaqua' is also found in neighbouring coastal languages: but the most likely explanation is that these writers were vague about the extent of the coast which took its name from a greeting in fact only met

around Grand Lahou. It will be noticed that Bosman limited the Quaqua coast to almost exactly the area of the two modern languages.

38. M. DE FIGUEIREDO, *Hidrographia*, 1614 edn., p. 54 ('costa dos Alares' from Sete Aldeas to Rio de Sueyro, because peopled with 'negros Alares'); BRASIO, op. cit., 3, item 15, 'Informação da Mina, 22.9.1572', on p. 93 ('Os alandes, que habitão quasi desde o Cabo das Palmas até perto de Axem . . .'): this writer was describing the coastal people who brought food by sea to the Portuguese at Axim and may have only guessed at the extent of the coast they occupied, particularly since it appears that the Portuguese had few contacts with the coast between Cape Palmas and River Fresco. If however his statement was correct and the 'alandes' were the inhabitants of almost the whole coast between Cape Palmas and Axim, then the term cannot have been an ethnonym. Bosman (see note 5) supplied another name for the people of the Quaqua coast, 'Adaouw': we have referred to this name in our first paper (p. 258 and note 38), but Bosman's reference hardly supports our suggestion that the Adaouw were the inland Adyukru. We previously overlooked a 1556 reference to 'Allowe', name of 'a place' (district?) about halfway between River S. André and Axim: HAKLUYT, 1589, p. 114.

39. CLARKE, op. cit. (1848/9), however, did slightly better, in publishing vocabularies of the Eastern Kru languages and of Avikam.

40. D. DALBY and P. E. H. HAIR, 'A Further Note on the Mina Vocabulary of 1479-80', *Journal of West African Languages*, 5, 1968, pp. 129-32. According to de la Fosse, the collector of this vocabulary, 'nous tirasmes vers la minne d'or . . . il y a une portz a ladite minne d'or, dont la premiere a en nom Chama et l'aultre quy est 6 lieues plus loing Laldee duos partz . . . et il m'escheut le lot d'aller les 6 lieues plus loing': R. FOULCHÉ-DELBOSC, 'Voyage à la côte occidentale d'Afrique . . .', *Revue Hispanique*, 4, 1897, pp. 175-201, on p. 182 (or p. 135/450 in the original MS.). The 'village with two parts' was in 1482 chosen as the site for the castle of São Jorge da Mina and is now Elmina; though de la Fosse of course meant by 'Mina' the whole neighbouring coast, it would appear that the vocabulary was collected at Elmina. In a personal communication (15.10.1966), Dr. J. M. Stewart of the University of Ghana has expressed doubts as to whether de la Fosse's vocabulary represents a true sample of a single language, since many of the recognizable items seem to Dr. Stewart to be as much Gã or Ewe as Twi-Fante: our own view is that the aberrance of many items derives from mis-recording.

41. On p. 259 and in n. 41: Professor Wilks' paper therein cited was given, not at the conference stated, but at the Third Conference on Africa History and Archaeology, S.O.A.S., London, in 1961. On de Marees' vocabulary (P.D[E] M[AREES], *Beschryvinge ende Historische verhael vant Gout Koninckrijck van Gunee . . .*, Amsterdam, 1602, and edited S. P. L'HONORÉ NABER (Linschoten Vereeniging), s-Gravenhage, 1912, pp. 125-9/255-9, 200 words and phrases: there are also many vernacular terms scattered through the preceding text), Dr. J. M. Stewart comments: 'if we take the main dialect division to be between Asante and non-Asante, it is fairly clear that the division was already marked by 1600, and that de Marees' vocabulary is non-Asante' (personal communication, 15.10.1966).

42. THEVET, op. cit., I, f. 67r: 'Vers castel de mine et Cap à trois poinctes, quand ils voyent quelque navire . . . [ils] trafiquent avec vous . . . il ne vous fault que mettre a terre . . . quelque piece de toile blanche, qui se nomme en leur langue *Elquethan* . . . Quant au Seigneur de castel de mine, il ne permet que pas un marchant ny autre estranger y entre: mais les Barbares y portent les grains d'or qu'ils tirent des rivieres . . . Lors vous verriez autour de vous un grand nombre de ces Mores . . . qui vous interrogent . . . *Tahob takul*, voulez vous manger? [i.e. Arabic *tuhibb ta'kul*] . . .', etc. Thevet had been to Arabia and therefore had some knowledge of Arabic: he is known to have visited Senegal (although the Senegal vocabulary he supplies is almost entirely Arabic or Berber), but it is less certain that he actually visited Gold Coast, though his text implies that he did. As the quotation shows, the conversation recorded between the informant and merchants from the interior is in Arabic. It is conceivable that some of the Dyula merchants visiting Gold Coast, being Muslims, knew this much spoken Arabic. But Thevet does not remark that Arabic is being used, rather he implies that this is the local vernacular. The possibility cannot be excluded that this passage,

like others in Thevet's writings, is wholly fictitious, or at least, fiction combined with material borrowed from earlier writers. If, however, it could be shown that Thevet or a direct informant had in fact visited Gold Coast, the passage might provide valuable evidence on the history of the use of Arabic as a lingua franca on this part of the Guinea coast. In J. O. HUNWICK, 'The Influence of Arabic in West Africa', *Transactions of the Historical Society of Ghana*, 7, 1964, pp. 24–41, although Dyula merchants on the coast and the use of 'pidgin Arabic' as a lingua franca are both mentioned, there are no pre-1700 references to Gold Coast.

43. H. MEGISER, *Thesaurus Polyglottus, vel, Dictionarium Multilingue*, Francofurte ad Moenum, 1603: we have not completed our examination of this work, but have noted that in the language termed 'Guineensium', the term for *aurum* 'gold' is *scheke*, i.e. Twi *s(h)ika*. We have not yet discovered where Megiser found this orthographical version of the term, but it was presumably a Germanic-language source. Another West African language occasionally cited in this work is 'Ialophorum', i.e. 'Jolof'.

44. Wilhelm Johan MÜLLER, *Die Africanische Landschafft Fetu*, Hamburg, 1673 (the recent German reprint has not been seen): on Müller, see H. DEBRUNNER, 'Notable Danish Chaplains on the Gold Coast', *Transactions of the Gold Coast and Togoland (later Ghana) Historical Society*, 2, 1956, pp. 13–30; BARBOT, op. cit., pp. 414–20—one section of the vocabulary 'being more particular to the Blacks of Axim and Anta' and another 'to those from Anta to Cormentyn' (p. 415). Neither vocabulary has yet received published study. Dapper (1668) also included a number of vernacular terms in the course of his account of Gold Coast (some borrowed from de Marees), hence the following comment in BOSMAN, op. cit., 1705, p. 131: 'And if the Negroes, which we daily converse with, who live about our Forts, expressed themselves as agreeable as the others, 'twould be no difficult matter to learn the Language in two or three years, which we find at present we can scarce do in ten, or at least not in any sort of Perfection. Some of us, amongst which I dare reckon my self, have made such a Progress, that we can understand the greatest part of it, though we can hardly hit the Pronunciation. The Sound of some words is so strange, that though we have often endeavoured to express them with our European letters, yet we have never been able to do so, and the Negroes can neither write nor read and consequently have no use of Letters, which renders it impossible for us to trace their Faults. Dr. Dapper, who never was here, hath adventured to express their Words; which, though I may pretend to some knowledge of their Languages, I dare not attempt, being assured I shall not succeed much better than he.' In contrast to this defeatist attitude, one of the earliest descriptions of a European engaged in learning an African language, using local informants, and with the difficulties precisely stated, relates to Gold Coast and Twi— T. Thompson, *Two Missionary Voyages . . .*, 1758, p. 70.

45. On the Guan languages, their present distribution and possible history, see J. R. GOODY, 'Ethnological Notes on the Distribution of the Guang Languages', *Journal of African Languages*, 2, 1963, pp. 173–89; C. PAINTER, 'The Distribution of Guang in Ghana and a Statistical Pre-testing on Twenty-five Idiolects', *Journal of West African Languages*, 4, 1967, pp. 25–78; C. PAINTER, 'The Guang and West African Historical Reconstruction', *Ghana Notes and Queries*, 9, November 1966, pp. 58–66 (turning on a limited and dubiously-based lexicostatistical analysis, this reconstruction is unconvincing in detail). But above all, on these subjects, and also on Twi and the Akan group, see a most important paper, J. M. STEWART, 'Akan History: Some Linguistic Evidence', *Ghana Notes and Queries*, 9, November 1966, pp. 54–8. This paper was not available to us when writing our first article. Dr. Stewart proposes a slightly different internal classification for the group of languages we have termed 'Akan', and also proposes a radical change of terminology, mainly for the following reason. 'Until recently, this language [Twi in our terminology] which is the mother-tongue of nearly half the population of Ghana, and which is spoken as a second language by a goodly proportion of the remainder, had no generally accepted name: it used to be customary to refer always to one or other of the two main dialects, namely Asante and Fante, and never to refer to the language as a whole. Now, however, the unity is admitted and the Asantes, the Fantes and the Government of Ghana are all agreed that the language should be called Akan. Linguists must clearly accept this development.' Whether or not the logic of the last sentence appeals to the body of linguists, there are certainly grounds for accepting some of the consequent changes Dr. Stewart

ETHNOLINGUISTIC INVENTORY—LOWER GUINEA COAST 245

recommends. It is not possible for us to alter terminology employed in the earlier papers of the series (thus, our Akan group corresponds to Dr. Stewart's 'Volta-Comoe', our Twi language to his Akan language), but we have accepted minor points, e.g. the term 'Guan' for the previous 'Guang'. Dr. Stewart argues on pp. 57–8 of his paper that 'the geographical positions of the Guan languages in relation to each other have remained largely unchanged since the original splitting up of Proto-Guan . . .'; and in a personal communication (15.10.1966) he adds—'I do not think that the present situation, whereby Twi-Fante is the dominant language throughout the areas of the southern Guan languages, is at all new. A study of the sound-correspondences suggests that Awutu and Larteh-Chirepon-Anum, unlike the more northerly Guan languages, have been under Twi-Fante influence for many centuries. Thus, if a Twi-Fante vocabulary was collected at a particular point on the coast at a particular time, it does not necessarily mean that Awutu [Afutu] was not spoken there at that time.' (This last point has reference to Müller's vocabulary.) Finally, on the subject of the Guan languages, Dr. Goody, in the paper cited above (on pp. 178–81), discusses the terms 'Brong' and 'Ntafo', and points out that 'Brong' does not necessarily indicate speakers of a Guan language, as we assumed in our first article (on p. 259): on this point, see also PAINTER, op. cit. (*G.N.Q.*, 1966), p. 65.

46. See the list of names in our first paper, p. 259: fuller references—PACHECO PEREIRA, op. cit., liv. 2, cap. 5, pp. 122, 124 ('. . . negros que de longuas terras este ouro aly trazem, os quaes sam mercadores de diverssas nasções, .s. Bremus, Atis, Hacanys, Boroes, Mandinguas, Cacres, Andeses ou Souzos e outros muitos . . .'); DAPPER, op. cit., p. 434/63, a list of 42 kingdoms. Add to the references in footnote 42 of our first paper, 'Map of the Gold Coast 1629' (map 743 of the Leupen collection, Algemeen Rijksarchief, The Hague, *Ghana Notes and Queries*, 9, 1966, pp. 14–15 and at end—showing the states of Anta, Abramboe, Acanij, Atij and Incassa. In this first paper (on p. 259) we stated that a Portuguese source of 1572 referred to the 'Taafo', five days journey beyond the 'Acanes': a re-reading of BRASIO, op. cit., 3, p. 110, shows that the last term is 'Asacẽs'—though this may well be a miscopying of 'Acanes', since it occurs in the form 'Asacẽs Grandes', and the term 'Acanes Grandes' appears on the map cited.

47. DAPPER, op. cit., p. 458/86: 'Het Koningrijk van Akanien . . . Hun tale is met die van Fetu, Atty, Sabou, Kommendo, en Abramboe, als ook Fantijn meest een en dezelve, doch wat liefelijker'; p. 480/107: 'De tale of sprake dezer volken is zeer verschillend: want van Kormantijn tot Akara, hoewel maer vijftien mijlen van elkandre gelegen, heeftmen vier onderscheidelijke talen. [Our comment in note 44 of the first paper was misconceived: this statement does not contradict the following one, since Kormantijn was the most eastern town of the most eastern Akan-speaking kingdom.] Maer d'Akanisten, Kormantijners, Fantijners, Moureers, Minaers, Kommendenaers; desgelijks die van Sama, Agitaki of Akitaki, Aguaffo, Futu, Igwa, Anemabo, Adja, Sabou, Abramboe, spreken een en dezelve tale: maer die van Anten verschillen van tale met de volken van Guaffo of Kommendo.' This statement means that the same language—or 'mostly' the same (perhaps the Twi-Fante dialects were indicated)—was spoken in the kingdoms and towns on the coast between Shama and Kormantin, in the neighbouring interior territories of Abramboe and Atty, and in their neighbour to the North, the 'Akanist' kingdom. The statement regarding Anta was omitted in the English translation of this passage (OGILBY, op. cit., p. 458): it indicates the difference between Twi/Akan and the Ahanta dialect of Anyi/Akan. Today, however, Shama lies just across the border, on the Ahanta side, whereas Dapper placed it within the Twi territory.

48. The text accompanying the Dutch map of 1629 (cited in note 46) states, in the published translation, 'Guaffo or great Comendo has another language than those of Anta'; cf. the statement in Dapper quoted in the previous note.

49. DE MAREES, op. cit., p. 42b/83: 'Berqu . . . dit volck spreken een ander tael, ende tot hier toe spreecken de voorgaende plaetsen al een spraecke'; DAPPER, op. cit., p. 453/82 is obviously quoting De Marees, but the reference appears as part of a description of the kingdom of Agwana, and it is therefore not clear whether the people of the new speech are the people of Berku itself, or the people of Agwana, i.e. from just beyond Kormantijn to Berku. On the modern boundary of Twi and Akan, see M. MANOUKIAN, *Akan and Ga-Adangme Peoples of the Gold Coast*, 1950, map. When De

Marees wrote—'De tellinghe van Anta tot Berque is een ghetal' (p. 128/258), he was presumably giving his view of the extent of the Akan languages, from Berque on the East to Anta on the West, though it is not clear why he failed to include Axim, which was known to the Dutch.

50. DAPPER, op. cit., p. 458/86, quoted in note 47. The 'four languages' are something of a puzzle: Twi and Gã of course make up two, but the third and fourth could only be separate pockets of Afutu/Guan. Dapper was perhaps drawing on, and exaggerating, De Marees (1602), who after stating that at Bereku a new speech was spoken, added that at Accra yet another was spoken: since the Accra speech was Gã, the Berku speech was presumably Guan. It is only fair to point out that, apart from these two references where the existence of a Guan language is implied—though the language is not named and no vocabulary is supplied—coastal Guan is undocumented in early sources. The purely linguistic evidence, however, as stated earlier, makes it almost certain that Afutu/Guan was spoken on or near the coast in earlier centuries. This is therefore very nearly an exception to our over-confident assertion in our first paper that every language of the coast could be documented in the early sources.

51. GOODY, op. cit., p. 175: the omitted section reads—'although there is plenty of evidence of displacement of languages *within* these larger groupings'. Inasmuch as this proviso applies to Akan, it presumably refers to the position of Guan, which Dr. Goody thinks shows evidence of expansion by migration in comparatively recent times; this view has, however, been strongly argued against, in STEWART, op. cit., pp. 57–8.

52. Ibid., pp. 56–7.

53. PACHECO PEREIRA, op. cit., liv. 2, cap. 6, pp. 126, 128: 'Adiante vinte leguoas do dito cabo Corço está hum promontorio que se chama ho cabo das Redes [exact identification uncertain] ... e toda a terra que vay do cabo Corço pera o cabo das Redes he Razoadamenta alta e montanhosa; e neste meo estam tres luguares povoados de pescadores .s. Fante o grande e Fante o pequeno, e Sabuu o pequeno [exact identification of these villages is uncertain, but they presumably lay within the later kingdoms of Sabu and Fanti, i.e. around Kormantin] ... e os negros d'esta terra falam a linguoajem dos da Mina ...' [The statement in the first article that Pacheco Pereira put the eastern boundary of the Mina language at Cape Redes was more definite than the quotation justifies.]

54. DE MAREES, op. cit., p. 43/89: 'Ackra ... sy spreken alhier wederom een ander tael'.

55. DAPPER, op. cit., p. 480/107: 'De volken van Akara, Nengo en Sinko hebben een verscheiden tale, en kunnen, hoewel zoo na d'een by den ander gelegen, elkandre niet verstaen'; DE MAREES, op. cit., p. 43b/90: 'Chinka ... sy hebben alhier een ander tael als die van Ackra doen, ende hoe luttel dat het scheelt van weechshalven van malcanderen, nochtans en verstaen sy malcanderen niet.' Note that we have modified the translation of Dapper given on p. 261 of our first paper. Today, Gã and Adangme are 'not completely mutually intelligible', but within each language all dialects are mutually intelligible—J. BERRY, in M. MANOUKIAN, op. cit., p. 69.

56. See p. 260 and note 48 of our first paper.

57. The translation—'*Doutrina Christiana, y explicacion de sus misterias, en nuestra idioma Español, y en la lengua Arda*, Madrid, 1658, pp. 26 (reprinted in the work cited in note 50 of our first article, and again in Mateo DE ANGUIANO, *Misiones Capuchinas en Africa*, 2, Madrid, 1958, pp. 251–66); BARBOT, op. cit., pp. 414–20, vocabulary of 'Fida and Ardra'. As explained in note 3 (p. 55) of our article on Upper Guinea in *African Language Review*, 6, 1967, we have treated 'Ewe' as a single unit, following Westermann and Bryan, although there are now appears to be agreement among linguists that some of the 'dialects' are in fact full languages. With regard to the study of earlier Ewe, the attention of linguists is drawn to a lengthy vocabulary and conversation manual in Gũ/Ewe, drawn up in 1731 and in 1741: L. SILVEIRA and E. CORREIA LOPES, editors, *Obra nova de língua geral de Mina de António da Costa Peixoto*, Lisbon, 1945. Portuguese contacts with Eweland in the eighteenth century are described in A. F. C. RYDER, 'The Re-establishment of Portuguese Factories on the Costa da Mina in the Mid-eighteenth Century', *Journal of the Historical Society of Nigeria*, 1, 1959, pp. 157–83 (but the vocabulary is not mentioned).

58. Dapper, for instance, described a stretch of coast on each side of the Volta River without naming the inhabitants (p. 488/115): he then described the kingdom of Arder, extending from East of Grand Popo (without discussing the Popo area in detail) to Aqua, whose precise location was not subsequently indicated (p. 488/115). Finally, he included in the description of Arder references to the coast beyond (and far beyond) the kingdom—references to Ba (? Badagry), to River Lagos, and to Kuramo (? a variant or misprint for Kurado, i.e. Ikurudu; see A..F. C. RYDER, 'Dutch Trade on the Nigerian coast during the Seventeenth Century', *Journal of the Historical Society of Nigeria*, 3, 1965, pp. 195–210, on pp. 196–7; and P. C. LLOYD, 'Osifekunde of Ijebu', in P. D. CURTIN, *Africa Remembered*, 1967, pp. 217–88, on p. 239), again without naming the inhabitants (p. 494/121). About the languages spoken in Arder, Dapper made a curious statement (p. 491/118): 'Hun eigen moederlijke tale of sprake is by hen weinigh geacht, dies zy die zelden spreken; maer meest Alkomijs, daer te lande voor een edele sprake gehouden.' The 'noble' speech Alkomy was apparently Locumi or Yoruba; Yoruba–Arda connections are examined, rather superficially, in I. A. AKINJOGBIN, *Dahomey and Its Neighbours 1707–1818*, 1967, p. 13 (note that the 'Yoruba–Aja Commonwealth' of the seventeenth and eighteenth centuries, extending as far as Benin, depicted in the map on p. 10, is an outrageous tribal-patriotic fiction).

59. According to AKINJOGBIN, op. cit., p. 13, 'the first known European notice of "Ardra" appeared on a map of 1596'. However, a toponym resembling Arda/Ardra had appeared on maps in approximately the location of Arda since 1500: e.g. B. M. Egerton MS. 2803, Italian map c. 1508, 'alhalondra'; A. Z. CORTESÃO and A. TEIXEIRA DA MOTA, *Portugaliae Monumenta Cartographica*, I, 1960, plate 39, Portuguese map of 1539, 'alladia', and plate 15, Portuguese map of 1540, 'alhandra' (many other instances could be given, but multiplication of examples does not strengthen the evidence as it is clear that these sixteenth century maps were copied from each other). While it is possible that the cited toponym was a corruption of the Portuguese 'aldea da' ('town of'), this is rendered less likely by textual evidence of the existence of Arda as early as 1539: BRASIO, op. cit., 2, item 29, 'Carta dos missionários do Benim a D. João III, 30.8.1539', on p. 82: '... pollo costume que tẽ de ma. tratar e cativar todos os ẽbaixadores dos Reis que lhe screvẽ, como fez aos do Labidā e aos d'Arida ...' (Labida was a Gold Coast kingdom [? Labadi], while Arida/Arda was a neighbour or near-neighbour of Benin). The form 'Arida' actually appears as a toponym in the approximate position of Arda, on a map of 1570: CORTESÃO and TEIXEIRA, op. cit., 3, 1962, plate 266, map by Fernão Vaz Dourado. The peoples on and neighbouring the Arda coast were listed in 1627 as follows: 'Las castas que de ordinario traen de aquellas partes [to São Thomé, as slaves] son Minas, Popoos, Fulacs ['otro Principe en medio de' Popo and Arda—modern ?], Ardas o Araraes [possibly a doublet for Arda/Allada, but as written elsewhere Axares, perhaps from the ethnonym 'Aja'], q̃ todos es uno, Offoons [Fõ], tambien casta Arda; Locumies ...', A. SANDOVAL, *Naturalez ... de todos Etiopes*, Seville, 1627, lib. 1, cap. 16, f. 59r, insert from cap. 14, f. 51v. The 'Fulaos' were apparently from 'Faloim': BRASIO, op. cit., 5, item 137, 'Relação da Costa da Guiné, 1607', on p. 381 ('O resgate de Arda ... O resgate de Faloim ... Os resgates de Benim e Poupo'). The Fõ were named in a slave trade document of 1690: R. RICHARD and G. DEBIEN, 'Les origines des esclaves des Antilles' *Bulletin de l'IFAN*, B, 26, 1964, pp. 167–211, on p. 181, 'Foins'.

60. The sources cited frequently in this list are as follows: DE LA FOSSE 1480 (see the article cited in note 40), a vocabulary of a score of words, apparently collected at Elmina; TOWERSON 1555, in R. HAKLUYT, *Principall Navigations*, 1589, p. 108, a vocabulary of eight words, collected apparently near Elmina; DE MAREES, op. cit., columns 125–9, pp. 254–9 of the modern edition, a vocabulary of about 300 words and phrases of 'de Swarten vande Gout-custe van Guinea (principael ontrent het Kasteel de Maine)'; MÜLLER, op. cit., an appendix of unnumbered pages entitled 'Vocabula oder Nenn-Wörter welcher sich die Fetuischen in ihrer Sprache gebrauchen', a vocabulary of about 400 words; BARBOT, op. cit., pp. 415–20, but we have preferred to quote most of the words from a manuscript source, J. BARBOT, 'Journal d'un voyage de Guinée' 1678–79, B.M. Add. 28,788, where the Akan vocabulary of about 250 words is to be found on pp. 79–82. The lexicographical sources quoted are J. G. CHRISTALLER, *Dictionary of the Asante and Fante Language*, 2nd edn., 1933, and J. BERRY, *English, Twi, Asante and Fante Dictionary*, 1960.

61. For a discussion of some terms containing *aburo-*, see J. N. MATSON, 'History in Akan Words', *Transactions of the Gold Coast and Togoland Historical Society*, 2, 1956, pp. 63–70, on pp. 63–5. The following terms derived from *bɔrɔfo* 'European' Christaller, are also to be found in DE MAREES 1602—*borfokango* 'Neerlanders', cf. *Kǎŋkǎŋ brɔfo* 'Dutch' Christaller; and *borfapa* 'Portuguesen', cf. *Butukesi-borɔfo* 'Portuguese' Christaller.

62. The modern source cited is F. W. H. Migeod, *The Languages of West Africa*, vol. 1, 1912: on p. 143, sets of Gã and Adangme numerals as collected by the author. The Gã numerals, when they differ from the Adangme ones, are added in the word-list in brackets. It will be noted that the earlier numerals are only very marginally closer to modern Adangme than to modern Gã.

63. On the Dutch, see RYDER, op. cit. (1965). The first vocabulary of Yoruba was published by Bowdich in 1819—see P. E. H. HAIR, *The Early Study of Nigerian Languages*, 1967, pp. 4–5.

64. PACHECO PEREIRA, liv. 2, cap. 7, p. 130: 'Rio do Laguo ... e doze ou treze leguoas por este Rio acima he achada hũa grande cidade, que se chame ho Geebuu ... e ho Rio d'esta terra aguora em nossos dias se chama Agusale'; 'in our day' suggests something more transient than a river, and since the ruler of Ijebu is today entitled *awujale*, the text should probably be amended to read 'Rey' (or perhaps 'Ro', i.e. 'Reino') for 'Rio': this emendation was tacitly made in A. F. C. RYDER, 'An Early Portuguese Trading Voyage to the Forcados River', *Journal of the Historical Society of Nigeria*, 1, 1959, pp. 294–321, on p. 306, and Dr. Ryder commented that 'the difference between [Agusale] and the present form may well represent a true change in pronunciation and not a Portuguese mistake'). Also ibid., p. 134: 'Ao levante d'este Reyno do Bemy cem leguoas de caminho no sertaão he sabida hũa terra, que em nossos dias teem hum Rey que se chama Licosaguou [? *orukɔ*, 'name', *Salakɔ* 'male name'], R. C. ABRAHAM, *Dictionary of Modern Yoruba*, 1958] ... e loguo junto com este estaa outro grande senhor, que ha nome Hooguanee [Edo, *oghene*, 'lord', title of the ruler of Ife]'; on *oghene* (*ɔghɛnɛ*), see A. F. C. RYDER, 'The Benin Missions', *Journal of the Historical Society of Nigeria*, 2, 1961, pp. 231–59, on p. 232, but also note the second thoughts in A. F. C. RYDER, 'A Reconsideration of the Ife-Benin Relationship', *Journal of African History*, 6, 1965, pp. 25–37, on p. 27. Pacheco Pereira's reference to two interior kings was incorporated in the roteiro published by M. DE FIGUEIREDO, op. cit., editions of 1614 and later, but with the names now appearing as 'Miosaque' and 'Agare': these forms were borrowed by the Dutchman RUITERS, op. cit., 1623, and by the Spaniard SANDOVAL, op. cit., 1627, the latter treating them as names of coastal peoples (e.g. lib. 1, cap. 16, f. 59r, 'Mosiacos, Agares').

65. Add to note 51 in our first paper: P. MORTON-WILLIAMS, 'The Ọyọ Yoruba and the Atlantic Trade 1670–1830', *Journal of the Historical Society of Nigeria*, 3, 1964, pp. 25–45, on p. 27; AKINJOGBIN, op. cit., p. 13, n. 4; RYDER, op. cit. (1961), p. 241, quoting a document now available in BRASIO, op. cit., 8, item 135, 'Carta de Frei Columbino de Nantes ao Prefeito da Propaganda Fide, 26.12.1640', on p. 464, a reference to 'Licomin', first as the name of a territory neighbouring Benin and then mistakenly as the name of a language spoken in Benin and neighbouring districts. The earliest known references to Locumi are in a work written in America describing the ethnic provenance of slaves: 'A un lado destos Ardas, estan situados la tierra adentro los Lucumies ... aunque estos Lucumies suelen diferẽciar entresi, y no entẽdesse, por ser de tierras muy apartadas', SANDOVAL, op. cit., lib. 1, cap. 14, f. 51v, and cap. 16, f. 65v. Today there are many Yoruba dialects, but these are in general mutually intelligible, hence it is likely either that Sandoval's information about non-intelligibility was wrong, or that he was using Locumi to mean other groups as well as Yoruba-speakers. Sandoval's list of coastal peoples, the first part of which was quoted in note 59, continues—'Locumies o Terranovas [this nickname is an indication that this part of the coast had not been well-known to European traders before 1600]; Barba [see below], Temnes [an error?: the Temne were omitted from an earlier list of Upper Guinea peoples], Binis, Mosiacos, Agares [for these two names, see the previous footnote], Gueres [Warri], Zarabas, Iabus [Ijebu], Caravalies ...'. Later, discussing tattoo-marks (a section of interest to ethnographers), Sandoval refers to 'los Lucumies Barbas' and 'los Lucumies Chabas' (cap. 16, f. 66v). Thus, the Locumi were distinguished from the Ijebu, but included the Barba (? Barba/Borgu, today the neighbours to the North West of Oyo Yoruba: if so, one of the earliest references in

European sources to a Gur language), and the Chaba (? Shabbe, a language related to Nupe, today lying between Yorubaland and Nupeland, North of Oyo, or ? Shabe, allegedly a Yoruba kingdom, West of Old Oyo, see AKINJOGBIN, op. cit., map on p. 10). A list of kinds of Locumi living in nineteenth century Cuba can be found in F. ORTIZ, *Hampa afro-cubana/Los negros esclavos*, 1916, pp. 39–41.

66. DAPPER, op. cit., p. 494/121: 'Het Koninghrijk van Ulkami of Ulkama, een machtigh gewest, leit gestrekt beoosten Arder, tusschen het Koninghrijk van Arder en Benijn, in 't Noord-oosten, doch 't komt niet aen strant uit'; p. 495/121: 'Het Koninghrijk van Benijn ... paelt in het Noord-westen aen het Koninghrijk van Ulkami, Jaboe, Isago en Oedobo, in 't Noorden aen dat van Gaboe, acht dagen reizen boven de groote stadt Benijn gelegen ...'. It is open to question whether in the last quotation there is any significance in Dapper's use of the singular in 'the kingdom of Ulkami, Joboe, Isago and Oedobo': cf. above, 'between the kingdom of Arder and Benijn'. If we allow that Ulkami did not include Ijebu, it is not at all clear whether Ulkami reached the sea, or was wholly interior; it is conceivable that at this date, the Yoruba states were cut off from the sea by Benin control of the coastal lagoons. As regards 'Oedebo', note that in Dutch, intervocalic /d/ is often pronounced as a *y*-glide: hence the term may approximate to the mysterious Oye-Eboe of Olaudah Equiano (P. EDWARDS, ed., *Equiano's Travels*, 1967, p. 7), as well as to Owo or Oyo. Dapper's information on Western Nigeria is discussed in RYDER, op. cit. (*J.H.S.N.*, 1965), pp. 197–8, where it is suggested that Gaboe may be an unrecognized variant of Jaboe/Ijebu.

67. PACHECO PEREIRA, op. cit., liv. 2, cap. 7, pp. 132, 134, 136 (he claimed to have visited Benin four times); R. EDEN, *The Decades of the newe worlde* ..., 1555, f. 345v–348v (voyage of 1553); R. HAKLUYT, *Principal Navigations*, 1598 (voyages of 1588–89 and 1590–91); DE MAREES, op. cit., the section by D. R. entitled 'Beschyvinghe ... vande groote Stadt Bennin'; RYDER, op. cit. (1961) and op. cit. (*J.H.S.N*, 1965).

68. On the Benin missions, see RYDER, op. cit. (1961), pp. 235, 238, 259: the 1539 letter translated on pp. 258–9 is in BRASIO, op. cit., 2, pp. 80–1, and on p. 391 of the same volume see the reference to a 'Cartilha da Doutrina Christã em lingoa do Congo' (which was apparently printed though no copy is known to exist). Ryder mentions the attempt of another party of missionaries to learn the Benin language in 1642 (p. 244).

69. DAPPER, op. cit., p. 495/121: 'Het Koninghrijk van Benijn ... paelt in het Noord-westen aen het Koninghrijk van Ulkami, Jaboe, Isago en Oedobo ... in 't Oosten aen het Koninghrijk van Istanna en Forkado of Ouwerre, en in 't Zuiden aen de zee'; p. 505/132: 'Isago, schatbaer aen den Koningh van Benijn, paelt in 't Westen aen de Benijn. Het lant is rijk van peerden ... De Koningh van Isago overtreft veerre in maght en mogentheit die van Jaboe en Odobo, en ontziet den Koningh van Benijn het minste van allen . . Het Koninghrijk van Istanna, gelegen om d'Oost van het Koninghrijk van Benijn, was wel eer een machtigh Koninghrijk'.

70. Etsako is N.N.E. of Benin, not N.W.—though some of the other compass directions are certainly inexact, e.g. Warri is said to be East of Benin whereas it lies to the S.E. The vegetation of the modern Etsako area is mainly orchard bush, and because of tsetse fly there are no horses today—R. E. BRADBURY, *The Benin Kingdom*, 1957, pp. 81–2. While the reference to horse-rearing suggests a savannah kingdom, probably North of the Niger, we are not convinced that Isago represents Isaji, supposedly an ethnic group in Nupeland, as proposed in RYDER, op. cit. (*J.Af.H.*, 1965), p. 33, and instead agree that the name is 'not easily identifiable'—R. E. BRADBURY, 'Chronological Problems in the Study of Benin History', *Journal of the Historical Society of Nigeria*, 1, 1959, pp. 263–86, on p. 276.

71. PACHECO PEREIRA, op. cit., liv. 2, cap. 8, p. 138: 'Ric dos Forquados ... Ha jente d'este Rio se chama Huela; e mais dentro no sertaão estaa outra terra que se chama ho Subou ...'.

72. Huela = Hwela = Hwera = Iwera = Iwere. We find Dr. Ruder's comment on Pacheco Pereira's names puzzling: 'Huela, a name that cannot be identified with any certainty, but probably related to the Urhobo or Isoko. Beyond them and further in the interior were the 'Subou' (Sobo)—a name which if erroneous is clearly also of some antiquity' (RYDER, op. cit., 1959, p. 296). Today, the Urhobo/Sobo still live 'further in the interior' than the Iwere: see the map in BRADBURY, op. cit., 1957.

The comment on p. 127 of this last work that Sobo 'a name often indiscriminately applied to the Urhobo and Isoko is a corruption of 'Urhobo' much disliked by the people themselves', and the remark in WESTERMANN and BRYAN, op. cit., p. 89—'The name Sobo is an anglicized form of Urhobo', both involve misconceptions. The term 'Sobo' is old and is merely a slight mispronunciation, and mis-hearing, of 'Urhobo': in the Urhobo language '*rh* is realized ... in careful speech as a voiceless alveolar tap. This sound is easily mistaken by an inattentive ear for *s*. ... Hence, 'Sobo' for "Urhobo" ' (J. KELLY, 'Urhobo in the *Polyglotta Africana*', *African Language Review*, 7, 1968, pp. 107-13, on pp. 109, 112). The Zarabas/Zarabus listed by Sandoval (see note 65) between the Warri and the Calabars may be the Sobo/Urhobo, if we can accept an extreme corruption of the ethnonym.

73. A. F. C. RYDER, 'Missionary Activity in the Kingdom of Warri to the early Nineteenth Century', *Journal of the Historical Society of Nigeria*, 2, 1960, pp. 1-26, on pp. 2-3; RYDER, op. cit. (*J.H.S.N.*, 1965), pp. 204-05; the name 'Oeyre' is recorded in a Portuguese document of 1522, but appears to relate to a port on the Benin River—this may have been within Iwere territory, but the later 'Warri' was on the Forcados River, RYDER, op. cit., (1959), p. 301, n. 2.

74. Most of the terms of the word-list are from DAPPER, op. cit. The modern sources are H. MELZIAN, *A Concise Dictionary of the Bini Language of Southern Nigeria*, 1937, and BRADBURY, op. cit. [See also Postscript below.]

75. In the section on the Ijɔ, detailed comments on linguistic points by Dr. Kay Williamson, and on toponyms by Mr. Robin Horton, both of the University of Ibadan, very kindly supplied in personal communications, have been incorporated in the text and have led us to modify or correct statements in our first paper.

76. PACHECO PEREIRA, op. cit., liv. 2, cap. 8, pp. 138, 140, 144: 'Rio dos Forquados ... Ha jente d'este Rio se chama Huela; e mais dentro na sertaão estaa outra terra que se chama ho Subou ... e adiante d'estes há outros negros que ham nome Jos e possuem grande terra e sam jente belicosa e comem os homeẽs ... Rio dos Ramos ... A jente desta terra sam chamados Jós ... Rio de Sam Bento ... Rio de Sant 'Ilefonso ... Rio de Santa Barbara ... Rio Pequeno ... estes quatros Rios ... sam abitados d'aquelles povoos a que chamam Jos ... Rio Real [Bonny River] ... A jente d'este Rio sam chamados Jos; estes e os de que atrás falamos, todos sam huũs e todos comem carne humana ...'. The form 'Jos' for 'Ijaws' was used at the end of the eighteenth century by a Frenchman, *Mémoires du capitaine Landolphe*, Paris, 1823, I, p. 134. We suggested in our first paper (p. 262) that the term 'Usa' (applied to pirates operating off the Benin and Forcados rivers: BOSMAN, op. cit., p. 430) was a corruption or misprint of Ijɔ; another explanation can be found in P. D. CURTIN, *Africa Remembered*, 1967, p. 243 (see also p. 236, n. 41 by P. C. LLOYD). But Dr Williamson has pointed out that the modern pronunciation of the ethnonym varies as between the dialects of Ijɔ, so that the Central Ijɔ call themselves *Izɔn*; and she suggests that 'Usa' might indicate an earlier form *Uzɔ. However, the form [I]jɔ must have been found in some dialects *c*. 1500, since, as we have seen, Pacheco Pereira used it to describe the people in all the rivers. His evidence incidentally raises doubts whether the term (in any form) 'was originally used only by the Central and Western groups and has been extended to include the Eastern Ijɔ by administrators and ethnologists' (K. WILLIAMSON, 'Ijɔ Dialects in the *Polyglotta Africana*', *Sierra Leone Language Review*, 5, 1966, pp. 122-33, on p. 124). Finally, Pacheco Pereira's evidence throws doubts on the too easily accepted traditions of migration of the Delta population from Benin (uncritically accepted, for instance, in K. O. DIKE, *Trade and Politics in the Niger Delta 1830-85*, 1956, p. 24), a point made in E. J. ALAGOA, 'Oral Traditions Among the Ijo of the Niger Delta', *Journal of African History*, 7, 1966, pp. 405-19, on pp. 416-7. In footnote 53 of our first paper, we suggested that Pacheco Pereira's reference to a country called Opuu 'one hundred leagues' up the Forcados River (liv. 2, cap. 7, p. 136—'... e hindo cem leguoas por ha madre d'este Rio Fermoso acima he achada hua terra de negros, a que chamam Opuu ...') probably referred to the Ijɔ, whose territory can be reached via the interior waterways from the Forcados. Dr. Williamson comments: '*opu* means "great" and is indeed common in place-names, e.g. Opu Dekema, "Great Degema", but is never used alone as far as I know. I wonder if "Opuu" could represent "Opughu", since -*gh*- is often very faintly pronounced. But this does not suggest any town to me, nor have I heard of such a name being used for the Ijɔ.'

77. RYDER, op. cit. (*J.H.S.N.*, 1965), pp. 205-07: this argues that the information in Dapper's 1668 account of this part of the coast refers in fact to the 1640s. A 'Bras' slave in Cuba in 1568 may have been from the Ijɔ town of Brass (disregarding the unproven etymology from English 'brass'-pans), but a corruption of Bran/Bram/Brame is perhaps more likely—ORTIZ, op. cit., p. 30.

78. DAPPER, op. cit., p. 509/135: 'Het lant van Kalbarien is gelegen om en by een reviere, na dit lant de reviere van Kalbarien by d'onzen, anders in 't Portugeesch Rio Reael genoemt ... Deze reviere ... heeft binnen haren tweden hoek, aen den westwal, een dorp leggen ... by d'Invvoonders Fokké [Ifoko] genaemt ... Aen de noort-zijde van den gemelden spruit [i.e. the western one] leit een dorp Kalbarien ... Acht mijlen bewesten het dorp Kalbarien leit een dorp Belli genoemt ... Ontrent veertien mijlen de reviere van Kalbarien opwaerts, loopt een spruit Oost-noord-oost op, aen den welken verscheide dorpen leggen [the distance is exaggerated, and the trend of all the channels is N.W., not E.N.E., but at least towns well in the interior, perhaps in the Degema area, must be indicated]. Aen de reviere Kalbarien, eenige mijlen Noortwaerts op, leit een lantschap, genaemt Kriké [Okrika], daer aen een ander paelt, Moko genaemt. Zuidaerts van Moko leit na den zeekant een Landschap Bani genaemt [around modern Bonny], daer in een tamelijk groot vlek is, genaemt Kuleba, daer zeker Kapitein of lantvooght woont, die wel acht of tien dorpen onder zich heeft, en met zijn gebiet wel drie mijlen verre strekt, te weten, van bewesten de reviere Kalbarien tot aen het dorp Sangma [? Sengana, West of Brass]. Al de zwarten, die den oostelijken oever der grote reviere van Kalbarien bewonen, en hoger Noortwaerts op leggen, zijn mensch-eters; te weten, zy eten hunne vyanden op, die zy doot in den oorlogh bekomen; maer brengen de genen, die zy levendigh gevangen krijgen, tot Kalbarien te koop. Het getal, een, heet by hen *Barre* ...'. It is thus not made clear precisely the extent of the language of the vocabulary: was it limited to the town of Kalbarien? or to the blacks on the east side of the river, and northwards, who were man-eaters? or was it the speech of the whole area described, from the east side of the mouth of the river (the modern Bonny area) along the coast to west of modern Brass, and northwards up to Okrika and perhaps to the Degema district? We think the latter extent fits the text best, but admit that some doubt remains. Today, Ijɔ is spoken in the Bonny, Brass and Okrika districts and in the southern part of the Degema district: see the maps in WILLIAMSON, op. cit., p. 123, and in D. FORDE and G. I. JONES, *The Ibo and Ibibio-speaking Peoples of South-Eastern Nigeria*, 1950. The numerals appear in the German and English translations of Dapper, but are missing in the French translation (p. 315); hence, the evidence they provide was not taken into account by G. I. JONES, *The Trading States of the Oil Rivers*, 1963, pp. 36–8, when discussing early Delta trade and peopling. Dr. Williamson states that the numerals are closer to those in the modern Bonny dialect of Ijɔ than to those in any other dialect.

79. BRASIO, op. cit., 6, item 138, 'Relação de Garcia Mendes Castel Branco' 1620, on p. 471: 'Tenemos otro rescate con el Rey de Calabar, jente belicosissima ... Tenemos otro rescate com al Rey del Rio Real', the latter perhaps at Bonny?; ibid., 8, item 92 'Consulta do Conselho de Estado' 16.1.1636, on p. 348: 'os portos de Arda e Calabar'; K. RATELBAND, *Vijf dagregisters van het kasteel São Jorge da Mina* 1645-7, 1953, pp. lxxxiv-v, map of the New Calabar River, showing Focko [Ifoko] at the mouth and Rio Calbaery [Buguma Creek] within, dated 1638. The origin of the name 'Calabar' is uncertain. According to Dapper, the capital of Bani state was called 'Kuleba' (see previous note). Since the mid-nineteenth century at least, the town called Bonny by Europeans (perhaps from its Igbo name *uɓani*, assuming that the Okrika Ijɔ name for it, *iɓani*, is also borrowed from Igbo, and not vice-versa) has been known to its Ijɔ inhabitants as *okoloma*, allegedly from *okolo* 'species of bird', *ama* 'town': S. W. KOELLE, *Polyglotta Africana*, 1854; p. 8: WILLIAMSON, op. cit., p. 122. Now, if Dapper's information was correct, it is possible that an older form of *okoloma* was *okoloba* or 'Kuleba' (perhaps *okolo-ibe*, from *ibe*, 'clan'—although it is possible that the *okolo* derivation of *okoloma* is a late folk-etymology). Europeans may have transferred the name from the town near the mouth, to the river down which the trade came, and ultimately to the interior market at 'New Calabar'. It is worth noting that Portuguese sources from 1514 give the Rio Real (Bonny River), or one of its streams, the name Rio do Carmo/Rio Carmo (e.g. D. PERES, *Os mais antigos roteiros da Guiné*, Lisbon, 1952, 'Roteiro de Jaõa de Lisboa' (1514), on p. 66; CORTESÃO and TEIXEIRA, op. cit.,

I, plate 15, Jorge Reinel 1540; on the 1538 Dutch map referred to above, 'Ryo Carone' is the channel to the East of Bonny island): a Portuguese derivation is possible, but there is some resemblance between 'Carmo' and *okolama*, which might deserve further investigation—if it could be shown that *okoloba* and *okoloma* were variants rather than successive forms. As for the alternative name of *okoloma*, Bonny, this too is perhaps not recent: a reference to a 'Bany' village in the Rio Real in 1659 can be found in E. DONNAN, *Documents Illustrative of the History of the Slave Trade*, I, 1930, p. 141.

80. SANDOVAL, op. cit., lib. 1, cap. 1, f. 7v: 'Y treinta leguas desviados destos Reynos [Guere/Warri and 'Zarabu'/? Sobo] estan en cinco grados y medio los Caravalies, a los quales se siguen quarĕta, o cincuenta aldeas de varias y diferentes castas, y naciones destos negros, que acà llamamos Caravalies particulares, aunque realmente no lo son: pero porque salen, y vienen al rescate con los caravalies, los tenemos por tales. A estos Caravalies no se les conoce Rey ... y todos comẽ carne humana. Passados estos, a poco espacio esta la isla de Fernando Po ...'; lib. 1, cap. 16, f. 59 [misnumbered]: list of tribes taken as slaves tó São Thomé, as quoted in note 65, continues—'Gueres, Zarabas, Iabus, Caravalies naturales, o puros que dezimos: y Caravalies particulares. Estos ultimos son innumerables, y que no se entienden unos con otros ni los entienden comunmente los Caravalies puros. v.g. Ambo Caravali particular, Abalomo [Abolama], Bila [Bile: Belli in Dapper], Cubai [? Kugbo, near Nembe], Coco [cf. Koko on the Benin River: perhaps the toponym also occurs further East], Cola [Kula], Dembe [Nembe], Done [? Andoni], Evo [? Evo/Sobo], Ibo, Ido [Ido, near Buguma], Mana [? Mene, according to Bile traditions, an enemy settlement destroyed during the slaving days], Moco, Oquema [Egwema, near Akassa], Ormapri [? Orupiri (Forest-of-gods), near Bonny, perhaps formerly Orumapiri (Forest-of-the-gods)], Quereca [Okrika: Dapper's Krike], Tebo [? Tabaugh, near Bari], Teguo [? Etegwe, near Yenagoa: today Edo-speaking but politically connected with Ijɔ]; y assi van diferenciando innumerables en nombres, assi como en lĕguas ...'. Also f. 66r: 'Los Caravalies tambien tienen sus señales muy distinctas, que assi como lo son las naciones, lĕguas, y castas que no las refiero por ser como ellos, innumerables'. Mr. Robin Horton has commented: 'Oral traditions and corrobative material evidence (captured sacred tusks) suggest that between 1500 and 1600, the town of Bile was at least as prominent as New Calabar and Bonny in the slave trade, and that Bile got its slaves by sacking neighbouring Delta villages, rather than by trade with the hinterland. The Sandoval reference corroborates this by mentioning Eastern Delta villages whose inmates would be unlikely to have appeared under the circumstances of later peaceful trade by New Calabar and Bonny.' This present note supersedes (and corrects) note 54 in our first paper.

81. To the references in notes 56 and 57 of our first paper, add BARBOT, op. cit., p. 462. Sandoval's 'Done' was misread in our notes and appeared in our first paper as 'Dare'.

82. See p. 263 and n. 55 in our first paper, and add: 'Eboes ... some of them ... called Mocoes', B. EDWARDS, *The History of the British Colonies in the West Indies*, 1793, 2, p. 49; but cf. 'The Quaws (or Moscoes of the West Indies) whom the Eboes regard with great aversion', H. CROW, *Memoirs*, 1830, p. 200 ['The Bonny Ibo call the Ibibio Kwa', FORDE and JONES, op. cit., p. 68]: 'the Andoni today call inhabitants of Ibibio territory Mbogo', M. D. W. JEFFREYS, note in *Africa*, 5, 1934, pp. 503–06, on p. 504: 'Mboko is the present-day Kalabari word for all Ibibio', R. Horton (personal communication).

83. DAPPER, op. cit., p. 511/137: 'Van den Oost-hoek van Rio Reael, tot aen de reviere van out Kalbarien, strekt de kust Oost-zuid-oost zestien mijlen.' The Dutch had little trade beyond the Bonny River—RYDER, op. cit. (*J.H.S.N.*, 1965), pp. 207–08. The 'Calabar' slaves of the eighteenth century were from both New Calabar and (Old) Calabar.

84. See p. 263 and n. 56 of our first paper, and add this reference: BARBOT, op. cit., p. 383. Some of Barbot's 'Old Calabar' words appear to be Duala (see the Duala word-list).

85. Ibid., p. 461 and the map following p. 462; more information about the Ibibio and Ibo may yet be obtained from mission records—in the 1690s, missionaries at a base in São Thomé were in contact with kings of Calabar, 'Farahu' (?), and neighbouring

lands, according to documents in the archives of Propaganda Fide, listed in R. GRAY and D. CHAMBERS, *Materials for West African History in Italian Archives*, 1965, p. 90, items 876, 878.

86. *Pertinente Beschryvinge van Africa . . . getrokken en vergadert uyt de Reysboeken van Johannes Leo Africanus . . . by-gevoegt een pertinente beschryvinge van de Kuste van Guinea soo als die hedensdaags bevaren word, en de Handelinge die daar op de Gout-kust word gedreven . . .*, Rotterdam, 1665, p. 319 'Woorden in de Cameronis, Rio d'Elrey en 't hooge Land van Ambosus': the additional material in this work on seventeenth-century Dutch trade on the Guinea coast is valuable, but its main matter (and title), a Dutch translation of Leo Africanus' account of North Africa and the Sudanic states, has led to its being overlooked, e.g. in J. BOUCHARD, *La côte du Cameroun dans l'histoire et la cartographie*, IFAN, Centre du Cameroun, Douala, 1952; E. ARDENER, *Coastal Bantu of the Cameroons*, Ethnographic Survey of Africa, 1956. Our attention was drawn to it by a note in the 1913 edition of BRUN (op. cit., p. 31, n. 9), by the learned editor, the late l'Honoré Naber. [P.S. This vocabulary has now been studied in detail in E. ARDENER, 'Trading Polities between Rio del Rey and Cameroons 1500–1650', in I. M. LEWIS, *History and Social Anthropology*, 1968, pp. 81–126; and in P. E. H. HAIR, 'The Earliest Vocabularies of Cameroons Bantu', *African Studies*, 28, 1969, pp. 49–54. Ardener's paper supplies a comprehensive analysis of the various European sources on the Cameroons before 1700, and his conclusions on ethnolinguistic points should be compared with those in the present paper, esp. his discovery of some Efik terms in the vocabulary.]

87. DAPPER, op. cit., p. 511/137: 'Na de reviere d'oude Kalborgh [Cross River], komt Rio del Rey te leggen, welke een groote en heel wijde reviere is . . . Het lant om en by de reviere del Rey is al laeg en waterigh lant . . . Aen den Noordelijken oever dezer reviere del Rey leit een dorp, daer voor eenige jaren zeker Overste . . . over geboodt, maer wiert verdreven door die van Ambo . . . De volken, die hooger de reviere op wonen, by hen genaemt Kalbongos, zijn kloeke mannen . . . [their habits described . . .] Dezelve maniere wordt aen het hooge lant van Amboises, in Ambo, en Boetery onderhouden; welker Inwoonderen geduurigh tegen de zwarten, aen Rio del Rey gelegen, oorlogh voeren . . . [p. 512/138] Tusschen Rio del Rey, en de reviere Kamarones, ontrent ten halven wege, leit een kleine en nauwe reviere . . . Van daer tot aen de Kamarones strekt de kust Oost-zuid-oost, ontrent drie mijlen . . . In deze reviere worden by d'onzen ook slaven gehandelt, voor een en de zelve waren, gelijk in Rio del Rey. Zy gebruiken met die van de Kamarones een zelve getal: *Mo* is by hen een [etc.] . . . Het lantschap van Ambosine . . . is gelegen tusschen de revieren del Rey en de Kamarone, met zijnen uithoek vier mijlen van Rio del Rey. Aen de West-zijde van dezen uithoek leggen verscheide dorpjes, onder andere een, genaemt Bodi of Bodiwa, anders Cesge [surely a misprint] genaemt . . . Vier mijlen in 't Zuid-oosten van den uithoek . . . en vijf van de reviere Kamarones, leggen drie kleine eilandekens in zee, d'Amboises genaemt . . . [p. 513/138] Ontrent vijf mijlen van het hooge lant van Amboises leit de reviere Kamarones, anders Jamoer genoemt . . . [p. 513/139] Aen den Noordt-wal der reviere Kamarones woont zeer veel volks, mede Kalbanges genoemt, die oorlogh voeren tegen die van boven, daer de handelingh valt.' Note that the French translation omits the numerals, and is incorrect at several points, e.g. (at the end of the extract) '. . . qui sont toûjours en guerre avecs leurs voisins qui portent le même nom' (p. 316). The 'high land of Ambo' is certainly Cameroons Mountain, but the other geographical references are less clear. Jamoer/Jamoor is today the name, not of the main stream of the Cameroons estuary (the Wuri), but of the stream entering it on the North side, just East of Cameroons Mountain (and alternatively called River Mungo). Dapper's 'Rio del Rey' was clearly one of the rivers flowing into the large bays South East of the Cross River and North West of Cameroons Mountain—but which one? All these rivers pass through a quasi-delta region of islands and channels (a 'low, watery' area), and before 1600 they were not known separately to Europeans; the bay which is fed by the delta was termed 'Angra del Rey' (TEIXEIRA DA MOTA, op. cit., pp. 305–06). However, seventeenth-century maps do show a Rio del Rey, a river heading due North, and therefore presumably the River Ndiang, not far from the Cross River and the furthest of the rivers of the bay from the Cameroons Mountain. If we suppose that Dapper meant the Ndiang, then his Kalbongo who lived 'higher up' would be located at least 70 miles North of Cameroons Mountain. Unfortunately Dapper nowhere states the distance between

the Cross and the Rio del Rey rivers, but this can be estimated approximately by working backwards from the Cameroons River, as follows: (*a*) From Cameroons River to Mount Cameroons is said to be 5 Dutch/23 English miles (correct). (*b*) From Cameroons River to the islets of Ambas Bay is also 23 miles (roughly correct). (*c*) From the islets to the 'uithoek' of Mount Cameroons is about 18 miles in a North West direction; the 'uithoek' is therefore probably Debunja Point, about 15 miles W.N.W. (*d*) From Rio del Rey to the 'uithoek' is about 18 miles; the nearest point of the quasi-delta is in fact 30 miles away, while the internal mouth of the Ndiang is 60 miles away, and the channel of the Cross River about the same. It would seem therefore that Dapper meant by 'Rio del Rey', not the Ndiang, but some waterway nearer Mount Cameroons; either the main channel through the complex of islands (which today bears the name), or perhaps the nearest of the rivers, the Meme, which flows westward into the bay from behind Mount Cameroons and whose internal mouth is less than 40 miles from Debunja Point. (*d*) The 'little river', about 15 miles from River Cameroons, must have been the Bimbia River; it cannot have been 'half way' to the Rio del Rey, however the latter is identified. While this argument is not conclusive, it raises the possibility that the Kalbongo on the 'Rio del Rey' were not, as supposed above, on the Ndiang, but on the lower Meme River, immediately to the North of Mount Cameroon. If this is so, then they were in appropinquity to the other Kalbongo on Mount Cameroons and along the Cameroons River, or, in other words, the Kalbongo were to be found in a relatively restricted area around Mount Cameroons. Today, the Duala group does not extend to the North quite as far as River Meme, nor does it hold the northern or S.W. slopes of Mount Cameroons, but it is to be found on the other slopes, South to the Ambas Islands, and East to the Cameroons River. If therefore the Kalbongo were the ancestors of the peoples today speaking Duala group languages (see p. 264 of our first paper), and if our second interpretation of their location in the seventeenth century is correct, there has been some retreat on the North perimeter, before speakers of Mbɔ group (A.15) languages. However, the positioning of the modern group strongly suggests a coast-wise expansion in the past (as do some of the traditions of origin), and it is perhaps unlikely—despite Dapper— that much interior territory was ever held. The attempt to analyse the earlier documents in BOUCHARD, op. cit., pp. 80–96, does not go far, relying as it does on the French translation of Dapper. For the modern position, see M. A. BRYAN, *The Bantu Languages of Africa*, 1959, pp. 3–8; I. RICHARDSON, *Linguistic Survey of the Northern Bantu Borderland*, 2, 1957, passim; E. ARDENER, op. cit., pp. 17–22. The last work is one of the few volumes of the Ethnographic Survey which attempts to incorporate information from earlier sources, commendably (despite an unfortunate reference to 'Dapper's voyage', p. 17).

88. In our first paper (p. 264 and n. 58), we mentioned the earliest reference to the inhabitants of the Mount Cameroons area, and now add details: PACHECO PEREIRA, op. cit., liv. 2, cap. 10, p. 148: '... esta serra e ilha estaa adiante do de Radeyro Rio, dos quatro de que atrás fallamos [immediately before Cross River], sinco [an error: actually 25] leguoas de caminho ... ha qual serra e ilha foy descuberta por Fernam do Poo ... E esta serra e muito alta, e quando faz tempo craro, parece a vinte e cinco e trinta leguoas; e ha ilha que estaa na boca d'esta emseada, he muito povorada ... e d'aly ha terra firme sam sinco leguoas [the correct distance between Fernando Po Island and the mainland below Mount Cameroons] ... Nesta terra há muytos e grandes alyfantes ... e ha jente d'esta terra lhe chamam em sua linguoajem "Caaboo" ...'.

89. The earliest cartographic reference to 'Ambous' seems to be on a map of 1561 (CORTESÃO and TEIXEIRA, op. cit., 2, plate 203, Bartolomeu Velho 1561), where it is marked in the large letters which normally indicate an ethnonym, in the interior on the upper reaches of River Cameroons. But on a map of 1571 (ibid., 3, plate 266, Fernao Vaz Dourado) the name is placed on the coast, in the form 'I[hla/s]. ambos': and on a printed map of 1596 (ibid., 3, plate 384, 'Typus orarum maritimarum Guineae ...' from Linschoten's *Itinerario*) we find 'Costa dos Amboas'. For the argument that 'Ambo' may be a corruption of a misplaced Portuguese toponym, see p. 265 of the first paper. But the 1561 map was one of the earliest maps of Africa to incorporate Abyssinian toponymy, which in error was stretched out to fill in the otherwise empty Southern and West-central interior regions (see W. G. L. RANDLES, 'South

East Africa and the Empire of Monotapa as shown on selected printed maps of the 16th Century', *Studia* (Lisbon), 2, 1958, pp. 103–63, especially p. 159 which examines the 1561 map; C. F. BECKINGHAM and G. W. B. HUNTINGFORD, *The Prester John of the Indies*, 1961, 2, pp. 526–6, a note by R. A. Skelton on Gastaldi's map of 1564)—so that, for instance, on Pigafetta's famous map of 1591, 'Damut' appeared in interior Gabon, with 'Amboas' a little to the North. If Ambous/Amboas had wandered from Abyssinia, did it begin as a reference to the '*amba*'s, on which royal princes were imprisoned? Various *amba* were depicted, for instance, on a map in SANUTO's *Geografia* of 1588, though here given not their vernacular name but the functional description 'Regalis Mons' (BECKINGHAM and HUNTINGFORD, op. cit., frontispiece). However, it is also possible that the term was a genuine West African one, and an ethnonym. The earliest known textual reference pre-dates any cartographic reference: 'De la riviere Royale iusques au cap de Lepogonsalves est la terre des Embours, qui est une nation de gens qui mangent leurs ennemis ... Leur Royaume entre en la terre bien trois cens lieues et font toujours la guerre aux Manycongres ...' (*Les voycges avantureux du Capitaine Ian Alfonce Sainctongeois*, Poitiers, 1559, f. 54r: this work was probably written around 1540—much of the information in it is unoriginal, and an earlier printed source supplying the information on the 'Embours' may be suspected). While it is impossible to accept the stated extent of the Embour territory—from Bonny to Gabon, and 300 leagues inland—it includes the later—and (perhaps) independently-documented Ambo coast and territory. Today, part of the Highland of Ambo (the northern slopes of Mount Cameroons) and part of the interior of the Cameroons estuary (again neighbouring Duala group languages) is occupied by speakers of languages (Balɔŋ and Bɔnkɛŋ) which linguists group under a name derived from that of a more interior member of the group, Mbɔ. Were these languages undifferentiated in the recent past, and was the name (A)mbo general?

90. The term *gayombo/*? *gajanlas* in the Duala word-list that follows was referred to by both sources when discussing the Highland of Ambo, and it may have been intended to suggest that it belonged to an interior 'Ambo' language, rather than to the coastal 'Duala' language. Unfortunately, the term is probably a variant of *gombo* 'hibiscus esculentus', which is fairly widespread in the Bantu languages.

91. Modern Ijɔ terms have been kindly supplied by Dr. Williamson.

92. The material in this list of vocabulary is drawn from P. E. H. HAIR, 'The Earliest Vocabularies of Cameroons Bantu' (*African Studies*, 28, 1969), in which all early vocabulary is examined. The select items in the present list are mainly from the vocabulary ('Woorden', cited in note 86. Comparison is made with terms in Isuwu and Mokpe as well as with terms in modern Duala; the three languages are believed to be closely related, but Isuwu and Mokpe are much less well known than Duala. The modern sources are S. W. KOELLE, *Polyglotta Africana*, 1854; A. SAKER, *Grammatical Elements of the Dualla Language with a Vocabulary*, 1855; T. CHRISTALLER, *Handbuch der Duala-Sprache*, Basel, 1892; E. DINKELACKER, *Wörterbuch der Duala-Sprache*, 1914; H. H. JOHNSTON, *A Comparative Study of the Bantu and Semi-Bantu Languages*, 1, 1919.

POSTSCRIPT

Since the earlier papers of this series were published and since the present paper was prepared, there has appeared an important study of Cameroons coastal history, Edwin ARDENER, 'Documentary and Linguistic Evidence for the Rise of the Trading Polities between Rio del Rey and Cameroons 1500–1650' (in I. M. LEWIS, ed., *History and Social Anthropology*, 1968, pp. 81–126). This contains an even more detailed examination of the early sources than that given in the present paper, and an independent identification of the vocabularies. The method of research and the general conclusions are very similar to those of the present author.

A comment on the Benin section of this paper, kindly supplied by Dr. R. E. Bradbury of the University of Birmingham, but received too late to be incorporated, includes the following important points. Note 64: Dr. Bradbury points out that what we term 'three Yoruba titles' are strictly 'three titles of interior states, probably expressed in the Edo language though conceivably relating to Yoruba kingdoms'. Notes 66, 70 and 72: Dr.

Bradbury suggests that Oedebo and Isago, which he does not think represent Owo/Oyo and Etsako, may represent Urhobo and Isoko (a group formerly considered as part of the Urhobo, but now considered a separate ethnolinguistic unit) [the suggestion is attractive, even although difficulties are raised over the geographical directions and other particulars given in the text]. Note 76: he notes that the Edo still call the Ijɔ, *Uzɔ*. Finally, in the Edo vocabulary, he identifies *mouponoqua* as *ukpɔ nɔxua*, 'big cloth'.

Etsako in the Polyglotta Africana

JOHN LAVER

THE LANGUAGE

Ɛgbeːle, V.B.2 in the *Polyglotta Africana*, is a dialect of Etsakọ,[1] an Ẹdo language. Etsakọ is spoken in and near Afenmai Division in Mid-Western Nigeria by over 120,000 speakers, and Greenberg (1959) includes it, as Kukuruku,[2] in the Kwa sub-family of the Niger–Congo grouping. **Ɛgbeːle** (Ẹkpẹri in the current orthography, and /ɛ̀kphwɛ̀lì/ in this author's phonemic transcription) is the dialect of the Ẹkpẹri clan, who live mainly in some fourteen villages round the town of Ugbẹkpẹ. The 1963 Nigerian Census gave a population figure for the clan of 8,243, which seems rather conservative.

THE INFORMANTS

Koelle's informant, from a village he calls **Iwieːta**, possibly came from Iwietẹkhu, a small village near Ugbẹkpẹ. My own principal informant[3] was Michael Ashedu, from Udaba, and some confirmatory material was obtained on a short field trip in April 1967,[4] mainly from Chief M. Y. Kanoba, the Igiegbai of Ẹkpẹri, in Ugbẹkpẹ. The informants state that there are no appreciable differences of accent between the villages.

THE PHONOLOGY

Koelle's analysis of the consonant-system of Ẹkpẹri can be seen in Table 1, which also gives some indication of the phonetic characteristics of the consonants.

Table 1

	b		t	d			k	g	kp	gb
f	v	th	s	z	sh					
	m			n		ny				
				r				gh		
				l						
pf			ts	dz	dj					
						y			w	

Table 2 is a similar presentation of the consonant-system in my own analysis:

Table 2

p	b		t	d		k	g	kp	gb
						kh	gh	kph	gbh
f	v		s						
	vh								
	m			n	ñ				ñh
	mh								
			r						
			rh						
			l						
			ts	dz					
					j				w
wh									

The differences between Table 1 and Table 2, and many of the divergences between the transcriptions in the *Polyglotta* and in my analysis, lie in the fact that Koelle failed to notice a phonological distinction which is exploited by many of the items in the word-list. Ẹkpẹri, like all Etsakọ dialects,[1] uses differences of muscular tension during the articulation of syllables as the basis of a tense-lax phonological opposition. In a phonemic solution such as the present one, the opposition can be shown typographically in the consonant symbols, and in Table 2 the digraphs which are made up of a consonant symbol followed by *h* are designed to indicate the lax phoneme in a tense–lax pairing. (The current orthography also makes use of this device, somewhat inconsistently.) The tense–lax opposition has considerable morphological significance, in that consonant harmony gives information about the morphological make-up of words: there are three distributional sets of consonants, a tense set /k, g, kp, gb, v, m, ñ, r, w/, a lax set /kh, gh, kph, gbh, vh, mh, ñh, rh, wh/, and a neutral set /p, b, t, d, f, s, n, l, ts, dz, j/. In any single morpheme there is no co-occurrence of tense consonants with lax consonants. Neutral consonants can occur with either tense or lax consonants. /w/ and /j/ are the only consonants which can occupy the second position in a syllable-initial two-consonant cluster, and in this case they take on the tension characteristics of the consonant they follow.

In general, the exponents of tense consonants are distinguished from their lax counterparts by being longer in duration as well as of tenser articulation.

It may be helpful at this point to offer a brief explanation of the phonetic specifications of some of the consonants in Table 2 which are involved in the tense–lax opposition.

/k, g, kp, gb/ are all tense plosives, while /kh, gh, kph, gbh/ show substantial free variation, phonetically, between lax plosives and homorganic lax fricatives; /v/ is a tense, slightly affricated labiodental plosive, and /vh/ is a lax labiodental approximant; /m/ and

/mh/ are both bilabial nasals, tense and lax respectively; /ñ/ is a tense palatal nasal, and /ñh/ is a lax labial-velar nasal; /r/ is expounded by a tense voiceless fricative tap, which can vary freely in location from alveolar to denti-alveolar or dental (with the dental tap being the most common), and /rh/ is a lax voiced alveolar tap without friction; finally, /w/ is a tense labialized labial-velar approximant, and /wh/ is a lax bilabial approximant without lip-rounding.

Apart from the tense–lax pairings of consonants in Table 2, there are some other discrepancies between Tables 1 and 2. Table 1 has **z**, which does not appear in Table 2. (In fact **z** only appears in two items in the *Polyglotta* list, in **aːkazi** 'horse', and **aːkazi ɔːgbutso** 'mare'). Similarly, **sh** and **dj** in Table 1 have no counterparts in Table 2. **sh** would be transcribed as /sj/, a cluster, in the present analysis, and would be expounded phonetically in present-day Ekperi by a palatalized palato-alveolar fricative, or by an alveolar fricative [s] followed by a palatal approximant [j], in free variation. The voiceless palato-alveolar affricate **dj** in Table 1 occurs in the *Polyglotta* list only in one item, **djiːkakere** 'outer hand', and is probably a mis-hearing for **ts**. (The current form for 'outer hand' is /ìtsíkóbɔ̀/,[5] and /ìtsíkàkèlê/ is said to mean 'calf'.) **gh**, the sound of the Arabic 'ghain' in Table 1, occurring only in one item **ɔ toghiːa** 'hot', does correspond, on the other hand, with the lax velar /gh/ of Table 2, in the modern /ɔ̀ tòghjâ/ 'it is hot'.

Table 2 has two entries without any equivalents in Table 1, namely /p/ and /ñh/. We shall see below that some *Polyglotta* items transcribed as **pf** are in the present analysis transcribed with /p/, and some with /v/. /ñh/ does not occur in the words in the lexical inventory of the *Polyglotta*, but does occur in the language in a word such as /èñhwὲ/ 'ashes', for example (contrasted with /èñὲ/ 'crocodiles').

It was stated above that most phonological divergences between the two lists concern the consonants which participate in the tense–lax opposition. Some of these divergences are consistent: Koelle's **v** is always /vh/ in my transcription, and vice versa, as in **aviːviː** for /àvhjὲvhjὲ/ 'butterfly'; his **d** is always /rh/, and vice versa, as in **eːdede** for /órhèrhê/ 'stranger'. One divergence is consistent, but one-way: Koelle's **th** always corresponds to /r/, but not necessarily vice versa, as in **eːtha** for /èrà/ 'father', but **utuːri** for /ùrì/ 'throat'.

Other divergences are the result of Koelle's simply not noticing the tension opposition and collapsing the two phonemes in a tense–lax pairing into one, as in the following examples: **aːki** for /àkì/ 'market', and **aːke** for /ákhè/ 'pot'; **uːgoːa** for /úgwàà/ 'bone', and **aːgū̃** for /àghù/ 'belly'; **oːgba** for /ɔ̀kpá/ 'one' (there are no examples in the comparison of the two lists where Koelle used **kp** to transcribe tense /kp/ in my system—perhaps the high degree of articulatory tension in some way aggravated his tendency to confuse voiced and voiceless consonants), and **u:kpea:me:o** for /úkphjámélɔ/ 'coal'; **i: gbi:miɛ: rɛ** for /ìi gbìimhì/ 'I do not dance', and, although there are no appropriate forms in the *Polyglotta* transcriptions, Koelle would presumably have transcribed the first consonant phoneme in /ègbhèèè/ or /ègbhèléè/ 'house', as **gb**; **amɛ** for /àmɛ̀/ 'water', and **o:guma** for /òghùmhà/ 'male slave'. These are all examples of under-differentiation of sounds which are auditorily rather similar in many respects, but Koelle also failed to differentiate between a tense–lax pair whose phonetic exponents are somewhat more distinct, auditorily, in writing both /w/ and /wh/ as **w**, as in **o:wɛ** for /òwɛ̀/ 'leg', and **iwa:wa** for /áwháwhà/ 'mosquito'.

The last important type of divergence of consonantal transcription involves Koelle's use of **pf** and **r**. **pf** sometimes corresponds to /p/ in the modern system, and sometimes to /v/. Examples are **o:pfe** for /ópè/ 'rat', and **e:pfa** for /èvá/ 'two'. **pf** for /v/ is only a matter of typography, as the phonetic exponent of /v/ is the (tense) labiodental affricate that Koelle presumably had in mind in writing **pf**, except for the confusion of voice-state. **pf** for /p/ is a different case: /p/ seems fairly rare in Etsakọ dialects, so perhaps a diversification of the previous **pf** is taking place.

Koelle's **r** usually corresponds to my /l/, which is phonetically a voiced alveolar lateral tap, in free variation with a voiced alveolar lateral approximant whose articulation is often characterized by a fast tap-like gesture towards the alveolar ridge, without enough approximation centrally for contact or friction. There are many examples of correspondences such as **amenyi:ri** for /áméñìlì/ 'milk', **e:se:ri** for /èsèlì/ 'fish', and so on. But, occasionally, Koelle's **r** corresponds to tense /r/, which is more usually matched with the *Polyglotta*'s **th**. An example is one given earlier, **utu:ri** for /ùrì/ 'throat'.

These divergences apart, the two lists show remarkably close consonantal similarity. The remaining differences can often be ascribed to misprints or slips of the pen, as in **ata:le** (which corresponds in the present system to /áràalì/ 'blood'), which presumably should have read (in transliteration) **atha:le**. Conversely, **o:tha** for the modern /ótà/ 'soap', should have read **o:ta**. In both cases, in the original non-transliterated forms, only the presence or absence of a dot under the **t** was involved, as a simple error of printing, or of notation by the author.

The vowel analysis in the two systems is nearly identical, with seven vowel phonemes /i, e, ɛ, a, ɔ, o, u/. The differences lie mainly in the way that vowel length and semi-vowels are handled. For convenience of tonal analysis, vowel length in my analysis is shown by doubling (or in some cases tripling) the vowel symbol, instead of adopting Koelle's usage of a length mark. In dealing with semi-vowels, the role of /j/ and /w/ in the present analysis as the second consonant of syllable-initial consonant clusters is taken over in the *Polyglotta* by close vowels, usually **i** and **u**.

Otherwise, the only difference of any significance, apart from slight disagreements about vowel height, is that Koelle noted some vowels in non-nasal environments as being nasalized, as in **eːwũ** 'shirt', and **oːkɔrĩ** 'war'. There is currently a slight tendency for closer vowels to be nasalized, but there is no phonological opposition involved. An additional factor is that both Ishan and Ora, Ẹdo languages to the south and west of Ẹkpẹri respectively, have phonologically distinctive nasalization of vowels, and may have exerted some influence.

MORPHOLOGY

Like other Ẹdo languages, Etsakọ uses vowels as number-prefixes in nouns. As John Kelly comments in his article on another Ẹdo language in this series, 'Urhobo in the *Polyglotta Africana*'[6], there is a tendency 'for plural noun-forms to be used where singular would seem to be indicated by the situation or is requested by the English-speaking investigator'. Many of Koelle's transcriptions show a plural Ẹkpẹri form for a singular English item, e.g.

ikumi is the plural of /ùkhùmhì/ 'medicine'
aːkɔ is the plural of /ɛ̀kɔ̀/ 'tooth'
iːthari is the plural of /èràlì/ 'fire'
eːbe is the plural of /óbè/ 'book'

Inconsistency of observation, and failure to penetrate the elision rules in compound word-formation, led to some obscuring of the morphology in the *Polyglotta*. In compound word-formation, where final and initial vowels are adjacent across the boundary between the elements, the final vowel of the first element is nearly always elided (unless it is /i/ or /u/, in which case it is replaced by /j/ or /w/). Even without knowing the elision rules, and not knowing the initial element, given that he knew the word **oːwɛ** 'leg', Koelle should not have misplaced the hyphen in **iːye-kowɛ**, 'foot'. There are morphological inaccuracies also in **kpuroː-wɛ** 'toe', **ɛkoloː-wɛ** 'thigh', and **eːtseroː-wɛ** 'heel'; more consistency of phonological observation in these three examples might have helped Koelle to the conclusion that he was dealing with words made up of three elements, an unknown, **l** as a genitival linker, and **oːwɛ** 'leg' (parallel to the use of *r* as a genitival link in John Kelly's article on Urhobo). Koelle was inconsistent in noting the juncture in only some compound words and not in others. He knew the word **oːthai** 'tree', but wrote 'root' as **uriːrioːthai**. A knowledge of the tense–lax opposition, and of the distributional fact that tense and lax consonants do not occur within the same morpheme might have enabled him to give a different morphological interpretation of **iː gbakɔ** 'I rise', where the **gb** (/kp/ in my analysis) is tense, and the **k** lax.

However, once the phonological and morphological inconsistencies are revealed, the differences between the two analyses are very much reduced, and as in the case of Urhobo, are chiefly lexical. Ẹkpẹri does not seem to have changed to any substantial degree, in the areas of phonology and morphology that Koelle was able to penetrate, since the time when the *Polyglotta* was written.

NOTES

1. See J. LAVER, 'A Preliminary Phonology of the Ayele Dialect of Esakọ', *J.W.A.L.*, 4, 2, 1967, pp. 53–6.
2. See J. GREENBERG, *The Languages of Africa*, Bloomington, 1959, pp. 1–88. Kukuruku is now a somewhat pejorative term, and Etsakọ (the plural form of Koelle's **Otsãːkõ**, Introd., p. 8), the label used by the language-users themselves, would be a much more acceptable form. There is no connection with Koelle's **Eshitaːko** (VI.3), however.
3. I gratefully acknowledge a grant in aid of research from the Institute of African Studies of the University of Ibadan, during the academic year 1965–66.
4. The trip was made with the aid of a Hayter Travel and Field Research Grant from the Centre of African Studies of the University of Edinburgh, for which I am very grateful.
5. The tone markings in the examples transcribed in my system are to be interpreted as follows: acute accent, high tone; grave accent, low tone; circumflex accent, high falling tone.
6. See J. KELLY, 'Urhobo in the *Polyglotta Africana*', *A.L.R.*, 7, 1968, pp. 107–13.

Le Gio dans la Polyglotta Africana

J. L. DONEUX

LE **giːo** est la langue **II.13** de la *Polyglotta*. Elle sera examinée ici à partir de deux documents récents. D'une part, une publication issue du Libéria: K. E. Griffes, *A Start in Gio*, Hartford (Conn.), 1959 (tentative edition), ronéo. D'autre part, des notes manuscrites personnelles dont une partie a servi pour une *Esquisse d'un dialecte dan*, à paraître en polycopie dans les Documents linguistiques de l'Université de Dakar.

Il n'y a pas de problème de caractérisation de la langue. La désignation de **giːo** par Koelle est celle même qui est utilisée par l'ouvrage de Griffes. Notre choix du terme « dan » était imposé par le fait que l'enquête avait lieu dans la ville de Danané en Côte d'Ivoire, où la désignation « yacouba » est refusée par les locuteurs comme d'origine étrangère (nickname: *yà po᷄ ɓo à?* « dit-il ainsi ? »), et la désignation « dan » communément acceptée. Si les variantes dialectales sont nombreuses, il s'agit bien de la même langue des deux côtés de la frontière, et puisque le linguiste ayant travaillé en Côte d'Ivoire suit sans difficulté le texte libérien, nous pensons qu'il doit en être de même pour les locuteurs. Nous avons d'ailleurs pu assister sur place à une longue conversation entre un Gio du Libéria et un groupe de villageois dan.

1. PHONOLOGIE

Les signes utilisés par Koelle pour cette langue sont les suivants:

Consonnes	**m**	**n**	**ny**	**ŋ**	**gm**
	p	**t**		**k**	
	b	**d**	**dj**	**g**	**gb**
	f	**s**	**sh**		
	v	**z**		**gh**	
		l			
		r			
	w		**y**		

Voyelles **i, e, ɛ, a, ɔ, o, u**, et les mêmes nasalisées.

K. E. Griffes donne pour son dialecte le système suivant:

Consonnes m   n   ny   ŋ
               p   t   k   kp
               b   d   g   gb
               ɓ   l
               f   s
               v   z
               w   y   x

Voyelles   i   ɥ   u   nasales   ĩ   ũ
              e   ö   o   ɛ̃   ɔ̃
              ɛ   ə   ɔ   ã
                  a

Le système proposé dans l'*Esquisse d'un dialecte dan* est le suivant:

Consonnes m   n
               p   t   k   kp
               b   d   g   gb
               ɓ   ɗ
               f   s
               v   z
                   l
               w   y
              (w̃)   (ỹ)

Voyelles   les mêmes que K. E. Griffes.

Si nous comparons le système de Koelle à ceux des documents contemporains, une seule question se pose, mais pour divers sons, à savoir: les divergences de notation à plus d'un siècle de distance traduisent-elles une évolution de la langue, ou des imperfections dans l'interprétation de Koelle ou dans la nôtre?

Voyons les différents points litigieux:

1.1. Les consonnes nasales chez Koelle. Sont en question: **ny**, **ŋ**, **gm**. La description de Griffes retient *ny* et *ŋ*. Par rapport au système proposé pour le dan, il semble qu'il s'agit soit d'une différence dialectale, soit d'une interprétation phonétique différente. Nous proposons pour notre part soit *ỹ* et *w̃*, soit *yṼ* et *wṼ*.

	Koelle	Griffes	dan
« nez »	**niːu**		ỹu, yũ
« œil »	**nya**	nya	ỹa, yã
« sein »	**iːnyõ**		ỹɔ, yɔ̃
« huile »	**nyɔː**	nyɔɔ	ỹɔ, yɔ̃
« cheveu »	**ŋu**		w̃u, wũ
« sacrifice »	**ŋuːa**		w̃ua, wũa

En ce qui concerne **gm**, il semble bien qu'il n'y a pas à retenir un phonème disparu. Koelle le donne d'ordinaire devant une voyelle nasale :

	Koelle	Griffes	dan
« épaule »	**gmã**		gbã
« fumée »	**siɛ:gmẽ**		siö-gbĩɛ
« chien »	**gmẽ:**	gbẽ	gbẽ

Il semble donc bien qu'il n'y ait pas lieu ici de parler d'évolution notable de la langue.

1.2. Absence de *kp* chez Koelle. Nous pouvons l'interpréter comme une faiblesse de notation chez l'auteur. Il faut sans doute rapprocher le fait de celui déjà signalé dans cette revue par G. Innes sur le mende ('Mende in the *Polyglotta Africana*', A.L.R., 6, 1967, p. 123) où Koelle paraît commettre la même erreur. En gio même, nous relevons plusieurs autres confusions, dans des syntagmes, entre consonnes sourdes et consonnes sonores :

« je cuis la nourriture » : **ma: bu:ɛ gba** pour *ma ɓö kpa*
« je danse » : **ma: taŋgɛ** pour *ma tã kə*
« je tue la poule » : **ma: tɔ: sɛ** pour *ma tɔ zə*.

1.3. L'absence des ingressives chez Koelle. On remarquera tout d'abord qu'il y a différence de systèmes dans les documents récents. K. E. Griffes donne *ɓ* et *ɗ* comme deux ingressives. Nous proposons dans l'*Esquisse* un système comprenant trois phonèmes : *ɓ*, *ɗ* et *l*. C'est Koelle qui va éclairer la diachronie sur ce point. Il n'a pas décelé les ingressives, mais elles existaient à son époque. Une règle de morphophonologie du dan actuel veut que nasale syllabique+ingressive devienne nasale. Or, la recension de Koelle dévoile cette règle agissante dans le gio il y a plus de cent ans :

« mère »	**deɔu** (**ndeɔu** et **ne:ɔu**)
« grand-mère »	**de:ye** (**nne:ye**)
« fils »	**nɛ** (**ma nɛ**)

Les éléments entre parenthèses signifient respectivement : ma mère, ma grand-mère, mon fils. La reconstruction des formes de base donnerait : *n ɗe*, *n ɗe yö* (*và*), *n ɓà nɔ́*, ceci pour le dan actuel. Il s'agit donc bien d'ingressives ; la contre-épreuve est fournie par « père » **dɛ** (**ndɛ**) où l'on voit que devant occlusive Koelle ne donne pas de variante avec assimilation. On notera avec intérêt en passant le petit point d'ethnolinguistique suivant : la construction déterminant-déterminé en dan est directe lorsque le rapport est « ontologique », introduite par *ɓa* lorsqu'il s'agit d'un rapport de propriété, de possession. Mais « mon fils » est *n ɓà nɔ́*, et non *n nɔ́*. C'était, on le voit, déjà le cas dans le gio de Koelle.

Deux ingressives existaient donc dans le gio du dix-neuvième siècle. Est-ce le système proposé par Griffes pour le gio du Libéria, ou celui du dan qui rend le mieux compte de la phonologie passée de la langue ? On aurait aimé quelques spécimens supplémentaires pour en juger, mais à notre avis les rares termes comparables dans les trois documents sont dirimants. Il n'y avait pas trois (ɓ, ɗ, l) mais deux phonèmes (ɓ, ɗ ou l) :

	Koelle	Griffes	dan
« arbre »	**giri**	xlɥ [xɥdɥ']	lɥ'
« mortier »		xlö' [xödö']	lö'
« lier »		xlö` [xödö`]	lö`
« soleil »	**nyira:**		lãa

Nous revenons ci-dessous sur la valeur disyllabique ou non de **giri** et de **nyira:** à l'époque de Koelle. Mais une chose paraît certaine, c'est que les langues mandé du groupe mana-busa offrent pour ces mots une forme avec consonne (j, y ?) précédant la liquide ingressive. Il n'est que de consulter A. Prost, *Les langues mandé-sud du groupe mana-busa*, Dakar, 1953, pour s'en convaincre. Soit « arbre » : *yili* (manon), *yiri* (ben), *yukwi* (gban), *yiri* (guro ; *yli* dans les listes communiquées aimablement par J. P. Benoist récemment). Quant au bambara, mandé central, il présente *dyiri*. Le dan actuel n'obtient donc son phonème supplémentaire que par une assimilation totale d'une séquence de deux sons dans une représentation unique, d'où :

	dan	
« mortier »	*lö'*	< *yle
« où ? »	*dö*	< *de
« avec »	*dö'*	< *le

1.4. **Deux glides chez Koelle.** Certains spécimens de la *Polyglotta* comportent un **r**, d'autres un **l**. Il faut distinguer deux cas. Dans quelques syntagmes ou morphèmes plurisyllabiques, **r** est mis pour **d** : **ma: ba a:bi re** « je prie Dieu », où **re** est le correspondant de *dö* dans les documents actuels. Dans les autres cas, à peu de chose près, la notation de Koelle correspond à la phonétique actuelle du dan : [*l*] après labiale ou vélaire, [*r*] après dentale ou palatale (*y*) :

	Koelle	dan
« petit frère »	**zera**	záá, zlá [zra]
« perroquet »	**sira**	
« se laver »	**suru**	zlú [zru]
« jeu »	**tiro**	tló [trɔ]
« six »	**sora:do**	sládo [srado]
« guerre »	**gulu**	glù
« riz »	**mili**	mlɥ`
« forêt »	**bili, bli**	ɓlɥ

Seul cas divergent: « chapeau » **gbira** (dan: *kplà*); quant à
« main » **kora** et « village » **gurɔ** il nous est impossible de juger de
leur composition, les termes actuels du dan étant respectivement
kɔ̀(-dɛ́) et *pö*.

On peut également se demander, comme G. Innes l'avait fait pour
le mende (article cité) s'il y a eu réduction d'éléments disyllabiques à
des formes monosyllabiques depuis un siècle. Notre impression est
qu'ils étaient déjà monosyllabiques à l'époque. D'une part, la
variante notée par Koelle pour « forêt » **bili, bli** semble l'indiquer,
d'autre part ses voyelles de première syllabe paraissent quelque peu
suspectes d'être des phénomènes d'anticipation dans l'écoute de
Koelle.

Enfin, on ne peut ramener à ces divers cas celui du terme pour
« deux »:

	Koelle	Griffes	dan
« deux »	**peːrɛ**	*pèètɛ*	*plɛ*

L'apparition de *t* dans le gio actuel, la voyelle longue en première
syllabe déjà présente dans la *Polyglotta* empêchent clairement de
ramener le terme à *plɛ.

1.5. La notation **gh** chez Koelle. Elle n'intervient, sauf erreur,
que deux fois: **yaːga, yaːgha** « trois » et **ma ŋgbaːgha** « je te
donne ». On ne voit pas quelle reconstitution faire du second groupe
(dan: *má ɥ gba* « je te donne », « je t'ai donné »). Le premier item
montre qu'il s'agit d'une variante. On la trouverait encore dans des
dialectes dan actuels.

1.6. La notation **sh** chez Koelle. Elle intervient une seule fois:
shuːe « ongle ». La palatalisation de *s* est une variante qu'on trouve
aujourd'hui dans le dialecte dan de Wa lorsqu'on se trouve en
présence d'un groupe S+/i, u/+V. Dans nos listes, le mot « ongle »
est rendu par *sòò*, mais *ʃuo, ʃoo, ʃuö* doivent se retrouver sans peine
dans le canton de Wa.

1.7. La notation **dj** chez Koelle. Pour d'autres langues de la
Polyglotta, ce problème doit être particulièrement délicat. Koelle note
lui-même: '**ds** is the sound of **ch** in "church" '. Nous permettra-t-on
de regretter en passant qu'on n'ait admis que **dj** pour en rendre
compte dans cette revue (*S.L.L.R.*, 3, 1964, p. 58) ? Il y a certainement des langues où Koelle s'est trouvé noter par ce digraphe soit des
palatales sonores, soit des palatales sourdes. Pour le gio, la com-
paraison avec les données actuelles donne les résultats suivants:

	Koelle	Griffes	dan
« lait »	**nyoo-dji** & **nyoo-gi**		ỹɔ́-yí
« malade »	**djɔ:a**	yúá	yúɔ́
« je ris »	**ma: dje:du:a**		má yéí tó
« je rêve »	**ma: djie:wo** & **ma gi:**		má yɔ́ ɓo
« je mange du riz »	**ma dja: bwe**		má yá ɓö
« je bois de l'eau »	**ma: dji mu**	má yí mɥ	má yí mɥ
« riz »	**dja, gia, igia**	yá	yá

Ainsi, **dj** de Koelle représente toujours *y* des documents actuels. Mais le phonème /y/ est en fait susceptible d'être représenté en outre dans la *Polyglotta* par **dy**: **dyu:o** « poisson » (gio: *yúɔ̀*; dan: *yúö*) et par **g**, comme le montre ci-dessus **gia** « riz » et comme l'indique en outre le mot pour « eau » choisi à un autre endroit de la recension de Koelle: **gi** « eau ». Nous pensons en outre que le cas est le même pour **giri** « arbre », déjà cité. Plusieurs fois, cependant, Koelle marque un **y**: dans **ya:ga** « trois » et dans **ma: yi sɛ** « je dors » (dan: *má yi zə*).

On peut cependant se demander si ces incertitudes de notation n'ont pas leur source dans le fait que la langue de l'époque comportait un /j/, ou peut-être même que des termes comme *yí* « eau » aujourd'hui renvoient à un **gí*, déjà très palatalisé du temps de Koelle.

1.8. L'absence des voyelles centrales chez Koelle. Rappelons brièvement que les deux documents contemporains utilisés proposent une série de trois voyelles centrales: ɥ, ö, ə. Absolument aucun des items de la *Polyglotta* ne comporte une de ces voyelles. Le problème sera que Koelle était parfaitement à même de les noter si elles existaient à l'époque, puisque sa table des sons établit « **è** and **à** are peculiarly pectoral **e** and **a** sounds, especially common in the Bornu language », mais se complique pour nous du fait que les centrales ne sont pas notées non plus par lui dans les langues de l'ouest-atlantique, où elles abondent.

	Koelle	Griffes	dan
« enfant »	**nɛ**	nɔ́	nɔ́
« père »	**dɛ**	də	də
« ventre »	**(n)gu(lo:)**	gɥ'	gɥ'
« cuiller »	**mi:a**	mìá	mìə
« feu »	**si:e**	sìè	sìö
« fer »	**pi:ɛ**	pìɛ̀	pìə̀
« pierre »	**gu:ɛ**	gùə	gùö
« fumée »	**siɛ:gmẽ**		sìö-gbĩ'ɛ
« hache »	**du:a**		dùɔ̀
« corde »	**bilɛ:**	ɓɥ`ə	ɓɥ`ə
« esclave »	**dɔ̃:ã, du:ã**		dũ`ə̀

	Koelle	Griffes	dan
« arbre »	**giri**	*xly'*	*ly'*
« palmier »	**se**		*sö*
« riz »	**milī**	*mly*	*mly`*
« forêt »	**bili, bli**	*ɓly*	*ɓly*
« poisson »	**dyuːo**	*yúò*	*yúö*
« éléphant »	**biːe**	*bìe*	*biö*
« bon »	**sɛ**	*sə̀*	*sə̀*
« tuer »	**sɛ**	*zə*	*zə*
« tomber »	**buːe**		*pyö*
« voir »	**diːe**	*ye*	*yo*
« prendre »	**si**	*sy'*	*sy'*
« faire »	**gɛ**	*kə*	*kə*
« manger »	**bwe**	*ɓö*	*ɓö*
« avec »	**re**	*lö'*	*dö'*

Un examen attentif de cette liste permet de constater que la centralisation dans les dialectes actuels est plus large en dan qu'en gio (cuiller, feu, fer, poisson, éléphant, voir). On s'en apercevra mieux en donnant quelques termes supplémentaires disponibles dans les deux documents :

	Griffes	dan
« le, la »	*ɓεε*	*ɓə* (ce ... là)
« lui »	*e*	*yö*
« jeter »	*zuo*	*zùö`*
« travail »	*yuo*	*ɟuö*
« au-dessus »	*lúo*	*dúö*

On peut donc se demander si effectivement la langue gio de Koelle comportait des centrales. Il semble y avoir évolution vers une centralisation de plus en plus poussée. Deux arguments complémentaires pourraient être donnés en ce sens : d'une part, le guro n'a pas de centrales ; d'autre part, dans les dialectes dan actuels, on peut toujours s'attendre à voir apparaître dans un endroit quelconque un morphème comportant la voyelle latérale et non la centrale. L'enquête comparative sur les facteurs de centralisation reste d'ailleurs à faire, et il semble que les séquences VV soient plus facilement atteintes que les morphèmes à CV.

2. TONOLOGIE

On pouvait se demander si la notation par Koelle d'une accentuation en gio servirait de point de repère pour un examen de la tonologie de la langue à son époque. Nos documents posent également pour les deux dialectes un système à trois tons : haut, moyen, bas. Nous admettons en outre pour le dan une chute tonale (ton descendant) qui n'est valable que dans des domaines liés à la grammaire.

Koelle place parfois une accentuation sur des morphèmes monosyllabiques. Il était intéressant de voir si cette notation correspondait à un ton particulier de nos morphèmes:

	Koelle	dan
« cheveu »	**ŋú**	*w̃u*
« nombril »	**bú**	*blù*
« couteau »	**dá**	*dàa*
« chat »	**nyá:**	*ỹáa*
« œuf »	**nyá:**	*ỹà*
« il est noir »	**é ti:**	*yö` tii*

On le voit, le résultat est décevant. L'accentuation de Koelle peut correspondre à n'importe quel ton des morphèmes actuels (il faut signaler que les tons des morphèmes sont d'une très grande homogénéité entre les deux documents actuels).

L'examen des termes disyllabiques et des syntagmes n'est pas plus satisfaisant. Dans les verbes conjugués, Koelle varie de notation d'une phrase à l'autre. Il met souvent une accentuation sur **má, má:** qui est effectivement à ton haut (dan, gio: *má* « je » au passé); il en met une autre sur **ŋá:** qui porte également le ton haut (dan: *ŋáá*, *n'ká* « je ne » au passé; gio: *n'ká*). Mais il a des traitements contradictoires:

« j'achète »	**má: dɔ**	(dan: *má dɔ́*)
« je vends »	**ma: gó**	(dan: *má gó*, mais: « je pars »)
« j'entends »	**má: ma**	(dan: *má ma*)

Lorsque la phrase comporte un complément d'objet, Koelle reporte sur ce dernier, aux dépens de *má* « je », toute accentuation:

« je pleure »	**ma: gbé:bo:a**	(dan: *má gbö ɓo*)
« je dors »	**ma: yísɛ**	(dan: *má yi zə*)
« je rêve »	**ma: djíe:wo**	(dan: *má yɔ́ ɓo*)
« je mange du riz »	**ma djá: bwe**	(dan: *má ya ɓö*)
« je bois de l'eau »	**ma: djí mu**	(dan: *má yí mɥ*)
« je bats l'enfant »	**ma: nɛ' ma**	(dan: *má nɔ́ ma*)
« je couds la chemise »	**ma sɔ' du:e**	(dan: *má sɔ kə*)

Il faut conclure, semble-t-il, que Koelle n'a pas été frappé en gio par le phénomène tonal, mais qu'il a noté des variations d'intensité, qui peuvent exister de fait, et c'est certainement le cas pour le complément d'objet venant avant le verbe.

3. LOCALISATION DU GIO DE KOELLE

C'est du Libéria que devraient venir les indications permettant de recouper les données géographiques apportées par Koelle sur l'origine de son informateur. Il semble en tout cas difficile qu'une région quelconque de Côte d'Ivoire parlant dan se trouve à « un jour de marche de la mer ». Ce n'est qu'au Libéria que la langue est parlée plus au sud. En outre, quelques éléments lexicaux montrent que le parler de l'informateur est plus proche de celui décrit par Griffes (et même très proche), que du dan de Danané. Enfin, le terme gio utilisé par Koelle renvoie clairement à un des dialectes proprement libériens de la langue. Comparez :

	Koelle	Griffes	dan
« deux »	**peːrɛ**	*pèètɛ*	*plɛ̀*
« six »	**soraːdɔ**	*sráàdo*	*sládo, fládo*
« dix »	**gɔː**	*gɔ́ɔ̀*	*gɔ́ɔ do*
« Dieu »	**aːbi**	*áàɓí*	*zlã̀*
« poivre »	**kiːe**	*kíè*	*lá*

La Langue de Tumbuktu dans la Polyglotta Africana

A. PROST

Dans la *Polyglotta Africana*, sous le titre **XII.C.** (Unclassified Central African Languages), Koelle donne la langue de Tumbuktu et Gene, c'est à dire le soŋay de Tombouctou et Dienné.

Il s'agit là du dialecte occidental de la langue soŋay, dialecte commun à quelques variantes près, à la région de Tombouctou et de Dienné. Il a été décrit par la suite dans : Dupuis-Yacouba, *Essai de méthode pratique pour l'étude de la langue songoï ou songaï*, Paris, 1917.

J'ai publié de mon côté « La langue soŋay et ses dialectes », *Mémoires de l'IFAN*, n° 47, Dakar, 1956, où est étudié le parler de Gao et les parlers du Niger.

Les mots enregistrés par Koelle sont bien notés et très facilement reconnaissables. Il y a une plus grande exactitude de la transcription dans le cas du soŋay que dans le cas du gourma ou du moré (cf. mon étude « La langue Gurma dans la Polyglotta Africana », *Sierra Leone Language Review*, 5, 1966, pp. 134-8).

Il reste cependant que Koelle n'a utilisé que la palatale sourde notée **dj** et que la sonore correspondante *j* est absente.

Nous avons noté :

w pour *b* intervocalique :
« coal » **dɛndji biːwi** pour *dendyi bibi*
« well » **iːsawi irkui** et *aː saːbi yɛrkoi* qui veulent dire littéralement « ils louent Dieu, il loue Dieu ». C'est la formule que l'on emploie pour répondre qu'on est en bonne santé, que tout va bien ; le verbe est *sabu*.
« tomorrow » **suːba** et **shiwa**, le premier terme est le bon.

gh pour *g* (occlusif) dans :
« ground-nut » **maːtigha** qui est en réalité *matiga*

k au lieu de *g* :
kɔrɔ pour *goro*

Souvent les palatales ne sont pas notées et sont remplacées par les occlusives **k** et **g** :
« salt » **kiːri** pour *kyiri*
« night » **kiːgi** pour *kyigin* à Gao et *tyidyi* à Tombouctou
« bird » **kiroːkeina** pour *kyiraw keyna*

EVOLUTION DE LA LANGUE DEPUIS UN SIÈCLE

Les palatales du soŋay ont été transcrites par moi *ky* et *gy* car elles me paraissent une réalisation palatalisée de *k* et de *g* devant *i* et *e*. Dupuis-Yakouba (D-Y) les a notées *ty* et *dy*. En outre, Tombouctou a plus de sons palatalisés que Gao, et notamment *z* est inexistant et, à Tombouctou, a pour correspondant *dy*. Une forme comme *zigi*, « monter » (Gao) est *dyidyi* à Tombouctou. Il me semble que l'évolution est dans le sens *zigi* > *dyidyi* et non l'inverse.

A l'appui de cette opinion, et pour autant qu'on peut se baser sur l'enregistrement de Koelle dans le détail, on trouve plusieurs fois dans la *Polyglotta*, non seulement des occlusives **k** et **g** pour les palatales actuelles, mais egalement des sons **z** alors que le Tombouctien actuel n'a que le son *dy*. On pourrait ainsi tenir que le passage de *z* à *dy* est relativement récent dans le dialecte tombouctien, sans doute influencé par le bambara et le peul qui ont tous deux *dy* et non pas *z*.

REMARQUES EN SUIVANT L'ORDRE DES MOTS DE KOELLE

(Nous indiquons le dialecte de Tombouctou en le faisant précéder de T. et en suivant l'orthographe adoptée par Dupuis-Yacouba; le dialecte de Gao sera précédé de G.).

Les Nombres

Ils sont précédés d'un « préfixe », sans doute un pronom qui est *a* à T. tandis qu'à Gao on a *a fo* « un », puis *i hinka, i hinza*, etc...
« quatre » est noté **a ta:ki** qui est excellent. D-Y a *tatyi*, et Gao aussi, mais le « défini » à Gao est *taka* et l'ordinal « quatrième » est *takanta*.

Pour les nombres intermédiaries (« onze, douze » etc.) le nombres des dizaines est suivi de **kindi** puis du mot représentant les unités. D-Y donne *tyinde*, Gao a *kyindi*.

Les Noms

« woman »	**woi**	T. *wey*	
« boy »	**i:za keina**	T. *idye keyna*	G. *iza keyna*
« son »	**i:za-har**	T. *idye har*	G. *izaru*
« daughter »	**i:za-woi**	T. *idye wey*	G. *izawey*

Il semble difficile de confondre le son *z* avec *dy*, et ces exemples portent a penser que le tombouctien ancien était plus proche du dialecte de Gao qu'actuellement. Parfois même, dans des exemples, Koelle donne **i:sha** au lieu de **i:za** (doublets: « son, daughter » **i:sha har** et **i:sha woi**), par contre on trouve « I flog a child » **ai kare djakeina** qu'il faut lire: *ay kar idya keyna*.

Pour les formes « my father, my mother, thy father » etc. l'informateur a parfois introduit après le pronom complément (donnant la valeur de possessif) une particule **ta** adoucie en **da** qui renforce ce pronom: *ay* « moi », *ay ta* « moi-meme, moi-là »; *nin ta, nta, nda* « toi-meme », c'est ainsi qu'on a les formes **aibaba, ainya, aika:ga** pour *ay baba, ay nya, ay kaga,* et **ninta baba, ndanya, ndankaːga** pour *ni(n) ta baba, n ta nya, n ta(n) kaga* (cf. D–Y, au mot *ta* dans le lexique).

« doctor »	**dawaːu** est le mot *dawā'* « médicament » en arabe; **teːbu** est peut-etre *ṭabīb* « docteur » en arabe.
« face »	**nigiːnɛ** sans doute *ni gyine (dyine)* « ta face », ton « devant »; **mɔː** en réalité « oeil ».
« forehead »	**teŋɛ, teːndje** T. *teŋe*.
« tooth »	**hiːnyɛ, hiŋgɛ** T. *inye* G. *hinye* et *hinge* (il est à noter que D–Y ne marque pas toujours les *h* initiaux).
« throat »	**ginde** T. *dyinde* G. *gyinde*.
« shoulder »	**gɛshɛ** T. *dyese* G. *gyese*.
« foot »	**kɛːdikul** & **ke** T. *tye* G. *kye* (Koelle ne marque pas la palatalisation; **ke + di + kul** signifie « pied + le + tout = tout le pied »).
« elbow »	**kambaː-biːri** « os du bras »; **sɔhonɛ biːri** T. *sokone-biri* os du coude.
« rib »	**kɛroː-biːri** T. *tyero-biri* G. *kyeraw biri* de *kyeraw* « côté » et *biri* « os ».
« heel »	**djɛː-korɛ** T. *tye kore* (ici Koelle a transcrit **djɛː** le mot **kɛː/ke** « foot » de la page 41.
« vein »	**liːŋgi** T. *lindyi* G. *lingyi*; **alasaːbu** est le mot arabe.
« small-pox »	**woihaigumo** T. *weyaygumo*; **masamasa** est la rougeole.
« hat »	**boŋa fɛndu** T. *boŋo fendu* « chapeau en paille tressée ».
« cap »	**fuːla kirei** T. *fula tyirey* « bonnet rouge, chéchia »
« village »	**koirɛ** & **koɛːra** T. *koyra*.
« door-way »	**huːmɛ** & **mɛː** signifient *me* « ouverture, bouche » et *hu-me* « ouverture de la case ».
« mat »	**tandjɛrɛ** T. *tendyere*.
« spoon »	**djoːto** T. *dyoto* « calebasse à manche ou calebasse-cuiller, cf. « calabash » below.
« armlet »	**kamba-ndjarfu** T. *kamba-ndyorfu* (*kamba* « bras », *ndyorfu* « argent, objet en argent »).
	soŋko T. *sonko* « bracelet en argent ».
« calabash »	**gaːsu** & **djoːto** T. *gasu* est la calebasse ordinaire, *dyoto*, la calebasse-cuiller vue precedemment.
« gun »	**marfa** T. *malfa*; **tshoudar** (? on ne voit pas ce que peut être ce mot).
« powder »	**albaːru** & **albaːdu** T. *albarudu*.
« bow »	**karaːlefɛ** & **karaː** (??)

« arrow »	**haŋgou** T. *toŋgow*, mais à Gao on a **hangaw** « pointe de flêche en pierre (préhistorique) » et également « harpon pour la chasse à l'hippopotame ».
« quiver »	**tuŋgohu** T. *toŋgow-hu*, c'est à dire la case (*hu*) des flêches; on retrouve là, dans Koelle, le mot **tuŋgo** pour « flêche ».
« God »	**yarkui, yɛrkoi** T. *yerkoy*, ce qui signifie « notre Maître » (*koy* « maître », *yer* « nous »).
« idol »	**kɔrtɛ** & **kɔte,** en réalité le mot est bambara, utilisé en pays soŋay pour désigner les maléfices, mauvais sorts, poisons.
« greegree »	**daba:ri-futu** signifie « manière mauvaise »; **se:he:ru** est un mot arabe *siḥr* désignant un gris-gris sur lequel on fait des sacrifices.
« heaven »	**aldjɛnnɛ** T. *aldyenne*.
« hell »	**dja:hanna** & **nu:nɛ** T. *aldyehennam* « enfer »; T. *nuṛe* « le feu » est employé aussi pour désigner l'enfer.
« sun »	**weinɛ** & **woinɛ** T. *weyne* « soleil ».
« day »	**dja:ri** & **dja:ri koro:no** T. *dyari* « jour » & *dyari korno* « jour chaud » ou *dyari koron* « chaleur du jour ».
« night »	**ki:gi** T. *tyidyin* G. *kyigin*.
« dry season »	**kɔrɔ nua:ti** & **koron,** le premier mot doit être lu T. *koron wati* « le temps de la chaleur », le 2eme T. *koron* « chaleur ».
« rainy season »	**kaidiawa:ti** & **kaidi:a** T. *keydia* (on retrouve dans le premier mot: *wati* « temps, époque de »).
« coal »	**dɛndji bi:wi** & **dɛngi biwi** T. *dendyi bibi* « charbon noir » (on retrouve là comme fréquemment dans Koelle un **w** au lieu d'un *b* intervocalique).
« chain »	**shɛsar** est la petite chaîne fine d'où **ginde-shɛsar** T. *dyinde sesar* « chaîne de cou, ornement »; **galaŋga** désigne les chaînes des prisonniers.
« walking stick »	**taŋkara** & **bundu** T. *tınkara* « longue canne ornée de cuivre ou d'argent portée par les notables »; T. *bundu* signifie « bois, tout objet en bois », aussi bien « bâton » ou « canne ordinaire ».
« palm-tree »	**garboi** T. *garbey* est en réalité le « balanites ægyptiaca » dont les fruits sont parfois appelés « dattes sauvages » car elles ressemblent aux dattes par l'aspect, elles ont une saveur à la fois sucrée et amère et sont recherchées par les gens du pays.

« palm-oil »	**bulaŋga kirei,** le mot a dû être inventé par les informateurs de Koelle, car l'huile de palme est inconnue a Tombouctou; le vocable fourni est composé de *bulanga* « beurre de karité » et de T. *tyirey*/G. *kyirey* « rouge ».
« kuskus »	**biːmbiri kirei** désigne simplement le gros mil rouge.
« cotton-tree »	**dambu**; le fromager est inconnu à Tombouctou mais peut-être connu à Dienné. On trouve dans D-Y *dambu* « amadou à briquet fait avec la beurre du fruit du fromager ou kapok ».
« rice »	**mɔː** (**moː-taːsu** « cooked ») T. *mo* « riz, plante et grains non décortiqués (paddy) »; *mo taso* « bouillie de riz ».
« yam »	**labdundu,** l'igname est inconnu dans le pays, *dundu* y désigne les tubercules de nénuphars, et le terme est aussi appliqué aux ignames venant de la Côte actuellement et mis en vente sur les marchés; **lab** + **dundu** « *dundu* de terre » semble être un mot fabriqué par l'informateur pour désigner un tubercule poussant dans la terre et non dans le fleuve.
« ground-nut »	**maːntighɛ** & **maːtigha** T. *matige*.
« pepper »	**dando** T. *dendi* « piment ».
« maize »	**masara haːma** T. *almasarhama*, le premier terme serait arabe *almasar*/*masara*, et on le retrouve dans Koelle même en kandin (tamacheq), mandara, hausa et peul; le 2ème terme signifie « gros mil, sorgho ». Le zerma a conservé ce mot en lui accolant celui désignant le petit mil (pénicillaire) *masar hayni*, le soŋay de Gao a actuellement *kotokoli*, mot étranger.
« cow »	**hɔu** T. *hau*.
« milk »	**waː** T. *wa*, surtout employé dans les composés *wa gani* « lait frais » etc., supplanté par le mot peul *kosam*; à Gao uniquement *wa*.
« butter »	**bara kura** (**siriːmɛ dji** « melted ») T. *barakura* « beurre frais », *silim dyi* « beurre (*dyi*) de l'outre (*silim*) »; le beurre fondu étant mis dans des outres pour être apporté des campements nomades au marché.
« sheep »	**feːdji** & **feːgi** T. *fedyi*, on remarquera que Koelle emploie ici **dj** pour un palatale sonore *dy*, et que la prononciation *fegi* était encore conservée. A Gao on a *fegyi* « mouton », le *g* étant palatalisé devant *i*, mais on a *fego* aussi bien que *fegyo* pour le défini « le mouton ».

« rat »	**ndjam** & **djam** T. *ntyom*.
« pig »	**alkinshir,** il s'agit du phacochère, le mot est arabe, *khinzīr*, noté par Koelle pour les parlers du Wadai, Adirar et Beran; aujourd'hui on n'emploie que T. *binka*.
« bat »	**teirasui,** sans doute T. *tyiraw-su* « oiseau mauvais ».
« pigeon »	**tuːdjul** & **tuːyun** T. *tudyun*.
« parrot »	**alhuːdi** T. *hudhudi*.
« bird »	**djirɔu** & **kiroːkeina** T. *tyirow* & *tyirow keyna* « petit oiseau ».
« butterfly »	**talaːla** T. *alfa-fatafela*.
« wasp »	**dondoːŋkariːa** (??)
« bee »	**yoːnya** et « honey » **yuː** il s'agit du même mot *yu* « miel », *yu-nya* « mère du miel ».
« frog »	**kɔːrobaːta** T. *korombata* G. *kormata*.

Les Adjectifs

Il y a en soŋay des verbes d'état ou de qualité « être grand, être long, être blanc, être rouge, etc. », et des adjectifs qui leur correspondent ou en sont dérivés « grand, long, blanc, rouge ». Koelle donne l'une ou l'autre forme, ou les deux formes: une forme verbale précédée du pronom personnel *a* (3ème personne du singulier); une forme adjectif souvent « défini » et précédée du pronom *i* qui lui donne cette valeur. Ainsi il donne **abeːr** « il est grand » et **ibeːr** « le grand »; **i kiːna** « le petit » et **a kiːna** « il est petit ». Parfois l'adjectif est donné dans sa forme « indéfinie » ou bien avec un nom, ainsi **kɔrei** « blanc », **boro korei** « white man »; « good » **abɔːri** « il est beau » & **aguma** « il est bon »; « bad » **ifutu** « le méchant » & **a meːr** « il est vilain »; « old » **iːdjɛn** (*i dyena*) « le vieux » & **aː gɛn** (*a dyen*) « il est vieux »; « new » **i taːo** « le nouveau ».

« well » **iːsawi irkui** & **aː saːbi yɛrkoi** (i.e. « thank God ») correspond à la réponse que font les Arabes quand on leur demande des nouvelles de leur santé: *alḥamdu lillāh* « louange à Dieu ». La première phrase peut s'entendre: *ir sab yerkoy* « nous louons Dieu » ou *i sab yerkoy* « ils louent Dieu »; la 2ème phrase est à la 3ème pers. du singulier.

« hot »	**akoron** « c'est chaud », **aːduŋgu** « c'est tiède ».
« cold »	**iːyei** « le froid (celui qui est froid) », **aː yei** « c'est froid ».
« dry »	**idaːo** « le maigre », **akɔː** « c'est sec ».
« greedy »	**borɔfutu** « homme méchant, coléreux ».
« stupid »	**fuyeːnte** & **nɛːri,** le premier signifie « paresseux, bon à rien », le 2ème « simple d'esprit, sot ».

« rich »	**almankoini** = *alman* « troupeaux » et par extension « cheptal/capital » + *koyni* « maitre de ».
« straight »	**isarɛ** (*i sare*) « le droit ».
« crooked »	**igum** (?) & **a goŋgoːri** (*a gongoli*) « il est courbé ».

Les Verbes

Koelle a recueilli deux formes à l'affirmation et deux formes à la négation : présent/progressif positif et négatif, parfait positif et parfait négatif.

« I go » **ai koi** *ay koy* « je suis allé »; **ai gaːkoi** peut-être une erreur pour *ai go koi* ou bien le *ga* est une forme de mise en vedette du sujet au parfait, actuellement c'est *nga* à Tombouctou, mais *ga* à Goundam et la phrase signifie « c'est moi qui suis allé » tandis que *ai go koi* signifie « je vais, j'irai ».

« I sit down » **ai goro** « je suis assis », **ai gogoːro** *ay go goro* « je m'assieds » ou « je vais m'asseoir ».

« I breathe » **ai gohĩːhã** *ay go hiha* « je respire ».

« I do not play » **ai na hɔːrei** « je n'ai pas joué » et **ai si hɔːrei** « je ne joue pas » ou « je ne jouerai pas ».

Avec ces données préliminaires, il est très facile de reconnaître les verbes données par Koelle. Nous ne ferons que quelques remarques :

« I run »	**ai sur** & **ai gaːd shur** T. *dyur* « courier ».
« I stop »	**ai kindiːnɛ** & **ai fara** *ay tyindi ne* « je suis resté ici »; *ay fara* « je suis fatigué ».
« I snore »	**ai kɔrɔ** T. *ay goro*.
« I weep »	**ai hoũ** & **ai goihɔũ** T. *hem/hum* « pleurer ».
« I kneel »	**ai guŋguːma** & **ai gorɛkandjɛːga**, *ay gunguma* signifie « je fais la prosternation pour le salam »; *ay gor'ey kandye ga* « je suis assis sur mes genoux ».
« I hear »	**ai moũ** T. *ay mom*.
« I beg »	**ai ŋaːreini** T. *ay ŋarey ni* « je t'ai prié ».
« I take »	**ai djɔuga** T. *ay dyow ga* « je l'ai saisi ».
« I buy »	**ai dei** & **ai koidei** T. *ay dey* « je l'ai acheté »; *ay koy dey* « je suis allé l'acheter ».
« I cut a tree »	**ai dumbu tuːri** & **ai kodumbu bundu** *ay koy dumbu turi* « je suis allé couper un arbre ».
« I flog a child »	**ai kare djakeina** *ay kar idya keyna*.
« I break a stick »	**ai hasara tuːriːdi**, *hasara* signifie « abimer », *turi di* « l'arbre » (*di* ajouté a un substantif indéfini en fait un « défini » comme l'article *the* : on a d'autres examples p. 183 **kusuːdi** « the pot », **dɛrbedi** « the cloth »).

A Bibliography of the Somali Language and Literature

JOHN WILLIAM JOHNSON

INTRODUCTION

In compiling this bibliography, I have used several libraries, including the Secretariat Library in Hargeysa, the United Nations Library in Mogadishu, the private library of Mr. Ariberto Forlani in Mogadishu, the Butler Library at Colombia University in New York, the Main Library at the University of Texas in Austin, the British Museum Library in London, and the Library of the School of Oriental and African Studies at the University of London.

I would like to make acknowledgements to several people who have helped greatly with the preparation of this work. Especial thanks are extended to Dr. B. W. Andrzejewski, Dr. David Dalby, Mr. Felix K. Knauth, Mr. Muuse H. I. Galaal, and Dr. B. G. Martin.

A special note must be given on the spelling used in the bibliography, for Somali has, as yet, no established orthography. Priority has been given to the spelling employed by each author. Where transcription was necessary because of the lack of special characters, I have used the Latin alphabet perfected by Mr. Muuse H. I. Galaal. An outline of this script may be found in his book *The Terminology and Practice of Somali Weather Lore, Astronomy, and Astrology*, Mogadishu, 1968, available from the New Africa Booksellers, P.O. Box 897, Mogadishu, Somali Republic. The alphabet used for transcribing Arabic is the internaticnally accepted one, while that used for Russian is as employed by the Library of the London School of Slavonic and East European Studies. The alphabetizing of the names of Somali and Arabic authors follows the practice of first name first, second name second, etc.

There are two codes employed in this bibliography. The publishers' and journals' names have all been coded. The subject matter of each entry has likewise been coded and is the last item of each entry. A complete list of codes follows this introduction.

Note that the names Muuse H. I. Galaal, Hhirsi Magan and Shirre Jama Ahmed have alternative spellings: Musa H. I. Galaal, Hirsi Magan and Shire Jaamac Achmed (or Axmed) respectively. The divergence is due to the above stated reasons.

CODE OF PUBLISHERS AND JOURNALS

Code	Publisher or Journal	Place of Publication
A.	Affrica	Rome
A.A.E.	Archivio per l'antropologia e l'etnologia	Italy
A.A.L.	Atti della Accademia dei Lincei	Rome
A.C.E.G.	A. Carcano: edizioni grafiche	Milan
A.F.	Afrika: German Review of Economic, Cultural, and Political Affairs in Africa and Madagascar	Germany
A.F.F.	Afrikanskaya Filologiya (African Philology)	Moscow
A.F.I.	Amministrazione Fiduciaria Italiana	Italy
A.H.	Alfred Hoelder	Vienna
A.K.I.	Abhandlung der kd. Institut	Hamburg
A.L.I.	Arab Language Institute of the University of Al-Azhar al-Sharīf	Cairo
A.L.R.	African Language Review	London
A.L.S.	African Language Studies	London
A.M.	Andrew Melrose, Ltd.	London
A.R.	Africa Report	Washington, D.C.
A.R.O.	Angus and Robertson, Ltd.	London
AUTH.	Published by the author	—
B.	Biettli	Milan
B.A.	Biblioteca africana	Italy
B.B.C.	British Broadcasting Corporation	London
B.F.B.S.	British and Foreign Bible Society	London
B.S.A.I.	Boll. soc. afr. ital.	Italy
B.S.G.I.	Boll. soc. geogr. ital.	Italy
B.S.L.P.	Bulletin de la société de linguistique de Paris	Paris
B.S.O.A.S.	Bulletin of the School of Oriental and African Studies	London
B.W.O.	British War Office	London
C.	Civilisations	France
C.A.	Crown Agents [for the Colonies]	London
C.E.I.	Casa editrice italiana	Rome
C.E.M.	Casa editrice mediterranea	Rome
C.E.S.	Casa editrice Sonzogno	Milan
C.P.	Compass Pub. Co.	New Haven, Conn.
C.R.G.L.	Comptes rendus du groupe linguistique d'études chamito-semitiques (Ecole pratique à la Sorbonne)	Paris

Code	Publisher or Journal	Place of Publication
C.S.	Corriere della Somalia	Mogadishu
C.U.P.	Cambridge University Press	London
D.	Dalka	Mogadishu
D.E.	Delaporte	Paris
D.R.	Dietrich Reimer	Berlin
D.M.	Dār al-Ma'ārif	Cairo
D.N.	Druzhba Narodov	Moscow
D.N.S.	Donum Natalicium Schrijnen	Nijmegen-Utrecht
D.Q.T.N.	Dār al-Qawmiyya lil-Ṭabā'a wa al-Nashr	Cairo
D.T.H.	Dār al-Ṭabā'at al-Ḥadītha	Cairo
E.	L'Esploratore	Naples
E.A.C.	Edizioni arte e cultura	Mogadishu
E.A.I.S.R.	East African Institute of Social Research	Kampala
E.L.	Ernest Leroux	Paris
E.L.E.	Edizioni 'le lingue estere'	Milan
E.P.	Eagle Press	Nairobi
E.S.P.	Education Society's Press, Byculla	Bombay
F.M.	Festschrift Meinhof	Germany
G.I.P.	Gregg International Publishers, Ltd.	Farnborough, Hants.
G.P.	Gregg Press	East Ridgewood, New Jersey
H.	Heffer	Cambridge
H.B.A.K.	Hamburger Beiträge zur Afrika-Kunde: Deutsches Institut für Afrika-Forschung	Hamburg
I.A.	The Indian Antiquary	Bombay
I.A.I.	International African Institute	London
I.P.S.	Istituto poligrafico dello stato	Rome
I.Q.	The Islamic Quarterly	London
I.U.P.	Indiana University Press	Bloomington, Indiana
J.A.L.	Journal of African Languages	East Lansing, Michigan
J.A.S.	Journal of the African Society	London
J.B.R.A.S.	Journal of the Bombay Royal Asiatic Society	Bombay
J.F.I.	Journal of the Folklore Institute	Bloomington, Indiana
J.M.A.S.	The Journal of Modern African Studies	London

Code	Publisher or Journal	Place of Publication
J.R.A.I.	The Journal of the Royal Anthropological Institute of Great Britain and Ireland	London
J.S.A.	Journal de la société des africainistes	France
J.S.S.	Journal of Semitic Studies	Manchester
K.A.W.	Kaiserliche Akademie der Wissenschaften	Vienna
K.P.T.T.	Kegan Paul, Trench, Truebner and Co.	London
L.	Language	Baltimore
L.C.	Library of Congress	Washington, D.C.
L.E.	Larose Editeurs	Paris
L.G.	Longman, Green and Co.	London
L.R.	Linguistic Reporter	Washington, D.C.
M.	Macmillan and Co., Ltd.	London, New York
M.B.H.	Muṣṭafā al-Bābī al-Ḥalabī	Cairo
M.C.	Mission Catholique	London, Berbera
M.G.M.	Al-Munshī Ghulām Muḥammad	Aden
M.I.	Maṭbaʿat al-Imām	Cairo
M.M.H.	Maṭbaʿat al-Mashhad al-Ḥusaynī	Cairo
M.P.	Maître phonétique	Nevilli
MS.(S)	Manuscript(s)	—
M.S.G.I.	Mem. soc. geogr. Ital.	Italy
M.S.O.S.B.	Mitteilungen des Seminars für orientalische Sprachen zu Berlin	Berlin
N.A.A.	Narody Azii i Afriki (Peoples of Asia and Africa). The Academy of Sciences of the U.S.S.R.	Moscow
N.M.P.	Nile Mission Press	Cairo
N.P.	The National Printers, Ltd.	Mogadishu
N.R.	The National Review: a Periodical Panorama of Somali Events. Ministry of Information, Somali Government	Mogadishu
N.S.	New Society	London
N.T.E.C.	National Teacher Education Center	Afgoi
O.C.P.	(Oxford) Clarendon Press	London
O.M.	Oriente moderno	Rome
O.U.P.	Oxford University Press	London
P.A.	Présence africaine	Paris

Code	Publisher or Journal	Place of Publication
P.A.Y.	*Problemy Afrikanskogo Yazykoznanya: Tipologiya, Komparativistika, Opisanie Yazykov* (Problems of African Linguistics: Typology, Comparative Studies and Descriptive Linguistics)	Moscow
P.B.G.S.	*Proceedings of the Bombay Geographical Society*	Bombay
P.F.C.	P. Fontana et Cie	Algers
P.M.P.	Pall Mall Press	London
P.O.	*Przegląd Orientalistyczny*	Warsaw
P.P.P.	Peter Pauper Press	Mount Vernon
R.A.L.	*Rassegna di Accad. Lincei*	Rome
R.A.S.	Royal Asiatic Society	Cambridge
R.C.S.M.A.	*Report of the C.C.T.A./C.S.A. Symposium on Multilingualism in Africa*	Brazzaville
R.F.F.	*Revue de folklore français*	France
R.K.P.	Routledge and Kegan Paul, Ltd.	London
R.M.F.I.	*The Reporter: the Magazine of Facts and Ideas*	New York
R.S.E.	*Rassegna di studi etiopici*	Rome
R.S.O.	*Rivista degli studi orientali*	Rome
S.A.F.I.S.	Stamperia AFIS	Mogadishu
S.A.W.W.	*Sitzungsberichte, Akademie der Wissenschaften in Wien, philosophisch-historische Klasse*	Vienna
S.C.	Stamperia della colonia	Mogadishu
S.D.O.	*Somalia d'oggi*	Mogadishu
S.E.	*Studi etiopici*	Rome
S.G.	Société géographique	Paris
S.I.P.A.	Somali Institute of Public Administration	Mogadishu
S.J.	*The Somaliland Journal*	Hargeysa
S.N.	*The Somali News*	Mogadishu
S.O.	Stationery Office	Hargeysa
S.O.A.S.	School of Oriental and African Studies, University of London	London
S.S.L.L.	Society for Somali Language and Literature	Mogadishu
S.T.M.C.	Scuola tipografica missione cattolica	Mogadishu
S.U.	Syracuse University	Syracuse, New York

Code	Publisher or Journal	Place of Publication
T.	Thacker	Bombay
T.B.G.S.	Transactions of the Bombay Geographical Society	Bombay
T.C.	Teachers College, Columbia University	New York
T.F.	Theodor Froehlich	Berlin
T.F.M.C.	Tipografia francescana, missione cattolica	Asmara
T.F.O.	Tipografia Ferrari, Occella and Co.	Alessandria
T.R.	Tipografia Raimondi	Asmara
T.R.I.	La tribuna: rivista mensile di attualita politica, economica e sociale	Mogadishu
T.R.U.	Truebner and Co.	London
U.H.	Ulrico Hoepli	Milan
U.L.P.	University of London Press	London
U.S.D.H.E.W.	United States Department of Health, Education and Welfare, Office of Education	Washington, D.C.
U.S.P.C.	United States Peace Corps	—
U.S.R.S.O.	Univ. degli studi di Roma, Scuola Orientale	Rome
V.A.M.	Vicariato apostolico di Mogadiscio	Mogadishu
W.A.R.	War Somali Sidihi (now The Somali News)	Hargeysa
W.Z.K.M.	Wiener Zeitschrift für die Kunde des Morgenlandes	Vienna
Y.A.	Yazyki Afriki: Voprosy Struktury, Istorii i Tipologii (Languages of Africa: Problems of Structure, History and Typology). The Publishing House 'Nauka'	Moscow
Z.A.O.S.	Zeitschrift für afrikanische und ozeanische Sprachen (Seidelsche Zeitschrift)	Berlin
Z.D.M.G.	Zeitschrift Dt. Morgenland. Ges.	Germany
Z.E.S.	Zeitschrift für Eingeborenen-Sprachen (formerly Zeitschrift für Kolonialsprachen)	Berlin
Z.K.	Zeitschrift für Kolonialsprachen (see: Zeitschrift für Eingeborenen-Sprachen)	Berlin
Z.P.	Zeitschrift für Phonetik	Berlin

SUBJECT MATTER CODE

Code   *Explanation*
bibl   Contains bibliography of linguistic and/or literary importance
dict   Dictionary
dict.w Word lists
ess   General essay on the language or culture
ess.l   Essay on a literary theory
ess.s   Essay on a linguistic theory
ess.w   Essay on a theory of writing Somali, or on the problem of writing Somali
gmr   Grammar
prd   Periodicals or newspapers published in the Somali language
prd.l   Periodicals or newspapers published in the Somali language, using a Latin script
prd.s   Periodicals or newspapers published in the Somali language, using the Somali writing system
rpt   Reports, e.g. societies' studies, progress reports, etc.
txt   Text
txt.a   Somali text in the Arabic language
txt.s   Somali text in Somali only
txt.t   Somali text in translation only
txt.st Somali text in both Somali and translation

(*Note:* In some cases, the subject matter code refers only to a section of a book in question, relevant to the scope of this bibliography, and *not* necessarily to the total content of the book.)

BIBLIOGRAPHY

ANONYMOUS, 'Boggii Murtida' ('The Page of Wisdom'), *D.*, i/6, December 1, 1965, p. 22. (txt.s)

——, 'Boggii Murtida' ('The Page of Wisdom'), ibid., ii/2, August 1, 1966, p. 9. (txt.s)

——, 'Boggii Murtida' ('The Page of Wisdom'), ibid., ii/3, September 1, 1966, p. 9. (txt.s)

——, 'Cultural Heritage', *N.R.*, v, July 1965, p. 34. (ess)

——, *Haj- Osaman-Eh (Gharko): A Heaven's Pilgrimage: an Attempt to Render (so far as may be) in Somali the First Part of Bunyan's 'Pilgrim's Progress'*, N.M.P., n.d., pp. 158. (txt.s)

——, 'A Nation of Poets', *S.N.*, 440, July 4, 1969, p. 11. (ess, txt.t)

Al-Shaykh 'ABD ALLĀH b. Mu'allim YŪSUF AL-QUṬBĪ AL-QĀDIRĪ AL-QALANQŪLĪ, *Al-Majmū'at al-Mubāraka (The Blessed Collection)*, M.M.H. for Islamiya Bookshop in Mogadishu, n.d. (txt.a)

Al-Shaykh 'ABD AL-RAḤMĀN b. al-Shaykh 'UMAR AL-'ALĪ AL-QĀDIRĪ, *Jalā' al-'Aynayn fī Manāqib al-Shaykhayn: al-Shaykh al-Walī Ḥājj Uways al-Qādirī wa al-Shaykh al-Kāmil al-Shaykh 'Abd al-Raḥmān al-Zayla'ī* (*The Opening of the Two Eyes Concerning the Miraculous Acts of the Two Shaykhs: The Saint and Pilgrim Shaykh Uways of the Qadiriyya Fraternity and the Accomplished Shaykh 'Abd al-Raḥmān of Zayla'*), M.M.H., *c.* 1954, pp. 103. (txt.a)

——, *Al-Jawhar al-Nafīs fī Khawāṣ al-Shaykh Uways* (*The Precious Jewel Devoted to Shaykh Uways*), M.M.H., 1964, pp. 240. (txt.a)

'ABD AL-ṢABŪR MARZŪQ, *Thā'ir min al-Ṣūmāl: al-Mullā Muḥammad 'Abd Allāh Ḥasan* (*The Revolutionary from Somalia: the Mullah Muhammad 'Abd Allāh Ḥasan*), D.Q.T.N., 1964, pp. 224. (txt.a, txt.st)

'ABDULLĀHI Hhāji MAHHAMŪD and PANZA, Bruno, *Afkayaga Hooyo*, E.A.C., 1960, pp. 118. (txt.s, gmr)

ABRAHAM, R. C., *Somali–English Dictionary*, U.L.P., 1962, pp. 332. (dict)

——, *English–Somali Dictionary*, U.L.P., 1967, pp. 208. (dict)

ABRAHAM, R. C. and SOLOMON WARSAMA, *The Principles of Somali*, London, AUTH., 1951, pp. 481. (gmr)

Al-Shaykh AHMAD b. ḤUSAYN b. MUḤAMMAD, *Manāqib al-Ustādh al-Shaykh Ismā'īl b. Ibrāhīm al-Jabartī* (*The Miraculous Acts of the Teacher and Shaykh Ismā'īl b. Ibrāhīm al-Jabartī*), M.B.H., 1945, pp. 8. (txt.a)

Al-Sayyid AHMAD b. ZAYNĪ DAHLAN, *Al-Durar al-Saniyya fī al-radd 'alā al-Wahhābiyya* (*The Flashing Pearls: a Refutation of the Wahhābiyya*), M.B.H., 1966. (txt.a)

ANDRZEJEWSKI, B. W., 'Is Somali a Tone-Language?', *Proceedings of the Twenty-Third International Congress of Orientalists*, R.A.S., 1954, pp. 367–68. (gmr)

——, 'Some Problems of Somali Orthography', *S.J.*, i/1, December 1954, pp. 34–47. (ess.w)

——, 'The Problem of Vowel Representation in the Isaaq Dialect of Somali', *B.S.O.A.S.*, xvii/3, 1955, pp. 567–80. (gmr)

——, 'Accentual Patterns in Verbal Forms in the Isaaq Dialect of Somali', *B.S.O.A.S.*, xviii/1, 1956, pp. 103–29. (gmr)

——, 'Pronominal and Prepositional Particles in Northern Somali', *A.L.S.*, i, 1960, pp. 96–108. (gmr)

——, 'Notes on the Substantive Pronouns in Somali', *A.L.S.*, ii, 1961, pp. 80–99. (gmr)

——, 'Speech and Writing Dichotomy as the Pattern of Multilingualism in the Somali Republic', *R.C.S.M.A.*, 1962, pp. 177–81. (ess)

——, 'Poetry in Somali Society', *N.S.*, i/25, 1963, pp. 22–4. (ess.l, txt.t)

——, *The Declensions of Somali Nouns*, S.O.A.S., 1964, pp. 149. (bibl, gmr)

——, 'Somali Stories', WHITELEY, W. H. (ed.), *A Selection of African Prose: 1. Traditional Oral Texts*, The Oxford Library of African Literature, O.C.P., 1964, pp. 134–63. (txt.t)

——, 'The Art of the Miniature in Somali Poetry', *A.L.R.*, vi, 1967, pp. 5–16. (ess.l, txt.st)
——, 'Inflectional Characteristics of the So-called Weak Verbs in Somali', *A.L.S.*, ix, 1968, pp. 1–51. (gmr)
——, 'Reflections on the Nature and Social Function of Somali Proverbs', *A.L.R.*, vii, 1968, pp. 74–85. (ess.l, txt.st)
——, 'Recent Researches into the Somali Language and Literature, *S.N.*, 439, June 27, 1969, pp. 4, 8. (rpt)
——, 'The Role of Broadcasting in the Adaptation of the Somali Language to Modern Needs', in WHITELEY, W. H. (ed.), *Language Use and Social Change*, O.U.P. (in the press). (bibl, ess.s)
——, 'Somali Modes of Thought and Communication', *Newsletter: a Quarterly Publication*, Mogadishu, S.I.P.A., 3, January–March 1969, pp. 1–9 [supplement]. (ess)
——, 'Somali Poetry', *Directory of Somalia: 1968–69*, London, Diprepu Co., Ltd., for 'Diplomatic Bookshelf and Review', 1969, pp. 22. (ess.l, txt.t)
——, 'Some Observations on Hybrid Verbs in Somali', *A.L.S.*, x, 1969, pp. 47–89. (bibl, grm)
ANDRZEJEWSKI, B. W. and LEWIS, I. M., *Somali Poetry: an Introduction*, The Oxford Library of African Literature, O.C.P., 1964, pp. 167. (ess.l, txt.st)
ANDRZEJEWSKI, B. W. and MUUSE H. I. GALAAL, 'A Somali Poetic Combat', *J.A.L.*, ii, 1963, part 1 pp. 15–28, part 2 pp. 93–100, part 3 pp. 190–205. Republished *in toto* by Michigan State University, n.d. (ess.l, txt.st)
——, 'The Art of the Verbal Message in Somali Society', LUKAS, Johannes (ed.), *Neue afrikanistische Studien*, *H.B.A.K.*, v, 1966, pp. 29–39. (ess.l, txt.st)
ANDRZEJEWSKI, B. W., STRELCYN, S. and TUBIANA, J., 'Somalia: The Writing of Somali', *Antologia storico-culturale*, 7–8, Mogadishu, Ministry of Education, 1969, pp. 214–34. (ess.w) (Reprint of U.N.E.S.C.O. Report WS/0866.90, CTL)
ARMSTRONG, Lilias E., 'The Phonetic Structure of Somali', *M.S.O.S.B.*, xxxvii/3, 1934, pp. 116–61. Republished by G.P., 1964, pp. 46. (gmr)
ARPINO, Ludovico d', *Vocabolario dall'Italiano nelle versioni Galla, Oromo, Amara, Dancala, Somala*, U.H., 1938. (dict.w)
BARRY, E., *An Elementary Somali Grammar*, T.R., c. 1937, pp. 106. (gmr)
BELL, C. R. V., *The Somali Language*, L.G., 1953, pp. 185. Republished by G.I.P., 1968, pp. 198. (gmr)
BERGHOLD, K., 'Somali-Studien', *Z.A.O.S.*, iii, 1897, pp. 116–98. (rpt, txt.st)
——, 'Somali-Studien', *W.Z.K.M.*, xiii, 1899, pp. 123–98. (rpt, txt.st)

BIRD, J., 'Abyssinia, Eastern Africa, and the Ethiopic Family of Languages', *J.B.R.A.S.*, 1845, pp. 294–309. (ess)

BRADEN, Tom and Sandra, 'Somali Stories', in their *Stories for Somali Students*, U.S.P.C., [1967], pp. 6–10, 65–9, 103–08. (txt.t)

BRITISH and FOREIGN BIBLE SOCIETY, *Anjilka Sidu 'Digey Marko (St. Mark's Gospel in Somali: Tentative Edition)*, B.F.B.S., 1915, pp. 57. (txt.s)

BRYAN, M. A., *The Distribution of the Semitic and Cushitic Languages of Africa*, O.U.P. for I.A.I., 1947, pp. 36 with map. (bibl, ess.s)

BUCHHOLZER, John, 'Tales the Somalis Tell', in his *The Horn of Africa*, A.R.O., 1959, pp. 98–105. (txt.t)

BURTON, Sir Richard Francis, *First Footsteps in East Africa or an Exploration of Harar*, London, 1856. Republished by R.K.P., 1966, pp. 320. (ess)

CARCOFORO, Enrico, *Elementi di Somalo e ki-Suahili parlati al Benadir*, U.H., 1912, pp. 154. (Reprinted in 1935) (gmr)

CARESSA, Ferruccio, *Dizionario africano*, C.E.S., 1938, pp. 283. (dict)

CERULLI, Enrico, 'Canti e proverbi Somali nel dialetto degli Habä'r Auwál', *R.S.O.*, xvii, 1918, pp. 797–836. (txt.st)

——, 'Di alcune presunte consonanti nei dialetti Somali', *R.S.O.*, xii, 1918, pp. 877–83. (gmr)

——, 'Somali Songs and Little Texts', *J.A.S.*, part 1, xix, 1919; part 2, xx, 1920; part 3, xxi, 1921. (txt.st)

——, 'Nota sui dialetti Somali', *R.S.O.*, viii, 1921, pp. 693–99. (ess.s)

——, 'Il gergo delle genti di bassa casta della Somalo', *F.M.*, 1927, pp. 99–110. (ess.s)

——, 'Per la toponomastica della Somalia', *O.M.*, xi, 1931, pp. 460–7. (ess)

——, 'Tentativo indigeno di formare un alfabeto Somalo', *O.M.*, xii, 1932, pp. 212–13. (ess.w)

——, 'Quelques notes sur la phonologie somali', *C.R.G.L.*, iv, 1947, pp. 53–7. (gmr)

——, *Somalia i: storia della Somalia, l'islam in Somalia, il libro degli zengi*, A.F.I., 1959, pp. 363. (ess, txt.a, txt.st)

——, *Somalia ii: diritto, etnografia, linguistica, come viveva una tribù Hawiyya*, ibid., 1959, pp. 392. (ess, txt.st)

——, *Somalia iii: la tribù Somala, lingua Somala in caratteri Arabi ed altri saggi*, ibid., 1959, pp. 230. (ess, txt.st)

CHIARINI, G., 'Raccolta di vocaboli dei Somali–Isa', *M.S.G.I.*, i, 1897, pp. 209–15. (dict.w)

CONOVER, Helen F., *Official Publications of Somaliland, 1941–1959: a Guide*, L.C., 1960, pp. 41. (bibl)

CONTI ROSSINI, Carlo, *Etiopia e genti di Etiopia*, Firenze, 1937. (ess.s)

CONTINI, Jeanne, 'The Illiterate Poets of Somalia', *R.M.F.I.*, xxviii/6, March 14, 1963, pp. 36–8. (ess.l)

——, 'Somali Republic: a Nation of Poets in Search of an Alphabet', *A.R.*, December 1963, pp. 15–18. (ess.l, ess.w)
COSTAGUTI, Marchesa Maria Afan de Rivera, *Manuale pratico di lingua Somàla ad uso dei viaggiatori nella valle di Giuba*, C.E.I., 1909, pp. 136. (gmr)
CUST, R. N., 'Language of Somali-land', R.A.S. (?), pp. 95–100. (ess.s)
——, *The Modern Languages of Africa*, T.R.U., 1883. (ess.s)
CZERMAK, W., 'Somali Texte im Dialekt der Habr-Ja'lo', *W.Z.K.M.*, xxxi, 1924, pp. 113–36. (txt.st)
——, 'Zur Phonetik des Somali', *W.Z.K.M.*, xxxi, 1924, pp. 82–102. (gmr)
——, 'Zum Gebrauch des Infinitivs als "Futurum" in Somali', *D.N.S.*, 1929, pp. 182–89. (gmr)
DRAKE-BROCKMAN, R. E., *British Somaliland*, London, 1912. (ess.s)
DRYSDALE, John G. S., *Some Notes for Beginners on the Somali Language*, S.O., 1953, pp. 67. (gmr)
——, *Somali Primer, Part 1*, S.O., 1959, pp. 40. (gmr)
DUCHENET, Edouard, *Histoires Somalies: La malice des primitifs*, L.E., 1936, pp. 191. (txt.t)
——, 'Le chant dans le folklore somali', *R.F.F.*, ix, 1938, pp. 72–87. (txt, ess.l)
FERRAND, Gabriel, *Notes de grammaire çomâlie*, P.F.C., 1886, pp. 28. (gmr)
——, 'Traditions historiques, linguistique et anthropologie', in his *Les Çomâlis*, E.L., 1903, pp. 64–84. (ess)
FERRARIO, Benigno, 'L'accento in Somâlo', *R.S.O.*, xi, 1914–15, pp. 961–7. (gmr)
——, ' "Ingir<*Ingi'il" in Somalo', *R.S.O.*, xii/1, 1916–18, pp. 717–19. (gmr)
——, 'Note di fonologia Somâla', *R.S.O.*, xii/1, 1916–18, pp. 199–217. (gmr)
FORLANI, Ariberto (ed.), *Bibliografia Somala*, S.T.M.C. for Camera di Commercio Industria ed Agricoltura della Somalia: Sezione Fiere e Mostre, 1958, pp. 138. (bibl).
FUNAIOLI, Ugo, *Fauna e caccia in Somalia: con 24 tavole colori dell'autore*, S.T.M.C. for Governo della Somalia, Ministero per gli Affari Economici, Dipartimento Agricoltura e Zootecnia, 1957, pp. 98. (dict.w)
GABRIELE DA TRENTO, P., 'Vocaboli in lingue dell'Etiopia meridonale', *R.S.E.*, i, 1941, pp. 203–07. (dict.w)
GAL, Durka Elia E., *La fronda: poesie della Somalia*, S.C., 1929, pp. 50. (ess.l)
GIRACE, Alfonso, 'Nomi di Luogo in Somali', *C.S.*, May 23, 1955, p. 3. (ess)
GLEASON, Joseph, OMER AWAD and RORICK, David, *Is ka Wahh u Qabso*, T.C., 1968, pp. 73. (gmr)

GLOVER, P. E., *Provisional Check-List of British and Italian Somaliland Trees, Shrubs and Herbs*, C.A., 1947, pp. 181. (dict.w)

GORLANI, Daniele, *Harùf: al Àlefba Somàlied*, V.A.M., 1941, pp. 61. (gmr)

GREENBERG, Joseph, *Studies in African Linguistic Classification*, C.P., 1955. (ess.s)

GUIDI, —, 'Somali-Texte', *Luigi Robecchi-Brichetti gesammelte Texte*, A.A.L., 1889, p. 219 ff. (txt)

HENRY, L., *Essai de vocabulaire pratique français issa (somali) avec prononciation figurée*, Melun, 1897. (dict.w)

HERZOG, Robert, see under: Hetzron, Robert

HETZRON, Robert, 'Les compléments verbaux en Somali', *C.R.G.L.*, viii, April 1960, pp. 92–5. (gmr)

——, 'The Particle *bàa* in Northern Somali', *J.A.L.*, iv/2, 1965, pp. 118–30. (gmr)

HHIRSI MAGAN 'IISE (ed.), *Horseed: Goosanka Afka iyo Suugaanta Soomaalida*, S.S.L.L., fortnightly, began January 29, 1957. (prd.s, txt.s)

HAMBURGER, L., *The Negro-African Languages*, London, 1949. (ess.s)

——, 'Elements dravidiens en Somali', *B.S.L.P.*, l/1, 1954. (ess.s)

HUNT, John A., *A General Survey of the Somaliland Protectorate: 1944–1950*, C.A., 1951, pp. 203 with maps. (bibl)

HUNT, John A. and Viney, N. M., *Gazetteer of British Somaliland Place Names*, MS., 1945. (dict.w)

HUNTER, F. M., *A Grammar of the Somali Language*, E.S.P., 1880. (gmr)

ḤUSAYN AḤMAD SHALABĪ, *Aqāṣīṣ min al-Ṣūmāl (Stories from Somalia)*, D.M., 1962, pp. 152. (txt.t)

IBN MUḤYĪ AL-DĪN QĀSIM AL-BARĀWĪ AL-QĀDIRĪ, *Majmūʿat al-Qaṣāʾid fī madḥ Sayyid al-Anbiyāʾ (Collection of Poems in Praise of the Lord of the Prophets)*, M.B.H., 1955, pp. 71. (txt.a)

IBRĀHĪM ḤĀSHI MAḤMŪD, *Al-Ṣūmāliyya bil-lughat al-Qurʾān: Muḥāwala Waṭaniyya li-Kitāba Lughat al-Umm (Somali Through the Language of the Koran: An Indigenous Attempt to Write the Mother Tongue)*, D.T.H., for A.L.I., 1963, pp. 91. (ess.w)

JAHN, A., 'Somalitexte: gesammelt und übersetzt', A.H. for *S.A.W.W.*, clii, 1906. (txt.st)

Shaykh JĀMAʿ ʿUMAR ʿĪSĀ, *Taʾrīkh al-Ṣūmāl fī al-ʿUṣūr al-Wusṭā wa al-Ḥadītha (History of Somalia in Medieval and Modern Times)*, M.I., 1965, pp. 256. (txt.a, txt.s)

JANSEN, Pietro Gerardo, 'Lingue e dialetti della Somalia', in his *Guida alla conoscenza dei dialetti de l'Africa orientale*, Quaderni di Cultura Linguistica 2, E.L.E., 1936, pp. 103–26. (ess.s, dict.w)

JOHNSON, John William, *A Bibliography of Somali Language Materials*, Hargeysa, U.S.P.C., 1967, pp. 12. (bibl)

JONES, D., *The Phoneme: Its Nature and Use*, H., 1950, pp. 267. (ess.s)

Jones, Ruth, *Africa Bibliography Series: North-East Africa*, I.A.I., 1959, pp. 51. (bibl)
Jones, S., 'Somali h and c', *M.P.*, 1934, pp. 8–9. (gmr)
Joppi, Raffaele, 'L'insegnamento della lingua Somala', *S.D.O.*, ii/1, January–February 1957, pp. 17–19. (ess.s)
King, J. S., 'Somali as a Written Language', *I.A.*, 1887, part 1, August, pp. 242–3; part 2, October, pp. 285–7. (ess.w)
Kirk, J. W. C., *Notes on the Somali Language with Examples of Phrases and Conversational Sentences*, London, 1903. Republished by G.I.P., 1968, pp. 94. (gmr)
——, 'The Yibirs and Midgàns of Somaliland, Their Traditions and Dialects', *J.A.S.*, iv/13, 1904, pp. 91–108. (ess)
——, *A Grammar of the Somali Language with Examples in Prose and Verse and an Account of the Yibir and Midgan Dialects*, C.U.P., 1905, pp. 216. (gmr, bibl, dict.w, txt.st)
Klingenheben, A., 'Ist das Somali eine Ton-Sprache?', *Z.P.*, iii/5, 6, 1949, pp. 289–303. (ess.s)
Koenig, E., *Vocabulaires appartenant à diverses contrées ou tribus de l'Afrique recueillis dans la Nubie supérieure*, D.E. (dict.w)
Koenig, M., 'Vocabulaire de l'idiome des Saumals', in his *Recueil de voyages et de mémoires*, S.G., pp. 35–46. (dict.w)
Lang, Carl, 'Repetition, Reduplikation und Lautmalerei in der Somali-Sprache', *B.A.*, i/2, 1925, pp. 98–104. (gmr)
Larajasse, Evangeliste de, *Somali–English and English–Somali Dictionary*, K.P.T.T., 1897, pp. 301. (dict)
Larajasse, Evangeliste de and Sampont, Cyprien de, *Practical Grammar of the Somali Language with a Manual of Sentences*, K.P.T.T., 1897, pp. 265. (gmr)
Laurence, Margaret, *A Tree for Poverty: Somali Poetry and Prose*, E.P. for the Somaliland Protectorate, 1954, pp. 146. (txt.t)
——, 'A Tree for Poverty', in her *The Prophet's Camel Bell* (American title: *New Wind in a Dry Land*), M., 1965, pp. 190–202. (txt.t)
Lederer, Tom and Shank, Mary Ann, *Stories Told by Somalis*, Baidoa, AUTH., May 1968, pp. 12. (txt.t)
Legum, Colin, 'Somali Liberation Songs', *J.M.A.S.*, i/4, 1963, pp. 503–19. (txt.t)
Leslau, Charlotte and Leslau, Wolf, 'Somalia', in their *African Proverbs*, P.P.P., 1962, pp. 55–56. (txt.t)
Lewis, I. M., 'The Gadabuursi Somali Script', *B.S.O.A.S.*, xxi/1, 1957, pp. 134–56. (txt.st, ess.w)
——, 'The Names of God in Northern Somali', *B.S.O.A.S.*, xxii/1, 1959, pp. 134–40. (ess)
——, *A Pastoral Democracy: A Study of Pastoralism and Politics among the Northern Somali of the Horn of Africa*, O.U.P. for I.A.I., 1961, pp. 320. (bibl, txt.st, dict.w)

——, *Marriage and the Family in Northern Somaliland*, East African Studies, No. 15, E.A.I.S.R., 1962, pp. 51. (dict.w)

——, 'Recent Progress in Somali Studies', *J.S.S.*, 1964, pp. 122–34. (bibl, rpt)

LIGHT, R. H., *English–Somali Sentences and Idioms for the Use of Sportsmen and Visitors in Somaliland*, T., 1896. (dict.w)

Seid MAHAMED ABDULLAH HASSAN, 'Poème Somalien', *P.A.*, xxxviii, 1961, p. 239. (txt.t)

MAINO, Mario, 'L'alfabeto "Osmania" in Somalia', *R.S.E.*, x, 1951, pp. 108–21. (ess.w)

——, 'Poesie e canti Somali', *C.S.*, xi/3, May 12, 1951. (txt.t)

——, 'I Somali e la loro lingua', *A.*, vii/2, February 1952, pp. 49–50. (bibl)

——, *La lingua Somala strumento d'insegnamento professionale*, T.F.O., 1953, pp. 111. (gmr, bibl, txt.st)

——, *Terminologia medica e sue voci nella lingua Somala*, T.F.O., 1953, pp. 358. (dict.w)

——, 'Breve storia della lingua Somala', *S.D.O.*, ii/2, June 1957, pp. 17–19. (ess.s)

MARIN, G., 'Somali Games', *J.R.A.I.*, lxi, 1931, pp. 499–511. (ess)

MEINHOF, C., *Die Sprachen der Hamiten*, A.K.I., ix, 1912, pp. 256. (ess.s, dict.w)

MINOZZI, Maria Teresa and TURRIN, Cinzica Poletti, *Dizionario Italiano–Somalo*, A.C.E.G., 1961, pp. 178. (dict)

MOHAMED FARAH ABDILLAHI, *Sheekooyin Fogaan iyo Dhowaan ba leh: Suugaanta Soomaalida Sheeko ahaan*, Mogadishu, AUTH., 1967, pp. 47. (txt.s)

MOHAMED FARAH ABDILLAHI and ANDRZEJEWSKI, B. W., 'The Life of 'Ilmi Bowndheri, a Somali Oral Poet who is said to have Died of Love', *J.F.I.*, iv/2, 3, June–December 1967, pp. 73–87. (ess, txt.t)

MOHAMED SCEK GABIOU, 'La lingua Somala', *C.S.*, May 24, 1954, p. 3. (ess.s)

MORENO, Martino Mario, 'Brevi notazioni di Ǧiddu', *R.S.E.*, x, 1951, pp. 99–107. (ess.s)

——, *Nozioni di grammatica Somala*, U.S.R.S.O., 1951, pp. 141. (gmr)

——, 'La modernisation et l'unification des langues en Somalie', *C.*, ii, 1952 pp. 61–6. (ess.s)

——, 'Il dialetto degli Ašrâf di Mogadiscio', *R.S.E.*, xii, 1953, pp. 107–38. (ess.s)

——, *Il Somalo della Somalia: grammatica e testi del Benadir, Darod e Dighil*, I.P.S., 1955, pp. 404. (gmr, txt.st)

MUHAMMAD 'ABDĪ MAKĀHĪL, *Inshā' al-Mukātabat al-ᶜAṣriyya fī Lughat al- Ṣūmāliyya* (*A Method of Modern Correspondence in the Somali Language*), M.G.M., 1932. (ess.w, txt.st)

Muḥammad Ṣūfī b. al-Shaykh Qāsim al-Barāwī and Ḥājj al-Shaykh Murīd Walī al-Barāwī al-Qādirī, *Al-Shajarat al-Qādiriyya al-Sharīfa* (*The Nobel Genealogy of the Qādiriyya*), Mogadishu, n.d. (txt.a)

Muuse H. I. Galaal, *A Collection of Somali Literature mainly from Sayid Mohamed Abdille Hassan*, Mogadishu, AUTH., n.d. (txt.s)

——, 'Arabic Script for Somali', *I.Q.*, i/2, 1954, pp. 114–18. (ess.w)

——, 'Somali Stories', *W.A.R.*, part 1, lxxviii, December 1955, p. 5; part 2, lxxix, January 1956, p. 6; part 3, lxxxi, February 1956, p. 11; part 4, lxxxii, February 1956, pp. 5, 8. (txt.st)

——, 'Folk Literature', *N.R.*, ii, March 1964, p. 19. (ess.l)

——, 'From the Somali Story Teller's Anthology', *N.R.*, v, July 1965, pp. 35–6. (txt.t)

——, 'Somali Poetry', *A.F.*, vii/2, 1966, pp. 43–6. (ess.l)

——, 'The Somali Pastoral Weather Lore System', *Perspectives on Somalia: Orientation Course* (*for Foreign Experts Working in Somalia*), S.I.P.A., 1968, pp. 56–73. (es.l, txt.st)

——, 'Some Aspects of Somali Pastoral Medicine', ibid., pp. 74–9. (ess.l)

——, 'Some Observations on Somali Culture', ibid., pp. 39–55. (ess)

——, *The Terminology and Practice of Somali Weather Lore, Astronomy and Astrology*, Mogadishu, AUTH., May 1968, pp. 77. (ess.l, dict.w, txt.st)

——, 'Traditional Somali Attitude Towards Foreigners', U.S.P.C. (cyclostyled), May 1969, pp. 9. (ess, txt.st)

Muuse H. I. Galaal and Andrzejewski, B. W., *Hikmad Soomaali*, Annotated African Texts, iv, O.U.P. for S.O.A.S., 1956, pp. 150. (bibl, ess.w, txt.s)

Orano, Marcello, *Elementi per lo studio della lingua Somala: grammatica con 65 verbi coniugati per esteso frasario e dizionario dei vocaboli più usati nelle due forme parlate più communemente*, U.H., 1931, pp. 264. (gmr, dict.w)

——, *Manuale della lingua Somala*, U.H., 1931. (gmr)

——, *La lingua Somala parlata nella Somalia settentrionale, nell'Ogaden*, C.E.M., 1936, pp. 182. (gmr)

Osman, 'To Be or Not to Be (The Somali Language)', *D.*, i/12, June 1, 1966, pp. 8–9. (ess.w)

Pace, A., 'Note e discussioni sulla lingua Somala', *S.D.O.*, ii/1, January–February 1957, pp. 14–15. (ess.s)

Palermo, Giovanni Maria da, *Grammatica della lingua Somala*, T.F.M.C., 1914, pp. 357. (gmr, txt.st)

——, *Dizionario Somalo–Italiano e Italiano–Somalo*, T.F.M.C., 1915, pp. 209. (dict)

Palmer, Joe Darwin, *A Comparison of Somali and English Phonemes* (*with a Note on the Intonation of Somali,*) N.T.E.C., 1967, pp. 20. (gmr)

PANZA, Bruno, 'Canti Somali', *S.D.O.*, i/2, December 15, 1956, pp. 14–16. (txt.t)

——, 'Canti Somali', *S.D.O.*, ii/1, January–February 1957, pp. 22–3. (txt.t)

PANZA, Bruno and YAASIIN 'ISMAAN KEENADIID, 'Gabai di Ina Abdille Hassan', *S.D.O.*, i/1, October 12, 1956, pp. 21–2. (txt.t)

PAULITSCHKE, Philipp, *Ethnographie Nordost-Afrikas: die Geistige Cultur der Danâkil, Galla und Somâl*, D.R., 1886. (bibl, ess.s, txt.st)

PEDERSEN, Holger, *The Discovery of Language: Linguistic Science in the Nineteenth Century*, I.U.P., 1962, pp. 360. (ess.s)

PIA, J. Joseph, 'Language in Somalia', *L.R.*, viii/3, June 1966, pp. 1–2. (ess.s)

PIA, J. Joseph, BLACK, Paul D. and DILLINGER, Dale, *Beginning in Somali: Drillbook*, U.S.D.H.E.W., 1964, pp. 210. (gmr)

——, *Beginning in Somali: Primer*, ibid., pp. 240. (gmr)

PIA, J. Joseph, BLACK, Paul D. and M. I. SAMATER, *Beginning in Somali: Revised Edition*, S.U., 1966, pp. 380. (gmr) (Prepared under contract with U.S.P.C.)

PIA, J. JOSEPH and MOLITOR, R. D., *Reading in Somali: An Elementary Cultural Reader, Volume I: Reader*, S.U. for U.S.D.H.E.W., 1969, pp. 224. (gmr, txt.st)

——, *Reading in Somali: An Elementary Cultural Reader, Volume II: Pony and Glossary*, ibid., 1969, pp. 192. (gmr, txt.st)

PIRONE, M., 'Leggende e tradizioni storiche dei Somali Ogaden', *A.A.E.*, lxxxiv, 1954, pp. 119–28. (txt)

——, 'La lingua somala e i susi problemi', *A.*, xxii/2, 1967, pp. 198–209. (ess)

PRAETORIUS, F., 'Über die Somalisprache', *Z.D.M.G.*, xxiv, 1870, pp. 145 ff. (ess.s)

REINISCH, Leo, *Die Somali-Sprache: i: Texte*, Südarabische Expedition, Band i, A.H. for K.A.W., 1900, pp. 287. (txt.st)

——, *Die Somali-Sprache: ii: Wörterbuch, Somali–Deutsch, Deutsch–Somali*, ibid., Band ii, 1902, pp. 540. (dict)

——, *Die Somali-Sprache: iii: Grammatik*, ibid., Band v, Teil 1, 1903, pp. 126. (gmr)

——, 'Der Dschäbärtidialekt der Somali-Sprache', A.H. for *S.A.W.W.*, cxlviii, 1904. (ess.s)

RICCI, Lanfranco, 'Corrispondenza epistolare in osmania', *R.S.E.*, xiv, 1959, pp. 108–50. (ess.w, txt.st)

RIGBY, Christopher Palmer, 'Specimens of the Languages Spoken on the Western Shore of the Red Sea and Gulf of Aden', *T.B.G.S.*, vi/6, 1844, pp. 93–4. (dict.w)

——, 'On the Somali Language', *T.B.G.S.*, ix, 1849. (ess.s)

——, *Outline of the Somali Language with Vocabulary*. (gmr, dict.w)

ROBECCHI-BRICCHETTI, Luigi, 'Testi Somali', *R.A.L.*, October–November 1889. (txt)

——, 'Lingue parlate Somali, Galla e Harari: note e studi raccolti ed ordinati nell'Harar', *B.S.G.I.*, 1890. (ess.s)

——, *Vocabolario Harari, Somali, Galla*, Rome, 1890. (dict.w)

——, *La grammatica Somala*, Rome, 1892. (gmr)

——, 'Note sulle lingue parlate Somali, Galla e Harrari, raccolte ed ordinate nell'Harrar', *B.S.A.I.*, xiv, 1895–97. (ess.s)

——, *Materiali linguistici dell'Africa orientale*, Naples, 1898. (ess.s)

SABBADINI, Ettore, 'Studi recenti di lingua Somala in Italia', *A.*, ix/2, February 1954, pp. 56–7. (rpt)

SACCONI, —, '[Vocabulary and Sentences in Somali]', *E.*, 1878, pp. 105–11. (dict.w)

SAEED ADEN ABDILLAHI, 'Somali Songs and Music', *S.N.*, 415, January 10, 1969, p. 6. (ess)

SAMATER, 'Proverbs as a Cultural Vehicle', *D.*, ii/11, May 1, 1967, pp. 14–16. (ess.l)

SAMPONT, Cyprien F. de, *Grammaire Somalie*, M.C., 1905. (gmr)

——, *Grammaire abrégée de la langue Somalie avec exercices et conversations*, R.A.L., 1920, pp. 237. (gmr)

SCHLEICHER, A. W., *Die Somali-Sprache: erster Theil; Texte, Lautlehre, Formenlehre und Syntax*, T.F., 1892, pp. 159. (gmr, txt)

——, *Somali Texte: Dr. Schleichers Somali Texte, herausgegeben von Leo Reinisch*, A.H. for K.A.W., 1900 p. 159. (txt)

SERRAILLIER, Ian, CROSSE, Gordon and GRIFFITHS, John, *Ahmet the Woodseller*, A B.B.C. Television Broadcast to Schools, B.B.C., 1965, pp. 23. (txt.t)

SHARĪF 'AYDARŪS b. AL-SHARĪF AL-'AYDARŪS AL-NADIRĪ AL-'ALAWĪ, *Bughyat al-Āmāl fī Ta'rīkh al-Ṣūmāl (The Focus of Hopes Concerning Somali History)*, S.A.F.I.S., 1955. (txt.a)

SHIRRE JAMA AHMED, *An Elementary Somali Phrase Drill Book*, Mogadishu, AUTH., c. 1964, pp. 131. (gmr)

——, *Gabayo, Maahmaah iyo Sheekooyin Yaryar*, N.P., May 1965, pp. 63. (txt.s)

——, *Iftiinka Aqoonta: Light of Education*, Mogadishu, AUTH., 1, November 10, 1966; 2, November 30, 1966; 3, December 25, 1966; 4, January 25, 1967; 5, February 25, 1967; 6, July 1967. (prd.l)

——, 'Il somalo scritto', *T.R.I.*, i/8, July 15, 1967, pp. 6, 9. (ess.w)

SHIRRE JAMA AHMED and KOZOLL, Charles, *An Elementary Somali Drill Book*, T.C., 1966, pp. 160. (gmr, bibl)

SMEE, Th., 'Specimens of Different Languages Used on the East Coast of Africa (Suaheli, Somali, Galla)', *P.B.G.S.*, vi, 1844, pp. 50–5. (ess.s)

SMITH, A. O., *Somali Vocabulary and Useful Terms: Handbook*, Genale, March 28, 1943, pp. 54. (dict.w)

SMOYER, Tom, et al., *Baadiye iyo Beled: The Interior and the City in Somalia*, U.S.P.C., 1969, pp. 50. (txt.st)

SOMALI GOVERNMENT, *Wargeyska Somaliyed* (*The Somali Messenger*), Mogadishu, March 1957 (only two editions published). (prd.l)

——, 'Il problema della lingua Somala (1)—estratti e articoli', *Somaliya-antologia storico-culturale*, 7–8, June 1969, Ministero Pubblica Instruzione, Dipartimento Culturale, Hamar [Mogadishu], pp. 266. (ess.w)

STEPANJENKO, D. I. and MOHAMED Haji Osman, *Kratkiy Somali-Russkiy i Russko-Somali Slovav* (*A Concise Somali-Russian and Russian-Somali Dictionary*), Moscow, Isdatel'stvo 'Sovetskaya Entsiklopediya', 1969, pp. 319.

STORACI, E., *Il poliglotta Africano: vademecum per l'Africa orientale: Italiano, Arabo, Suahili, Somalo, Galla, Tigrino, Tigrè: raccolta dei vocaboli più usati*, B., 1935. (dict.w)

SYAD, William J. F., *Khamsine: poèmes*, P.A., 1959, pp. 70. (txt.t)

——, 'Poème', *P.A.*, xxxviii, 1961, p. 238. (txt.t)

——, 'Rozhdenye strany-stikhi somaliyskovo poeta' ('Birth of a Country: Poems of a Somali Poet'), *D.N.*, ii, 1962, p. 130. (txt.t)

TILING, Maria von, 'Die Vocale des bestimmten Artikels im Somali', *Z.K.*, ix, 1918–19, pp. 132–66. (gmr)

——, 'Adjektiv-Endungen im Somali', *Z.K.*, x, 1919–20, pp. 208–40. (gmr)

——, 'Die Sprache der Jabarti, mit besonderer Berücksichtigung der Verwandtschaft von Jabarti und Somali', *Z.E.S.*, xii/1, 1922, pp. 17–162. (ess.s)

——, 'Jabarti Texte', *Z.E.S.*, xv, 1925, pp. 50–64, 139–58. (txt.st)

——, 'Somali-Texte und Untersuchungen zur Somali-Lautlehre', *Z.E.S.*, viii, 1925, pp. 1–156. (gmr, bibl, txt.st)

——, 'Ein Somali-Text von Muhammed Nur', *Z.E.S.*, xviii/3, 1928, pp. 231–3. (txt.st)

TRENTO, Gabriele da, 'Vocaboli in lingue dell'Etiopia meridionale', *R.S.E.*, i/2, 1941, pp. 203–07. (dict.w)

TUCKER, A. N., 'Problèmes de typologie dans la classification des langues non-bantu de l'Afrique du nord-est', *J.S.A.*, 1961, pp. 59–74. (ess.s, bibl)

——, 'Fringe Cushitic: an Experiment in Typological Comparison', *B.S.O.A.S.*, xxx/3, 1967, pp. 655–80. (ess.s)

TUCKER, A. N. and BRYAN, M. A., *The Non-Bantu Languages of North-Eastern Africa*, Handbook of African Languages iii, O.U.P. for I.A.I., 1956, pp. 228 with map. (ess.s, bibl)

——, *Linguistic Analyses: the Non-Bantu Languages of North-Eastern Africa*, Handbook of African Languages, O.U.P. for I.A.I., 1966, pp. 627 with map. (ess.s, bibl)

VINEY, N. M. *A Bibliography of British Somaliland*, B.W.O., 1947, pp. 36. (bibl)

VYCICHL, Werner, 'Zur Tonologie des Somali: zum Verhältnis zwischen musikalischem Ton und dynamischem Akzent in afrikanischen Sprachen und zur Bildung des Femininums in Somali', *R.S.O.*, xxxi, 1956, pp. 221–7. (gmr)

WALSH, L. P., *Under the Flag and Somali Coast Stories*, A.M., 1937. (txt.t)

YAASIIN 'ISMAAN KEENADIID, 'La funzione sociale del linguaggio', *S.D.O.*, i, 1956, p. 28. (ess.s)

——, *Buug koowaad kii Soomaali ga* (*The First Book of Somali*), S.S.L.L., 1958, pp. 38. (gmr) (Published in Somali Script)

——, *Af Soomaali: koowaad* (*The Somali Language: Vol. 1*), S.S.L.L., 1966, pp. 30. (gmr) (Published in Somali Script)

——, *Cir iyo Dhul: Buug koowaad* (*Sky and Earth: Book One*), S.S.L.L., 1966, pp. 33. (txt.s) (Published in Somali Script)

——, *Sheekada Yabka le oo Dadka* (*The Glorious Story of the People*), S.S.L.L., 1966, pp. 20. (ess) (Published in Somali Script)

——, 'Il Somalo scritto', *T.R.I.*, i/7, June 15, 1967, pp. 8–10, 13. (ess.w)

YUSUF OSMAN (with the collaboration of MUUSE H. J. GALAAL), 'When the Camel Chews the Cud', *D.*, ii/11, May 1, 1967, pp. 17–18. (txt.t)

ZABORSKI, Andrzej, 'Opowieści i bajki Somalijskie' ('Somali Stories and Fables'), *P.O.*, iii/59, 1966, pp. 217–24. (txt.t)

——, 'Arabic Loan-words in Somali: Preliminary Survey', *Folia Orientalia*, Cracow, Poland, 8, 1967, pp. 125–74. (ess.s)

——, 'Six Short Somali Texts', *Folia Orientalia*, Cracow, Poland, 10, 1969, pp. 231–43. (txt.st)

ZHOLKOVSKI, A. K., 'Posledovatel'nosti predglagolnykh chastits v yazyke somali' ('Sequences of Preverbal Particles in the Somali Language'), *Y.A.*, 1966, pp. 143–66. (gmr)

——, 'K leksikograficheskomu opisaniyu somalyskikh sushchestvitelnykh' ('Towards a Lexicographic Description of Somali Nouns'), *N.A.A.*, 1967, pp. 93–102. (gmr)

——, 'Materiyaly k russko-somaliyskomu slovaryu' ('Materials for a Russian–Somali Dictionary'), *A.F.F.* (in the press). (ess.s, gmr)

——, 'Stroenie nezavisimogo utverditel'nogo predlozheniya v somali' ('The Structure of the Independent Affirmative Sentence in Somali'), *P.A.Y.* (in the press). (gmr)

RESEARCH REVIEW

THIS section of the *African Language Review* is available in each volume for the announcement of research and publication projects, and for the presentation of research reports and questionnaires. Items for inclusion should be submitted to the Editor.

West African Linguistic Society: Scholarship Grants

[Communicated by Professor Ayọ Bamgboṣe, University of Ibadan]

The West African Linguistic Society invites applications for grants, under its scholarship scheme, from African students studying for a higher degree or diploma in Linguistics, especially at universities in West Africa. These grants, which are intended to encourage the training of African linguists, will normally not exceed $1000 per person. Applications should be addressed to Professor Ayọ Bamgboṣe, Secretary-Treasurer, West African Linguistic Society, University of Ibadan, Ibadan, Nigeria, with a copy to Professeur M. Houis, 1 Rue des Eglantines, 91 Ris Organis, France.

The Language Map of Africa

[Communicated by the Editor]

The Language and History in Africa Seminar, which has been meeting at the School of Oriental and African Studies in London since the end of 1966, is currently embarking on a consideration of the historical, cultural and ethno-linguistic implications of the present geographical distribution of African languages, under the general theme 'The Language Map of Africa'. The Seminar provides an interdisciplinary forum for academic staff and research students, especially but not exclusively in the fields of history and language study, and an associated one year M.A. course is to be introduced as one of the options for the University of London M.A. in African Studies ('Introduction to the Language Map of Africa'). Meetings of the Seminar are open to members of other universities, and further particulars on both the Seminar and the M.A. in African Studies may be obtained from the Centre of African Studies, S.O.A.S., University of London.

An earlier series of papers presented to the Seminar is being published by Frank Cass & Co. Ltd., under the title *Language and History in Africa*, and it is hoped to follow this eventually with a second volume of collected papers, *The Language Map of Africa*. An actual map of linguistic distribution in Africa is also in course of compilation in London, and any individuals or institutions who wish to collaborate in this project, or to contribute data, are invited to contact the Centre of African Studies at the above address.

Inter-University Communication
(with particular reference to the exchange of Creole language recordings)

[Communicated by H. D. Perraton, Director, Inter-University Research Unit, Cambridge]

The Inter-University Research Unit of Cambridge is carrying out a feasibility study into the use of television and similar aids as a means of exchanging teaching materials internationally. The aim of the research is to discover how far the exchange of recordings, on television, film, or tape, is a practical way for universities to share their resources, alongside the traditional exchange of staff. If the one-year study justifies it, the Unit hopes to follow this with a five year period of experiment. At this stage the Unit is working most closely with the University of Guyana and developing a programme based on its interests, needs and specialisms; as time goes on, it is hoped to involve other English-speaking universities.

Over the last ten years, the advent of language laboratories and closed-circuit television has given universities experience in the use of educational technology to improve and enrich their teaching. Since 1965 the Inter-University Research Unit has been concerned with the use of educational technology in higher education, but from a different angle: our interest has been not so much in improving teaching on a single campus as in the possibility of using communications technology for the *exchange* of teaching between universities or colleges. Between 1967 and 1969 the Unit set up and evaluated a series of experimental links between British universities; the techniques used varied between telephone seminars, the production of television programmes and the exchange of sound tapes with slides.* This has led on to the new research on links between British and overseas universities.

The Unit is now working out plans for its first exchanges, in the light of discussions with academic staff at the University of Guyana. One of the most important aspects of these exchanges will be their orientation: in many different fields teachers at the University of Guyana urged that exchanges should be with other developing universities in tropical countries. For—ironically—it is often easier for a teacher in a new, tropical, university to find out what is happening at British or American universities than to keep in touch with developments at other universities like his own. And yet there are many fields where universities in the third world are facing the same problems, doing the same kind of research, and developing parallel expertise. One of the first exchanges we hope to develop will, therefore, be of this east-west kind, in the field of Creole languages.

The University of Guyana offers a course on sociolinguistics which uses a range of recordings on Caribbean Creole languages. The Department of English there is interested in exchanging recordings (and transcriptions) of Creole languages in order to develop that course, and to help in linguistic research on Creoles. The Unit is therefore beginning to seek materials that might meet the needs of Guyana—and, at the same time, to discover whether other universities could use recordings from Guyana. We want to discover not only something about the feasibility of doing this from the scholar's point of view—how easy it is to fit materials into a curriculum at a university thousands of miles away—but also to sort out the key technical problems of sound-quality, postal and customs regulations and so on (easier for sound tape than for television). Our previous experience suggests that these practical, apparently trivial, problems are the ones which tend to make unorthodox forms of communication often too inconvenient to be of much value.

Looking further ahead, the Unit hopes to be able to work in a range of subjects and with a number of universities. Our long-term interest is to see how far the newer forms of communication can be used to make contact between universities easier, and less haphazard. To do this we want to establish a situation where it is as straightforward for universities to exchange teaching recorded on tape or film or television as it already is for them to exchange books or people. Once we get towards that situation, it will be easier to make sound decisions about the academic needs best met by these new techniques.

Enquiries, either about the inter-university programme in general, or about the exchange of Creole language material in particular, should be addressed to the Director, Inter-University Research Unit, 32 Trumpington Street, Cambridge, CB2 1QY, England.

*Cf. H. D. Perraton, et al., *Linking Universities by Technology*, National Extension College, 1969.

Association of Africanists in Germany

[Communicated by Professor Hermann Jungraithmayr,
University of Marburg]

The Association of Africanists in Germany held its first annual conference in Marburg/Lahn from July 18–20, 1969. The conference was devoted to 'Problems and Implications of Inter-disciplinary Co-operation within African Studies'.

In his opening address Professor Ernst Dammann (Marburg) welcomed the initiative of the rising generation of German Africanists in examining the practical and theoretical possibilities of co-operation across the boundaries of the established disciplines. In the past such co-operation had almost been non-existent in African Studies in Germany.

Wilhelm Seidensticker (Hamburg) presented a paper on some aspects of the theory of inter-disciplinary co-operation. Bernd Heine and Bernd Wiese (Cologne) offered an analysis of the distribution of Swahili in Western Kenya. In their paper quantitative field data supplied by a socio-linguist were discussed by a geographer within the terms of his discipline. The results suggested that the spreading of Swahili as a lingua franca in Western Kenya had been strongly influenced in the past by ecological factors and administrative boundaries.

H. J. Greschat and Thilo C. Schadeberg (Marburg) proposed new university curricula for M.A. degrees in African Studies and in the History of Religions, which were to combine a multi-disciplinary training with a specialisation on African materials. The implications for historical research in Africa of interdisciplinary co-operation between linguists and ethnologists were outlined by Brigitta Hennen-Benzig (Mainz) in a paper on the problems of interpretation presented by oral traditions.

W. J. G. Möhlig and J. C. Winter (Cologne/Oxford) exemplified problem-orientated co-operation between a linguist and a social anthropologist. They contributed a semantic analysis of the membership in different noun-classes of kinship terms among the Dciriku, a South-West African Bantu-speaking tribe. Their analysis suggested that there is a positive correlation between Dciriku kinship terms belonging to different noun-classes, on the one hand, and the kind and degree of intrusion into ego's personal sphere which on grounds of social structure is allowed to the bearer of a given kinship term, on the other. Thomas Maler and Artur Simon (Marburg/Hamburg) presented a discussion of the phenomena of spirit cults among the Digo (Tanzania), in which they combined the approaches of the history of religions, ethno-musicology, medicine, psychology, linguistics, sociology and history, in order to achieve a synthetic, ethnological view of the phenomena.

The Association of Africanists in Germany (Vereinigung von Afrikanisten in Deutschland, VAD) was founded in March 1969 by a number of mostly junior German Africanists. At present it has some fifty members, including several professors in German and African universities. It was organized to provide a forum for the studies of African cultures and societies in order to assist in integrating African Studies in Germany into the world-wide development of Africanist research, and in order to promote more intensive and efficient communication and co-operation across the boundaries of the various established disciplines in Germany, such as African linguistics, ethnology, ethno-musicology, history, sociology, political studies, religious studies, law, etc. Natural scientists whose research interests impinge on the work of Africanists are also invited to participate in the work of the VAD.

The chief purposes of the new association are:

—to facilitate communication among scholars who are doing research or who are teaching in the Africanist field, no matter whether they are affiliated to a university or not.

—to provide assistance in interdisciplinary projects within the field of African studies.

—to assist in developing contacts with foreign scholars who have research interests in Africa.

—to promote relations with scholars and institutions in Africa.

—to prepare information for the German public about the development of African studies in Germany and about the work of the VAD.

Professor Hermann Jungraithmayr, University of Marburg, was elected secretary of the VAD. The regular activities of the VAD include an annual conference, the proceedings of which are published in a special series. *The proceedings of the first annual conference have been published by HELMUT BUSKE VERLAG HAMBURG, under the title 'Probleme interdisziplinärer Afrikanistik', pp. 140, price DM 14.—*

Correspondence should be addressed to the Vereinigung von Afrikanisten in Deutschland, 355 Marburg, Am Krummbogen 28, Germany.

Benue-Congo Comparative Wordlist and Noun Class Systems

[Communicated by T. L. Cook, University of Ibadan]

The *Benue-Congo Comparative Wordlist* includes 198 languages, with representatives of the Plateau, Jukunoid, Cross River and Bantoid branches of the Benue-Congo language group. Responses from over 150 glosses are presented in 117 entries with identification of likely cognates among languages and comments on the distribution of the various roots. Volume I, edited by Kay Williamson and Kiyoshi Shimizu, appeared in 1968 and includes entries for English glosses A–L; Volume II (M–Z), edited by T. L. Cock, will appear shortly.

Benue-Congo Noun Class Systems, edited by Jan Voorhoeve and P. P. de Wolf, presents descriptions of the noun class systems of thirty-seven languages (Part I) and a comparative study of these systems (Part II). This volume appeared in March, 1969.

All three volumes are the product of the activities of the Benue-Congo Working Group of the West African Linguistic Society. The purpose of the group is to bring together and to analyse data relevant to an investigation of the position of Bantu within the Benue-Congo group and of the internal relationships (sub-groupings) of the Benue-Congo languages in general.

The *Noun Class Systems* volume may be ordered from the Afrika Studiecentrum, University of Leiden, Stationsplein 10, Leiden, The Netherlands. The price is U.S. $2.00 or 16/8d. (Sterling). A special reduced price of U.S. $1.20 or 10/– (Sterling) is offered to members of the West African Linguistic Society and to educational institutions.

The *Comparative Wordlist* may be ordered from the West African Linguistic Society, University of Ibadan, Nigeria. The prices, including surface postage, are as follows:

	Both Volumes	One Volume Only
£ Nigerian	3:6:–	2:–:–
£ Sterling	4:–:–	2:10:–
U.S. $	10.00	6.25

For members of the West African Linguistic Society:

	Both Volumes	One Volume Only
£ Nigerian	3:–:–	1:15:–
£ Sterling	3:12:–	2:5:–
U.S. $	9.00	5.60

Studies in African Linguistics

[Communicated by the Department of Linguistics, University of California, Los Angeles]

Announcement is made of the publication of the first number of a new journal in African Languages and Linguistics, *Studies in African Linguistics*, ed. Talmy Givón, devoted to articles of theoretical linguistics using the data of African languages as its point of departure. The journal is published by the Department of Linguistics and the African Studies Centre, University of California, Los Angeles.

The contents of the first issue (vol. 1, no. 1) are as follows:

Larry M. Hyman, THE ROLE OF BORROWING IN THE JUSTIFICATION OF PHONOLOGICAL GRAMMARS

William E. Welmers, THE DERIVATION OF IGBO VERB BASES

Herbert Stahlke, SERIAL VERBS

Isaac George, NUPE TONOLOGY

Subscription per volume (3 issues): $6.00 U.S. and Canada, $7.00 elsewhere. Single issues are available at $2.50 each. Cheques are payable to the African Studies Centre, UCLA, and orders and articles for publication should be sent to the Editor, *Studies in African Linguistics*, c/o Department of Linguistics, University of California, Los Angeles, Calif. 90024, U.S.A.

Recent Publications Received

BENTON, P. A., *The Languages and Peoples of Bornu*, with an Introduction by A. H. M. Kirk-Greene, Frank Cass, London, 1968, Vol. I, pp. 34, viii, 304 (84/–), Vol. II, pp. 124, 130, 119 (105/–). A new collection of four of Benton's previously published works, comprising his *Notes on Some Languages of the Western Sudan*, 1912 (in Vol. I), *Kanuri Readings*, 1911, *Primer of Kanuri Readings*, 1917, and *Bornu Almanac*, 1916 (in Vol. II); a modern critical introduction has been provided by A. H. M. Kirk-Greene.

BURSSENS, Amaat, *Problemen en Inventarisatie van de Verbale Strukturen in het Dho Alur (Nordoost-Kongo)*, with an English Summary, Kon. Vlaamse Academie voor Wetenschappen, Brussel, 1969, pp. 31 (95 BF). A description of the verbal morphology of Dho Alur, a Nilotic language of N.E. Congo.

HAIR, P. E. H., *The Early Study of Nigerian Languages: Essays and Bibliographies*, C.U.P., London, 1967, pp. xiv, 110 (50/–; $6.50 in U.S.). Three detailed essays, with accompanying bilbiographies, devoted to the early study of Yoruba (1825–50), of Hausa and Kanuri (1840–90), and of Nupe, Igala, Ibo and Ijaw (1840–90).

HARRIS, W. T., and SAWYERR, Harry, *The Springs of Mende Belief and Conduct*, Sierra Leone University Press, Freetown, and O.U.P., London, 1968, pp. xvi, 152 (35/–). A discussion of the influence of belief in the supernatural among the Mende, compiled originally by the late Rev. W. T. Harris and now substantially edited, revised and amplified by the Rev. Canon H. A. E. Saywerr.

HEINE, Bernd, *Die Verbreitung und Gliederung der Togorestsprachen*, Dietrich Riemer, Berlin, 1968, pp. 311, 22 maps. This first volume of the Kölner Beiträge zur Afrikanistik (edited by Oswin Köhler) is devoted to a detailed comparative and historical study of the so-called Togo Remnant Languages.

HOLSOE, Svend E., and FOLEY, David M., eds., *Liberian Studies Journal*, African Studies Centre, DePauw University, Greencastle, Indiana, 1968, ff., $5.00 p.a. A biannual journal devoted to studies of Liberia, especially in the fields of the social sciences and humanities, including linguistics.

INNES, Gordon, *A Mende-English Dictionary*, C.U.P., London, 1969, pp. 155 (100/–; $16 in U.S.). A tone-marked dictionary of Mende, based on the up-country Kɔɔ Mɛnde dialect and using the standard orthography of the Sierra Leone Provincial Literature Bureau.

[KOUNTA, BALENGHIEN, BIRD, et al.] *Lexique Bambara*, Ministère de l'Education Nationale, Bamako, 1968, pp. v, 33 (duplicated). Bambara-French word-list, including short introduction and key to the total pattern of lexical entries, produced for purposes of vernacular literacy teaching in Mali.

MANESSY, Gabriel, *Les Langues Gurunsi*, Société pour l'Etude des Langues Africaines, Paris, 1969, Vol. I, pp. 80, Vol. II, pp. 102 (Klincksieck, dépositaire). An essay in the application of the comparative method to the Gurunsi group of 'Voltaic' languages, including the establishment of phonological and morphological correspondences.

MAW, Joan, *Sentences in Swahili: a Study of their Internal Relationships*, S.O.A.S., London, 1969, pp. 142 (Luzac & Co. Ltd., 50/-). A syntactic description of spoken Swahili, based on the theory and methodology of M. A. K. Halliday.

MOLNES, Angela, *Language Problems in Africa*, East African Research Information Centre (Circular No. 2), 1969, pp. 62 (obtainable from EARIC, P.O. Box 30756, Nairobi). A study of language problems in African development, with special attention to the present situation in Kenya, Tanzania and Uganda, and with a general bibliography.

PIETERSE, Cosmo, and MUNRO, Donald, eds., *Protest and Conflict in African Literature*, Heinemann Educational Books, London, 1969, pp. 127 (25/-, paperback 12/-). A collection of papers devoted to the theme of protest in the work of modern African writers, ranging from the politics of negritude to protest against apartheid, and from cultural conflict to satire against African elites.

TERPSTRA, Gerard, *English-Tiv Dictionary*, Institute of African Studies (Occasional Publ. No. 13), University of Ibadan, 1968, pp. 120 (duplicated). A provisional tone-marked English-Tiv glossary, originally produced in 1959 as an expansion of W. A. Malherbe, *Tiv-English Dictionary*, Lagos, 1934 (with incorporation of additional items from R. C. Abraham, *Dictionary of the Tiv Language*, London, 1940).

WHITELEY, W. H., *Some Problems of Transitivity in Swahili*, S.O.A.S., London, 1968, pp. 110 (Luzac & Co. Ltd., 50/-). An exploratory study into the neglected areas of transitivity and extended verbal radicals in Swahili (cf. Whiteley and Mganga, 'Focus and entailment: further problems of transitivity in Swahili', published in this volume of *A.L.R.*).

WHITELEY, Wilfred, *Swahili: the Rise of a National Language*, Methuen, London, and Barnes Noble Inc., New York, 1969, pp. 128 (25/-, paperback 13/-). A study of the historical growth of Swahili as a language of literature and of trade, and of its present role as the national language of Tanzania.

NOTES FOR CONTRIBUTORS

Contributions, which may be in either English or French, should be typed with double spacing and wide margins on one side of the paper only. Title and author's name should appear at the beginning of the typescript; if the title is long, a shortened version should also be submitted for use as a running headline. Notes should be numbered in a single series throughout the article (*not* restarting at '1' with each page of copy), and should preferably be typed on a separate page or pages at the end of the article; they should be referred to as 'notes' rather than 'footnotes'. Special characters should be written in by hand unless they can be reproduced exactly on the typewriter; attention should be drawn to them in a separate covering note.

Contributors are asked to observe as closely as possible the typographical conventions of the *African Language Review*, which are briefly stated below; a more detailed statement can be obtained from the Editor.

Linguistic data should be indicated by single underlining in typescript, for printing in italics. (Italics are not used for quotations from foreign authors, however, unless introduced as specimens of the language concerned.) Glosses should be set within quotation marks. Bold type (indicated on typescript by wavy underlining in red) is reserved for studies of S. W. Koelle's *Polyglotta Africana*; details of the conventions proposed for the transliteration of Koelle's data are set out in the *African Language Review*, 3, 1964, p. 58 (and in 6, 1967, pp. 109–110).

The conventions for bibliographical references may be observed in the current volume of the *African Language Review*. The author's surname (or the distinctive part of the name used for alphabetization) is underlined twice in the typescript (initial letters three times) for printing in large and small capitals; prenames or initials are not underlined. Titles of monographs, periodicals or collective volumes are underlined once for printing in italics; titles of contributions to periodicals or collective works are placed within single quotation marks, and are not underlined.

Major cross-headings (introducing major sections of an article) are underlined twice for setting in small capitals, subsidiary cross-headings (introducing sub-sections) are underlined once for setting in italics. Internal cross-references should be ringed.

Contributions should be addressed to:

Dr. David Dalby, *African Language Review*,
School of Oriental and African Studies,
Malet Street, London WC1E 7HP.

It will facilitate editing if typescripts can be submitted in duplicate, and contributors should in any case retain a carbon or photostat copy of any typescript submitted: this will enable minor editorial queries to be raised with the contributor without the necessity of returning a copy of his typescript.